A Theory of Corporate Crime

OXFORD MONOGRAPHS ON CRIMINAL LAW AND JUSTICE

This series aims to cover all aspects of criminal law and procedure including criminal evidence. The scope of this series is wide, encompassing both practical and theoretical works.

OTHER TITLES IN THIS SERIES

Victims as Agents of State Accountability
A Comparative and Normative Analysis
Marie Manikis

How Juries Work
And How They Could Work Better
Rebecca K. Helm

Civil Recovery of Criminal Property
Colin King, Jennifer Hendry

The Insanity Defence
International and Comparative Perspectives
Ronnie Mackay, Warren Brookbanks

Justice In-Between
A Study of Intermediate Criminal Verdicts
Federico Picinali

Criminal Fraud and Election Disinformation
Law and Politics
Jeremy Horder

Policing the Borders Within
Ana Aliverti

Criminalizing Sex
A Unified Liberal Theory
Stuart P. Green

Reasons to Doubt
Wrongful Convictions and the Criminal Cases Review Commission
Carolyn Hoyle and Mai Sato

Fitness to Plead
International and Comparative Perspectives
Ronnie Mackay and Warren Brookbanks

Criminal Misconducts in Office
Law and Politics
Jeremy Horder

The Preventive Turn in Criminal Law
Henrique Carvalho

Criminal Justice and Taxation
Peter Alldridge

In Search of Criminal Responsibility
Ideas, Interests, and Institutions
Nicola Lacey

Preventive Justice
Andrew Ashworth and Lucia Zedner

Character in the Criminal Trial
Mike Redmayne

Homicide and the Politics of Law Reform
Jeremy Horder

The Insecurity State
Vulnerable Autonomy and the Right to Security in the Criminal Law
Peter Ramsay

Manifest Madness
Mental Incapacity in the Criminal Law
Arlie Loughnan

The Ethics of Plea Bargaining
Richard L. Lippke

Prosecuting Domestic Violence
A Philosophical Analysis
Michelle Madden Dempsey

Abuse of Process and Judicial Stays of Criminal Proceedings
Second Edition
Andrew L.-T. Choo

A Theory of Corporate Crime

JEREMY HORDER
Professor of Criminal Law, School of Law, London School of Economics, London, UK

OXFORD
UNIVERSITY PRESS

OXFORD
UNIVERSITY PRESS

Great Clarendon Street, Oxford, OX2 6DP,
United Kingdom

Oxford University Press is a department of the University of Oxford.
It furthers the University's objective of excellence in research, scholarship,
and education by publishing worldwide. Oxford is a registered trade mark of
Oxford University Press in the UK and in certain other countries.

Published in the United States of America by Oxford University Press
198 Madison Avenue, New York, NY 10016, United States of America.

British Library Cataloguing in Publication Data
Data available

Library of Congress Control Number: 2026933221

ISBN 9780198936503

DOI: 10.1093/9780198936534.001.0001

Printed and bound by
CPI Group (UK) Ltd., Croydon, CR0 4YY

FSC
www.fsc.org
MIX
Paper | Supporting
responsible forestry
FSC® C013604

The manufacturer's authorized representative in the EU for product safety is
Oxford University Press España S.A. of Parque Empresarial San Fernando de Henares,
Avenida de Castilla, 2 – 28830 Madrid (www.oup.es/en or product.safety@oup.com).
OUP España S.A. also acts as importer into Spain of products made by the manufacturer.

This book is dedicated to the memory of Professor Leonard Leigh (1935–2025), who served as Lecturer and later Professor of Criminal Law at the London School of Economics from 1962 until 1997. His book, The Criminal Liability of Corporations in English Law (London, 1969) can justifiably be regarded as the foundational scholarly work on this subject in the United Kingdom.

PREFACE

The origins of this book lie in the Law Commission work in 2007–08 on the development of an offence capable of capturing companies' involvement in bribery committed by employees, agents, and subsidiaries.[1] The 'failure-to-prevent' model of corporate involvement in fault-based offending, which emerged as part of that process,[2] has rapidly been applied to other economic crimes[3] and also adopted in some jurisdictions overseas (in Australia, South Africa, and in the Republic of Ireland). The main task of this book is to provide a theoretical basis for the model, and to explain the role it plays alongside other modes of corporate criminal responsibility in a liberal-welfarist state. Amongst other things, I defend the model as one capable of application to companies large and small, and to both fault and no-fault offences, and hence as providing the basis for a general theory of corporate crime, even though I also defend the use of other models of corporate criminal liability in particular circumstances. Central to my defence of the model will be an analysis and justification of a defence of 'all reasonable precautions taken and all due diligence exercised' to an allegation of corporate failure to prevent crime. This defence, the wording of which should replace that of 'adequate' or 'reasonable' procedures, is central to the failure-to-prevent model, by way of contrast with (for example) the vicarious liability model in the United States or with the 'identification' model in the United Kingdom and elsewhere. In that regard, the defence is emblematic of what I argue is an important underlying political commitment in the liberal-welfarist state. This is the commitment to see companies (the vast majority of which are one-person or micro companies) less as amoral profit-seeking behemoths, and more as HLA Hart's famous 'puzzled' citizens, perfectly prepared to do what the law requires and committed to the values underlying it,[4] if (1) they can be given clear guidance on compliance and (2) there is a reasonable prospect that corporate lawbreakers will in appropriate cases face the right kind of punitive justice.

[1] Law Commission (2008).
[2] Embodied in the Bribery Act 2010, s 7.
[3] Including fraud, fraud-related offences, and the facilitation of tax evasion.
[4] HLA Hart (1961), 40. The 'puzzled man' is equivalent to John Finnis' '[citizen] who is willing to advance the common good', and so needs precise direction in that regard: see John Finnis (1980), 361.

ACKNOWLEDGEMENTS

I have incurred many debts in the years it has taken to write this book. The Corporate Law group and the Criminal Law and Justice group at London School of Economics (LSE) have been unfailingly patient, as different chapter drafts have headed down various blind alleys. Mark D'Souza, University College London, kindly provided invaluable insights on some of the philosophical claims in Chapter 1. Alex Sarch, Surrey University, cast his acute eye over what I have to say about Parliament's recent forays into corporate criminal law reform; and my work on that would also have come to little were it not for the support and expertise of Gabriele Watts, Barrister at 2 Hare Court, London. I have also benefitted greatly from discussions with Alison Cronin, Peter Ramsay, Heli Korkka-Knuts, Sam Hickey, and members of the International Academy of Financial Crime Litigators, whose knowledge of how different liability models work in practice around the globe is unparalleled. Mehar Suri, LSE, provided research assistance and perceptive comments which have been invaluable. Finally, I am more grateful than I can possibly say to my wife, Naomi, whose love, support, and faith consistently refresh my own.

CONTENTS

TABLE OF CASES

UK CASES

INDIA CASES

REPUBLIC OF IRELAND CASES

US CASES

TABLE OF LEGISLATION

UK LEGISLATION

AUSTRALIAN LEGISLATION

CANADIAN LEGISLATION

DUTCH LEGISLATION

EUROPEAN UNION LEGISLATION

FRENCH LEGISLATION

REPUBLIC OF IRELAND LEGISLATION

USA LEGISLATION

INTRODUCTION

I.1 An Overview of the Argument

In this book, my principal task will be to explain and defend a particular model of corporate criminal liability. This is what has come to be known as the 'failure-to-prevent' model.[1] Under this model, the main concern of corporate criminal liability is not the substantive criminal wrongdoing engaged in by the person (director, employee, agent, or subsidiary) acting on company business.[2] Instead, the two focal points of criminal liability are the company's failure to prevent the occurrence of that substantive wrongdoing, and its efforts more generally to avoid failures of that kind.[3] Why should these points of liability be so significant?

So far as a focus on the failure to prevent wrongdoing is concerned,[4] one advantage of such a focus is that it permits the failure-to-prevent model to be a general theory of corporate criminal liability. For example, it has traditionally always been accepted that companies cannot be convicted of certain crimes,[5] meaning that such crimes must be excluded from the scope of any theory of corporate criminality. Examples are murder (where the sentence is mandatory life imprisonment[6]), a range of sexual offences contrary to the Sexual Offences Act 2003,[7] or offences such as (say) being drunk and disorderly in a public place,[8] or wearing a UK military uniform without being a member of His Majesty's military forces.[9]

[1] This wording used to describe the relevant offence comes from the heading given in the statute to the first such offence, created by section 7 of the Bribery Act 2010: 'Failure of commercial organisations to prevent bribery'.

[2] Under the failure-to-prevent model, the role of the substantive wrongdoing is to act as a predicate offence. That is one way in which the failure-to-prevent model is theoretically distinct from the more widely discussed (and critiqued) model of vicarious liability, under which the company is convicted of the same offence as the associated individual.

[3] The idea that a company should have some kind of 'reasonable procedures' defence to a criminal charge is, of course, not a new one: see, e.g., Note (1979) and Brent Fisse (1983). However, less well explored has been the theoretical distinction between the corporate efforts made to prevent the particular wrongdoing 'token' and the systems put in place to prevent wrongdoing of that 'type': see the discussion in chs 1 and 4.

[4] The importance of a focus on efforts to avoid wrongdoing of the relevant type is addressed in the next section.

[5] See the discussion in Amanda Pinto QC and Martin Evans (2008), 1.1.

[6] *Hawke v Hulton & Co* [1909] 2 KB 93.

[7] Amanda Pinto QC and Martin Evans (2008), 1.1.

[8] Criminal Justice Act 1967, s 91. See, further, the discussion in Section 1.3.

[9] An offence, contrary to Uniforms Act 1894, s 2.

A Theory of Corporate Crime. Jeremy Horder, Oxford University Press. © Jeremy Horder 2026.
DOI: 10.1093/9780198936534.003.0001

In relation to the latter three types of examples, the traditional argument is that the nature of the conduct involved in such offences means that they require a corporeal entity to commit them.[10] So, they cannot be committed by a company—an abstract legal entity—as a principal offender, even when a corporeal individual representing the company itself engages in the relevant conduct.[11] However, the scope of the excluded category is uncertain,[12] even though determining its scope may be important. Suppose that an employed doctor on duty rapes someone in his organization's care,[13] or representatives of a defence contractor illegally dress as UK military personnel to boost company sales at an arms fair.[14] We are entitled to know what legitimate scope there might be for extending the criminal law to reflect the responsibility of the employing organization for the occurrence of the wrongdoing.

In such cases, the organization's key responsibility should be understood as the responsibility for failing to prevent the substantive offending. To begin with, a company can clearly be convicted and punished for failing to prevent an offence, even when the substantive offence in question attracts a mandatory sentence of imprisonment. So, a company could theoretically be convicted of and punished for failing to prevent a murder, even if a conviction of the company for murder would leave the law powerless to punish the company itself through application of the prescribed penalty.[15] More broadly, a failure to prevent an act is necessarily something analytically separate from engagement in the act itself, and different evaluative considerations may apply to the failure as opposed to the act. As I have just indicated, the nature of some substantive offences, such as many sexual offences, or (say) being drunk and disorderly in a public place,[16] may make it seem as if they can necessarily only be perpetrated by a human individual.[17] However, that point seems less significant in the case of a failure to prevent the occurrence of such offences. That is because such a failure is a piece of conduct at one remove from the substantive offence itself.[18]

[10] The nature of the 'person' presupposed by the criminal law is briefly considered in Section 1.3, where the 'corporeal entity' constraint will in fact be challenged.

[11] In the case of murder, the argument is that, as an abstract entity, a company cannot be imprisoned, and so cannot be convicted of a crime attracting a mandatory prison sentence.

[12] See further the discussion in Section 1.3.

[13] This important example is further discussed in chs 1 and 5. See also the discussion of model 'D' liability in Section I.4 below, and Jeremy Horder (2025b).

[14] This example is further discussed in ch 1.

[15] In *Fidelity Industries v State* (2004) 03 MAD CK 0179, the High Court of Madras declared that it had the inherent power to punish companies by way of a fine in such cases, but it seems unlikely that a UK court would follow suit in that regard. See Jeremy Horder (2025b).

[16] Criminal Justice Act 1967, s 91.

[17] As we will see in Section 1.3, it is arguable that all offences (especially fault-based offences) presuppose a human perpetrator, even though the law is selective about when it permits this presupposition to affect the scope of corporate criminal liability.

[18] Such a failure must itself, of course, be made manifest through the omission(s) of relevant individuals associated with the company. In that respect, I will argue below, and more fully in ch 1, that the ultimate responsibility for every corporate omission lies with the director—or directors

In that regard, where the liability of companies is concerned, the more important distinction is between substantive offences (such as fraud or bribery) committed in order to benefit the company commercially and substantive offences (such as sexual offences) committed for other—perhaps more personal—reasons. Suppose that a predicate offence, such as fraud, is committed by an associated person in order to benefit the company. Then, it is arguable that the normative connection with the company generated by such a person's intent when acting justifies conviction of the company for failing to prevent the offence, whether or not the company was aware that such offending might be taking place. The key question will be whether or not appropriate procedures were in place to prevent offending of that kind.[19] However, is a company also fairly labelled as having criminally failed to prevent offending, in the absence of an intent to benefit the company on the part of the associated person? An example already mentioned involved the offender who is an employed doctor and uses his position to engage in sexual offending for purely selfish reasons.[20] In accordance with what I refer to as the '*Alford* Principles',[21] in a restricted range of circumstances, the answer to that question can be 'yes'.

Considered more broadly, as a general theory of corporate criminal responsibility, the failure-to-prevent model is far better suited to describing and labelling a company's typical involvement in all kinds of offending—including financial crimes—than the substantive wrongdoing that constitutes the predicate offence:

> A local sales manager (X) working for a UK-wide housing firm (Company Y) bribes contractors to prioritise Company Y's building contracts, intending to benefit Company Y (while also making her role appear crucial).[22]

Is it only X in an individual capacity who commits bribery in this example, or does Company Y also do so through X's actions? In truth, there is simply no uncontroversial way of resolving this age-old conundrum. Modern UK law further complicates giving a clear answer to the question by making the answer turn on the resolution of what may be a highly contested further issue: whether, at the relevant time, X was a 'senior manager' at Company Y.[23] By contrast, it is clear that Company Y in this example fails to prevent the bribery committed by X, bribery

collectively—whose failures (being at the highest level) gave that omission the most significant normative expression in the world.

[19] The issue of 'intent to benefit' is discussed more fully in ch 5.

[20] See further the analysis of model D in Section I.4 below, and the discussion in ch 5.

[21] *JF Alford Transport* [1997] EWCA Crim 654, discussed in ch 3.

[22] See also the case of *R v Andrews Wetherfoil* [1972] 1 WLR 118, discussed further in ch 2.

[23] See, further, Jeremy Horder (2025a) and Jeremy Horder (2025b). Under section 196 of the Economic Crime and Corporate Transparency Act 2023, other things being equal, Company Y will itself be guilty of bribery in the example if X is determined to be a senior manager. The 2023 Act is discussed in detail in ch 2.

that embodied—alongside X's selfish motive—an intention to benefit the company. Given the 'relational' nature of corporate activity (described below), it is submitted that it is hard to think of a better understanding of the nature of the company's responsibility in this example, both in terms of an analysis of (in)actions or events and in terms of 'fair labelling'.[24]

There are further advantages to analysing corporate criminal responsibility in terms of a company's failure to prevent crime. As we will see in Chapters 3 and 4, analysis in such terms is based on principles of control over associated persons who engage in wrongdoing, rather than on the causing of those wrongs.[25] Accordingly, the failure-to-prevent model can be applied with equal theoretical justification to strict liability crimes, crimes of negligence, and crimes involving a free deliberate and informed act (such as fraud or bribery) on the part of the associated person. That makes the applicable principles of liability clearer, fairer, and more consistent in a range of cases. Consider some examples illustrating the lack of clarity about the application of existing principles. For example, imagine a case in which a court is asked to apply the presumption of fault to an ostensibly strict liability offence allegedly committed by a company. It is claimed (inter alia) that the stigma attaching to conviction must mean that Parliament intended the offence to be interpreted as requiring proof of a fault element.[26] Under the current law, unless and until the court applies the presumption, it cannot be known in advance what principles of corporate liability are relevant. If the presumption is applied and fault must be proved, then, controversially, the fault must have been that of someone at director (or possibly senior manager) level.[27] If the presumption is not applied and liability is strict, then—equally controversially, albeit for different reasons[28]—liability can be vicarious, and the company's fault or involvement (if any) becomes irrelevant. The law would be simpler and fairer if the relevant questions, whether or not the offence is held to be fault-based, were: (1) 'did the Company fail to prevent the commission of the offence by an associated person?' and (2) 'did the company have robust procedures in place to prevent offending of that kind?'.

It is not only in this unusual type of case that it can be hard to defend the need to draw distinctions fundamental to the current law. Suppose that a small- or medium-sized finance company's (low-level) employee commits an offence by distributing promotional material that is false and likely to mislead the average

[24] For a good discussion of this concept and of its importance to the criminal law, see James Chalmers and Fiona Leverick (2008). The model fills what Sam Buell has aptly described as the 'responsibility gap' between persons associated with the company who engage in wrongdoing and the top-level executives who may not have known about but could have prevented that wrongdoing: Samuel W Buell (2017).

[25] See also text at n 42 below.

[26] Imagine, for example, that the defendant in *Sherraz v DeRutzen* [1895] 1 QB 918 was a corporate public house owner, and that the person who served the police officer on duty was an employee.

[27] See Economic Criminal and Corporate Transparency Act 2023, s 196, and Crime and Policing Bill 2025, cl 196.

[28] See the discussion in chs 3 and 5.

consumer.[29] Then, the company also commits that offence through the operation of the doctrine of vicarious liability, because the offence in question is one of strict liability.[30] However, suppose that evidence came to light suggesting that the employee acted dishonestly when distributing the material to consumers, and so the prosecution charged fraud instead. Ironically, far from being made worse, the company's legal position (given the employee's low-level status) is now greatly improved, in spite of what might in practice be great similarity between the offences. The company can point to the need to prove that someone at directorial or senior manager level engaged in (or was complicit in) the fraud before criminal liability can be extended to the company for that offence.[31] The position should be that, in each case, whatever the size of the company, whatever the status of the employee within the firm, and whether or not the offence in question was one of strict liability, the company's wrong is its failure to prevent the offence taking place. In that regard, an overall scheme illustrating the way that corporate criminal liability works, when focused on the failure-to-prevent model, is provided in Section I.4.

The creation of a general principle of corporate liability for failure-to-prevent offences is appropriate, in part, because other than in the case of one-person companies (about which I will say more in due course), the commission of offences in a corporate context is almost inevitably 'relational' in character. In other words, responsibility for what happened stems from a key (failure of) interaction between different persons associated with the company. In corporate contexts, when someone associated with a company commits a substantive offence in the course of company business, another person or people associated with the company will either (1) have commanded, encouraged, or assisted its commission; (2) have tolerated its commission; or, more commonly, (3) have unwittingly done nothing (or not enough) to safeguard against wrongdoing of that type when they could or should have taken safeguarding steps.[32] Acknowledging this point, in the way that corporate liability is understood, fills the so-called responsibility gap between offending employees or agents and high-level executives in a position to control or influence them.[33] Only a lingering attachment to an individualistic model of fair labelling makes it seem as if the priority must be to put aside the relational aspect of corporate criminal wrongdoing, in analysing the nature of such wrongdoing, and

[29] Contrary to the Consumer Protection from Unfair Trading Regulations (2008), s 5.

[30] See, e.g., *Provincial Motor Cab Company v Dunning* (1909) 2 KB 599.

[31] To complicate matters further, if the company was in law a large company, it would commit the offence of failing to prevent fraud in this example. See the discussion in ch 2.

[32] The sophisticated account of corporate liability developed by James Gobert and Maurice Punch rests on the idea, alluded to here, that a company is complicit in the crimes committed by its employees and agents: see James Gobert and Maurice Punch (2003). However, the difficulty for their theory is that it is hard to square the notion of 'complicity' in crime with a simple failure to prevent it, in the absence of knowledge, intention, or awareness: *Johnson v Youden* [1950] 1 KB 544.

[33] On the 'responsibility gap', see Samuel W Buell (2017).

try to find a way of saying that the corporate person somehow itself committed the substantive offence in question.[34]

So far as the relational aspect of corporate wrongdoing is concerned, and in particular a company's failure to prevent a substantive crime it could have prevented, whose failure is the one that matters? My argument will be that, for fair labelling purposes, the most important prevention or (as I will call it) 'safeguarding' failure is that of a company's director or directors. Theirs is the most important safeguarding failure, no matter how distant from day-to-day directorial concerns the crime of a person associated with the company might (appear to) have been. The reason for taking such an approach, in which the 'buck stops' with the director or directors in every case of failure to prevent crime, is quite simple. It is that all lines of executive authority within a company lead ultimately to the company directors, the persons within a company constitutionally granted supreme executive authority as a matter of company law.[35] All persons associated with the company, whatever the position they occupy within it, just like all systems and processes on which the company relies, are ultimately under the supervisory control (however attenuated, and whether or not delegated[36]) of the directors. In any case, then, in which a crime is committed by an associated person at whatever level,[37] it is true to say that the directors *collectively* have not used their supreme executive authority to prevent that happening. Accordingly, in such a case, the focus in point of liability can—and should—switch to the adequacy or reasonableness of the procedures that the directors had in place (including the nature of any delegation of crime-prevention responsibilities) to prevent crimes of that kind.

The failure-to-prevent model has a crucial advantage over alternative models that have emerged in recent years, such as models focused on corporate culture or on corporate systems and processes.[38] However sophisticated one's account of corporate liability in terms of a firm's 'culture' or its 'systems and processes', such an account will always be vulnerable to potential criticism on fair labelling grounds.[39] It will be vulnerable in that way, if the culture, system, or process was operative at (say) local or regional level or at an overseas branch, but was not known about, not approved, or perhaps had even been disavowed at the highest executive level

[34] I say that, whilst acknowledging the extraordinary sophistication of recent efforts to show that companies themselves, through their culture, systems, or processes, commit substantive offences: see, e.g., Elise Bant (2023) and James Gobert (1994).

[35] See the discussion in ch 3.

[36] Delegated powers are subject, in law, to requirements of directorial oversight of their use, underlining the importance of the directors' position as supreme executive authorities: see the discussion of this point in ch 1.

[37] Including a case in which a director commits an offence, if the director was acting under the authority of the board: see *SFO v Barclays* (2018) EWHC 3055 (QB).

[38] Elise Bant (2023), 187–88; James Gobert (1994).

[39] The same goes for Mark D'Souza's account of corporate criminal liability in terms of what he calls the 'comprehensive identification' of the company with any crime committed by one of its employees acting within the scope of their actual or ostensible authority: see Mark D'Souza (2020).

within the company or group of companies.[40] So, where defective or malevolent corporate culture, systems, or processes at any level within a firm or network of firms have led to criminal wrongdoing, what is the relevance of this to corporate liability? It is the failure of the supreme executive authorities—the directors—to have done enough to root out or negate that culture, system, or process, as a manifestation of the inadequacy of the procedures they had in place to prevent such wrongdoing.

Alongside an explanation and defence of the failure-to-prevent model, I will also be concerned to provide a theoretical basis for a reinterpretation of the traditional 'identification' doctrine. This is the doctrine used to find companies directly liable for substantive fault-based crimes where (in short) those crimes were committed by the most senior company officers.[41] The overwhelming majority of UK firms are comprised only of a sole director or small number of directors. This means that the identification doctrine is still a potentially potent weapon in the armoury of corporate criminal law in many cases. However, the doctrine is to some extent unduly wedded to the bureaucratic structure of formal office-holding within companies: the crime must be committed by a 'director' (or, in many instances, a 'senior manager'[42]), if the company is itself to be found liable. Accordingly, the doctrine is not open to a more substantive interpretation, in which a court looks at the roles taken on over time by, say, a highly trusted long-standing employee or an influential spouse working more informally for the firm, and asks whether, in practice, such a person's conduct should be identified with the company. Such a substantive account of the identification doctrine would make it better able to reflect the reality of many small-firm business practices, where the business is organized on a more horizontal 'Durkheimian' than a vertical 'Weberian' basis. In such businesses, solidarity or attitudes of deference between family members may play a more significant normative role than bureaucratically organized lines of authority.[43] The importance of this issue should not be underestimated. In 2020, there were 4.8 million family businesses in the United Kingdom, making up 85.9 per cent of all private sector businesses.[44]

To return to the failure-to-prevent model, the argument hitherto presented makes the model appear equally dependent on a 'vertical' (Weberian) model of

[40] A point acknowledged by Celia Wells (2001), 155–59.

[41] See, e.g., *Tesco Supermarkets v Nattrass* [1972] AC 153 (HL).

[42] See the discussion in ch 2.

[43] See the discussion in ch 3.

[44] In 2022, these businesses employed 13.9 million workers (51.5 per cent of all private sector employment) and contributed £575 billion to the UK economy: https://commonslibrary.parliament.uk/research-briefings/cdp-2022-0241/#:~:text=Oxford%20Economics%20estimates%20that%20there,billion%20to%20the%20UK%20economy. Similarly, in the United States, over 80 per cent of all businesses are sole enterprises with no employees, and the numbers of businesses employing more than 20 employees pales into insignificance compared to the number employing fewer people: https://www.forbes.com/advisor/business/small-business-statistics/#:~:text=Recent%20data%20from%20the%20U.S.,99.9%25%20of%20all%20U.S.%20businesses (last accessed 28/02/2024).

corporate structure. On that model, I argue that what matters to corporate liability is the inaction of persons in supreme authority (the directors), in that they have ultimate supervisory power over what goes on in the company through the conduct of employees and agents. Liability based on a failure to use such supervisory power is liability based on what I will refer to as the 'control principle' of liability. As discussed in Chapter 3, the application of this principle depends on a (corporate) person having a control right and duty to prevent wrongdoing by associated persons.[45] However, as I have just indicated, many firms are comprised only of directors (commonly a small number, as in the case of a family firm), and it might be misleading to describe the relationship between them as characterized by 'control'. On my account, as between directors, however many there may be and whatever their status (executive or non-executive), their relationship is formally one of what I will call 'influence' rather than one of control. A non-executive director, say, cannot control the actions of an executive director, or vice versa, even though both may have similar corporate legal responsibilities.[46] However, each type of director is in a position to—and should seek to—influence the other director, and each type of director is under a duty to pay at least some heed to the influence of the other director. This is what understanding their relationship in terms of what I will call the 'influence principle' involves.[47] In cases of companies comprised only of directors, it is the influence principle that provides the foundation for failure-to-prevent liability: the failure on the part of the other directors to use their influence to stop the commission of a crime by a fellow director.

Most importantly, whether it is the control or the influence principle that is in issue, failures to prevent crime in companies with more than one director should be regarded as a *collective* failure on the part of the directors as a body. Individualist models of corporate criminal liability—models that seek to identify the company with the commission of the substantive offence—inevitably struggle to explain how such identification can provide a fair and accurate label for offending, when one is dealing with, what in Chapter 1 I will call, an ethically 'heterogenous' company. This is a company in which, at different levels, there is diversity in terms of knowledge and opinion within the company about what is (and ought to be) company practice. An example would be where one third of the company board suspects that offending is going on, a different third of the board has no idea it is going on, and the final third of the board has been wrongly assured that there are procedures in place to ensure that it cannot be going on. In such an example, on what basis can offending fairly be attributed to the company? Such a puzzle about fair labelling is dissolved once one appreciates that, whatever their individual states of mind in

[45] See also Jeremy Horder (2024).

[46] See, e.g., https://www.handbook.fca.org.uk/handbook/COCON/1/Annex1.html (last accessed 19/02/2025).

[47] See the discussion of *Powers v Greymountain Management* [2022] IEHC 599 in ch 3.

relation to the substantive offending, the directors collectively failed to prevent the crime being committed; and in labelling terms, that is what should matter.

I.2 Liability Theories: Moral and Politico-Economic Foundations

The kind of analysis that brings us to this point is what might in broad terms be considered applied moral philosophy. The influence of such an approach will also be clear in the account that I give in Chapter 1 of why a company can be held criminally liable even though it is not itself a moral agent: because its existence confers corporate status on certain kinds of legally significant human action. It will also shape the nature of the account that I give in Chapter 6 of justifications (there are a number of such justifications) for punishing companies.[48] Nonetheless, this work also relies on politico-economic foundations, in pursuit of its thesis. Different bases for holding companies to account in criminal (or regulatory) law reflect changing political understandings of the role of companies in modern capitalist economies and of the role of the state in relation to companies. For example, augmenting a classical nineteenth-century individualist concern with the 'identity' of the company in law, for the purposes of finding companies criminally liable for traditional forms of wrongdoing, is now a liberal-welfarist concern with what are taken to be the broader responsibilities of a company. These are the responsibilities (anathema, in general, to the old common law[49]) involved in safeguarding against wrongdoing and inappropriate risk-taking engaged in by people associated with the company: in particular, those—such as employees—subject to the company's control or influence. These responsibilities—reflected in potential criminal liability—may nowadays extend not only to the free, deliberate, and informed conduct of a company's employees, agents, and subsidiaries, but also to the trading and employment practices of a company's contracting partners in the marketplace.[50]

What shape is given to the criminal law by the adoption of a broadly liberal-welfarist set of assumptions? A liberal-welfarist approach involves the use of law to prioritize incentivizing companies themselves to see virtue in taking a creative and committed approach to compliance, to shouldering some of the burden of addressing what is, increasingly, a complex and multifaceted (as well as specialized) world of adequate risk reduction and harm prevention.[51] So, for example, liberal-welfarist laws commonly (1) exonerate companies who, although guilty of

[48] Briefly discussed in the next section.

[49] See, e.g., the discussion of *Chisholm v Doulton* (1889) 22 QBD 736 in ch 3.

[50] See, generally, the discussion in chs 4 and 5.

[51] Discussed in ch 4. See Tom Crook (2007), 371: 'Liberal governance, in short, involves multiple strategies of ordering, of which the liberal subject is at once the object and subject: simultaneously a target of regulation and an active agent of self-regulation and governmental critique'.

wrongdoing, made sufficient efforts to comply with the law's demands and (2) use a system of punishment not primarily to take retribution or shame wrongdoers but in a forward-looking way to induce them to adopt penitential attitudes, to engage in systematic reforms, and to engage in reparations, as part of their rehabilitation as responsible, compliance-oriented corporate citizens. Liberal-welfarism, in law, thus occupies theoretical and political space between two rival theories. On the one hand, there is classical liberalism, the philosophy of the old common law.[52] As a part of its robust individualism, classical liberal theory takes the view that altruistic attitudes and welfare-oriented practices[53] in the marketplace should not be promoted through 'administrative coercion . . . [or] . . . direct state controls'.[54] Instead, classical liberalism undergirds its voluntarism, in respect of welfare promotion, through an emphasis on the retributive and deterrent effect of only a narrow range of generally applicable prohibitions. These are prohibitions—such as *mala in se* crimes governing fraud or bribery—that criminalize companies on the same basis as individuals for engaging in a limited number of unacceptably harmful or excessively risky forms of conduct.[55] As Hayek put it: 'As a true law should not name any particulars, so it should especially not single out any specific persons or groups of persons [such as companies].'[56]

On the other hand, there is the dirigiste social-democratic preference for micromanagement (so distrusted by Hayek[57]), in the form of direct state enforcement of high welfarist standards.[58] Like classical liberalism, dirigiste social-democratic theory places emphasis on deterrence and retribution, but it does so for very different reasons. On dirigiste social-democratic accounts of corporate activity,[59] companies cannot be trusted not to seek systematically to evade demands to pursue the welfare goals the accounts hold dear.[60] On such accounts, it thus falls to state officials directly to enforce compliance with those demands, through the taking of deterrent and retributive enforcement steps against offending companies. Liberal-welfarism may share a broadly similar understanding with dirigiste social-democratic thinking about the appropriateness of particular welfare goals, such as the need to operate in an environmentally sustainable way and the importance of

[52] See the discussion in ch 3.

[53] Which no lesser figure than FE Hayek described as 'that hodgepodge of ill-assembled and often inconsistent ideals': FE Hayek (2007), 44.

[54] Ibid. For Hayek, welfare was to be promoted solely through non-coercive means, such as financial incentives.

[55] See, e.g., Milton Friedman (1970), 17: 'there is one and only one social responsibility of business—to use its resources and engage in activities designed to increase its profits so long as it stays within the rules of the game, which is to say, engages in open and free competition without deception or fraud'.

[56] FE Hayek (1960), 154.

[57] FE Hayek (2007).

[58] My distinctions here are inspired by, but do not directly track, Esping-Andersen's distinction between the 'liberal' and the 'social-democratic' understandings of how to promote welfare: see Gøsta Esping-Andersen (1990).

[59] Discussed further in ch 6.

[60] See the discussion in, e.g., Angus Nurse (2022), Steve Tombs and David Whyte (2015), and in ch 6.

a zero-tolerance approach to human rights abuses in the supply chain.[61] However, by contrast with dirigiste social-democratic thinking, under a liberal-welfarist approach, the criminal law should be more concerned with incentivizing sound corporate attitudes and practices in relation to compliance, and with shaping responsible corporate preferences in that regard, than with taking retribution for departures from prescribed standards; and that is true, whether those standards are the minimalist ones of classical liberalism or the maximalist ones of dirigiste social-democratic philosophy. The belief in liberal-welfarism is represented in this work by two key features of the argument. First, as I have just indicated, there is the central place given to the role of defences, such as having had in place at the relevant time adequate or reasonable procedures, or the more broadly applicable defence—which I ultimately prefer—of having taken all reasonable precautions and exercised all due diligence.[62] Secondly, there is the emphasis placed, in relation to the state's response to corporate wrongdoing in serious cases, on a move away from achieving so-called just deserts.

In Chapter 6, I argue that the state's response to serious corporate failures to prevent crime should be concentrated on (1) systematic reforms to corporate attitudes and practices bearing on compliance and (2) securing medium- to long-term victim or community-focused penitential reparation, or commitment to the creation or sustaining of what I call 'materially contextual' common goods. In relation to (1), the central place given to defences focused on 'striving' for compliance, in defining the scope of liability for corporate crime, involves an appeal to the corporate body as a responsible citizen of the welfarist state. In relation to (2), the focus on penitential activity of different kinds, as a response to corporate crime, involves an emphasis on the capacity of corporate wrongdoers to prove themselves to be worthy members of and contributors to the welfarist state. The empirical justification for this approach to liability and punishment is that, although the figures will obviously differ from one commercial sector to the next, (1) most firms are more likely than not to seek to be by-and-large compliant with regulatory requirements, (2) most firms are likely to support regulatory investigation and criminal prosecution when law-breaking has been discovered, and (3) firms will, on becoming aware of regulatory or criminal proceedings against lawbreakers, commonly review the adequacy of their own processes and procedures.[63] That is so, even though, of course, many firms—just like many individuals—become involved in criminal wrongdoing, whether sector-specific (such as breaches of food-safety

[61] See, e.g., Joseph Raz (1979), 228: '[W]elfare law and governmental manipulation of the economy also increase freedom by increasing—if successful—people's welfare.'

[62] See the discussion in ch 4. The use of the phrase 'exercised all due diligence' as a defence to a (regulatory) offence was relatively infrequent before 1972, with well under 100 UK instances—and none in statutory instruments—coming before 1972. By way of contrast, since 1972, there have been over 2,000 uses of the phrase to define such a defence, with over 1,000 uses appearing in statutory instruments.

[63] See the evidence cited in Section 4.2 and, e.g., in Financial Conduct Authority (2023), 54–59.

legislation) or more general in nature (such as tax evasion or breaches of health-and-safety law).[64]

A common trope of modern corporate criminal law scholarship, heavily influenced by the dirigiste social-democratic approach, is that liability structures and punishment practices must be shaped by reference to a particular central case of the company. This is the (large) company concerned only with amoral growth-driven profit-seeking, governed by 'structures of irresponsibility',[65] and having a 'calculative orientation': an orientation that leads it to adopt a more general political strategy of 'block[ing] the use of the law to hold [it] to account'.[66] Some firms do indeed fit this stereotype, and are capable of doing—and have done—great harm. However, that does not mean that the existence of such firms, and the impact of such harm, should closely shape our underlying assumptions about and approach to corporate wrongdoing.[67] One problematic feature of giving pride of place to such a perspective on corporate crime is that it tends to isolate wrongdoing in corporate settings from wrongdoing in institutional settings (including within public bodies) more broadly. Features of corporate crime such as 'structures of irresponsibility' and obstructing legal intervention, leading to systematization of wrongdoing, have been found consistently in both political and non-profit public or charitable bodies as well as in private market-based bodies.[68] That makes the relevance of a private corporate setting to systematic wrongdoing less clear in its significance.[69] More importantly, in this context, central case analysis based on the model of an amoral, rapacious larger firm greatly misrepresents the nature of the typical firm in the United Kingdom and across the world.

Focusing on the United Kingdom, whilst large UK companies (with over 250 employees) account for just under half of all revenue, employees, and physical capital,[70] that still leaves just over 50 per cent of these crucial elements being provided by small- and medium-sized entities. What is more, in the United Kingdom today, of the 5.4 million registered businesses, no fewer than 4.1 million (74 per cent) had no employees, and 3.1 million (56 per cent) were unincorporated sole

[64] See, e.g., the discussion in Hazel Croall (1989).

[65] Steve Tombs and David Whyte (2015), 128.

[66] Ibid., 121–23.

[67] Just as we would not judge the adequacy of the criminal justice system's response to individual offenders across the board, by reference to its approach to high-level organized crime.

[68] Recent examples include the systematic neglect and ill-treatment of patients at Stafford Hospital: https://www.thelancet.com/journals/lancet/article/PIIS0140-6736(13)60264-0/fulltext (last accessed 02/12/2024). See also https://www.oxfam.org.uk/mc/npwwwq/ (last accessed 02/12/2024). For a more recent example, Sussex police widen inquiry into Brighton hospital deaths: https://www.brightonandhovenews.org/2025/02/07/police-explore-cover-up-claims-over-hospital-deaths/ (last accessed 01/01/2026).

[69] GCJ Bennett (1999); Jeremy Horder (2012), ch 4.

[70] https://www.money.co.uk/business/business-statistics#:~:text=The%207%2C960%20large%20firms%20%28250%2B%20employees%29%20in%20the,industry%20%E2%80%93%2076%25%20of%20the%20overall%20business%20population (last accessed 01/04/2025).

proprietorships almost all of which had no employees.[71] Quite simply, the micro, small-scale director-led company or proprietorship forms the biggest single proportion of UK firms. There is also a significant fragility to the existence of these small firms: no less than 60 per cent of companies will fail to survive past three years of existence.[72] Further, whilst there were only just over 2,000 company liquidations in 1963, by the 1990s the figure was regularly exceeding 15,000 annually,[73] and reached 22,109 in 2022.[74] These facts make contentious the image of the archetypal firm as a committed and systematic medium- to long-term wrongdoer. The image of the criminally pathological corporate offender, seeking profits through growth at any human or environmental criminal cost, simply does not fit the (self-) image of the typical micro UK or US firm. Such a firm—operating overwhelmingly from a sole, local site (or from home)—is much more likely to be driven predominantly by a desire to provide an opportunity for family members to achieve personal autonomy through worthwhile work, or—even when work itself provides only a subsistence living—at least to enjoy a sense of the republican freedom that comes with being one's own boss.[75] Accordingly, a theory of corporate crime that takes as its starting point the 'othering' of companies as a socio-political enemy, to be held in (criminal law or regulatory) check by whatever means possible, will simply find itself theoretically ill-equipped to account for the lived experience, aspirations, and ideals of the majority of UK firms (and, indeed, firms across the Western world).

The adoption of this politico-economic background leads me to take as my central case a different model of corporate attitudes to law-abidingness, for the purpose of developing a theory of corporate crime. This is model of the firm that is a corporate representation of HLA Hart's 'puzzled man [*sic*]' of legal theory. The focus on (1) corporate striving to secure regulatory compliance (e.g. manifested in robust safeguarding procedures and the exercise of all due diligence) and on (2) the encouragement of penitential attitudes and reparative conduct when wrongdoing has been done builds on what HLA Hart rightly claimed should be the key concern of a theory of law more generally. This is not the ill-disposed would-be lawbreaker, an excessive concern with whom distorts analysis by over-emphasizing taking retribution through the infliction of punitive sanctions. Instead, it is the 'puzzled

[71] https://www.gov.uk/government/statistics/business-population-estimates-2022/business-population-estimates-for-the-uk-and-regions-2022-statistical-release-html (last accessed 11/06/2023). Only 2 per cent of UK businesses trade from more than one site.

[72] https://www.resolvefinancial.co.uk/startup-failure-statistics/ (last accessed 13/04/2023). Only 28 of the UK FTSE 100 companies from thirty-three years ago are still around as many merged or failed: David Brett (2017).

[73] https://webarchive.nationalarchives.gov.uk/ukgwa/20140716212200/http://www.insolvencydirect.bis.gov.uk/otherinformation/statistics/historicdata/HDmenu.htm (last accessed 13/04/2023).

[74] https://www.gov.uk/government/statistics/company-insolvency-statistics-october-to-december-2022/commentary-company-insolvency-statistics-october-to-december-2022 (last accessed 13/04/2023).

[75] In that regard, it is significant that a greater proportion of women and ethnic minorities have directorial status in small than in large businesses. These points are discussed in more detail in ch 2.

[business] man or ignorant man [*sic*], who is willing to do what is required, if only he can be told what it is',[76] and is hence willing to make amends, change attitudes, and improve practices when wrong has been done.

I.3 The Key Arguments of Chapters 1–6

Fair labelling of a company, in respect of criminal wrongdoing engaged in by an associated person, is a potentially complex task, because wrongdoing perpetrated in the course of business may not represent—indeed it may betray—the company's values. In Chapter 1, I present in a detailed form the arguments to address this problem (amongst other problems) by tackling corporate crime through the failure-to-prevent offence, with its defence focused on the steps taken to safeguard against wrongdoing of the relevant type.[77] The failure-to-prevent model can straightforwardly be applied to all offences, including fault-based offences, reflecting the different roles that the company and the offender played in the commission of the offence. In that regard, evaluation of the company's involvement, in terms of *directorial* failure to prevent the wrongdoing, is the closest that we are likely to get to achieving fairness in labelling. That is because at whatever level within the firm wrongdoing took place (and even if it reflected a minority practice), the fact remains that the directors are the persons with supreme executive authority to change attitudes and practices and to put a stop to wrongdoing.[78]

In pursuit of the argument, I suggest that analysis of corporate crime would be greatly assisted by clearer distinctions drawn between different conceptions of the company, each of which may have a role is explaining different aspects of the justification for liability and punishment. I distinguish four such conceptions: the company as an abstract legal entity, as a concrete legal entity, as a real entity, and as an entity led by a supreme authority. For example, my focus on the director or directors, as the person or persons ultimately responsible for failures to prevent crime, draws on the conception of a company as an entity led by a supreme authority. By contrast, we will see that the conception of the company as a real entity—instantiated by living systems, practices, and culture—is of central relevance to safeguarding defences. Defences such as 'due diligence shown', 'adequate',

[76] HLA Hart (1961), 40. The 'puzzled man' is equivalent to John Finnis' '[citizen] who is willing to advance the common good', and so needs precise direction in that regard: see John Finnis (1980), 361.

[77] In Chapter 2, I will also explain how the traditional identification doctrine should be understood in a more substantive way to capture the activity of the smallest (family) firms.

[78] Even when the attitude, commitment, or understanding of an employee who offends happens to be aligned with that of a person or persons in supreme authority within the company, it is still not a person or persons in authority who (short of involvement through complicity) engages in the wrongdoing itself. So, failure-to-prevent offences are equally appropriate in such instances. An example might be the attitude towards safety of both management and employees in the lead-up to the Herald of Free Enterprise disaster: See the discussion in Celia Wells (2001).

or 'reasonable' procedures are concerned not (or not merely) with what should be done on paper but with what is and should be done in practice, in the way that the company actually imbues its trading practices with values associated with compliance. However, I will criticize real entity-based accounts of corporate liability that seek to shape the practice of *in*culpation, as opposed to exculpation, by reference to the company as a real entity. Inculpation is best understood in terms of the company as an entity led by a supreme authority.

I conclude Chapter 1 with an examination of the challenge presented to theories of corporate criminal liability for fault-based offending by the involvement of artificial intelligence (AI) in corporate business systems.[79] I describe the challenge as analogous to the issue of how fairly to label a company in respect of harmful workplace accidents. In both instances, what should be in focus, in point of liability, is the company's failure to prevent (and its procedures for preventing) the 'outcome'—external—elements of the offence. So, just as the law might be reformed such that a company can be held liable for failing to prevent (say) a serious injury or death at work, so it could be reformed such that a company may be held liable for failing to prevent (say) a fraud or bribery *outcome*—the external element of those offences—brought about by a system of AI.

In Chapter 2, I use the recent passage into law of the Economic Crime and Corporate Transparency Act 2023 as a basis for a broader exploration of the way in which the law can and should approach the liability of companies of different sizes. I start with a critique of the 2023 Act, and of the parts of that Act to be replaced and extended by clause 196 of the Crime and Policing Bill 2025. In this context, the most important changes made by the 2023 Act are that (1) it extends direct corporate liability for substantive offences to instances in which a 'senior manager' in a firm of any size (and not merely a director) engages in a fault-based economic crime and (2) it introduces an offence of failing to prevent fraud (including a range of fraud-related crimes) applicable only to the largest companies. I criticize the first of these changes on three grounds. First, it exposes a firm to unfair labelling when, for example, a senior manager acting in the course of their employment commits a crime in contravention of 'zero tolerance' policy towards crime wholeheartedly endorsed and vigorously supported by the directors.[80] Secondly, it leaves the notion of 'senior manager' unclear: crimes committed by 'managers' will not necessarily be attributable to the company, but those of 'senior managers' will. Finally, in relation to small firms, the new basis for liability is particularly unclear, because in such firms employee roles are much more commonly less well defined, and—unlike failure to prevent offences—the new basis for liability has no applicable

[79] The issue of the use of AI in business compliance is touched on in ch 4.

[80] So, in effect, the 2023 Act imposes vicarious liability on firms for economic crimes committed by senior managers, even though this kind of liability was clearly and rightly rejected by the Law Commission in its Report on which the 2023 Act was based: Law Commission (2022). See the discussion in chs 2 and 5, and in Jeremy Horder (2025a).

defence of 'reasonable procedures'. I suggest that it would have been better to apply the new offence of failure-to-prevent fraud to all firms, of whatever size, as this offence comes with the benefit of defences unavailable in cases of direct, substantive liability.

In Chapter 3, I consider in depth the theoretical basis for finding companies liable for failing to prevent crime by associated persons. This kind of liability stems historically from welfarist Parliamentary intervention during the Victorian period, intervention (ostensibly in the form of vicarious liability) aimed at overcoming deficiencies in the individualist approach of the common law to corporate criminal liability. After setting the discussion in the context of liability for failing to prevent crime more generally, I go on to distinguish three bases for justifying the imposition of criminal liability for a corporate failure to prevent liability. These are the control principle, the influence principle[81] (both discussed briefly in Section I.1 above), and what I call the 'oversight' principle. The latter is distinct from both control and influence principles, in that it is not an 'interventionist' supervisory duty. In relation to the oversight principle, the overseen entity may not be under a duty to behave in accordance with any expectations that the overseeing entity has of them, nor to be influenced in what they do by that entity; and correspondingly, the overseeing entity may have no right to exercise control or influence over the overseen entity. Instead, where there is an oversight duty, there is a duty to maintain a 'watching brief' over another person, without an accompanying control or influence-based right to intervene if it seems that the other person is committing or is going to engage in wrongdoing. I argue that oversight duties, without a right of control or influence, are an important way in which one can understand the emerging duties of 'due diligence' placed on companies with respect to the observance of respect for human rights by contracting partners in the supply chain.[82] An oversight duty gives rise to duties on the overseer to have regard to their *own* conduct, in the light of what they learn through overseeing another person, and does not give rise to supervisory duties to control or influence the person being overseen.

In Chapter 4, I examine in detail and argue in favour of the defence, to a failure-to-prevent offence, of having 'taken all reasonable steps and exercised all due diligence' to prevent wrongdoing. Such a defence is central to my account of corporate crime. It places at the theoretical and moral heart of that account the idea of the company as the 'puzzled citizen' who wishes to do what the law requires, and beyond that, more importantly, as the citizen who wishes to honour and promote the workplace and trading values (as I call them) that underpin legal intervention in pursuit of a liberal-welfarist ideology. Historically, I locate the rise of

[81] For the very particular way in which I define these notions, see Sections 3.2, 3.3 (control), and 3.7 (influence).
[82] An issue considered in more depth in ch 5.

this defence to its current prominence in United Kingdom, to efforts to provide a legislative framework for UK corporate compliance with EU safeguarding standards. Theoretically, I analyse the defence of 'all reasonable precautions and all due diligence', a safeguarding defence, as a second-order defence: concerned less with first-order success in prevention, and more with second-order success in trying or (as I prefer to call it) 'striving' hard enough for prevention. The main focus, by way of contrast with most criminal law defences, is on assessment of the robustness of safeguarding procedures and processes manifested over time, and not on explanations for why things went wrong at the very moment that the wrongdoing occurred. However, in that respect, the defence is not one to be analysed solely by reference to technical 'industry standards'. Overall, taking account of expert standards, the issue should always be whether, in spite of having failed to prevent wrongdoing, a company has (over the relevant period) shown adequate *commitment* to safeguarding, and hence to the values that underpin the legal requirement to engage in it. In pursuit of the argument, I discuss various corporate perspectives on safeguarding. These involve evaluative ideal types, as a way of analysing how the courts have implicitly understood safeguarding issues when interpreting the scope of offences applicable to companies. They include the 'minimalist reactor', the 'positive responder', and the 'pro-active learner',[83] alongside a contrast between what I call the perspective on safeguarding of the 'risk-embracing but ethical Chief Executive Officer' and what I call the perspective of the 'risk-averse, perfectionist compliance officer'.

In Chapter 5, I consider what I call the 'reach' of corporate criminal liability. A company must act through its associated persons, whether these are directors, employees, agents, subsidiaries (in a formal legal sense), or other bodies in which the company has an ongoing interest, such as special purpose vehicles, or other companies in which it has a minority stake. However, with respect to the criminal activities of such persons or entities, there are limits to what a company will be held to have itself done, or to what it will be held responsible for having failed to prevent. For example, whilst it is trite law that someone engaging in wrongdoing can still be acting in the course of employment even when disobeying instructions, it is also common for there to be a requirement that fault-based wrongdoing has been engaged in in order to benefit the company if the company is itself to be fixed with liability.[84] I consider the role of the requirement that a wrongdoer be acting 'in order to benefit' a company to be principally a normative constraint on the scope of corporate liability for the predicate offence in question, rather than as an individual fault element. I contrast it with other state-of-mind focused (potential)

[83] These are drawn from Ian Vickers et al (2005), 160–65.

[84] Clearly, an associated person can also be both disobeying instructions *and* simultaneously acting in order (as they see it) to benefit the company, something that may be true even in the case of strict liability offences. See, further, the discussion in ch 5.

normative constraints on corporate liability. Two such constraints, applicable when an offence committed by an associated person was *not* intended to benefit a company, are (1) that the company knew about the offending or (2) was aware that offending of that kind might be going on but had failed to put in place proper procedures aimed at preventing it.[85]

This analysis forms part of a broader discussion of the restrictive view that must be taken of the connection between companies and associated persons, when deciding whether or not a company can be held vicariously liable for the latter's wrongdoing. By contrast with this restrictive view, a more dynamically principled set of criteria of association govern whether a company may be found responsible for having failed to prevent wrongdoing. The latter basis for corporate responsibility can embrace, in a way vicarious liability cannot, a company's associations with subsidiary companies and other bodies or purpose trusts in which the company has only a minority interest. There are, though, limits to the criteria of association triggering responsibility for failing to prevent wrongdoing. In particular, I argue that contracting partners in a supply chain should ordinarily or presumptively not be regarded as 'associated persons' for the purposes of liability for failing to prevent wrongdoing, in so far as they are freely contracting partners.[86] Nonetheless, a company may be (criminally) responsible for failing to check whether its contracting partners have proper procedures in place to avoid wrongdoing, such as human rights abuses. In such a case, responsibility is for a breach of what I called above an oversight duty; but such a duty is not, unlike a duty to prevent human rights abuses, an interventionist duty relating to the conduct of the other party.

Finally, in Chapter 6, I consider the appropriate response of the state to corporate criminal wrongdoing, and in particular to failures to prevent crime. To begin with, I set out a general justificatory theory of punishment—special to companies—focused on breach of corporate 'membership' rules for participation in the marketplace. These membership rules include rules outlawing failures in point of probity, integrity, and law-abidingness, just as the rules of the road include prohibitions on unsafe driving practices as a feature of the 'membership' conditions for a group of persons licensed to drive. I then go on to develop a more specific theory of punishment particularly appropriate (albeit not confined) to more serious cases of corporate wrongdoing. This is a theory of victim- and community-focused penitential activity. Drawing on an argument in Chapter 1, I focus on the fact that, in some cases (if far from all), the guilty company—with all the human, organizational, and financial resources commonly at its disposal—will be in a

[85] See, further, Section I.4 below.

[86] Although, as we will see, it is important to qualify this claim by saying that a company that is especially dominant or influential over its supply chain may in effect make its contracting partners associated persons for these purposes.

position to deliver not just better safeguarding culture and processes throughout the firm, but systematic victim- or community-based penitential reparation on a medium- to long-term basis. That may be the morally soundest way in which to respond to a company's wrongdoing. No matter how many people within the company are themselves punished individually and however severely,[87] other than in simple cases such individual punishments are highly unlikely to lead either to an enduring culture of and commitment to compliance throughout the firm, or to the delivery of a comprehensive, organizationally sophisticated and enduring penitential response that serves victims and affected communities.[88] So, the state's focus, in responding to (serious) corporate wrongdoing, should—beyond requiring the development of a culture of compliance—be the harnessing of a company's organizational and executive capacities to deliver positive benefits to victims and the broader community on an ongoing—sometimes, on a lifelong—basis, as its penance for engagement in wrongdoing.

I.4 A Scheme of Corporate Criminal Liability

A key classical liberal concern of corporate criminal liability is an individualist concern with establishing the true 'identity' of the company for that purpose. That concern is reflected in the doctrine of 'identification' (model A below). Bridging the gap between the classical liberal approach and a more modern concern with the broader responsibilities of companies in the liberal-welfarist state is a willingness to hold companies to account for failings in what might be called their basic 'proprietary' responsibilities for their premises and business systems (models B and G below).[89] That liberal-welfarist concern is also evident in the state's willingness to hold companies liable vicariously (model F) for the wrongdoing of a limited range of associated persons, and in its willingness to hold them liable for failing to prevent the free, deliberate, and informed wrongdoing of a wider range of associated persons including subsidiaries (models D and E below). The liberal-welfarist model is even more clearly manifested by the state's preparedness to hold companies accountable for the business standards observed by their independent contracting partners (model C below). I will now give a brief account of the different bases for, or models of, criminal liability—or, at the very least, for exposure to regulatory penalties—that do or should exist in some form in a liberal-welfarist

[87] Not uncommonly, key executives involved in historical corporate wrongdoing will have left the company, and will thus have power to change its attitudes and conduct.

[88] That is not to deny that there may, of course, be a strong case for the punishment of individuals involved in corporate wrongdoing.

[89] The emergence of this trend will be charted in ch 3.

or welfare capitalist state, even though some models are more controversial than others, and not all will be discussed in depth.[90]

(A) *Direct Liability for a Substantive Criminal Offence.* Liability of this kind is currently confined to cases in which a director or senior manager (or someone with fully delegated powers) commits an offence when acting with authority. In cases of no-fault crimes, this kind of liability poses relatively few problems. However, in cases involving fault-based crimes, acute fair labelling issues may arise when a senior officer's criminal conduct does not represent the view or approach of the board. Accordingly, for fault-based crimes, I suggest that direct liability should be centred on cases in which (1) the company is comprised of a sole director who commits the offence; (2) the board (in a firm of any size), by majority, consents to or connives at the commission of the offence; and (3) in a small, close-knit firm, any decision by one associated person is regarded in practice by all the others as a representation of the firm itself ('all for one and one for all'), thus implicating all firm members in the commission of an offence by one of their number.

(B) *Liability for a Failure Respecting a Dangerous 'Internal' State of Affairs under Company Control or Influence.*[91] This basis for liability is focused on ongoing risk management and not harm done. It concerns, for example, the use of land or business systems and practices that belong to or are under the direct control of the company (hence, the reference to an 'internal' state of affairs). This basis for liability tends to be found as part of a regulatory scheme, involving either or both of administrative penalties and criminal sanctions. The Health and Safety at Work Act 1974 is the primary example, covering risks to human physical or mental health and security in the workplace.[92] A more modern example is the set of safety obligations imposed on online platforms by the Online Safety Act 2023.[93] Where the internal state of affairs under the company's control concerns its employment of a business system that poses risks of customer financial or data loss (as opposed to risks of physical or mental harm), stemming from poor design or management, penalties are more likely to involve only regulatory fines rather than criminal sanctions.[94]

[90] The models below expand on Gobert's seminal discussion of models of corporate criminal fault: see James Gobert (1994).

[91] I will not be centrally concerned with forms of wrongdoing falling under (B) in this work, but some discussion of the issues can be found in Section 1.8.

[92] Another example is provided by the Environmental Protection Act 1990: section 33 includes a prohibition on keeping controlled waste in a way that 'could' harm human health or cause environmental pollution.

[93] The Online Safety Act 2023 creates a mixture of regulatory penalties, criminal offences, and other sanctions, rather than relying on only one form of punishment.

[94] The Financial Conduct Authority's 'Principle 3', governing the regulated sector (https://www.handbook.fca.org.uk/handbook/PRIN/2/?view=chapter), makes it possible to impose penalties on

(C) *Liability for a Failure Respecting a Dangerous 'External' State of Affairs Open to Company Control or Influence.* This basis for liability is also focused on on-going risk management and not harm done. It is more controversial than (B) above, because a company is being held responsible for overseeing or monitoring not its own but a different, independent body's activity (hence, the reference to an 'external' state of affairs). Such a basis for liability is uncommon but may be found as part of a regulatory scheme involving either or both of administrative penalties and criminal sanctions.[95] An important modern example involves a 'due diligence' failure to monitor possible human rights violations committed by independent contracting partners,[96] or a failure to check that supply chain consumables producers are observing quality standards.[97]

(D) *Liability for Failing to Prevent a Free, Deliberate, and Informed Criminal Act (Not Intended to Benefit the Company) of an Associated Person.* The closest English law currently comes to acknowledging this basis for liability is in the rules governing corporate complicity in crime.[98] Under these rules, in very limited circumstances, a company may be found to have been complicit in a substantive offence committed by an associated person, whether or not that offence was intended to benefit the company;[99] but the rules are unclear. It would be better if it were possible to analyse such cases in terms of failures to prevent offending. However, when an associated person's wrongdoing was not intended to benefit the company, a distinctive normative basis must be found for any corporate liability respecting that wrongdoing. This can be found in an analogy with the civil law doctrine of 'actual notice'.[100] Developing this analogy, corporate liability for failure to prevent wrongdoing not intended to benefit a company can be justified where there is proof either that the company knew at the highest level of an associated person's offending and did nothing, or that it was aware that offending of that kind might be going on but had no systems in place to prevent it. These are what I call in Chapters 3 and 5 the '*Alford*' principles of liability.[101]

regulated companies that did not have adequate 'risk-management' systems. For an example of regulatory penalties for a failure to keep data secure, see https://www.bbc.co.uk/news/technology-54568784 (last accessed 21/05/2025).

[95] https://www.europarl.europa.eu/news/en/press-room/20231205IPR15689/corporate-due-diligence-rules-agreed-to-safeguard-human-rights-and-environment (last accessed 21/05/2025).
[96] Discussed in ch 5.
[97] See the discussion in ch 4.
[98] *JF Alford Transport* [1997] EWCA Crim 654. See the discussion in chs 3 and 5.
[99] *Gaunt* [2003] EWCA Crim 3925, discussed in ch 5.
[100] *Hunt v Luck* [1902] 1 Ch 428.
[101] See the discussion of *JF Alford Transport* [1997] EWCA Crim 654 in ch 3 and *Gaunt* [2003] EWCA Crim 3925, [2004] 2 Cr App R (s).

(E) *Liability for Failing to Prevent the Free, Deliberate, and Informed Criminal Act (Intended to Benefit the Company) of an Associated Person.* Most of the discussion and analysis in this book will concern this basis for corporate conviction. The fact that the criminal act is perpetrated by an associated person acting as such and is intended to benefit the company (even if that intention is, for the offender, secondary to some other intention)[102] is—subject to a safeguarding procedures defence—an adequate normative basis for implicating the company in a criminal failure-to-prevent the wrongdoing, whatever its state of knowledge or awareness in relation to the offending.[103]

(F) *Vicarious Liability (or Failing to Prevent a Strict Liability Offence).* The welfare-driven development of vicarious corporate liability for the strict liability offending of employees or agents is well established but remains controversial. In the interests of fair labelling, vicarious liability would be better reimagined as an instance of corporate failure to prevent wrongdoing. As an aspect of this development, when an associated person has deliberately ignored procedures or instructions, and intentionally committed a relevant offence, the company should not be liable if all reasonable steps had otherwise been taken and all due diligence exercised to avoid such conduct.

(G) *Liability for Failing to Prevent a Significant Non-Criminal Harm.* It would be desirable to create an offence of failing to prevent a non-criminal but significant harm, such as a preventable accident at work, or the bringing about—through a company's use of artificial intelligence or other analogous processes—of the external elements of an offence.[104]

Currently, English law makes space for (A), (B), (E), (F), and also for (C) and (D) to a much more limited extent, but does not recognize (G). In this work, I will not be primarily concerned with fully defending the scheme just outlined, such as the more extensive basis for liability in case (D) and for liability in case (G), although I do support such an extended basis for liability. Instead, I will concentrate on defending the failure-to-prevent model that I place at the heart of (E).

[102] These concepts are analysed in ch 5.

[103] A company should have a defence that it had taken all reasonable steps and exercised all due diligence to avoid offending of that kind. This more demanding defence should replace the less demanding 'adequate' or 'reasonable' procedures defences: see the discussion in ch 4.

[104] See the discussion in ch 1. This offence would be subject to a defence that all reasonable steps had been taken and all due diligence exercised to avoid the harm occurring.

1
ACCOUNTING FOR CORPORATE CRIME

1.1 The Corporate Crime of Failing to Prevent Crime

PROBLEMATIC EXAMPLE: Company C, a finance advisory firm, has long had a director-led and actively policed policy of 'zero tolerance' towards financial crime engaged in by members of the firm. Unknown to the directors, D, a C company senior manager, nonetheless commits false accounting in order to win a major advisory contract for the firm. The Company itself is charged with having committed false accounting, in accordance with to section 196 of the Economic Crime and Corporate Transparency Act 2023.

A theory of corporate criminal responsibility must meet the challenge of explaining the grounds on which companies can properly be convicted of crimes. What makes companies legitimate candidates for criminal liability and punishment? The task undertaken in this book is to develop a clearer and more theoretically secure basis for holding corporate organizations to account in criminal law. In doing so, I hope to shed light on certain key puzzles about corporate criminal responsibility, a phenomenon that fits uneasily within a criminal law system of official labelling and condemnation designed primarily for human individuals. Central to my theory will be an explanation and defence of the failure-to-prevent model of corporate criminal responsibility. On that model, a company stands to be convicted not of the substantive offence committed by someone (P) engaged in business on company's behalf, but of the separate crime of 'failing to prevent' P committing the substantive offence, subject to a defence that the company had taken sufficient care to prevent offences of that type being committed.[1]

This model of responsibility has rapidly gained ground in the United Kingdom, as the basis for imposing criminal liability on companies respecting serious fault-based crimes such as bribery and fraud committed by associated persons,[2]

[1] Such a defence is discussed in detail in ch 4, where the proper wording of the defence is considered.
[2] Bribery Act 2010, s 7; Economic Crime and Corporate Transparency Act 2023, s 199. See also the Criminal Finances Act 2017, ss 45 and 46 (failure to prevent the facilitation of tax evasion).

A Theory of Corporate Crime. Jeremy Horder, Oxford University Press. © Jeremy Horder 2026.
DOI: 10.1093/9780198936534.003.0002

although it remains under-theorized. A well-known example is failure to prevent bribery, contrary to section 7 of the Bribery Act 2010:

> (1) A relevant commercial organisation ('C') is guilty of an offence under this section if a person ('A') associated with C bribes another person intending—
> (a) to obtain or retain business for C, or
> (b) to obtain or retain an advantage in the conduct of business for C.
> (2) But it is a defence for C to prove that C had in place adequate procedures designed to prevent persons associated with C from undertaking such conduct.

Liability under section 7 arises where A (an associated person[3]) commits bribery to benefit C commercially, and C cannot show that, at the relevant time, it had adequate procedures in place to prevent conduct of that kind being engaged in by persons such as A.

The growth of the failure-to-prevent model is in part a reflection of a long-term socio-economic trend in medium- to large-sized corporate business operations: their reliance on hierarchy, on delegation of discretionary decision-making, on divisions of labour, and on the provision of specialized services by third parties.[4] In such circumstances, for senior personnel, alongside direct involvement in achieving day-to-day corporate goals comes a key form of indirect involvement: seeing to it that such goals are achieved by others (not 'rowing' but 'steering'[5]), and accepting responsibility when they are not. However, the growth of the failure-to-prevent model is also in part due to a much longer-standing legal-theoretical difficulty. This is the difficulty involved in making companies of different shapes and sizes fit the individualistic central case of criminal wrongdoing: the engagement in the wrongful act itself. Judges and theorists have struggled to account adequately for the fact that fault-based wrongful acts in corporate contexts may be committed through the free, deliberate, and informed acts of individual employees, agents, or subsidiaries. Rejecting the (morally crude) deployment of vicarious liability to make companies liable for such kinds of criminal wrongdoing,[6] great effort has accordingly been expended on finding ingenious ways to say that a company—through the way in which it was connected to the individual offender—itself also actively engaged in fault-based criminal wrongdoing, through that

[3] The meaning of 'associated person' is considered in ch 5.

[4] For a broader discussion, see Ronald Coase (1937). See also Sergio Conti and Paolo Giaccaria (2001), 35, contrasting modern companies with 'the manufacturing economy of past centuries, peopled with small independent producers usually working on a single product and in a restricted geographical area'.

[5] https://nonprofitquarterly.org/distinguishing-a-boards-steering-and-rowing-work/ (last accessed 20/02/2025).

[6] Other than in cases of no-fault liability. See *Tesco Supermarkets v Nattrass* [1972] AC 153 (HL).

individual.[7] Yet, an offending employee, agent, or subsidiary is a person who—unlike a director—may not feature constitutionally as an officer of the company.[8] So, if an individual offender (such as an employee), even though contracted to the company, is not constitutionally an officer of the company, how can the company itself also be fairly labelled as the offender, respecting the individual's (ex hypothesi) free, deliberate, and informed act of wrongdoing? It seems a better reflection of the constitutional basis of companies to say, respecting the crimes of such individuals, that a company—through a collective failure on the part of its constitutional agents or officers: the directors—simply failed to use their powers to prevent the wrongdoing, than that the company somehow—through the employee, agent, or subsidiary—itself committed that wrongdoing; or so I shall argue.

The failure-to-prevent model is sometimes considered to be an outlying species of corporate criminal offence, a poor substitute for ever more sophisticated doctrines that identify the company with the commission of substantive offences.[9] 'Identification' doctrines try to make plausible the conviction of the company for substantive fault-based offending, by regarding the criminal conduct of individual company officers as the conduct of the company itself.[10] By way of contrast, the argument of this work is that liability based on identification doctrines works only in a limited—albeit significant—class of cases.[11] The failure-to-prevent model should instead become the exemplar of the way in which companies themselves stand in relation to all crimes, whether or not fault-based, committed by persons engaged on company business.[12] There are several advantages (some have already been mentioned in the Introduction) to such a paradigm shift, of which two should be mentioned here.

First, the failure-to-prevent model better reflects the reality of criminal offence-creation as it commonly bears on companies. So far as the basis of liability is concerned, as individuals, we are primarily (and normally, solely) responsible for our

[7] See, e.g., Mark D'Souza (2020).

[8] See Companies Act 2006, s 12: 'The statement of the company's proposed officers required to be delivered to the registrar must contain the required particulars of information about—

(a) the person who is, or persons who are, to be the first director or directors of the company;
(b) in the case of a company that is to be a private company, any person who is (or any persons who are) to be the first secretary (or joint secretaries) of the company;
(c) in the case of a company that is to be a public company, the person who is (or the persons who are) to be the first secretary (or joint secretaries) of the company.'

[9] See, in particular, Mark D'Souza (2020).

[10] *Tesco Supermarkets v Nattrass* [1972] AC 153 (HL). See, further, the discussion in Section 1.4 below and ch 2.

[11] The role of the identification doctrine, in relation to the liability of small firms, is described in Section 1.7 below.

[12] The failure-to-prevent model can also be applied to public bodies, but that argument will not be pursued here.

own conduct. By contrast, if they are responsible at all, companies are responsible for the conduct of other people legally connected to them: directors, employees, agents, or subsidiaries. The concept of failure-to-prevent captures this point quite naturally, in a way that theories concerned to show that the company itself is the perpetrator struggle to do. The failure-to-prevent model thus provides a more appropriate label for a company's involvement in the commission of a crime, and that is true whether or not the crime is fault-based. As we saw in the Introduction, a company can fail to prevent the commission of fraud in much the same way that it can fail to prevent the commission of a strict liability trade descriptions offence, or indeed a harm that is (setting aside the company's involvement) in itself non-criminal, such as harm stemming from an accident at work or from a malfunctioning artificial intelligence (AI) system.

Turning to consider the mode of liability, the failure-to-prevent model fits well with the fact that companies are far more commonly regulated than individuals through exposure to criminal liability for omissions. Companies are exposed to many kinds of omission-based offence that have few (if any) parallels in the realm of individual liability. For example, under the Companies Act 2006, companies face liability for, amongst other things:

Failing to send the registrar a copy of amended articles,
Failing to forward resolutions or agreements affecting the company's constitution to the registrar,
Failing to give the registrar notice of changes made to the company constitution by court order,
Failing to keep a register of members and their particulars,
Failing properly to keep a register of directors containing requisite information,
Failing to hold annual general meetings for a public company, or as required by the articles or the members in the case of a private company,
Failing to prepare a strategic report,
Failing to comply with the approval and signing of the directors' report and accounts,
Failing to send out copies of reports to those entitled to receive them.

There are many other examples,[13] such as the key offences under sections 23 and 118 of the Environmental Protection Act 1990 that almost all make it an offence for someone—commonly a company—to 'fail to' comply with a requirement under

[13] For example, hundreds of companies have accepted penalty notices for omissions offences (typically, concerning registration and due diligence failures), contrary to the Money Laundering, Terrorist Financing and Transfer of Funds (Information on the Payer) Regulations 2017: See https://www.gov.uk/government/publications/businesses-not-complying-with-money-laundering-regulations-in-2018-to-2019/list-of-businesses-for-tax-year-2019-to-2020-that-have-not-complied-with-the-2017-money-laundering-regulations--2?preview=5095232 (last accessed 02/06/2023).

the Act. Many of these offences are in essence regulatory offences. Even so, it seems clear that the ideal type of liability mode that is familiar from the realm of individual liability, involving a wrongful *act* rather than an omission, is commonly subverted in the realm of corporate criminal liability. Against this background, although it is not primarily regulatory in nature, the failure-to-prevent model of offending goes with rather than against the grain, holding out the prospect of very substantial simplification of the principles of corporate criminalization across the board.

A second advantage of the failure-to-prevent model is that it makes central to an analysis of liability the efforts that a company has made to prevent offending, through the provision of a 'reasonable precautions', 'due diligence', 'adequate', or 'reasonable' procedures defence.[14] Such defences do not feature in identification doctrine-focused theories of liability, which treat such efforts as necessarily bearing only on mitigation at the sentencing stage. Accordingly, particularly in the case of fault-based offences, identification doctrine-focused theories struggle to make sense of a liability paradox to which those theories give rise. This is the paradox that arises when it is claimed that company D itself (as opposed simply to an individual director within the company) engaged in a criminal act, in circumstances where it must also be admitted that at the very same time company D disavowed such conduct and was committed to upholding and enforcing robust procedures to prevent it.

Consider a case in which whilst the directors are engaged in actively reinforcing a robust 'zero-tolerance-to-fraud' policy, a senior manager commits fraud to benefit the company. Was the company the person who committed the fraud? Or, was the company the person who was engaged in stamping out the practice of fraud? In point of identification and of fair labelling, you cannot have your cake and eat it too, by answering 'yes' to both questions, because the 'identification' of a company with a criminal act means the identification of the company *as a whole*. Accordingly, what is the right approach for those inclined to 'cakeism', who wish to say that one part of the company in this example was engaged in fraud, whilst another part was engaged in stamping out fraud? The answer to that question, and the way to dissolve the liability paradox, is to adopt a doctrine of liability that accommodates and is shaped by the fact that any company involving more than one person can be a heterogeneous entity, in terms of outlook, activity, and outcomes.[15] A company's heterogeneity—its diversity in terms of the attitudes, conduct, and goals of its associated persons—may be made manifest in different ways.

[14] See the discussion in ch 4.

[15] See, further, Grahame Thompson (1982). The following analysis makes use of some elements of the so-called structural reform model of companies, developed by US theorists, according to which a company is, as Wray puts it, 'a complex entity in which subunits, auxiliary divisions, and middle managers pursue their own "subgoals", which often clash with the aims of the corporation as a whole': Christopher A Wray (2017), 2020. See, e.g., John C Coffee Jr (1981), 393 onwards.

In a dysfunctional organization, different individuals or groups of persons associated with the company adopt different outlooks (some ethical, some unethical) when pursuing company business, and supposedly authoritative standards—if any exist—will only sporadically or inconsistently be enforced, or will not be enforced at all.[16] Alternatively, in a perhaps more likely scenario, heterogeneity may be manifested asymmetrically, in the course of company business. When heterogeneity is manifested asymmetrically, an ethical outlook is demonstrated by (more or less adequately systematized and vigorously enforced) corporate efforts to prevent offending, but offending manifesting a different ethical outlook nonetheless takes place.[17] John Coffee Jr gives some examples, including the following:

> [T]he executive vice president who is a candidate for promotion to president may be willing to run risks which are counterproductive to the firm as a whole because he is eager to make a record profit for his division or to hide a prior error of judgment.[18]

In such a case, there may be a top-level commitment to making high ethical standards authoritative and high safety standards the norm, along with robust procedures in place to make good on those commitments, but either (1) wrongdoing nonetheless sometimes occurs through individual instances of carelessness[19] or (2) there are individuals within the firm who have the capacity and determination to act in the belief that the company would be best served by engagement in certain kinds of wrongdoing.[20] Clearly, in examples of asymmetric heterogeneity, there will be many cases in which top-level commitment to high ethical or safety standards is not as strong as it ought to be, or where in spite of strong commitment, procedures in place to follow through on those commitments are not as good as they should be.[21] In such cases, whether or not the company can be blamed for the occurrence of any given instance of wrongdoing (the actual outcome), it can clearly be blamed for failing to try hard enough more generally to prevent outcomes of that type.

In this work, other than when discussing morally homogenous firms such as one-person firms (discussed briefly below[22]), I will take as my working model underpinning failure-to-prevent offences the asymmetrical case of corporate

[16] See, e.g., *R v Her Majesty's Coroner for East Kent, ex parte Spooner* (1989) 88 Cr App R 10. See also Peter Cleary Yaeger (1995), 154: 'Corporations implicitly house a division of moral labour according to which managers at different ranks are inclined to perceive dilemmas from differing moral angles.'

[17] As in the problematic example at the start of this chapter.

[18] John C Coffee Jr (1981), 393.

[19] See, e.g., *Harrrow London BC v Shah* [2000] Crim LR 692.

[20] *SFO v Barclays* (2018) EWHC 3055 (QB) is a possible example of such a case.

[21] See, e.g., *SFO v Airbus SE* (2020), https://www.judiciary.uk/wp-content/uploads/2020/01/Director-of-the-Serious-Fraud-Office-v-Airbus-SE-1.pdf (last accessed 21/09/2025).

[22] See the discussion in ch 2.

heterogeneity. In part, that is because such a model reflects the way that the law understands the supervisory relationship between a company's supreme executive authorities—its directors—and the company employees or agents beneath them. For example, in explaining the supervisory duties imposed on company directors respecting powers delegated to employees, in a famous passage Mr Justice Parker said:

> Whilst directors are entitled (subject to the articles of association of the company) to delegate particular functions to those below them in the management chain, and to trust their competence and integrity to a reasonable extent, the exercise of the power of delegation does not absolve a director from the duty to supervise the discharge of the delegated functions.[23]

Whether or not the capacity in which someone committed a crime means that the company itself can be identified with its commission, it is open to the criminal law to identify a company with, or judge it by, the efforts it has made to abide by supervisory ethical duties placed by law on company directors to take responsibility for the integrity (to use Mr Justice Parker's term) of those who act in its name. This 'supervision duty' approach to the role of directors is, of course, of particular importance in relation to safeguarding against wrongdoing. In the regulated sector, it is a commonplace that a firm must adequately supervise processes designed to ensure that wrongdoing does not take place. For example, in fining Starling Bank £28,959,426 for breach of its safeguarding requirements, the Financial Conduct Authority highlighted a finding that 'Starling's senior management failed to adequately oversee and monitor the day-to-day compliance with (a voluntary requirement) . . . Starling's senior management did not provide effective challenge and oversight of those responsible for the day-to-day implementation of the [voluntary requirement]'.[24]

What is important about the rise to prominence of directorial supervisory duties is that they provide a different way of understanding how an ethically heterogenous company relates to wrongdoing committed by an associated person in the course of its business practices. For example, suppose that a managing

[23] *Secretary of State for Trade and Industry v Baker (No. 5)* [1999] 1 BCLC 433, 436, and 489.

[24] Financial Conduct Authority (2024), 12. In the United States, directors have been placed under fiduciary duties to supervise corporate compliance, the 'Caremark' duties: *In re Caremark International Inc Derivative Litigation*, 698 A 2d 959 (Delaware Chancery 1996). Breach of these duties (involving a betrayal of fiduciary status) occurs when 'the directors utterly failed to implement any reporting or information system or controls; or . . . having implemented such a system or controls, [the directors] consciously failed to monitor or oversee its operations thus disabling themselves from being informed of risks or problems requiring their attention': *Stone v Ritter*, 911 A 2d (Delaware 2006) 362, 370. See also *In re The Boeing Company Derivative Litigation*, C A 2019-0907-MTZ, 67 (Delaware Chancery 7 September 2021).

director (MD) commits a fraud to benefit the company in the course of business negotiation, using a blank cheque from a supply provided to MD to carry out company business by a trusting director or directors.[25] In such a case, the fraud is committed by a director; but how important really is this traditional 'identification' process to an evaluation of the responsibility of the company itself for what happened? One might argue that a focus on MD's—the offender's—status within the company is largely a distraction. Whatever MD's status within the company, MD is individually guilty of fraud. So, the key question in relation to the corporate dimension to the fraud, given that it was ex hypothesi committed in the course of employment to benefit the company,[26] is why and how the company enabled it or failed to stop it being committed. On my account, the involvement of the company itself in such an example is best represented as a (collective) failure to prevent the crime, on the part of the directors: an involvement that is criminal in nature if the directors had not ensured that robust procedures were in place to prevent offending of this type.

Where does this approach leave the traditional identification doctrine? This doctrine can still be relevant and decisive, in describing a company's involvement in a crime, in a numerically significant number of cases. These are cases where the company can be described as ethically homogenous. In such a company, there is no ethical space for the coexistence of (1) corporate commitment to prevent the commission of certain types of crime and (2) the commission of such a crime. An obvious example of such ethical homogeneity in the organization is where the wrongdoer, D, is the sole proprietor-director of a firm with no employees, as in *Lennard's Carrying Company Ltd v Asiatic Petroleum*.[27] Another example is where all the directors agree on or acquiesce in a course of criminal conduct.[28] However, interpreting the identification doctrine as a doctrine concerned with ethically homogenous firms means that the doctrine may have a wider application. I will consider other examples in due course but they include, for example, the numerically significant case of family firms in which the close relationship and bond between the parties means that, whatever the formal status of any individual family member (director, employee, and manager), the acts of one are regarded within the family as the acts of all.

[25] For an analogous case, *Dorchester Finance Co Ltd v Stebbing* [1989] BCLC 498.

[26] It is, of course, trite law that someone may still be acting in the course of their employment even though they are disobeying instructions or going against the prevailing ethos of the company: *Coppen v Moore* (No 2) [1898] 2 QB 306; *United States v Hilton Hotels Corp*, 467 F 2d 1000 (9th Cir 1972).

[27] [1915] AC 705 (HL).

[28] For a possible example, see https://www.justice.gov/opa/pr/airbus-agrees-pay-over-39-billion-global-penalties-resolve-foreign-bribery-and-itar-case (last accessed 21/10/2024): 'Airbus SE, the second largest Aerospace company world-wide, engaged in a systematic and deliberate conspiracy, that knowingly and willfully violated U.S. fraud and export laws', said Special Agent in Charge Peter C Fitzhugh of US Immigration and Customs Enforcement's Homeland Security Investigations New York.

1.2 Four Meanings of 'Company' in Criminal Law

If the failure to prevent crime model is principally focused on the collective failures of directors, with respect to crime prevention, does that imply that corporate criminal law and punishment in failure-to-prevent cases are addressed only to company directors, in their corporate capacity? Alternatively, are corporate criminal law and punishment addressed not only to the individuals who engaged in the wrongdoing but also to other (innocent) employees? To answer these questions, we need to understand the way in which the criminal justice system addresses companies in different guises. Discussion of corporate criminal liability and punishment has been hampered by a failure to distinguish these different guises, and explain which of them is relevant and when. Accordingly, in this section and in Section 1.3, I will set out different understandings of a 'company' that have influenced or underpinned theories of corporate criminal liability and punishment, and explain briefly how each is relevant to my discussion.

The company as an 'abstract legal' entity. It is trite law that a company may be regarded as in an important sense a 'myth and a fiction',[29] a 'legal abstraction',[30] a 'mere machinery',[31] or an 'abstract conception'.[32] As Lord Hoffmann put it, '[t]here is in fact no such thing as the company as such, no *ding* and *sich*, only the applicable rules [of attribution]'.[33] Adopting this conception of a company, when liability and punishment are imposed on a company, the moral message involved (if any) must be aimed at the company's human agents: its directors, employees, and so on. So much is relatively uncontroversial. Even so, the fact that companies have an existence as purely abstract legal entities has led some commentators to express scepticism about the (moral) point of corporate criminal law and of punishment in general.[34] GR Sullivan, for example, has argued that, '[t]here is no conceptual basis for a retributivist response to corporate illegality and no basis . . . for the claim that corporations are substantive moral agents which may perpetrate specifically corporate wrongs'.[35] However, such scepticism stems from a misunderstanding about the focus of liability in cases involving companies, and from an unduly restrictive view of how and when criminal liability and punishment may legitimately be imposed. The existence of the abstract corporate entity may play a significant role in offending, making the imposition of criminal liability on it permissible, even if the entity itself can neither think nor act. Further, the imposition of punishment on an

[29] *Broderip v Salmon* [1895] 9 Ch 323, 330–31, and 341.
[30] *Continental Tyre and Rubber (GB) Ltd v Daimler Co Ltd* [1916] 1 KB 893, 916.
[31] *Daimler Co v Continental Tyre and Rubber Co* [1916] 2 AC 307, 316.
[32] *Houghton and Co v Nothard, Lome and Wills Ltd* [1928] AC 1, 14.
[33] *Meridian Global Funds Management Asia Ltd v Securities Commission* [1995] 2 AC 500, 506–07, cited by GR Sullivan (1996), 516.
[34] See, e.g., Manuel Velasquez (2003).
[35] GR Sullivan (1996), 516. See also Samuel W Buell (2020), Susan Wolf (1985), and Manuel Velasquez (2003).

abstract corporate entity does not require a retributivist justification. The imposition of punishment on such an entity can be justified because it is the best way to serve important forward-looking moral purposes of the criminal justice system, such as ensuring systematic reforms are made, and that there is institutional commitment to medium- or long-term victim or community-focused penitential activity required at the sentencing stage.[36] I will explain these claims further and in Section 1.3.

To set the conception of the company as an abstract legal entity in a moral context, it is important to bear in mind that the way we treat inanimate entities or objects—including subjecting them to adverse treatment—can be rich in moral significance. This is evident from the way that, for example, we show concern at the desecration of graves or war memorials, or for the pollution of true wildernesses, and from the way that buildings or other landmarks associated with horrific crimes or regimes are often demolished rather than merely refurbished. Such concern is genuine moral concern, a concern to promote the quality of the conditions in which humans flourish. It does not merely reflect a negative or positive emotional reaction.[37] The existence of companies, as entities, is obviously not a general prerequisite for human flourishing.[38] Indeed, corporate activity (like the activity of the state itself, or of some charities) may threaten human flourishing through, for example, the use of dubious employment practices threatening the health, safety, and life-chances of employees.[39] Nonetheless, corporate activity—activity that the existence of the abstract corporate legal entity makes possible—can also be evaluated positively from a moral point of view, and the company as a legal entity plays a key part in that. For example, the continued existence of a company, as a matter of law, may underpin the realization of personal value for millions of people,[40] through the active and flourishing business, professional, or commercial lives they live whilst engaged in business activity on its behalf.[41] It follows that, far from being a matter of moral indifference, the conviction and punishment of (abstract and legal) companies can be of momentous significance in the personal lives of those connected to it, as a concrete entity.

[36] This issue is addressed in depth in ch 6.

[37] See Stephen Shute, John Gardner and Jeremy Horder (1993), introduction.

[38] Although their enduring significance in the public mind is demonstrated by the number of Facebook pages devoted to long defunct companies.

[39] For example, according to Office for National Statistics, over a million people in the United Kingdom were employed on a zero-hours contract from April to June 2024: https://www.ons.gov.uk/surveys/informationforhouseholdsandindividuals/householdandindividualsurveys/labourforcesurvey (last accessed 05/03/2025). Further, according to the Health and Safety Executive, 1.7 million working people suffering from a work-related illness in 2023–2024, and 604,000 working people sustained an injury at work: https://www.hse.gov.uk/statistics/overview.htm (last accessed 05/03/2025).

[40] The private sector accounts for 83.5 per cent of all employment: Office for National Statistics (2019), 11.

[41] See text at n 91 below.

So far as in-principle criminal liability is concerned, the importance of the company as an abstract legal entity is not that such an entity can think and act. Clearly, it cannot. The importance of a company's existence as an abstract legal entity has to do with the special normative status that it confers on conduct. The existence of the abstract legal entity makes it possible for human agents legally connected to it to engage in a distinctive form of activity: corporate activity. It is this kind of (in)activity that is in issue in corporate cases. 'Corporate activity' is not simply individual human activity motivated by benefitting the company. Any customer who intentionally shops at their local store to help to keep it in business engages in activity of that kind. The 'corporate' nature of activity is a normatively distinctive feature of that activity, even if the activity can also be described in individualized terms. So, winning a contract for my company, making a donation to charity on its behalf, or improving the health and safety rules governing my workplace are examples of (valuable) corporate activity, even if they clearly involve a series of individual actions. What instantiates such activity as corporate activity is that, when I engage in the actions, I do so by using a corporate capacity I possess (something considered in more depth in Chapter 5). Accordingly, the involvement of the abstract company does not come through deliberation or action (an impossibility) but through the conferral of the distinct normative status—corporate status—on the human activity.

The importance of this is that it is the prosecution of the company itself—either for the substantive offence or for failing to prevent that offence—that commonly best reflects the 'corporate' nature of activity undertaken in a corporate capacity. The prosecution of an individual director or employee, even when they were motivated to benefit the company through their crime, typically reflects—and is intended to reflect—only their individual involvement in the wrongdoing. In fair labelling terms, the conviction of the individual may thus less adequately reflect, and may not be intended (fully) to reflect, the involvement of a separate—corporate—person. Importantly, that is so, even if—indirectly—the company as a whole may be tainted by the individual conviction of a director or employee who committed a crime on company business. Moreover, the possibility of convicting the company for an offence committed by an associated person, in the course of business, plays an important protective role in point of justice and fairness. Suppose that an offence would not have been committed were it not for some organizationally significant feature of the way in which associated persons are permitted to (or must) engage in activities on the company's behalf. Then, the lower in the hierarchy the associated person-offender is, and the less freedom they have to depart from institutional norms or orders, the stronger the case for the company being required to face justice instead of the associated person themselves.[42]

[42] See, further, on this point, the discussion in Section 3.5.

To understand better the role of corporate capacity, consider this example:

> It is clear beyond doubt that someone at directorial or senior manager level within Company X committed fraud in their capacity as a company director or senior manager. However, because of the way in which the fraud was committed, it is impossible to know which of over 100 directors and senior managers at Company X was responsible.

The nature of this example means that no individual wrongdoer, even though there certainly was one, can be identified. Does that mean, other things being equal, that no prosecution of any person for fraud, or of the company for failure to prevent fraud, can properly follow? It does not. In such a case, liability is based on the fact that the fraud was undoubtedly committed by a relevant person (director or senior manager) acting in a corporate capacity. In that respect, who that person was, individually, is neither here nor there. In such a case, the existence of the company as an abstract legal entity plays a crucial role in the offence, conferring the appropriate normative status ('corporate activity') on the unknown fraudster's acts. That makes prosecution of the abstract corporate legal entity an entirely legitimate way of serving the moral purposes of the criminal justice system, in bringing the (failure to prevent the) fraudulent conduct to account.

I now turn to the issue of punishment, the justice of which in part presupposes that in-principle liability has a sound basis. An analogous argument to the one just made applies here. In Chapter 6, I will put on one side 'backward-looking' just deserts or retributive accounts of the justification for punishment, accounts tied to the notion of righting a wrong through supposedly proportionate hard treatment.[43] It is simply not plausible to suppose that an abstract legal entity can be made to 'suffer' retribution.[44] However, moving beyond GR Sullivan's exclusive concern with retribution,[45] there are some morally valuable punitive goals that may be achieved by imposing punishment on the company itself, as a means to achieving those ends.[46] The imposition of punishment on the abstract legal entity triggers fiduciary duties binding on relevant persons to exercise their corporate capacities to achieve those goals, even if they are themselves innocent of

[43] As HLA Hart rightly observed of just deserts theories, '[r]etributivists [just deserts theorists] appear to believe in 'a mysterious piece of moral alchemy in which the combination of the two evils of moral wickedness and suffering [through punishment] are transmuted into good'': HLA Hart (2008), 234–35. In adopting such a view, Hart was—improbable though it sounds—bringing himself broadly in alignment with the views of Karl Marx, for whom, '[W]hat a state of society is, that which knows of no better instrument for its own defence than the hangman, and which proclaims through the "leading journal of the world" [*The Times*] its own brutality as eternal law?': Karl Marx (1853), 25–26.

[44] See Samuel W Buell (2020).

[45] See GR Sullivan (1996), 516.

[46] As no more than an abstract legal entity, a company may permissibly be used purely as a means to a morally valuable end.

wrongdoing. In that regard, the forward-looking punishment theory on which I will rely is focused (especially in serious cases) on securing corporate commitment to morally worthwhile victim and community-focused penitential activity, alongside internal reform of company processes and attitudes. A case employing the latter kind of forward-looking punishment of a company is *United States v Mitsubishi International Corporation*.[47] In this case, in addition to a fine, the company was required to loan executives for one year to help the development of community organizations.[48] With respect to such a forward-looking theory, it is certainly true to say that where a company is comprised of a sole director, or of a small handful of individual directors, action taken against an individual corporate wrongdoer may serve the ends of criminal justice as well or better than action taken against the company. However, it is important to understand the proper explanation for this. In the case of micro-company wrongdoing, the punishment of the individual directorial or managerial wrongdoer involves the punishment of someone with a high degree of (or even sole) control over corporate ethos and conduct. Prosecuting that person individually may thus be the best way to achieve reformed corporate behaviour in future, along with victim or community reparation, as opposed to punishment of the company itself. By contrast, this may be far less likely in the case of a medium- to large-sized company.

Consider a case in which a multinational corporation failed to prevent systematic bribery throughout the world over many years.[49] The conviction and punishment of particular directors or employees (some or all of whom may have left the company) for their individual role in events has no necessary connection with, and may be highly unlikely in itself to lead to, any vital systematic reform of the company. Likewise, individual convictions may do little or nothing to facilitate global restitution to victims or long-term corporate commitment to (say) community rebuilding in affected jurisdictions. Under a forward-looking theory of punishment, these critical goals of the criminal justice process can only realistically be achieved by imposing such measures—*qua* punishments—as requirements demanded of the company itself, and thereby in particular of the existing directors as fiduciaries, whether or not the existing directors knew of or played any part in the wrongdoing (a point addressed in the next section).[50] In such cases, then, the moral purposes of the criminal justice system are served by punishment of the company, punishment

[47] 677 F 2d 785, 788 (9th Circuit 1982).

[48] See also *United States v Danilow Pastry Company* 563 F Supp 1159 (1983).

[49] For a not dissimilar case, see Deferred Prosecution Agreement—SFO v Rolls Royce PLC—Serious Fraud Office—Serious Fraud Office: https://assets.publishing.service.gov.uk/media/67c061c475083 7d7604dbc66/DPA_-_Rolls_Royce_-_170117.pdf (last accessed 31/08/2024), discussed further in ch 6.

[50] As Sam Buell puts it, 'prosecutors are more concerned—at least in the . . . cases involving FCPA violations, pharma marketing practices, bank money laundering, environmental offenses, and the like—with the organizational dynamics that generate corporate crime than they are with the individuals who execute the criminal acts': Samuel W Buell (2018), 29.

that involves and requires a collective (and director-driven) institutional response. I return to this issue in Section 1.3 below, but discussion of it brings me naturally to the next conception of the company.

The company as an entity led by a supreme executive authority. A company has by law a constitution, the essence of which is set out under the Companies Act 2006. Under that legal constitution, a company must have a director or directors, persons given special executive status by the 2006 Act. That brings me to the next corporate guise, the company as an entity led by a supreme executive authority. Constitutionally, it is the director or directors who are the company officers who must be appointed, as part of the process of setting up any company, however small or large. Further, it is the director or directors who have ultimate executive authority under a company's constitution, in relation to company decision-making. That is so, even if (from the perspective of the company as an 'owned' entity) the directors are accountable to shareholders for the company's overall performance, and even though they stand to be appointed or dismissed at the (proprietary) behest of shareholders.[51] As suggested in Section 1.3, concerning the company as an abstract legal entity, the ultimate executive authority possessed by directors makes them key players in securing compliance with the criminal law's guidance demands, and in securing forward-looking punitive demands for long-term institutional reform, victim reparation, and community service. An emphasis on this way of conceiving of a company—as an entity with supreme (executive) leaders—is hence an important part of the argument in this book.[52]

Corporate (in)activity may be engaged in by different types of persons—shareholders, employees, and agents—other than directors. However, in failure-to-prevent cases, the key pieces of corporate inactivity are the (collective) directorial failure to prevent the crime, and—where relevant—the failure to put in place proper procedures to prevent crime. Even when, as is customary in medium- to large-sized firms, the design and implementation of such procedures is delegated by directors to managers, this does not obviate the need for directors to exercise oversight functions in respect of that delegation. As Mr Justice Parker observed, 'the exercise of the power of delegation does not absolve a director from the duty to supervise the discharge of the delegated functions'.[53] Moreover, subject

[51] *Gramophone and Typewriter Ltd v Stanley* [1908] 2 KB 89 (CA), 105–06 per Buckley LJ: 'The Directors are not servants to obey directions given by the shareholders as individuals; they are not agents appointed by and bound to serve the shareholders as their principals. They are persons who may by the regulations be entrusted with the control of the business, and if so entrusted they can be dispossessed from that control only by the statutory majority which can alter the articles. Directors are not, I think, bound to comply with the directions even of all the corporators acting as individuals.'

[52] The idea of the company as a 'led' entity has some similarities with the 'trust' theory of the company, focusing on the fiduciary duties owed uniquely by directors to the company. However, whilst fiduciary duties are relevant to my account of the company as a 'led' entity (as we saw earlier), they do not play a pivotal role. That role is played by the supreme executive position occupied by directors.

[53] *Secretary of State for Trade and Industry v Baker (No. 5)* [1999] 1 BCLC 433, 436, and 489. See text at n 23 above.

to what I will say about this issue in Section 1.3, it is the company as an entity with a supreme executive authority that is necessarily addressed by the criminal justice system ex post, at the sentencing stage. It must ultimately be for the company directors (albeit through their managers, in appropriate cases) to authorize or approve the payment of fines, and—where so ordered—to arrange for the performance of victim- or community-focused reparation.

This, 'Weberian' understanding of a company and its directors, and of the identification doctrine, in terms of constitutionally empowered supreme executive authorities will be contrasted in Chapter 2 with a more Durkheimian understanding of the company in terms of 'mechanical' solidarity. As we will see, the Durkheimian understanding is more appropriate for small family firms. Putting that distinction on one side for now, we should note the basis for resistance to placing emphasis on the role of directors, in point of liability.[54] Such resistance is commonly driven by fears that giving a pivotal role to directors, in the determination of liability, will entail too little criminal responsibility being attributed to companies, given that much wrongdoing occurs out of directorial sight and out of directorial mind.[55] However, such fears presuppose that what is in issue is the application of an orthodox and individualistic form of criminal liability: liability for an act of substantive wrongdoing in itself (fraud, bribery, causing pollution, etc.), something with which directors of larger firms may never themselves sully their hands. By contrast, the failure-to-prevent model of criminal responsibility is not so crudely individualistic, because it turns on a recognition of the relatedness of corporate criminal wrongdoing: for every perpetrator of wrongdoing in the course of their employment, there is someone—or a group of persons—whose responsibility it was to prevent that wrongdoing. So, if one places failure-to-prevent crime at the heart of corporate criminal forms of responsibility, the fears referred to above can be allayed. By taking the view that the 'buck stops' with company directors respecting failure to prevent a crime, whatever the level within the company at which that crime was in itself committed, the criminal law regards the company as constitutionally engaged with that criminal wrongdoing.

The company as a real entity. A company may become a so-called real entity. This is an entity with a distinctive character or modus operandi developed out of its abstract legal form. In analysing this conception of a company, we should start by noting that there is an overlap between the real entity conception of a company and other conceptions of the company. For example, although a private company may start life with the legal minimum of one director, it may grow to be run exclusively by a number of directors. Its growth in this respect reflects its evolution as a real entity, even though the legal focus may be on its character as an entity led by a supreme executive body (the directors collectively). Similarly,

[54] See, e.g., Celia Wells (2001).
[55] See, e.g., the discussion in ibid.

a company may evolve by taking on one or more employees, or by using agents and subsidiaries. Such evolution reflects its growth in real entity terms. However, as I will explain, what makes such growth important is that the firm has evolved into what I call a 'concrete legal entity', an entity binding individuals together by contract. An important example of such evolution is the tendency of medium- to large-sized firms to appoint senior managers to play a key role in running the company. In response to this development, a number of jurisdictions have made it possible to identify the company itself with the wrongdoing of such persons, in addition to the wrongdoing of directors.[56] The United Kingdom has followed suit, in relation to financial crimes, in virtue of section 196 of the Economic Crime and Corporate Transparency Act 2023 (hereinafter 'the 2023 Act'), and clause 196 of the Crime and Policing Act 2025,[57] having already in effect made such an extension in corporate manslaughter cases.[58] So understood, corporate liability is real-entity-based, in that liability is being shaped in response to the way in some companies are now commonly run (in whole or in part).

Even so, such a real-entity-driven understanding of who can be identified with the company itself should be regarded as unsound, in point of fair labelling. That is because in companies employing senior managers, the company will commonly be morally heterogenous, and there will be a leadership tier above the senior managers with ultimate responsibility for guaranteeing the integrity and probity of a company's actions (including the integrity and probity of senior managers' actions). As explained in Section 1.1 above, in accordance with a conception of the company as an entity with a supreme executive authority, it is the discharge of that ultimate responsibility that ought to be in criminal law focus, from a fair labelling point of view, and that entails a principal focus on directorial failure to prevent crime, including crime committed by senior managers.[59]

Putting aside these cases of overlap, a company may also evolve as a real entity by developing characteristics less easy to capture in legal form: for example, its policies, systems, culture, and way of doing business.[60] As Eva Micheler has recently described the real entity theory:

> [F]irms . . . are more than the sum of the contributions of their participants. They also act independently of the views and interests of their participants. This occurs

[56] See, e.g., Criminal Code (Canada), s 22.2, as applied to the Corruption of Foreign Public Officials Act (Canada) 1999; Articles 121 and 122 of the French Criminal Code.

[57] See, further, the detailed discussion in ch 2.

[58] Corporate Manslaughter and Corporate Homicide Act 2007, s 1(4).

[59] Even so, as we will see in ch 6, that does not mean senior managers cannot or should not play a special role in criminal proceedings. For example, as a part of criminal punishment, it ought to be possible to issue binding (civil) orders to persons occupying certain key managerial roles, such as chief financial officer, requiring them to take personal responsibility for (say) making restitution, performing reparations, and reforming the way that a company does its business.

[60] Eva Micheler (2021).

> because human beings change their behaviour when they act as members of a group or an organization. In a group we tend to develop and conform to a shared standard. When we act in organizations habits, routines, processes, and procedures form and a culture emerges. These take on a life of their own affecting the behaviour of the participants.[61]

Thus understood, real entity theory has a bearing on failure-to-prevent offences in two ways. First, it has some bearing on the inculpatory, offence requirement in such offences that the associated person who engaged in (say) bribery or a fraud offence have done so with an intention to benefit the firm or one of its customers.[62] The notion of 'intention to benefit' can be given a largely contractual interpretation, as when D commits fraud in order to meet a performance target. Even so, it would be appropriate to interpret it more broadly: to encompass an associated person's intention to further the evolving plans and goals of the company at a strategic level, which means interpreting the notion of 'benefit' in terms of the company as a real entity.[63]

Secondly, real entity theory comes into its own when applied to common exculpatory defences to corporate crime, such as the failure-to-prevent defences that 'adequate' or 'reasonable' procedures were in place to avoid wrongdoing. When companies rely on such defences, they commonly rely on being able to point to the existence of in-house systems and processes for, and perhaps a culture of, safeguarding against wrongdoing (a safety-focused modus operandi) even though it is admitted that a given instance of wrongdoing slipped through the net. The company's defence is assessed in terms of whether it was doing enough, judged by the standards of a real entity committed to robust safeguarding practices and culture, to prevent or (acceptably) to reduce the risk of offences of the relevant type being committed.[64] In that regard, in Chapter 4, I will analyse what is at stake in satisfying defences of adequate or reasonable procedures, or (my preferred formula) of having taken all reasonable precautions and exercised all due diligence, in terms of a corporate real entity operating either as a 'positive responder' or as a 'pro-active learner'.[65]

More problematic have been some recent arguments that the core *in*culpatory principles of the criminal law should be adapted to account for the existence of a company as a real entity, in terms of its systems, culture, and modus operandi.[66] It

[61] Ibid., 1.

[62] The offences of failing to prevent bribery and failing to prevent fraud both require that the associated person who committed the offence have acted in order to benefit the company. By contrast, the crime of failing to prevent the facilitation of tax evasion does not require the associated person to have intended by that crime to benefit the company. See the discussion in Karl Laird (2017).

[63] I will return to this point in ch 5.

[64] See the more detailed discussion in ch 4.

[65] For this terminology, see Ian Vickers et al (2005), discussed in ch 4.

[66] Celia Wells (2001); Elise Bant (2023).

has long been possible to make a negative evaluation of a company's culture and systems—its existence as a real entity—central to inculpation in some instances. One example, found in section 1 of the Health and Safety at Work Act 1974, is in effect the obverse of the adequate or reasonable procedures defence: where an offence is committed if a (corporate) employer fails 'to ensure, so far as is reasonably practicable, the health, safety and welfare at work of all his [*sic*] employees'. An example from the regulatory sector is principle 3 of the Financial Conduct Authority's rules binding on regulated companies, namely that 'a firm must take reasonable care to organise and control its affairs responsibly and effectively, with adequate risk management systems'.[67] In these instances, liability may not be determined synchronically, turning solely on what happened—a lapse of some kind—at a given moment in time. Instead, liability may be determined diachronically. In that latter case, liability turns on a judgement about a 'state of affairs', and is focused on whether the company failed over time to develop, sustain, and foster a modus operandi, culture, or system adequately conducive to safety, health, or crime prevention.

In that regard, a state of affairs ('In the UK, companies are inadequately policed') is commonly an evaluative phenomenon, in itself lacking a unique spatio-temporal location, and hence in itself having no causal impact as such:

> A state of affairs lies there, placidly and quietly. If a state of affairs is to cause an outcome O, some . . . event has to occur, such that it causes O. This is crucial to an understanding of how states of affairs cause things.[68]

So, having (say) an unsafe system of working practices is something that, to use Thomson's terminology, may simply lie there 'placidly and quietly'. It is only brought into play causally when an event occurs that makes that happen: such as someone falling against a working machine that has had no safety shield fixed on it to prevent contact. However, no proof of such an event is required, to trigger liability for having an unsafe system of working practices under the 1974 Act. So, we may say that in-principle liability under the Act is not necessarily event-based and is non-causal in nature. The focus is on the ex hypothesi dangerous state of affairs that the company allowed to develop in the way that it manages its premises or runs its business: liability model B, as described in Section I.4.

However, many crimes, including those at issue in failure-to-prevent cases, are not amenable to proof simply in terms of a diachronic assessment of a continuing 'state of affairs', such as having inadequate risk-management practices or an unsafe system of working practices. Such crimes rely on proof of the manifestation of a so-called act-token, a unique space-time particular in a causal chain.[69] For

[67] Financial Conduct Authority (2023).
[68] J Jarvis Thomson (2003), 81, cited in Jeremy Horder (2024), 237.
[69] Linda Wetzel (2018).

example, in corporate cases, the offences of fraud, bribery, and failure-to-prevent fraud and bribery all require proof inter alia that someone associated with the company engaged in an act of bribery or of fraud. Such a crime involves a causally impactful 'act-token', something that occurred at a moment or series of moments in space-time. Naturally, the commission of such a criminal act-token engaged in on company business may be explained by, for example, a corrupt corporate culture within the firm. The act(-token) of bribery or fraud may—on the principles explained by Thomson in the passage cited above—bring the corrupt corporate culture of a firm into play.[70] It is on this basis that, for example, in relation to an unlawful act-token of corporate killing, section 8(3) of the Corporate Manslaughter and Corporate Homicide Act 2007 makes it clear that

> [t]he jury may also ... 'consider the extent to which the evidence shows that there were attitudes, policies, systems or accepted practices within the organisation', in so far as these may have encouraged a health and safety failure bearing on the company's breach of its duty of care, 'or to have produced tolerance of [that failure].

However, the key point is that, by its nature, an act-token, such as a corrupt act, cannot be identified or equated with (even if it can be explained by) a corrupt culture. That is because the continued existence of a corrupt culture, reprehensible and conducive to the commission of criminal act-tokens though it may be, is as such acausal. 'Lying placidly and quietly', such a culture has no status or identity as a unique act or omission taking place at a moment in space-time. Instead, the identification of a corrupt culture, as such, involves a diachronic value judgement about a persisting state of affairs, a judgment that may not be linked to a very definite time period and a fortiori not to a particular moment or moments in time.

If that analysis seems abstract, consider the failure of legislation aimed at equating act-tokens and states of affairs. Section 12(3)(1) of the Australian Criminal Code Act 1995 provides that a company will be taken to have had the intention, knowledge, or reckless state of mind of a human person, if it 'expressly, tacitly or impliedly authorised or permitted the commission of the offence'. Under the Code, such authorization or permission may be found to have been given if, amongst other things, 'a corporate culture existed within the body corporate that directed, encouraged, tolerated or led to non-compliance with the relevant provision'.[71] The provision has not been a success in bringing companies to justice,[72]

[70] For an analysis of how individual act-tokens bring states of affairs into (causal) play in criminal law contexts, see Jeremy Horder (2024).

[71] Australian Criminal Code Act 1995, s 12(3)(2)(C).

[72] Australian Law Reform Commission (2020), https://www.alrc.gov.au/news/corporate-criminal-responsibility-the-case-for-reform/ (last accessed 26/03/2024): 'Part 2.5 has been excluded from multiple Commonwealth statutes. In fact, Part 2.5 has been very rarely used, resulting in extremely limited judicial guidance.'

and that is not surprising. If a criminal law requires proof that an act was engaged in intentionally, knowingly, or recklessly, it requires proof, other than in exceptional circumstances, of a causally significant, unique space-time particular, of an act-token embodying that state of mind. A 'corporate culture', even one that 'encouraged, tolerated, or led to non-compliance', simply fails to meet that criterion. In its paper that formed the basis for the 2023 Act reforms considered in Chapter 2, the Law Commission rejected a 'real entity' basis for inculpation,[73] and this rejection reflects the difficulties with it outlined here. By contrast, as we will see in Chapter 4, evidence of a 'state of affairs' constituted by (sound) procedures, processes, and culture can be potent *ex*culpatory evidence, of a kind directly relevant to defences such as the defence of having had 'adequate procedures' to prevent wrongdoing.[74]

The company as a 'concrete legal' entity. A company is being considered as a 'concrete' legal entity when it is considered as a legal whole, including all those who are legally a part of it, such as directors, employees, shareholders, and in some instances subsidiary companies. The notion of the company as a concrete legal entity, a manifestation of its evolution as a real entity, is in some ways similar to the 'nexus of contracts' view of the company, favoured by some economic analysts;[75] but there is a crucial difference. The nexus of contracts view includes contractual relations between the company and customers. By contrast, on the theory of the firm as a concrete legal entity, such relations are external to the company itself. The company as a concrete legal entity is comprised only of a legal network of persons in some sense working for (or owning) it. Too little attention has been paid to the instances in which the criminal justice system addresses a company that has evolved as a real entity into a concrete legal entity.[76] When the criminal law addresses a company as a concrete legal entity, it reflects the 'relational' reasons that all legally connected persons have not to commit the substantive offence.[77] A relational reason is a specific kind of reason not to commit an offence that a third party, such as a mischievous customer swapping price labels on goods for amusement, does not have. In what instances is the conception of a company as a concrete legal entity at work?

To give a simple example, suppose that an employee (Z), in a branch of X Company's firm, commits a strict liability trade descriptions offence.[78] Do we need to decide, as between X and Z—as between the company as an abstract conception

[73] Law Commission (2022), paras 6.39–41.

[74] See also Celia Wells (2001), 156.

[75] FH Easterbrook and DR Fischel (1991).

[76] But see the discussion by Syliva Rich (2024) of the idea of the 'moral entanglement' with the company of those involved in companies.

[77] On the role of relational reasons, see RA Duff (2012). The nature of the connection between the company and its employees, agents, and subsidiaries is considered in depth in ch 5.

[78] See *Tesco Supermarkets v Nattrass* [1972] AC 153 (HL), and the discussion of such an example in the Introduction.

and the individual employee working for it—who was being addressed by the trade descriptions offence in performing its guidance function? We do not. In this example, X Company is being addressed as a concrete legal entity, as a network of legally connected persons required by contract to perform functions for the company. So, when any one of these persons commits an offence when performing such a function, they are taken to engage the company itself, in point of liability.[79] English criminal law addresses the company as a concrete legal entity in strict liability cases (and in simple negligence-based cases), because such offences may occur, over time, simply as a more or less predictable side effect of the conduct of any person within the company when purporting to fulfil their corporate duties or exercising their corporate powers: the offences are, in a sense, accidents 'waiting to happen' over the course of a company's life.[80] The imposition of liability on X Company for Z's conduct comes, of course, through the courts' employment of the doctrine of vicarious liability.[81] That doctrine treats employee-perpetrators as at one and the same time persons manifesting corporate activity in action, and as persons separate from the person—the company—to whom liability is (vicariously) attributed. However, the use of the doctrine of vicarious liability to convict the company is controversial in criminal law cases.

FB Sayre put this point vividly, in saying that vicarious liability 'violates the most deep-rooted traditions of criminal law [and is] a conception repugnant to every instinct of the criminal jurist'.[82] It is arguable that vicarious liability is not truly repugnant in this way in corporate criminal cases. That is precisely because, in such cases, the company is addressed as a concrete legal entity any of whose legally associated persons may, over time, bring about strict liability offences as a side effect of their corporate activities. So, it should not be open to the directors—as part of that concrete legal entity themselves—to disassociate the company they represent from the actions of fellow members of that concrete legal entity: their employees. However, it is nonetheless submitted that there is a better analysis of examples of this kind. The basis of liability should be reconceived so that the offences are regarded as offences addressed primarily to the company as an entity led by a supreme executive authority.

Such a reconception is being employed when one says that what explains the company's conviction, when a trade descriptions (or other strict liability) offence

[79] See, further, Mark D'Souza (2020), who implicitly draws on the conception of the company as a concrete legal entity in arguing for the view that the acts of employees in the course of their employment can be treated as the company's own acts, dispensing with need for the doctrine of vicarious liability.

[80] In the United States, companies are also addressed as concrete legal entities, through the doctrine of vicarious liability, in cases where wrongdoing is a free, deliberate, and informed effect of conduct; but that approach fails to take seriously the separateness of persons (when not acting in concert), even persons bound together in an organization, separateness manifested by their knowing and intentional conduct. A company may (more or less culpably) fail to prevent such wrongdoing (and be held liable for that), but it does not engage in it itself.

[81] See, e.g., *Coppen v Moore (No 2)* (1898) 2 QB 306.

[82] FB Sayre (1930), 702.

has been committed by someone associated with the company, is (1) that the directors of the company collectively failed to prevent the commission of the offence and (2) that—ex hypothesi—the directors had not put in place robust procedures to prevent offending of that type. According to this reconception, a substantive offence committed by someone associated with the company is presupposed, and plays the role of predicate offence, rather than being the sole focus *via* the doctrine of vicarious liability. Apart from the basic fair labelling advantages of such a reconception of the basis of corporate liability, analysing corporate criminal liability in failure-to-prevent terms has the advantage that, in principle, it can explain the basis of corporate liability for a strict liability offence when such an offence is engaged in deliberately, perhaps in defiance of company policy or instructions.[83] In such a case, the company's failure to prevent the offence, giving rise to in-principle liability, would fall to be judged in the light of the adequacy of its procedures for preventing such offending, procedures that may include the giving of the instructions on how to perform duties or exercise powers that were subsequently disobeyed.

1.3 Punishment and the Company as an Entity

Discussion of companies conceived of as entities of different kinds provides an opportunity to consider the question of who is addressed by the punishment that follows a corporate conviction.[84] To set this question in context, it is important to keep in mind that the conviction and punishment of a company, when understood as a concrete legal entity, may threaten the value of the personal stake that associated individuals (including those unconnected to the wrongdoing) believe they have in the company's good name and in its continued commercial viability.[85] It is not enough, in justifying corporate criminal liability and punishment, to point to its purely instrumental value as a way of motivating relevant individuals involved in the company to avoid wrongdoing, in the way that (say) chaining a vicious dog next to my neighbour's fence might dissuade him from encroaching over the border between us.[86] Corporate liability and punishment require moral justification.

In that regard, for Antony Duff, a communicative account of punishment is:

> an attempted dialogue with the offender. Two crucial features of the account are that, first, it gives offenders an active role in the process—they are not merely to

[83] *Coppen v Moore* (No 2) [1898] 2 QB 306; *United States v Hilton Hotels Corp*, 467 F 2d 1000 (9th Cir 1972).

[84] See, further, John Hasnas (2009). Broader issues about the justification for the punishment of companies are addressed specifically in ch 6.

[85] Se the discussion of this point in Section 1.2 above. I return to the point in ch 6.

[86] For an account of the justification for corporate punishment that is broadly instrumentalist in character, see VS Khanna (1996).

> suffer punishment, but to undertake it; and second, it portrays punishment as an attempt to engage with offenders not just as responsible agents (who were responsible for the crimes for which they are punished, and are capable of responding appropriately), but as fellow members of the polity.[87]

Duff's concern is, of course, with individual offenders, and his highly moralized account of punishment in terms of a two-way communication of censure might thus seem inappropriate in the case of an inanimate body, albeit one run by individuals. Accordingly, it is unclear whether his theory legitimates only the conviction and punishment of individuals acting in a corporate capacity, or whether it extends to the conviction and punishment of companies themselves. After all, it seems doubtful if, in the sense Duff intends, a company is a 'fellow member of the polity'.

Even so, we can deploy Duff's account to good effect in this context, if we regard his account as engaging the company as an entity led by a supreme executive authority. In Duff's terms, an attempt at 'dialogue' with the company will lack authority and significance, unless the person or persons with whom the dialogue is engaged speak for the company as a whole. As I indicated in Section 1.2, only directors (or persons to whom they have explicitly delegated this task) have the authority to speak in that way. The directors' ultimate executive authority makes them, normatively, the focal point in securing the conformity of the company not only with the criminal law's ex ante guidance demands but also with its ex post punitive demands.[88] It is the directors, and not managers or employees, who must fulfil fiduciary obligations to the company in these respects. It must ultimately be to the directors, as the embodiment of supreme executive authority within a company, that the criminal justice system looks for guarantees that court orders, fines, or the terms of deferred prosecution agreements—including reforms to corporate governance structures—are authoritatively complied with.[89] This claim is

[87] RA Duff (2024), 100.

[88] Clearly, the less serious the offence, the more reasonable it will be to leave issues of punishment resolution to members of the company further down in the chain of command. So, the directors of a major supermarket cannot in practice be expected themselves to initiate action respecting a minor trade descriptions offence committed in a regional branch; that would involve a disproportionate burden. However, were no action to be taken further down the chain of command, the responsibility *would* ultimately fall to the directors.

[89] For example, under the Companies Act (Ireland) 2014, s 53: 'Any judgment or order against a company wilfully disobeyed may, by leave of the court, be enforced by . . . (b) attachment against the directors or other officers of the company, or (c) sequestration against the property of such directors or other officers.' See also, to similar effect, the UK case of *ADM International SARL v Grain House International SA & Anor* [2024] EWCA Civ 33, at para 53 (per Lord Justice Popplewell): 'Directors and officers of a corporation have been treated as a special category where [an] order is made against the corporation. At least since 1860 . . . they could be treated as responsible as civil contemnors for breach of an order made against the corporation where they were culpably responsible for the corporation's failure to comply with the order.'

bolstered by the fact that in cases of vicarious liability, or of failure-to-prevent, the person within the company who committed the substantive offence—assuming it is known who they are—may play no role in the criminal proceedings or punishment at any stage, whatever their level of seniority. In that respect, as indicated earlier, the role of corporate criminal liability, and the focus on directors, is to some extent to shield (lower-level) employees from criminal investigation, conviction, and punishment, where what they did reflects much more badly on the company than it does on them.

Moreover, the emphasis Duff rightly places on the need for offenders not just to endure but to undertake punishment themselves provides a sound theoretical basis for criticism of what is in effect the laissez-faire attitude frequently taken by the criminal justice system to the way that companies respond to and implement punitive demands. The system permits them simply to contract for other persons to meet such demands, without becoming involved themselves in any way. I will argue in Chapter 6 that the law should favour punishments that actively engage the company in victim reparation and broader community-focused activity, as both an entity with a supreme executive authority and as a concrete legal entity. At the punishment stage, it should be possible for the courts to address the company, understood in terms of both of these guises, by requiring the personal involvement of company directors, managers, and employees, as a penitential response to wrongdoing: if not in actual reparation and victim- or community-focused service, then in the committed and creative supervision of the delivery of such service.[90] As we will see, in that way, the justice system moves away from seeing punishment purely in terms of outcome value-generating (such as resource reallocation from the offender to some other person or body), to viewing it in terms of intrinsic value-generating (involving the engagement of the offender in the generation of lasting victim or community benefit).

For the purposes of punishment, a company may be treated as more than just (in Lord Hoffmann's words) a set of 'rules of attribution'. In the case of a failure-to-prevent crime, it is my argument that directors collectively (whether or not individually guilty of any crime) represent the guilty company itself: the grain of truth in the identification doctrine. So, there is nothing wrong in saying that when we require all directors to be the object of the criminal law's punitive demands of the company, we treat them perfectly fairly; but what about innocent people who

[90] For example, if a transport company is ordered as part of its punishment to decontaminate land, it is unlikely to be appropriate for the directors or employees themselves to don hazmat suits and attempt to fulfil their obligations. The directors may be perfectly within their rights to hire specialist outside contractors: Environment Agency (2016). However, what will be necessary is that the company show commitment to an active and creative role in overseeing the restoration work being done by the specialists at the company's expense. By contrast, if an accounting firm has defrauded vulnerable customers, it may be perfectly appropriate to require the firm to engage in direct victim reparation or generation of public good: for example, by itself establishing and running (with its own personnel) an advice line for customers in financial difficulties.

legally form part of the company, such as employees, but who do not represent it in this formal sense? Does the punitive dimension to the criminal law also address such persons? Answering that question requires consideration of whether people can be officially addressed by the punishment system, without being the people—directors or their delegates—with whom the formal punitive dialogue (in Duff's sense) takes place in relation to a company. It is arguable that the censuring message of criminal conviction and punishment can be intended to have an effect on people who are themselves innocent but are legally connected to the person or people required to take part in the punishment dialogue described by Duff.

To recall the analysis from Section 1.2, the idea of a company as a 'concrete legal' entity is the idea that all of the persons involved by law in the company, whatever their role, make up the 'company'. A censuring punitive message may be conveyed to all of a company's associated persons, as a necessary and indeed as an intended part of (and no mere side effect of) what it means to punish a company. This is not the same point as the point being made when, for example, we say that if one member of a family is punished, all members of the family may consequently feel ashamed and suffer. In such a case, the suffering of the innocent family members is a tragic side effect of the punishment of the guilty individual who is the focus of censure. Other family members are not intended by the legal system to be tainted by the censure of the guilty family member.[91] Developing this point requires an appreciation of the need for a somewhat broader understanding of who is addressed by the censuring aspect of punishment, and in what way, than is provided by the individual human–offender-based accounts given by Duff and others. Consider this analogy, far-fetched though it appears to be at first sight. Under section 34A of the Children and Young Persons Act 1933, when a child under the age of sixteen appears in court charged with an offence, they must be accompanied by their parents, guardians, or carers. There is, of course, a strong welfarist justification for such a requirement that is not relevant to this context, but there is also a further possible justification to the provision. This is that the parent, guardian, or carer, although innocent of any offence themselves, should be exposed to the taint of censure, to a sense of responsibility, guilt, and shame that will or should accompany the child's conviction. Such an interpretation of section 34A is buttressed by subsequent legislative intervention making it possible to impose civil legal orders on parents or guardians requiring them, upon pain of penalty for breach, to take positive steps to improve their child's behaviour.[92] Parents are morally 'entangled' with the fate of their children, and such moral entanglement is the basis on which these legal measures may be justified.[93]

[91] It is uncommon for an offender's punishment to be affected by the suffering their family will have to endure following the offender's conviction: *Grant* (1990) 12 Cr App R (S) 441.

[92] Crime and Disorder Act 1998, s 8, discussed in Kathryn Hollingsworth (2007).

[93] For a discussion of 'moral entanglement' as a way of describing the relationship between individuals associated with a company and the company itself, see Sylvia Rich (2023).

The point of this analogy is to suggest that there may be a special punitive principle governing cases in which rights and duties are in law shared between persons, one of whom has committed an offence arising from or in relation to those shared rights and duties, a principle that reflects to some extent the 'moral entanglement' of such persons with one another. In such cases, it may be appropriate, as part of the censuring process, formally to address some or all of the right and duty holders other than the offender. For example, according to such a principle, one could legitimately require an innocent landlord to appear in court (or in some other way participate in the proceedings) when their tenant is accused of using the premises to engage in crime or engage in antisocial behaviour. Of course, in a criminal case against a company, few members of the company (if any) will appear in court themselves, but that is not the lesson to be learned from the analogy. The lesson is that everyone who is or becomes legally associated with a company—whether or not involved in the company's offending—may be expected to share in the censure involved in punishment, just as a parent may be made to endure the same experience at a trial of their child. Everyone involved in a company may similarly be intentionally exposed by the law to guilt and shame at the company's conviction, even though it is only the company directors (or their delegates) who must formally respond to and decide how best to comply with the law's punitive demands.

What follows from this point about the range or scope of the law's censuring message, conveyed in the punishment of companies? As I have already said, it should be the directors' primary role to secure compliance with punitive measures, if not necessarily through their own actions (in the way that an individual offender is required to do), then through the engaged and creative supervision of compliance secured by a third party. Even so, by analogy with the civil orders that can now be imposed on parents respecting their children, it seems plausible to suggest that whilst compliance with corporate punishment is a matter ultimately for directors, it should be open to a court (as an ancillary aspect of corporate punishment) to impose a civil order on any person legally associated with a company as a concrete legal entity to take steps to engage in—say—securing the performance of restorative or reparatory actions.[94] For example, a firm may have largely passive, inexpert directors, but may also employ a highly capable senior manager who effectively runs the firm and takes all its decisions. In such a case, whether or not the manager was themselves involved in the company's offending, it would be appropriate to empower a court to impose a civil order on the manager—or their successor—requiring them to take certain steps to (say) improve regulatory compliance, especially if it seems likely that the directors themselves will fail adequately to ensure that such steps are taken.

[94] For so long as that person remains in association with the company. It will always be open to an employee to resign from the firm rather than comply with such an order.

However, as indicated at the start of this section, there is another side to the point about the range or scope of censure in corporate cases and its extension to employed persons. So far as employment is concerned, by 2018, the UK private sector had reached its highest level of 27 million people who made up 83.5 per cent of all employment.[95] Bearing in mind the centrality of the 'world of work' to people's lives, that means that millions of people in the United Kingdom (and vast numbers worldwide) thus live in a state of what one might call a 'partial dependency' for a key element of the value in their lives: dependency on the flourishing of the private sector in general and of their firm in particular, and on the quality of their lived experience at work. A company (as both a real and a concrete legal entity) should be regarded, ideal typically, as a locus of personal capital built up by those who have invested time and effort in the company, the value of which for all those associated with it—not just the wrongdoers—is put at risk by the conviction of the company. Corporate criminal liability is thus a liability that exposes a company to a morally significant (risk of) damage, damage to the collective value of the personal capital invested in the company by those involved in it.[96] When the criminal law strikes a blow at a company, it is striking a morally significant collective blow at all those who have made a personal—not just an economic—investment in it.

In that regard, the welfare of even just the sole (innocent) employee in a firm is of moral significance to the sentencing process. Quite plausibly, a company's only employee may, over time, have come to identify themselves and their efforts with the success of the firm. Its demise or loss of good reputation, as result of the conviction of the company in virtue of a crime committed by a director, might hence come as a devastating personal—not just economic—blow. For many of those involved in sustaining a company as a going concern, the effect of criminal conviction can be compared to the stigmatizing impact on those involved of business failure. Business failure has been associated with, for example, self-imposed social withdrawal, and with a range of emotions including grief, remorse, shame, humiliation, anger, guilt, and blame as well as the fear of the unknown.[97] In consequence, as Deniz Ucbasaran et al put it, 'experiencing failure can have adverse motivational effects by generating a sense of "helplessness", thus diminishing individuals' beliefs in their ability to undertake specific tasks successfully in the future'.[98] That is not, of course, a reason to avoid prosecuting and punishing a company for its criminal

[95] Office for National Statistics (2019), 11.

[96] It goes almost without saying that a criminal conviction may have a severe impact on a firm's reputation and on its ability to continue trading successfully, or at all. For example, regulatory bodies may have to be notified of company convictions, convicted companies may be excluded from public procurement exercises, and in some industries, companies are likely to look carefully at the safety record of potential business partners, and requests for details of any safety convictions have become standard on tender questionnaires. Accordingly, the loss of business caused by a reputation damaged by a criminal conviction could have a much longer lasting impact that any fine or other penalty in itself.

[97] Dean A Sheppard (2003).

[98] Deniz Ucbasaran, Dean A Shepherd, Andy Lockett, and John Lyon (2012), 24.

wrongdoing. Just as well-run companies have become a key provider of economic, social, and personal value for employees and directors alike, in different domains, so badly run companies have the capacity through their agents—sometimes, in pursuit of those very values—to cause underappreciated but significant and widespread harm, as well as creating unacceptable risks.[99] Even so, the moral significance of the personal capital invested by associated persons in their companies is of particular concern when we consider that a conviction has the potential to impact on the innocent as much or even more than it does on the guilty who, perhaps having little loyalty to the firm, may simply move on to or start up other firms.[100]

Against that background, let us suppose that we take the fundamental rationale of sentencing to be the imposition of a sentence that is proportionate to the seriousness of the offence, but that we also accept the relevance of aggravating and mitigating features even if they have no bearing on this rationale (in other words, they do not impact on the seriousness of the offence).[101] According to the Sentencing Council, a court *should* 'take into account . . . factors which may reduce seriousness or reflect personal mitigation'.[102] There is, in other words, a duty to take into account matters of 'personal' mitigation, as well as matters affecting offence seriousness. I suggest that, in corporate cases, this duty translates into a duty to take into account the impact of the sentence upon persons legally associated with the firm conceived of as a concrete legal entity, persons who—for example—may find their jobs under threat or their conditions of employment worsened as a consequence of corporate compliance with a proposed sentence. There is a duty to take such factors into account precisely because, legally speaking, employees are part of the company that is being sentenced but in all probability innocent themselves of any offending. By contrast, whilst it is always open to a court to take into account the impact of a corporate sentence on consumers, subcontractors, market conditions, and so on, this is and should remain a wholly discretionary matter, precisely because individuals falling within these categories are not part of the firm being sentenced.[103]

[99] See, generally, Lieselot Bisschop et al (2025). This is something that will frequently go unnoticed or receive little publicity. For example, whilst there were 132 murders in London in 2021, generating significant public and political outcry: https://www.bbc.co.uk/news/uk-england-london-64183759 (last accessed 12/06/2023). However, the 123 work-related fatalities that occurred in 2021–2022 received nothing like the same attention or treatment: https://www.hse.gov.uk/statistics/fatals.htm (last accessed 12/06/2023). See, e.g., Steve Tombs (2005) and Celia Wells (2001).

[100] As is well known, convictions of the individuals involved, following corporate convictions, are rare indeed: Spotlight on Corruption (2024).

[101] Andrew Ashworth (2005), 151–52.

[102] https://www.sentencingcouncil.org.uk/overarching-guides/magistrates-court/item/general-guideline-overarching-principles/#Step%202%20Aggravating%20and%20mitigating%20factors (last accessed 14/03/2024).

[103] By contrast, in Sentencing Council guidance, no distinction is drawn between categories of third party, for the purposes of assessing the impact of a sentence. The Council says simply that the court should take into account the '[i]mpact of fine on employment of staff, service users, customers and local economy (but not shareholders)': https://www.sentencingcouncil.org.uk/offences/magistrates-court/item/corporate-offenders-fraud-bribery-and-money-laundering/ (last accessed 14/03/2024).

1.4 The 2025 Bill and a Threshold Puzzle in Corporate Criminal Liability

As indicated in the Introduction, it is often stated that there are some crimes a company simply cannot commit.[104] It is commonly supposed that a company cannot be convicted of murder or any other crime for which the only possible sentence is imprisonment,[105] that it cannot engage in bigamy,[106] and that there are some sexual offences (including those requiring an intent to obtain sexual gratification)[107] and driving offences[108] that it cannot commit. However, the scope of these exclusionary rules is beset by uncertainty and lacks clear principles. Clause 196 of the Crime and Policing Bill 2025 purports to sweep away all such restrictions on the scope of corporate wrongdoing, but only when the wrongdoing is engaged in by 'senior managers':

> (1) Where a senior manager of a body corporate or partnership ('the organisation') acting within the actual or apparent scope of their authority commits an offence under the law of England and Wales, Scotland or Northern Ireland, the organisation also commits the offence.

How sensible is such a simplification of the law? This provision appears to make companies guilty of any criminal offence (including murder and rape) when committed by a senior manager, when they would not be guilty if those same offences were committed by ordinary employees or agents.[109] In sexual offence cases, such an approach is doubly insulting to victims. First, it creates a mere criminal law fiction to describe the corporate dimension to the wrongdoing against the victims, by saying that the company *itself* raped or sexually assaulted them. Secondly, by implication, it wrongly suggests that when such wrongs are committed against victims by more junior employees, this is of less significance to the criminal law. That is because in such cases the traditional exclusion of corporate liability still applies, and so the company itself will face potential criminal liability—at best—for having failed to ensure that the place of work was as safe for patients as it could reasonably practically be made.[110]

[104] Amanda Pinto QC and Martin Evans (2008), 1.1.

[105] *Hawke v Hulton & Co* [1909] 2 KB 93, and the discussion in the Indian case of *Fidelity Industries v State* (2004) 03 MAD CK 0179 (Madras High Court). In the *Fidelity Industries* case, the High Court asserted the power to impose a fine in corporate cases, even when the only sentence provided for by statute was imprisonment. It is doubtful whether a UK court would take such a step.

[106] Amanda Pinto QC and Martin Evans (2008), 1.1.

[107] Ibid.

[108] *Richmond upon Thames LBC v Pinn and Wheeler* (1988) 7 LGR 659 DC.

[109] It is possible that the courts would read clause 196 as subject to the proviso that the 'offence under the law of England and Wales, Scotland or Northern Ireland' means an offence that is, in law, regarded as one that a company is capable of committing, but that is not a natural reading of the wording.

[110] See the Health and Safety at Work Act 1974, s 1.

A suggestion made in the Introduction was that a number of key sexual offences[111] involve the use or display of some part of the human body, something a company necessarily lacks; and so, offending of this kind is limited to 'corporeal entities'. However, a corporeal entity theory raises as many questions as it solves. Fraud and false accounting, crimes a company may certainly commit, necessarily involve at least some use of part of a human body by a relevant person, as when a director or senior manager types false details about the company's transactions into the company's accounts.[112] Why, then, given that the use of the hand can also implicate someone in the commission of (say) assault by penetration contrary to section 2 of the Sexual Offences Act 2003, can a company be guilty of fraud or false accounting but—it would seem—not of the offence contrary to section 2? Moreover, necessary though it may be in practice, it seems arbitrary to place a bar on conviction for certain crimes simply because statute provides only for imprisonment as the penalty. Even murder can be committed in a corporate capacity[113] and in order to benefit a company: consider a case in which a company's controlling officers shoot with lethal intent at trespassing protestors bent on destroying a company's vital commercial animal experimentation centre.

It might seem that these exclusionary rules are tied to a lingering sense that if companies themselves—purely legal entities with 'neither bodies to be punished, nor souls to be condemned'[114]—cannot be put in prison, cannot marry, cannot pursue sexual gratification, and cannot drive, then they cannot be convicted of offences dependent on proof of these activities. However, if that is the justification for the exclusionary rules, then—as I have just indicated—it threatens almost all forms of corporate criminal responsibility. For, as a purely abstract legal entity, a company cannot engage in any kind of voluntary conduct or possess a state of mind, and so cannot commit any offence involving proof of such an element: the vast majority of offences. To avoid being driven to such a conclusion, we might adopt the view embodied in clause 196 of the Crime and Policing Bill 2025—in respect of the conduct of senior managers acting with authority—that, if a company is regarded as acting solely through such human agency, there need be no limits to offences for which it can be convicted. Yet, whilst that provides a case for abolishing the exclusionary rules entirely (with such adjustment as to available penalties upon conviction as might be necessary), an argument remains from 'counter-intuitiveness', in point of fair labelling. Does it really make sense in labelling terms to say that a company *itself*—albeit through human agency—can engage in (say) bigamy, indecent exposure, being drunk, and disorderly in a public place, that it can wear a uniform

[111] And also offences involving the wearing of uniforms, or the like.

[112] It was made clear in *Tesco Supermarkets v Nattrass* [1972] AC 153 that, in order to be guilty of a fault-based crime, both the conduct and the fault element must be engaged in by a relevant senior officer.

[113] See the illuminating discussion of the issue in Alan Norrie (2018).

[114] Edward Thurlow, 1st Baron Thurlow, cited in John Poynder (1844), 268.

signifying association with a banned political organization;[115] or can beat or shake a carpet in a London street;[116] and what is truly gained by so finding?[117]

The key to unlocking this puzzle lies in acknowledging the importance to the justification for criminal conviction of fair labelling.[118] The possibility that a company may be convicted in any instance of failing to prevent an offence gives us a sounder basis for labelling companies appropriately. If a general offence of corporate failure to prevent crimes (of all kinds) were created, we would not then need to delve too deeply into whether, for example, bigamy and sexual offences presuppose a capacity for the kind of personal 'intimacy' (of which abstract legal entities are incapable) that is violated by the offender in such cases, or whether being drunk and disorderly presupposes the possession of certain physiological features not possessed by abstract legal entities. It would be enough to say, when making a decision on what offence to charge, that—morally speaking—the company's responsibility is best described in terms of having failed to prevent the offending in question by an individual associated with the company.[119] Let us go back to the example of a doctor working for a private medical company who (say) persuades innocent and trusting patients that they need to undergo a 'treatment' for their illness that he—but not they—realizes is sexual intercourse.[120] It may be morally counter-intuitive (and hence involve inappropriate labelling) to convict a company of the substantive offence of rape in such a case, as clause 196 of the 2025 Bill dictates. However, it is less counter-intuitive to propose that a company could be criminally liable for a separate offence of failing to prevent rape, in circumstances where the company knew about the offending and did nothing, or was aware that offending of that kind might be taking place but had no proper procedures in place to prevent it from taking place.[121] In such circumstances, the directors' knowledge or awareness arguably changes their normative position with regard to offending that, in the absence of such knowledge or awareness, would not fairly be regarded as attributable to them in criminal law because it was not intended to benefit the company.

[115] Public Order Act 1986, s 1.

[116] Metropolitan Police Act 1839, s 60.

[117] There are additional problems with clause 196, such as its failure to say what happens when a company's senior manager commits murder, or what the relationship will be between a corporate conviction for manslaughter, through the conduct of a senior manager, and corporate manslaughter under the Corporate Manslaughter and Corporate Homicide Act 2007: see the discussion in ch 5.

[118] See, e.g., James Chalmers and Fiona Leverick (2008).

[119] Liability would then fall to be determined in accordance with whether the offence was intended to benefit the company (model E from Section I.4), or if it was not intended to benefit the company, with whether the company at the highest level knew about the offending and did nothing, or was aware that this type of offending might be taking place but had no procedures in place to prevent it (model D from Section I.4).

[120] On the status of such cases as rape cases, see *Flattery* (1877) 2 QBD 410.

[121] This is 'model D' from Section I.4, in which corporate fault (of the kind described) at the highest level must be proved, as an appropriate alternative normative foundation for the absence of any intention on the associated person's part to benefit the company through their wrongdoing.

Even so, in Chapter 5, my argument will be that the strongest case for failure-to-prevent offences is in relation to offences that involve '*commercially* intrinsic risks' of trading, such as bribery, fraud, and false accounting. In the absence of knowledge that offending is going on, or awareness that offending of that type might be going on (coupled with an absence of proper procedures for preventing it), the case for imposing liability on companies for offences involving 'intrinsically *human* risks', like the risk of sexual offending in the course of employment, is less strong. Be that as it may, my argument concerns what is to count as a fair label for a company's responsibility, when offending occurs in the course of company business. Whilst the human individual associated with the company who engages in the criminal wrongdoing is the person rightly labelled as the 'fraudster', the 'briber', the 'polluter', the 'sex offender', and so on, the company is more accurately labelled as a 'safeguarding shortcomer' with respect to the engagement in the particular crime by the individual in question. There will, of course, in every case be a link between the two labels, reflecting on the company as wrongdoer. The more serious the crime that the company failed to prevent, the more stigmatic the label attached to the company respecting its safeguarding shortcoming. In that regard, far from involving a mis-labelling of the corporate offender, once one accepts that the central role of the 'company' is to set the framework within which individuals (and groups) may engage in company-related conduct, sometimes including wrongdoing, the failure-to-prevent model of corporate liability is the very embodiment of fairness in labelling.[122]

1.5 Committing a Corporate Crime

Fair labelling arguments are also important in unlocking a second puzzle about corporate criminal liability. This is the puzzle, considered briefly in Section 1.2 above, concerning how to understand when a company itself 'commits' a crime. This issue did not arise for so long as courts were content to find companies vicariously liable for offences created by statute committed by company employees.[123] However, the issue became significant when courts came to insist that a crime involving proof of a state of mind (and hence involving a free, deliberate, and informed act) could not be attributed to a company unless the crime was committed by someone who was 'identifiable with' or an 'embodiment of' the company.[124]

[122] For a contrary argument, that failure-to-prevent offences are not a fair label for the company's involvement, see Mark D'Souza (2020).

[123] See the discussion in Amanda Pinto QC and Martin Evans (2008), 39.

[124] Perhaps influenced by the German company law distinction between persons who are 'organs' of a company and persons who are mere corporate 'agents'. See the discussion in Amanda Pinto QC and Martin Evans (2008), 46; *DPP v Kent and Sussex Contractors Ltd* [1944] 1 KB 146, 154–55 (Viscount Caldecote LCJ); *Tesco Supermarkets v Nattrass* [1972] AC 153, 170E-G and 173 (Lord Reid).

This was held to be someone who was 'the directing mind and will of the corporation',[125] or 'the very ego and centre and personality of the corporation'.[126] In practical terms, what that meant was that a fault-based crime could not be regarded as having been committed by a company, unless it was committed by 'the board of directors itself, or . . . [the] person [with] an authority co-ordinate with the board of directors given to him under the articles of association', someone who 'can only be removed by the general meeting of the company'.[127] I will treat that as a requirement—commonly known as the 'identification doctrine'—that a fault-based crime can be committed by a company only when it has been committed by one or more persons at directorial level, acting in that capacity.[128]

From 1844 onwards, it became possible to create a company with distinct legal personality through a much simpler public registration process, as opposed to (say) using a private Act of Parliament. The Joint Stock Companies Act 1844 put on a statutory footing the powers hitherto normally conferred on directors of unincorporated companies (with limited liability for companies following from 1856).[129] Crucially, the 1844 Act granted key legal permissions to company directors to take the most important operating decisions on behalf of the company: section 3 defined directors as 'the persons having the direction, conduct, management or superintendence of the affairs of a company'. The 1844 Act built on the use by unincorporated companies of the trust in equity—and its deed of settlement—to recognize the separation of ownership of company assets from their management by the directors, in the interests of the company. By section 27 of the 1844 Act, directors were empowered:

> To conduct and manage the affairs of the company according to the provisions and subject to the restrictions of this Act, and of the deed of settlement . . . and for that purpose to enter into all such contracts and do and execute all such acts and deeds as the circumstances may require.

The implication was clear: a company acts through its executive arm, namely the directors.[130] As Cairns LJ was to put it not long afterwards, 'a company cannot act in its own person for it has no person; it can only act through directors who are

[125] *Lennard's Carrying Co Ltd v Asiatic Petroleum* [1915] AC 705 (HL), 713 (Viscount Haldane).
[126] Ibid.
[127] Ibid.
[128] I put on one side, for the moment, the changes to the identification doctrine brought about by the Economic Crime and Corporate Transparency Act 2023, and clause 196 of the Crime and Policing Bill 2025, considered in depth in ch 2.
[129] In itself, the 1844 Act was not to have as great an impact as the 1856 Act: MS Rix (1945). Even so, within fourteen months of enactment, 1,639 provisional registrations had been made. Nearly 5,000 limited liability companies had been established in England by the end of 1856, reaching 10,619 by 1883, and 50,000 by 1910: PW Ireland (1984).
[130] The importance, in that regard, of managing directors, as opposed to 'patron directors' (mere owners), was emphasized by Baron Parke in *Lane v Wilson* (1846) 7 LT 236.

agents of the company'.[131] What is more, in practice, section 27 powers were in fact regarded as duties. The courts' view was that, in accepting office, a director undertook to give their fullest attention to company affairs: even, if need be, all of their time.[132] By contrast, in virtue of section 27, company members (shareholders) should *not* be able 'to act in their own behalf in the ordinary management of the concerns of the company otherwise than by means of a director'.[133] Ownership, in other words, does not confer an executive function in corporate contexts,[134] even if it may confer some degree of supervisory control over company executives. In the unincorporated form of the company (prior to 1844), directors could be drawn from the body of trustees who owned the company assets, but the directors were still separate in law from the trustees, creating the potential for confusion over who had authority to deal with the company assets. After 1844, although directors retained their fiduciary status,[135] the assets could straightforwardly be owned by the company itself, making the formal position of trustee redundant and enhancing the executive importance of directors.[136]

It is against that historical background that we should consider what Lord Haldane said of 'the company', in *Lennard's Carrying Company v Asiatic Petroleum Company Ltd*:

> its active and directing will must consequently be sought in the person of somebody who for some purposes may be called an agent, but who is really the directing mind and will of the corporation, the very ego and centre of the personality of the corporation. That person may be under the direction of the shareholders in general meeting; that person may be the board of directors itself, or it may be, and in some companies it is so, that that person has an authority coordinate with the board of directors given to him under the articles of association ... [that person] is the life and soul of the company.

In his thinking, Lord Haldane was much influenced by the Hegelian theory of subject–object relations, having himself published work addressing the issue.[137] In Hegel's theory, the subject ('I') is not an a-historical entity detached from material phenomena but constituted and expressed through them.[138] So, applying

131 *Ferguson v Wilson* (1866) LR 2 Ch App 77, 89.
132 *York and North-Midland Ry v Hudson* (1853) 16 Beav 485, 500.
133 See the discussion in MS Rix (1945), 248.
134 Contrast the position under the Factory Act 1833, an Act necessarily drafted, at that time, on the assumption that factory 'owners' were the ones with responsibility for the running of factories.
135 *York and North-Midland Ry v Hudson* (1853) 16 Beav 485, 491 (per Lord Romilly MR).
136 Sealy (1967). Section 29 of the 1844 nonetheless acknowledged the fiduciary position occupied by directors as agents of the company. It recognized their fiduciary obligations to avoid direct or indirect conflicts of interest when contracting on behalf of the company: a contract made in breach of this provision could be avoided by the company, unless ratified by a general meeting of shareholders: *Aberdeen Rly Co v Blaikie Bros* (1854) 1 Paterson 394.
137 Richard Burdon Haldane (1921).
138 See the discussion in Todd Hedrick (2018), ch 1.

this theory to the company, Lord Haldane conceives of my identity (*qua* company director) as being expressed through the company, and the company as finding its identity in the material world through my conduct.

The difficulty with Lord Haldane's approach is that it does not provide a satisfying explanation of why the company, as opposed to the individual directors to whom the elements of the crime can be attributed, should be found criminally liable. To be sure, when a director, possessing the fault element (if any), engages in the conduct element of a crime, they may in some circumstances be said to commit the crime in their capacity as a director. In such cases, in a Hegelian spirit, perhaps we could go so far as to say that the abstract legal notion of 'director' is materially made manifest in the concrete criminal action, but that is not the same thing as saying that the company itself commits the crime. Company directors, and directorial 'capacity', are both concepts that presuppose companies, but presupposition implies difference. The fact that a director is an agent of the company establishes that the director's act in that capacity can bind the company, but it does not establish that the act is engaged in by the inanimate company itself. So, the attribution of crime to the company in such cases still looks like a form of vicarious liability.[139]

Yet, ironically, in approving of the decision in *Lennard's Carrying Company*, the House of Lords in *Tesco Supermarkets Ltd v Nattrass* saw itself as rejecting vicarious liability for fault-based crimes, on fair labelling grounds. In *Tesco Supermarkets v Nattrass*, Lord Reid was clear that when corporate liability is based on the conduct of a director, in so far as the director is acting 'as the company and his mind which directs his act is the mind of the company', then 'there is no question of the company being vicariously liable'.[140] To the same effect, Lord Morris added:

> In general, criminal liability only results from personal fault. We do not punish people in criminal courts for the misdeeds of others. The principle of *respondeat superior* is applicable in our civil courts but not generally in our criminal courts.[141]

In a way, thus, the identification doctrine can be considered to be the product of an argument for traditional constraints on (corporate) criminalization that is a moral argument 'by proxy'. Company directors are moral agents and so, if a company's acts are identified with the acts of such persons, then the same (moral) constraints on criminalization will apply to the company as apply to its directors.

A well-known and important objection to the identification doctrine is that it makes it impossible or very difficult to convict companies of crimes when they are committed by senior or middle managers with significant responsibilities or

[139] See the argument of GR Sullivan (1996) and Brent Fisse (1983).
[140] *Tesco Supermarkets v Nattrass* [1972] AC 153, 170E-G.
[141] Ibid., 179F.

discretionary powers.[142] Just as important, though, is the fact that the need to show that a fault-based crime was committed by someone at directorial level, who 'embodies' the company itself, is a requirement beset by theoretical confusion. To begin with, if, as Lord Morris suggests, vicarious liability should be rejected because we do not punish people in criminal courts for the '*misdeeds* of others', then such liability should be rejected in all cases where a crime involves a conduct element (a 'deed'), and not only where there is in addition a fault element. As Viscount Haldane rightly suggested in *Lennard's Carrying Co*, not only does a company have 'no mind of its own' but in addition it has 'no body of its own'.[143] So, considering the matter in terms of fair labelling, how can it be right to say that the company itself engages in the conduct element of a no-fault crime when the conduct is that of an employee, as opposed to someone (at directorial level) who 'embodies' the company? No doubt, common sense and public policy dictate that where a company relies on associated persons to carry out its business, it should not then be able—when such persons commit a crime in the course of company business—simply to disassociate itself from the commission of the crime.[144] Even so, that leaves as an open question the best way to understand the association between the company and the crime.

In that respect, of crucial importance to the argument of this book will be the conception of the company as an entity led by a supreme executive authority,[145] an entity in which the directors occupy a unique constitutional position in that regard. As Eva Micheler puts it:

> The directors are nominated as the holders of master authority that is outside the reach of . . . shareholders. Giving the directors of companies unlimited authority has an important stabilizing effect. Whenever the directors act, the company is bound. In addition, and perhaps even more importantly, whoever the directors authorize can bind the company. This gives the organization run by a company a stable connection point. All delegations that derive from the directors provide office holders with authority in their interaction with third parties. It supplies the organization run by a company with a 'Grundnorm' that is outside the reach of the shareholders.[146]

[142] See, generally, the discussion in Celia Wells (2001). In ch 2, I will consider whether the relevant provisions of the Economic Crime and Corporate Transparency Act 2023, and clause 196 of the Crime and Policing Bill 2025, do enough to address that problem.

[143] *Lennard's Carrying Co Ltd v Asiatic Petroleum* [1915] AC 705 (HL), 713.

[144] *Pearkes, Gunston & Tee v Ward* [1902] 2 KB 1. As indicated in Section 1.2 above, when the criminal law addresses a company in strict liability cases, it addresses it as a concrete legal entity, comprised of all those legally attached to the company, including employees alongside directors.

[145] See the discussion in Section 1.2 above.

[146] Eva Micheler (2021), 78–79.

Employees, however senior and influential in practice, are not constitutionally fundamental to a company in the way that directors are. The unique constitutional position of directors means that their own wrongdoing, or their failure to prevent the wrongdoing of others, has a legal significance and normative status that employee wrongdoing—or the failure to prevent it—does not. The key dimension to the constitutional position of directors is that they exercise supreme executive authority within a company.[147] Understood against that background, the so-called identification doctrine can be understood primarily as a doctrine about fair labelling. It is a doctrine that stands for the view that, in relation to fault-based crimes, unless someone possessing supreme executive authority was the one who committed the crime, it is not fair to label the company itself as (vicariously) having committed it.

Yet, even that reinterpretation cannot save the identification doctrine from grave theoretical difficulty. Until the matter arose for decision in *SFO v Barclays*,[148] the leading authorities on the identification doctrine gave no indication of what was to happen when someone at directorial level committed a fault-based crime when on company business, and in order to benefit the company, but did so without the knowledge or consent of (all) other directors. In such circumstances, can the company itself be regarded as having committed the crime?[149] The fair labelling problem posed by this issue has been magnified by the extension of the identification doctrine, under section 196 of the 2023 Act (and under clause 196 of the Crime and Policing Bill 2025), to include non-directors: 'senior managers'.[150] As indicated in Section 1.1 above, in an ethically heterogenous company, it is quite possible to imagine circumstances in which senior managers (or 'rogue' individual directors) exploit a broad commercial authority granted to them, to engage in criminal activity to benefit the company,[151] at the same time as the board of directors is actively seeking to enforce its 'zero tolerance' policy towards criminal activity in any form committed by associated persons.[152] If the company is found criminally liable in such circumstances, that looks like nothing more or less than unfair labelling stemming from the brute application of vicarious liability. Brent Fisse put the point well over forty years ago:

[147] In order to acknowledge this, it is not necessary to deny that directors act as agents, making the company vicariously bound by and liable for their actions: see the discussion in GR Sullivan (1996).

[148] *SFO v Barclays* (2018) EWHC 3055 (QB).

[149] This issue was raised as long ago as 1983 by Brent Fisse: Brent Fisse (1983).

[150] For detailed discussion, see ch 2.

[151] Thus exposing the company to primary liability for the substantive offence.

[152] Such a situation might easily arise if the relevant senior managers regard the directors as weak and insufficiently ruthless commercially. As indicated earlier, it is trite law that someone associated with a company can be regarded as acting on company business even when they disobey company policy: *Coppen v Moore* (No 2) [1898] 2 QB 306; *United States v Hilton Hotels Corp*, 467 F 2d 1000 (9th Cir 1972).

> To establish fault on the part of a director or manager is not necessarily to establish corporate fault. Fault on the part of one aberrant director or manager may exist despite exemplary behaviour elsewhere in the organization.[153]

Once again, an answer to this fair labelling conundrum is close to hand, in the form of liability for corporate failure to prevent crime.

To begin with, we should take note of the fact that the legal concept of a person's 'failure to prevent crime' draws attention, in a way that identification doctrines do not, to the fact that (other than in a one-person firm) a corporate crime is typically relational.[154] Such a crime commonly involves both (culpable) wrongdoing by X *and* (culpable) responsibility on Y's part for failing to stop X engaging in wrongdoing of that kind.[155] We can set this point in a context in which the criminal law is understood in part as a way in which to articulate a prohibition, an ex ante guide to what must (not) be done.[156] A guide to conduct must be addressed to those subject to it who are capable of initiating action, exercising restraint (on themselves and others), and so on, in the light of what the guide requires. In that respect, in the case of any company other than a one-person outfit, it is reasonable to think that the criminal law's guidance message is, in effect, two-sided. On the one side, the law is addressed (albeit indirectly) to the company as a concrete legal entity,[157] and hence to anyone legally associated with the company whose conduct in a corporate capacity—their corporate activity—may involve offending, including directors, employees, agents, and subsidiaries.[158] People falling in this category are required to shape their conduct, in a corporate capacity, according to the law's requirements.

On the other side, the law is directly addressed to the company as an entity led by a supreme executive authority. It is addressed to the persons with legal authority or influence over *every* other person associated with the company whose conduct may involve such offending, and that is ultimately the board of directors. The criminal law is addressed to the board, because individual corporate agents' offending on company business reflects a failure in point of an authority held over such persons (the relational point made above), and respecting such failures, the 'buck stops' with the board. That remains true, whether or not the board legitimately tasked someone else with overseeing the prevention of crime within the

[153] Brent Fisse (1983), 1187.

[154] See the discussion in Section 1.1 above.

[155] The bass for Y's responsibility—control or influence over X—is explained in ch 3.

[156] AP Simester (2021), 64–65. Of course, the criminal law also provides guidance on what is permitted (such action in self-defence or prevention of crime) and on what is excused.

[157] See the discussion in Section 1.2 above.

[158] In most instances, the criminal law will simultaneously address such persons directly, in an individual capacity. For example, someone who commits fraud on company business can be charged individually with fraud.

company.[159] Suppose, then, that a director, senior manager, or employee commits fraud when on company business, in order to benefit the company, but in circumstances where that is tantamount to a betrayal of company policy and ethos.[160] The question should not be, 'Did the company itself commit fraud?', an almost impossible question to answer satisfactorily in terms of fair labelling. The question should instead be, 'Was there a (collective) failure on the part of the board to prevent the fraud, and did the board fall short in terms of providing proper fraud-prevention procedures?'. Far from being a second-best compromise, in terms of criminal liability, it is submitted that in such circumstances it would be hard to find a fairer and more representative way of describing the company's connection to the crime. That is true, whatever the nature of the crime: fault-based or strict liability, *malum prohibitum* or *malum in se.*

One important reason for focusing on company failures, with respect to wrongdoing engaged in by persons associated with it, is that it is easier to find that a large number of people—such as a board of directors—collectively shared in a failure, than it is to find that they shared in a positive action. Suppose that a dishonest practice has grown up amongst a company's employees of improperly exploiting weak corporate accounting practices to add an extra 10 per cent to customers' bills, in the expectation that the customers will not notice. To recall an example given in the Introduction, suppose, further, that some directors knew about this practice but kept it secret, whilst other directors did not know about it, even though the practice had been going on for some time. Identification doctrine enthusiasts might encourage us to find that the company itself was complicit in these frauds, in virtue of the tolerance of it by some at directorial level; and of course, the doctrine of complicity applies to corporate persons as much as it does to individuals.[161] However, in this example, even if the stringent requirements of proving complicity can be made out, with respect to the directors who knew about the frauds, the fact is that some directors—perhaps a majority of them—did not know about them. Indeed, those directors who did not know about the frauds might plausibly regard the conduct of those who kept the practice secret as guilty of betraying both the company and their fellow directors. So, why should those who did not know about the frauds be implicated in their actual perpetration, through the conviction of company they direct?

The answer to that conundrum is that the wrongdoing of the company in this example is not that it shared in or connived at the perpetration of the frauds. The company's wrongdoing lies in the failure on the part of the directors to prevent the frauds and (ex hypothesi) adequately to safeguard generally against the

[159] In such a case, the board has still failed to prevent the crime, and the issue of delegation (and of its supervision) will form part of any investigation into whether or not the board had in place adequate procedures to prevent offending.

[160] As in *SFO v Barclays* (2018) EWHC 3055 (QB).

[161] *JF Alford Transport* [1997] EWCA Crim 654, discussed in detail in ch 3.

commission of fraud by employees. Such failures are *collective* failures at directorial level, failures that must be admitted even by those directors who were unaware that wrongdoing was taking place. In that respect, it does not matter whether there are two directors, or two hundred. They all share equally in the safeguarding failure, in a way they manifestly do not all share (if any do) in the perpetration of the frauds. Accordingly, they must all endure the stigma associated with such a failure. So, even if they escape conviction for 'fraud', as such, the company and its directors do not thereby escape all of the stigma associated with the commission of that offence. Brent Fisse once claimed: 'The concept of managerial *mens rea* is not a concept of genuinely corporate *mens rea* at all'.[162] But however accurate that claim may be in relation to the current understanding of the identification doctrine, it overlooks the possibility that fault may be found in collective directorial failures, and not just in discrete, individual directorial acts of wrongdoing.

An approach focused on collective directorial failure is also both simpler and fairer, in terms of labelling, than seeking to identify the substantive offence with the company through treating it as a real entity, through an analysis of its 'culture'[163] or of its 'systems'.[164] In so far as companies have a clearly identifiable culture or systems,[165] and such a culture or system explains offending by associated persons, then that is best regarded simply as an indication or as evidence that the company (meaning the directors, collectively) has culpably failed to prevent the offending, through a failure of crime prevention efforts and procedures. It is broadly that kind of approach that we find, for example, in section 8 of the Corporate Manslaughter and Corporate Homicide Act 2007. As we saw in Section 1.2 above, by virtue of section 8, evidence of dangerous corporate culture is treated simply as evidence pointing towards a gross breach of a duty of care by the company, but is not legally constitutive of such a breach. Such a breach only occurs, contrary to section 1 of the 2007 Act, if 'the way in which [a company's] activities are managed or organised (a) causes a person's death, and (b) amounts to a gross breach of a relevant duty of care owed by the organisation to the deceased'.

More broadly, on the point about the pivotal role of directors, as GR Sullivan has put it:

> [T]he current board of company X may have inherited and uncritically adopted the current trading patterns [culture and systems] of the company; they may be, as it were, on automatic pilot. Yet that very state of affairs is attributable to their agency and is a state of affairs that could be changed or adjusted if they so chose.[166]

[162] Brent Fisse (1983), 1187.
[163] See, in particular, Celia Wells (2001).
[164] Elise Bant (2023).
[165] In the case of one person or micro companies (the overwhelming majority of companies), that may be doubted.
[166] GR Sullivan (1996), 536.

Sullivan's analysis here bears some comparison with development of the *Caremark*[167] duty in the United States, outlined in section 1, under which civil liability may be imposed on senior company officers if, amongst other things, they failed in their (fiduciary) supervision duty and allowed a corporate culture to develop that condoned wrongdoing.[168] In pointing to the crucial role, in point of accountability, of a company board's ultimate responsibility for what goes on in its name, Sullivan implicitly draws here on what I will be calling the 'control principle'.[169] This principle, central to the theoretical foundation of an offence of failing to prevent crime, is not a principle that is focused on the causal role that someone had in bringing about wrongdoing. Instead, it is focused on the power and responsibility that someone in authority had to prevent that wrongdoing occurring. It is the company board, at the constitutional heart of the company, that has the ultimate responsibility and power to prevent wrongdoing by associated persons connected to the company, and the failure-to-prevent model is designed to capture and build on this insight. I will now try to shed more theoretical light on the case for saying that fair labelling of a company for a failure to prevent crime involves proof of a (collective) failure at board level.

1.6 The Company as an Abstract Legal Entity and Directorial Control

We saw in Section 1.2 above that companies have been variously described a 'myth and a fiction',[170] a 'legal abstraction',[171] 'mere machinery',[172] 'an abstract conception',[173] a 'mere alter ego',[174] 'an abstract being',[175] 'a hollow sham',[176] and 'an abstraction . . . with no mind of its own'.[177] Such statements reflect, amongst other things, the fact that the legal existence of a company does not necessarily turn on the continuous presence of human shareholders and directors. Even when the

[167] *Re Caremark International Inc Derivative Litigation* 698 A 2d 959 (Delaware Chancery, 1996).
[168] *In Re McDonald's Corporation Stockholder Derivative Litigation*, No 2021-0324, 2023 WL 407668 (Delaware Chancery 25 January 2023).
[169] As we will see in ch 3, the control principle can be buttressed by what I call the 'influence principle', concerned with cases where C can and should exercise influence (as opposed to control) over D, with regard to offending behaviour. The influence principle captures better than the control principle the relationship between equals such as company directors or partners, and the relationship between parent and subsidiary companies not under the direct control of the parent company.
[170] *Broderip v Salmon* [1895] 9 Ch 323, 330–31, and 341.
[171] *Continental Tyre and Rubber (GB) Ltd v Daimler Co Ltd* [1916] 1 KB 893, 916.
[172] *Daimler Co v Continental Tyre and Rubber Co* [1916] 2 AC 307, 316.
[173] *Houghton and Co v Nothard, Lome and Wills Ltd* [1928] AC 1, 14.
[174] *Pegler v Craven* [1952] 2 QB 69, 79.
[175] *Austin Reed Ltd v Royal Assurance Co Ltd* (18 July 1966, CA, not reported; but cited [1966] 3 All ER 699).
[176] *Re Bugle Press Ltd* [1961] Ch 270, 288, and 289.
[177] *Lennard's Carrying Company Ltd v Asiatic Petroleum Company Ltd* [1915] AC 705, 713.

director of a one-person company dies, the company continues to exist in law (the director's personal representatives have the power to appoint a new director or directors).[178] Considered as an abstract legal entity, a company provides a legal foundation for a framework of powers and duties to be exercised or performed by the directors (or their delegates, employees, etc.) in the company's name. The powers include the power to own or transfer property, to enter in contracts (or to accept gifts), to delegate to or share functions with certain others, and to create a network of legal relations. The exercise of such powers underlies the 'control' principle, as described in Chapter 3.

In that regard, it is obviously perfectly acceptable to speak as a form of shorthand of 'the company itself' doing X or failing to do Y, or as intending R or being reckless as to Z, so long as that is understood only as a shorthand for a particular legal understanding given to the (in)actions or mental states of individuals or groups within the company.[179] However, it cannot be stressed often enough that whilst an individual or group can—with legal consequences—act in the name of an abstract entity such as company (and hence bind the company in law),[180] it is not the company that acts or that possesses the mental state. As a formal, abstract legal entity, a company—unlike the human beings who populate it—cannot meet, for example, Searle's test for consciousness, intentionality, or thought processes.[181] The legal entity that is a company cannot feel pain or hear a sound (conscious states). It cannot want to eat food or believe that someone is approaching (intentional states), and it cannot figure out how to get to a banana that is out of reach (thought process).[182] Gobert and Punch suggest that although a company may not have the capacity to engage emotionally, it nonetheless has 'the rational capacity to understand that [its] actions [can] cause injury to innocent victims, and the physical capacity to refrain from engaging in those actions'.[183] However, taken literally, such a view lacks plausibility. It can only be individuals associated with the company who have rational and physical capacities, not companies as legal entities: the bloodless, mindless entities registered at Companies House.[184] It is this point that explains the importance of having a sound theory of *who*—be it individual or group—represents a company in law, when, and for what purpose. The limited relevance to liability of evidence concerning corporate culture or system must be understood in that context. For example, some 56 per cent of UK business

178 *Elliott v Cimarron UK Ltd* [2017] EWHC 3872.

179 See, generally, Manuel Velasquez (2003).

180 And whilst a failure to act on the part of an individual or group, or a mental state possessed by an individual or group, can in law be attributed to a company.

181 John R Searle (1994).

182 Ibid., 206.

183 James Gobert and Maurice Punch (2003), 48. For a similar argument, see CMV Clarkson (1996).

184 *Meridian Global Funds Management Asia Ltd v Securities Commission* [1995] 2 AC 500, 506–07, cited by GR Sullivan (1996), 516.

enterprises are one-person outfits.[185] Regarding such businesses, it is just a distortion to seek to analyse their activities in terms of corporate 'culture' or 'systems' as opposed to analysing them straightforwardly in terms of the relevant individual's conduct undertaken in the name of the business.

For the purpose of finding blameworthy corporate states of mind, some theorists have sought to elide the distinction between (abstract, inanimate) companies and (flesh and blood) individuals and groups, when it comes to inferring states of mind from conduct.[186] Mihailis Diamantis, for example, relies on evidence that, in empirical tests, when asked how to describe the same action undertaken by an individual, and alternatively by a company, ordinary people use the same language of mental states in relation to both the individual and the company.[187] However, such tests inevitably beg the key question: *whose* actions were involved, when evidence was presented as evidence of the 'company' having engaged in an action? Was it an employee's action, or a director's, or perhaps a middle manager's? As we have seen, companies comprised of more than one person have the potential to be ethically heterogeneous. This means that a company (in the form of its directors) can intelligibly seek to deny that a wrong done by an employee—or even by a director—should be attributable to the company, because the company was at that very moment following through more broadly on a commitment to implement robust procedures to prevent such wrongdoing.

A company's ethical heterogeneity is associated with or emerges from the efficiency-based divisions of labour that a corporate structure enables, on an ongoing basis, a point long ago explained by Ronald Coase and his followers.[188] First, it may be more efficient to have people who can be directed reliably to perform tasks (or to exercise powers) on a continuous basis as and when required, or to have people who can be trusted as equal partners in the division of labour, than it is to have to go to market to negotiate individual deals with strangers for these tasks to be performed.[189] As Coase put it:

> [T]he operation of a market costs something, and by forming an organisation and allowing some authority (an 'entrepreneur') to direct the resources, certain marketing costs are saved . . . A firm, therefore, consists of the system of relationships which comes into existence when the direction of resources is dependent on an entrepreneur.[190]

[185] https://www.money.co.uk/business/business-statistics#:~:text=More%20than%20half%20%2856%25%29%20of%20the%20businesses%20in,region%20in%20the%20UK%20%281%2C477%20per%2010%2C000%20residents%29 (last accessed 02/03/2025).
[186] Mihailis E Diamantis (2023).
[187] Ibid., 224–25.
[188] Ronald Coase (1937).
[189] Ibid.
[190] Ibid., 390.

To give a simple example, my office files may frequently need organizing, the office plants may regularly need watering, and the telephone must be answered during office hours; but it makes little sense to go to market to negotiate deals for each of these individual tasks to be done, when they could all done by an employee under my immediate direction. Secondly, such employment contracts may, legally, be more efficiently housed within an enduring corporate structure, a structure that—for example—survives the death or departure of any individual employing director or manager.

Key, though, to the dynamic efficiency of the division of labour, in any network of legal relationships established by their link to a company, will necessarily be the establishing of a hierarchy of such relationships. This will mean that (say) even if Z has been given the power to do A, that power may legitimately be changed in scope or cancelled by Y, whose power to act in that way may, in turn, be changed or determined by X (and so on). Who is at the top of this chain of authorization? Whilst shareholders might appear to be the correct answer, that is so only if the exercise of proprietary power is taken to be the key case of the exercise of corporate power, but proprietary rights (whilst obviously protected by the criminal law) are not a key focus in point of corporate wrongdoing. Criminal wrongdoing is primarily a matter of responsibility for (in)action and consequential events, and in the case of companies, what matters in that respect is who is at the top of the chain where *executive* power is concerned. This is the director or directors of the company. So far as the running—as opposed to ownership—of a company is concerned, the need to have directors is a corporate constitutional fundamental, in a way that the need (if any) for employees, however high ranking, is not.[191]

In that regard, directors have a special executive status granted to them by legislation. For example, section 40 of the Companies Act 2006 says, 'in favour of a person dealing with a company in good faith, the power of the directors to bind the company, or authorise others to do so, is deemed to be free of any limitation under the company's constitution'. In consequence, as Micheler puts it:

> The directors play a dual role. They are agents, but they also act as principals. They act as top-level superior agents who hold master-authority, the scope of which the shareholders cannot modify. They act as 'quasi-principals'.[192]

[191] Section 12 of the Companies Act 2006 states: 'The statement of the company's proposed officers required to be delivered to the registrar must contain the required particulars of—

(a) the person who is, or persons who are, to be the first director or directors of the company.'

[192] Eva Micheler (2021), 79.

The Prentice Report remarked to similar effect: 'The board is clearly the principal organ for conducting [a company's] business activities, something which is reflected in the fact that the board has almost invariably conferred upon it the widest jurisdiction possible to manage the company's affairs.'[193] It is, thus, understandable that the criminal law has regarded the criminal actions of directors, acting within the scope of their authority, as constituting the actions of the company.

By virtue of section 154 of the Companies Act 2006, a company must have at least one director (who must be a natural person). By virtue of section 172 of the Companies Act 2006, it is directors who are obliged to act in such a way as they consider in good faith promotes the success of the company. Further, it is directors who have ultimate responsibility for the day-to-day running of the company, and (where non-executive directors normally come in) for the monitoring of the way in which the company is run. It is, of course, typically during such day-to-day activity that offences come to be committed. In terms of accountability for such offences—in my terms, for the failure to prevent the offending—the 'buck stops' with the directors; and, as we saw in the discussion of *Secretary of State for Trade and Industry v Baker (No. 5)* in Section 1.1 above,[194] this remains true whether or not they delegate the task of preventing offending to one of their number or to some other person. So, it makes perfect sense, in fair labelling terms, to regard the (in)action of directors as the crucial focus, when considering the circumstances in which the company itself should be regarded as open to criminal liability. This is the core of good sense in *Lennard's Carrying Company, Ltd v Asiatic Petroleum Company, Ltd*,[195] which equated the conduct of the company with the conduct of directors. Once this focus on directorial responsibility is broadened to include conduct that the company (i.e. the directors) failed to prevent, then the core of good sense in that decision is given a morally and legally powerful manifestation, for labelling purposes. Accordingly, in answer to the question, 'whose failure is it that represents the failure of the company itself to prevent wrongdoing?', I give the unequivocal answer that the relevant failure is the failure of the company's director (in a sole director company), or of the directors collectively, as the supreme executive decision-taking and decision-monitoring agent(s) of the company.

1.7 Small Firms and Direct Corporate Liability

Although it is perfectly capable of application to small or one-person outfits, the main theory of criminal responsibility developed in this work, the failure-to-prevent theory, is well suited—indeed, designed—to capture the way in which

193 Department of Trade and Industry (1986), para 24.
194 [1999] 1 BCLC 433, 436 and 489, discussed in Section 1.1 above.
195 [1915] AC 705 (HL).

medium- to large-sized companies goes about their business. Even so, my focus on corporate failure to prevent crime does not entail that a company can never itself commit a substantive offence. What must on my account be true, in point of fair labelling, for a company itself to have committed a substantive offence? The principal condition that must be satisfied is what can be called the moral homogeneity condition. The crime must have been committed in circumstances effectively excluding any possible simultaneous commitment at the highest level to the prevention of such crimes. This means that a company is likely to be in a position to be regarded as actually committing a crime, as opposed to merely failing to prevent its occurrence, only when:

1. the company is a sole director company, and the director commits the crime;[196] or
2. a majority on the board has collectively consented to or connived at the commission of the crime; or
3. on particular facts (especially where very small, close-knit family firms are concerned) company directors or partners, and in some cases also employees, can be regarded as operating with a collective mindset, on the basis of which the acts of one are regarded as the acts of all.

Bases 1–3 for establishing criminal liability are aimed primarily at the small firm. It is essential not to neglect the phenomenon of small firm activity in the field of corporate crime. A very small 'micro' firm—with a turnover of £632,000 or less, £316,000 or less on their balance sheets, and ten employees or fewer[197]—is far more likely to be organized predominantly on *gemeinschaft* rather than *gesellschaft* lines.[198] That means such a firm will, in all probability, rely far more on placing trust in other members of the firm (including employees) to act properly, rather than on formal procedures.[199] A small, family firm is also more likely to understand its responsibilities as shared or collective in nature ('all for one, and one for all'). That makes formal bureaucratic distinctions between directors, managers, and employees less significant in practice than they commonly are in larger firms. Accordingly, on the one hand, in the case of very small firms, it may be possible to identify the criminal acts of company employees with the company itself, and not just the criminal acts of directors; but on the other hand, there is a strong case for permitting such firms to deny liability, especially in the case of fault-based offences, on the grounds that they entirely reasonably placed trust in an offending employee

[196] As indicated earlier, sole person enterprises constitute 56 per cent of the total of such enterprises in the United Kingdom.
[197] https://www.gov.uk/annual-accounts/microentities-small-and-dormant-companies (last accessed 17/11/2023).
[198] See, further, the discussion of these concepts in ch 2.
[199] JP Kennedy (2016).

not to offend. However, that is something that, under the recent 2023 reforms of corporate criminal liability (and under clause 196 of the Crime and Policing Bill 2025), they are unable to do. I return to this point in Chapter 2.

1.8 The Failure-to-Prevent Model and Risk-Based Offences

Notwithstanding the arguments made so far, it is important to be clear that the failure-to-prevent model is not (and is not intended to be) an all-purpose solution to corporate wrongdoing. The failure-to-prevent model is a model designed, first and foremost, to provide a 'best fit' in terms of criminal labelling for corporate involvement in substantive offending (polluting, bribing, defrauding, facilitating tax evasion, false accounting, etc.),[200] or in the causing of unacceptable harms that are non-criminal in themselves such as accidents at work or AI-generated wrongs.[201] As indicated earlier, such offences or harms are offences or harms involving act-tokens: casually impactful events that are unique in space-time.[202] However, in relation to the ex hypothesi unwitting posing of unacceptable risks, it is clear that companies fall to be judged in criminal law by reference to what were referred to earlier as a-causal, judgemental criteria. An example from health and safety regulation is when the law asks, 'Did the employer allow a situation to arise which the safety, health or welfare of persons in the workplace were not, so far as reasonably practicable, ensured?'.[203] Such offences apply a 'risk-management' model to the evaluation of corporate conduct,[204] and are commonly integral to a regulatory scheme aimed at standardizing and improving corporate compliance with key values.[205] Consequently, such offences are very commonly dealt with as much through penalties administered by the regulator as by criminal prosecution. In that regard, in the Introduction, I distinguished two types of offence: (1) liability for a failure respecting a dangerous 'internal' state of affairs under company control or influence[206] and (2) liability for a failure respecting a dangerous 'external' state of affairs open to company control or influence.[207]

The failure-to-prevent model is effectively embodied in offences of this kind (pure risk-taking), in that such offences could be expressed in terms of a failure to prevent unacceptable risk arising. However, there is an element of superfluity

200 Or in inchoate offences aimed at committing such offences.
201 See the discussion in Section 1.9 below.
202 See the discussion in Section 1.2 above.
203 See Health and Safety at Work Act 1974, s 1.
204 This model is discussed in ch 2.
205 See the discussion in ch 2.
206 Including health and safety at work, or systems addressing platform online safety: model B, as described in Section I.4.
207 A topical example being the obligation to monitor the observance of human rights standards by contracting partners (model C, as described in Section I.4). See the discussion below and the more detailed analysis in ch 5.

or redundancy in explaining such offences in terms of the failure-to-prevent model. That is because, to say that a company failed to prevent an unacceptable risks arising is simply another way of saying that an unacceptable risk was posed by the company. If that seems right, then in cases where the wrongdoing consists in nothing more than wrongful risk-taking, criminalization has no need to rely on the failure-to-prevent model. However, the moral purchase that the failure-to-prevent model can independently gain in risk-based cases can depend on the degree of specificity with which the risk is defined. Where a risk-based obligation is to avoid specific 'act-types', the failure-to-prevent model may play a morally more significant role in criminalization. Consider again the administrative offence—mentioned earlier—committed when a regulated company in the financial sector fails to 'take reasonable care to organise and control its [financial] affairs responsibly and effectively, with adequate risk management systems'.[208] If turned into a generally applicable corporate offence, such a provision would encompass and go (well) beyond all instances in which failures to prevent financial crime have now been criminalized. So, why not enact such a provision? A risk-based offence couched in such evaluative terms gives very substantial discretion to enforcement authorities to determine when an investigation should be launched and when a breach has taken place. It gives little guidance on what kinds of specific risk are to be guarded against, or on what taking 'reasonable care' involves, even if such guidance can be filled out through soft law developed by regulators or industry organizations.[209] That is acceptable in a regulatory context, in which the regulator is as much concerned to help regulated businesses improve their conduct, as it is to punish misconduct. However, it is far more controversial in a criminal law context where the focus is purely on investigation and prosecution of suspected wrongdoing.[210]

An illustrative example from the field of international bribery is the so-called internal controls provision of the Foreign Corrupt Practice Act (USA) 1977 (FCPA), discussed by Karen Woody.[211] This requires that every issuer of publicly traded securities 'devise and maintain a system of internal accounting controls sufficient to provide reasonable assurances' that (inter alia) 'transactions are recorded as necessary to permit preparation of financial statements in conformity with generally accepted accounting principles or any other criteria applicable to such statements, and to maintain accountability for assets'.[212] In accordance with the principle of vicarious liability applied in corporate criminal cases in the United States, if an

[208] Financial Conduct Authority (2023). See the discussion in Section 1.2 above.
[209] In that respect, the Corporate Governance Code is, for example, thin on detail: see Financial Reporting Council (2024), s 4.
[210] See further the discussion in ch 2.
[211] 15 USC § 78m(b)(2)(B); Karen Woody (2017).
[212] Section 13(b)(2)(b) of the Exchange Act (15 USC § 78m(b)(2)(A)).

employee knowingly violates this provision, then the company also does so.[213] Yet, in the view of one US court:

> the main problem with the internal accounting controls provision of the FCPA is that there are no specific standards by which to evaluate the sufficiency of controls; any evaluation is inevitably a highly subjective process in which knowledgeable individuals can arrive at totally different conclusions.[214]

Where there is a lack of clarity over regulatory demands, firms' inability to distinguish between behaviour that falls short of what is required, behaviour that is compliant, and behaviour that goes beyond what is required leads to inconsistency and unpredictability of responses. Some firms will go beyond what is required (playing safe by overspending on compliance), whereas others will take the opportunity to minimize what they do whilst claiming to be compliant (playing the system).[215]

Woody suggests[216] that 15 USC § 78m(b)(2)(B) would be fairer and more proportionate, as a basis for prosecution, if placed in the context of an actual violation by a company of the bribery provisions of the FCPA, or of the submission of false or misleading accounts: in other words, against the background of a failure to prevent an act-token of the relevant kind. However, one need not necessarily go this far to satisfy the demands of fairness and proportionality in relation to offences of risk-taking. These demands can be satisfied, so long as the unjustified risk in question relates to a sufficiently definite act-type (bribery, false accounting, pollution, etc.). For example, as we have seen, it is a defence to a failure-to-prevent bribery offence that a company had in place adequate procedures to prevent bribery, as an act-type, taking place.[217] It would have been possible (additionally, or instead) to have made the failure to put such procedures in place a substantive offence in itself, an offence committed whether or not any act of bribery to benefit the company took place.[218] Such a 'precursor' offence suffers from some of the problems of uncertainty just mentioned, and it lacks the power of labelling involved when a company is convicted of having failed to prevent a relevant act-token (say, an act of bribery). Even so, by confining the focus of a firm's preventative efforts to a specific risk in the form of an act-type, such as 'bribery', some clarity is given on the kinds of steps that might be relevant to avoidance of such offending.

213 *New York Central & Hudson River Railroad Co v US* 212 US 481 (1909).
214 *SEC v World-Wide Coin Invs* 567 F Supp 724, 751 (ND Ga 1983).
215 Lamia Chourou, Darlene Himick, and Samir Saadi (2023).
216 Karen Woody (2017), 1753–55.
217 Bribery Act 2010, s 7. See discussion in Section 1.2 above.
218 Such an offence would fall into the category of liability that in Section I.4 I called 'liability for a failure respecting a dangerous internal state of affairs under company control or influence' (model B).

That is significant, in that it explains the approach of some states in relation to the prevention of human rights abuses in the supply chain.[219] It is becoming increasingly common for 'due diligence' obligations to be imposed on (large) companies, with a view to ensuring that companies make sufficient efforts to ensure that there is no human rights abuse in their supply chains anywhere in the world.[220] The United Nations has identified four core components to this due diligence obligation:

(a) Identifying and assessing actual or potential adverse human rights impacts that the enterprise may cause or contribute to through its own activities, or which may be directly linked to its operations, products or services by its business relationships;
(b) Integrating findings from impact assessments across relevant company processes and taking appropriate action according to its involvement in the impact;
(c) Tracking the effectiveness of measures and processes to address adverse human rights impacts in order to know if they are working;
(d) Communicating on how impacts are being addressed and showing stakeholders—in particular affected stakeholders—that there are adequate policies and processes in place.[221]

When a company is in breach of such obligations, it may very well be right to impose criminal liability on the company.[222] As an act-type, though, an 'abuse of human rights' has potentially wide and uncertain scope, raising some of the issues of regulatory uncertainty just mentioned. Even so, if—as suggested by the Law Commission[223]—due diligence need be exercised only in relation to a narrow range of the most serious such abuses (as act-types), then the potential for such uncertainty is reduced, and the moral imperative to pursue due diligence vigorously is sharpened.

[219] See further the discussion in ch 5.
[220] See https://www.ibanet.org/article/0B9779EE-5105-4A43-B92E-EF4536E664F9 (last accessed 19/07/2023).
[221] United Nations (2018), 10.
[222] For example, in relation to child labour, Dutch law makes it a criminal offence for a company to fail in its due diligence obligations, under the *Wet Zorgplicht Kinderarbeid* 2019 (Dutch Due Diligence Act 2019). As part of its due diligence, companies must investigate whether there are reasonable grounds to suspect that a product or service in their supply chain has been produced using child labour. If, following this investigation, a company has reasonable grounds to suspect that goods and/or services have been procured with the use of child labour, it must develop and implement an action plan to ensure that child labour is prevented in its supply chains in the future. There are fines for failing to file a declaration that the company has exercised an appropriate level of supply chain due diligence, and penalties increase for companies found to have an inadequate due diligence process to detect and prevent child labour. Companies that fail to comply with the Dutch Due Diligence Act can be fined up to EUR 870,000 or 10 per cent of the company's total worldwide revenue. See, further, the discussion in ch 6.
[223] Law Commission (2022), ch 8.

In relation to human rights abuse, it has also been suggested by some bodies that the United Kingdom should go beyond a requirement for large companies to show due diligence in monitoring their supply chain, and in addition apply the failure-to-prevent model in such cases.[224] As we will see in Chapter 5, the issue of principle involved in such a proposal is whether (say) an independent supplier in the supply chain, who engages in the relevant abuse, can be considered to be sufficiently 'closely associated' with a UK-based company to make it appropriate to say that the UK-based company itself—and not just persons running the independent supply company—failed to prevent the human rights abuse. That, in turn, depends on whether the relationship between the (ex hypothesi, overseas-based) entity engaged in the abuse of human rights and the UK company with which the entity was doing business fell within the scope of one or other of two principles governing such relationships. These are the 'control principle', which involves a hierarchical supervisory relationship between two (corporate) people, and the 'influence principle', which involves a horizontal relationship in which one (corporate) person can and should seek to exercise influence for the good over another (corporate) person, even when they are not necessarily in a supervisory relationship with that other person.[225] In some instances, the relationship between UK companies and overseas entities engaging in human rights abuse will meet the criteria involved in applying these principles, meaning that it is permissible (other things being equal) to impose liability for a failure to prevent human rights abuses. However, in Chapter 5, I argue that in many cases the relationship between the companies in question (main company and independent contractor) will not meet either of these sets of criteria. In such cases, the focus should be on the discharge by the main company of what I call an 'oversight' duty, a duty to monitor the conduct of the independent contractor, and shape the main company's own contracting behaviour accordingly, but in the absence of any duty to intervene and prevent abuse by the independent contractor.

1.9 The Failure-to-Prevent Model, AI, and Non-Criminal Harms

The failure-to-prevent model is a general theory applicable to the commission of criminal offences. However, in some circumstances, the cause of unjustified harm or risk might be linked to the running of a company, even though the causing of the harm itself may not involve the commission of a criminal offence. Here are two examples:

[224] See, generally, the discussion in British Institute of International and Comparative Law (2020).
[225] The control and influence principles are discussed in ch 3.

1. A deep hole is mistakenly left in a floor by someone installing pipes at company premises, and the room is not subsequently checked by the company's safety inspectors. A worker suffers a serious injury when they fall down the hole.
2. A company uses an AI system to market its financial products to customers. For unknown reasons, the system begins to employ a financial fraud technique described in its data sources, and hence secures more investors by falsely misrepresenting the nature of the financial products.

In the first example, the criminal law has long taken the view that what matters in this example is simply whether or not the company failed in its duty to ensure (in so far as was reasonably practicable) that the company's premises were safe.[226] As is well known, a breach of that duty is a criminal offence even if no harm occurs.[227] Criminal liability is based on a 'risk-management' model of a kind common when regulatory agencies proactively govern the field of activity in question.[228] Even so, in pursuit of more accurate labelling, it would clearly be possible additionally to create an offence applying the failure-to-prevent model to cases of this kind, in which non-criminal unjustified harm has occurred.[229] So doing would mean that, in example (1), the company would be exposed to liability for an offence of 'failing to prevent serious injury', subject to a defence that it had in place adequate or reasonable procedures to prevent such harms: model G, as described in Section I.4.

The second example has the potential to pose a different, albeit analogous kind of problem, although the solution is similar.[230] As we saw earlier, it is a strict liability offence to provide consumers with false information about products, under the Consumer Protection from Unfair Trading Regulations 2008, in so far as so doing amounts to an unfair commercial practice. It is, of course, perfectly possible to argue that the company itself straightforwardly commits this offence in the circumstances described in example (2), because the company 'caused' the false information to be provided to customers.[231] The company caused the false information to be provided, in much the same way that I cause a wrong answer to be given when the answer is generated by my use of a calculator that turns out to have been faulty.

[226] See the discussion in Jeremy Horder (2025a) and Health and Safety at Work Act 1974, discussed further in ch 2.

[227] Unless a victim is killed, bringing the offence of corporate manslaughter into play.

[228] See the discussion in ch 2.

[229] For an argument along such lines, in relation to harm done through health and safety failures, see Peter Glazebrook (2002).

[230] In the discussion that follows, I assume that the company was unaware of the prohibited outcomes being produced by the AI system, as on the facts of example (2). Clearly, if the company was aware that the outcomes were being produced but did nothing, then the possibility of direct liability for fraud arises.

[231] A direct casual analysis of this kind avoids what would otherwise be difficult questions about whether the information was provided through a voluntary act of a kind that is arguably needed in cases where it is alleged that the company is vicariously liable for the strict liability offence.

Potentially more difficult is the question of whether the company is guilty of fraud contrary to the Fraud Act 2006, an issue that might easily arise in a non-consumer context not covered by the 2008 regulations. A sophisticated AI system has—in common with, for example, some species of bird and whale—the so called level D consciousness ability: 'the function of adapting behaviour to a specific purpose and the ability to produce a specific result based on the identification, judgement and evaluation of objective causes'.[232] It follows that a sophisticated company AI system does not simply execute individual human commands mechanically and is in that sense different from, say, the simple working of a (faulty) calculator. That is so, even if the results it produces stem from the actions of individuals associated with the company putting in place and overseeing the maintenance of the AI system. In example (2), the false information may have been provided 'intelligently', in the sense of having been provided to a sufficient degree independently of any particular human action or command, and that entails the application of a different kind of analysis.

Some scholars argue that systems and processes, including AI systems, should be regarded as the extended mind (and body) of the company.[233] So, if an AI system 'commits' fraud, so does the company. Clearly, even with an intelligent AI system, some contentious metaphysics is involved in such a claim.[234] Is it really appropriate to describe an AI system itself (as opposed to those in charge of it) as 'dishonest'? One should perhaps not rule out such an analysis completely,[235] although the issue remains of whether the company should still be liable for the supposed fraud if the AI system was introduced and run by a mere lower-level manager. Even so, in example (2), the company has clearly failed to prevent what might be referred to as the 'fraud outcome', the external elements of the offence in the form of delivery in the course of company business to the consumers of a false financial representation. By analogy, if an AI system were to offer a potential customer a sum of money in exchange for their improper commitment to sign a contract, it could be said that the company had failed to prevent a 'bribery outcome': the promise or giving of a bribe being in part an external manifestation of the offence of bribery. Subject to a defence that adequate procedures were in place to prevent such outcomes, more accurate labelling of the company's involvement is arguably achieved by a focus on a company's failure to prevent the occurrence of the external element of certain kinds of offence (the offence outcome),[236] when this occurs through the operation of non-human company systems or processes.[237] Outside the financial

[232] Jianhua Xie (2021), 125. Xie identifies seven levels of consciousness, with D being a mid-range level.
[233] Michailis E Diamantis (2020).
[234] See the discussion in Law Commission (2022), 6.39–41.
[235] It has the advantage that no new legislation would be needed to deal with the issue.
[236] Such as fraud, bribery, false accounting, or money laundering.
[237] Model G, as described in Section I.4.

crime context, this model of liability might also prove significant. Suppose that an AI chatbot encourages or assists a vulnerable person to commit suicide.[238] In such a case, the chatbot produces the offence outcome—the acts of encouragement or assistance—even if it cannot be said to have the fault element. The person or body operating the chatbot service fails to prevent that outcome. Accordingly, the key liability issue will be whether the operator has adequate systems in place to prevent such outcomes. Nonetheless, as my focus in this book is on offences committed by human individuals, I will not pursue this point further.

[238] https://www.msn.com/en-us/technology/artificial-intelligence/a-teen-contemplating-suicide-turned-to-a-chatbot-is-it-liable-for-her-death/ar-AA1MEiJc?ocid=BingNewsSerp (last accessed 19/09/2025).

2

THE 2023 ACT

LIABILITY AND THE (CLASS) POLITICS OF FIRM SIZE

2.1 An Outline Critique of the 2023 Act

PROBLEMATIC EXAMPLE: Company C, a car sales company, is comprised of a sole director (X). X's long-term domestic partner, D, is not employed by Company C but has always helped X with different aspects of the business. Worried about the firm's debts, but without telling X, D makes a false statement about the company's finances to a creditor, to secure an extension of credit. Company C is charged with fraud. The prosecution claims that, over the years, D has carved out a role as, in effect, a 'senior manager' of Company C, and so D's fraud is also committed by Company C, in virtue of section 196 of the 2023 Act. X denies that D is a 'senior manager' of the company, and says that, whilst Company C would have been guilty of failing to prevent D's fraud, contrary to section 199 of the 2023 Act, C company is a 'small' company to which this offence does not apply.

In this chapter, I explore the changes made to corporate criminal liability by the Economic Crime and Corporate Transparency Act 2023 ('the 2023 Act')[1] and, where relevant, the potential successor provisions of the Crime and Policing Bill 2025 ('the 2025 Bill'), in the light of the theory of corporate crime developed in this work. Alongside the introduction in section 199 of the 2023 Act of a new specific corporate offence of failing to prevent fraud, section 196 of the 2023 Act, to be replaced by clause 196 of the 2025 Bill, has extended the reach of corporate criminal liability in relation to crimes in the United Kingdom more generally.[2] I will argue that the extended reach of corporate liability for economic crimes created by section 196 and clause 196 falls between two stools. On the one hand, it effectively

[1] The broad aim of which was 'to prevent organised criminals, fraudsters, kleptocrats and terrorists from using companies and other corporate entities to abuse the UK's open economy ... to strengthen the UK's broader response to economic crime ... [and to] support enterprise by enabling Companies House to deliver a better service for over four million UK companies': Russell Taylor (2023), 2. This chapter sets out and then builds on arguments first developed in Jeremy Horder (2025a).

[2] Clause 196 of the Crime and Policing Bill 2025 will extent corporate liability, through the actions of senior managers acting within the scope of their authority, to all offences in UK jurisdictions.

A Theory of Corporate Crime. Jeremy Horder, Oxford University Press. © Jeremy Horder 2026.
DOI: 10.1093/9780198936534.003.0003

creates a kind of vicarious corporate liability for fault-based crimes such as fraud. The doctrine of vicarious corporate liability, familiar to US lawyers as a generally applicable doctrine,[3] has historically been applied only to no-fault strict liability offences in the United Kingdom.[4] The doctrine traditionally involves the automatic attribution of criminal liability to a company when, in the course of their employment, an employee or agent—no matter how low in status—commits a criminal offence.[5] On the other hand, by way of contrast with the position generally in the United States,[6] and with the position in relation to no-fault offences in the United Kingdom,[7] the scope of this new form of vicarious corporate liability is limited by the 2023 Act and the 2025 Bill to the criminal activity of a firm's 'senior managers' (the definition of which is considered in Section 2.2).[8] However serious it is, a fault-based crime committed by a lower ranking employee, below senior manager, will not automatically be attributable to the company, even if the crime was intended to benefit the company. Why not?

The limitation in the 2023 Act and 2025 Bill has been influenced by principles associated with a quite different doctrine of corporate criminal liability in English law. This is the 'identification' doctrine, introduced in Chapter 1. As we saw, perhaps influenced by the German company law distinction between persons who are 'organs' of a company and persons who are mere corporate 'agents',[9] the identification doctrine was developed by the courts to determine when a company itself commits a fault-based crime such as fraud or false accounting. In that regard, unlike the doctrine of vicarious liability, the identification doctrine is not ostensibly concerned with when a crime committed by a separate person can simply be attributed to the company.[10] In *Tesco Supermarkets Ltd. v*

[3] See *New York Central R Co v United States*, 212 US 481 (1909), imposing vicarious liability on a company for crimes (including fault-based crimes) committed by an employee or agent intending to benefit the company.

[4] *Mousell Brothers Ltd v London and North West Railway* [1917] 2 KB 836; *James & Son Ltd v Smee* [1954] 3 WLR 631.

[5] The Law Commission rejected the adoption of such an approach to govern crimes more generally: see Law Commission (2022) and ch 5.

[6] The classic statement is to be found in *New York Central & Hudson River Railroad Co v United States*, 212 US 481 (1909), 495 (Day J): 'We see no valid objection in law, and every reason in public policy, why the corporation, which profits by the transaction, and can only act through its agents and officers, shall be held punishable by fine because of the knowledge and intent of its agents to whom it has entrusted authority to act.'

[7] See, e.g., *Coppen v Moore (No 2)* [1898] 2 QB 306.

[8] We should note that the US Model Penal Code adopts a broadly similar approach to that embodied in section 196. Under the MPC § 207(1)(c), a company may be guilty of a fault-based offence if 'the commission of the offense was performed, or at least authorized, commanded, or recklessly tolerated by the board of directors or by a high managerial agent acting in behalf of the corporation within the scope of his office or employment'.

[9] See the discussion in Amanda Pinto QC and Martin Evans (2008), 46 and *DPP v Kent and Sussex Contractors Ltd* [1944] 1 KB 146, 154–55 (Viscount Caldecote LCJ).

[10] *Lennard's Carrying Co Ltd v Asiatic Petroleum Co Ltd* [1915] AC 705. It can, of course, be argued that the 'identification doctrine' is a fiction that simply conceals the fact that a company is being held vicariously liable for a crime committed by a director: see, e.g., GR Sullivan (1996). See the discussion in ch 1.

Nattrass,[11] Lord Morris explains the key question under the identification doctrine: 'When is some act the act of the company, as opposed to the act of a servant or agent of the company?'[12] As indicated in Chapter 1, before the coming into force of the 2023 Act, the only persons regarded under the identification doctrine as the embodiment of the company, and hence whose fault-based crimes are *ipso facto* committed by the company itself, have been the company's directors.[13] It is this rule which is changed by section 196 and clause 196. The change involves a modest extension to the range of persons who are to be treated as the embodiment of the company, to include its 'senior managers' (whether or not directors).[14] Henceforth, when a non-director senior manager (acting within the actual or apparent scope of their authority[15]) commits a fault-based crime, it is also to be regarded as the company's criminal act. That is so, even though senior managers, unlike directors, may be mere employees having no constitutional role within the company at all. Outside the regulated sector where certain individuals must be designated as 'senior managers',[16] there are few criteria for determining who is (apart from a director) to count as a 'senior manager' within a firm.[17] That poses a rule-of-law problem, in terms of lack a certainty over when a company itself stands to be convicted of a fault-based crime if one of its significant employees commits such a crime. As we will see, the lack of certainty is likely to bear down hardest on small firms. These are firms more likely to be run by skilled working or lower-middle class people, women or ethnic minority business people, where staff roles are not defined bureaucratically in unambiguous terms, in the way that they are more likely to be in larger firms more commonly run by tertiary educated middle class people.[18] Moreover, the lack of certainty itself stems from a deeper theoretical ambiguity about the 2023 and 2025 reforms and about the meaning of the identification doctrine.

[11] *Tesco Supermarkets Ltd v Nattrass* [1972] AC 153.

[12] Ibid., 178 (my emphasis). See also the speech of Lord Diplock at 199–200.

[13] *Tesco Supermarkets Ltd v Nattrass* [1971] UKHL 1.

[14] The extension of a company's identity to include 'senior managers' has been endorsed by Celia Wells, whose path-breaking work has done much to shape the course of scholarly argument, and ultimately legal reform: Celia Wells (2001), 155–56.

[15] This phrase, used in section 196 to determine the limits to a senior manager's representation of the company itself, was used for the first time in a criminal law context in *SFO v Barclays* (2018) EWHC 3055 (QB), and is drawn from the civil law of agency. Its use is deeply problematic in this context: see the discussion in ch 5.

[16] https://www.fca.org.uk/firms/senior-managers-certification-regime (last accessed 22/09/2025). See also the treatment of 'senior managers' in the Online Safety Act 2023.

[17] Under the Model Penal Code section 2.07(4)(c), 'high managerial agent means an officer of a corporation ... or any other agent of a corporation or association having duties of such responsibility that his or her conduct may fairly be assumed to represent the policy of the corporation or association'. This is clearly a very vague definition, and as we will see, the 2023 Act seeks to improve on it.

[18] Ethnic minority entrepreneurs are responsible for about 10 per cent of business start-ups, and self-employment is more common among such groups than for the white population: Anuradha Basu and Eser Altinay (2002).

Let me now turn to the introduction of an offence of failing to prevent fraud, in section 199 of the 2023 Act. That change is welcome[19] and consistent with the main proposition of this work: that the use of a failure-to-prevent model is the best way to conceive of and implement corporate criminal liability. However, the 2023 Act makes no effort to harmonize the provisions of this new offence with the existing corporate offence of failing to prevent bribery, or even with the new extended form of general corporate criminal liability in section 196. This creates unnecessary uncertainty and complexity. Moreover, in an effort to avoid regulatory burdens on the vast majority of (smaller) businesses,[20] the failure-to-prevent fraud offence is, unlike other existing failure-to-prevent offences, confined to so-called large organizations under the Companies Act 2006.[21] In itself, that restriction breaches what ought to be a general criminal law principle that if wrongdoing is worthy of criminalization, then that wrongdoing should in principle be criminal whether it is committed by the weak or the strong, and when it is committed by the economically insignificant as well as by the economically powerful. A small firm is perfectly capable of either committing or failing to prevent a massive fraud, as in some instances of so-called startup company frauds.[22] Further, the refusal to extend the failure-to-prevent offence to smaller firms creates the risk of entrenching class bias in the enforcement of corporate criminal law. Far from benefiting from an exemption from the failure-to-prevent fraud offence, its inapplicability means (1) that procedures the small firms have put in place to prevent or minimize the risk of wrongdoing will be irrelevant to their potential liability, and (2) they are more likely than a large firm to face direct corporate or individual prosecution for the substantive offence. All in all, an opportunity was missed by the 2023 Act to put corporate criminal liability on a theoretically and practically sounder footing, by making the failure-to-prevent model the centrepiece of corporate criminal liability in general.

2.2 Extended Corporate Criminal Liability under the 2023 Act

Section 196(1) of the 2023 Act—to be replaced by clause 196 of the 2025 Bill which is worded in similar terms[23]—provides that:

[19] See, further, Celia Wells (2010).

[20] The Government's impact assessment for the bill estimated the total cost of the corporate transparency and Companies House reforms at £289 million. It also estimated the annual cost to businesses at £18.9 million: Russell Taylor (2023).

[21] Unless the company in question is a subsidiary of a 'large' company, in which case it is in scope, whether or not it is itself a large company.

[22] Kimberly Gleason, Yezen H Kannan, and Christian Rauch (2022).

[23] But which extends the reach of the identification doctrine to all offences in UK jurisdictions.

> If a senior manager of a body corporate or partnership ('the organisation') acting within the actual or apparent scope of their authority commits a relevant offence ... the organisation is also guilty of the offence.

In relation to the concept of a 'senior manager', section 196(4)(c) provides that:

> 'Senior manager' in relation to a body corporate or partnership, means an individual who plays a significant role in—(a) the making of decisions about how the whole or a substantial part of the activities of the body corporate ... are to be managed or organised, or (b) the actual managing or organising of the whole or a substantial part of those activities.

These reforms stem from a recent examination of the issues by the Law Commission, in the course of which the Commission set out the 'senior manager' provisions as one of a series of options for reforming the traditional basis for attributing fault-based crimes to companies.[24] In that regard, as Elise Bant and Rebecca Faugno rightly point out, 'In an age of massive trans and multi-national corporations ... the adequacy of traditional corporate liability mechanisms is being increasingly questioned'.[25] Corporate structures and modes of operation create opportunities for offending on a much larger or widespread scale than could ever be achieved by an individual or group of individuals: through the dynamic use of delegated authority and of internal culture, through the creation of multiple forms of presence (such as subsidiaries), and through organized teamwork. It is this kind of problem to which section 196(1)—and hence clause 196 of the 2025 Bill—is meant to provide a solution.

As we have seen, at common law, prior to the 2023 Act, only persons with 'directing mind and will' status were persons whose words and actions were identified with the company and hence were regarded as the words and actions of the company itself.[26] The common law insisted that, with fault-based crimes, the prosecution show that all the elements of the offence (be they culpable words or actions) were identified with the company in this sense. So, for example, in order for a company to be convicted of fraud, contrary to section 2 of the Fraud Act 2006 (a fault-based crime), the traditional version of the identification doctrine required any false representation dishonestly made to have been made by someone (in effect) at directorial level, acting within the scope of their authority.[27] The making

[24] Law Commission (2022); ch 4.

[25] Elise Bant and Rebecca Faugno (2024), 348. See also the 2022 House of Commons Library Research Briefing (Ali Salach, 2022), 4: 'Successfully prosecuting *large* companies has been challenging' (my emphasis).

[26] *Lennard's Carrying Co Ltd v Asiatic Petroleum Co Ltd* [1915] AC 705. See, in particular, the speech of Lord Diplock in *Tesco Supermarkets Ltd v Nattrass* [1972] AC 153, discussed in ch 1.

[27] *SFO v Barclays PLC & ANR* [2018] EWHC 3055 (QB).

of such a false representation by any other person in the company, no matter how high-ranking, would not—unless someone with directing mind and will was complicit in its making—implicate the company itself. Once the identification doctrine became authoritative at common law, older cases—in which a fraud perpetrated by a senior manager (below board level) in the course of their employment was attributed to the company—were no longer to be regarded as sound in law.[28] Accordingly, section 196 (and hence clause 196) will, in all probability, have the effect of producing a different outcome in cases with facts such as those in the well-known case of *R v Andrews Wetherfoil*.[29]

In that case, a company's managing director, a 'technical' director, and the manager of a housing division had been involved in corrupt contractual dealings. The question was whether that meant their company was also guilty of corruption. The Court of Appeal quashed the company's conviction, holding:

> It is not every 'responsible agent' or 'high executive' or 'manager of the housing department' or 'agent acting on behalf of a company' who can by his actions make the company criminally responsible. It is necessary to establish whether the natural person or persons in question have the status and authority which in law makes their acts in the matter under consideration the acts of the company so that the natural person is to be treated as the company itself.[30]

The outcome would in all probability now be different, in such a case, in that it is likely that the managing director, the technical director, and even the manager of the housing division would all be regarded as in law 'senior managers', in accordance with the definition given in section 196(1) of the 2023 Act. In broad fair labelling terms, you might at first blush think it plausible to suppose that if (say) a firm's regional manager engages in fraud or corruption to benefit the company, the company itself should also be regarded as committing those crimes through the manager's acts, but such a conclusion may be doubted.

What makes such a conclusion troubling is the problem posed for fair labelling by corporate (ethical) heterogeneity, described in Chapter 1. To recall an example from Chapter 1, suppose that a senior manager (such as one of those in *Andrews Wetherfoil*), acting within the scope of their authority, engages in corruption to win business for their company, but the board of directors not only knew nothing of the manager's intentions but had also recently embarked on a systematic programme of action at all levels to reinforce the company's long-standing commitment to 'zero tolerance' of corruption in any form. In such circumstances, whether

[28] See, e.g., the discussion of *Moore v I Bresler* [1944] 2 All ER 515, in *St Regis Paper Company Ltd v R* [2011] EWCA Crim 2527.

[29] [1972] 1 WLR 118. The reform would also in effect reinstate the decisions in cases such as *Moore v I Bresler*: see n 28 above.

[30] [1972] 1 WLR 118, 122.

or not the senior manager is acting within the scope of their authority, is it really fair to label the company itself as guilty of corruption, in virtue of the manager's actions? The common law's former focus on directors, whatever its limitations, was designed—for the most part—to avoid this problem. That is because, as we saw in Chapter 1, such a focus was meant to ensure that, in committing a crime, a director would not be betraying a higher authority within the company.[31] Viscount Dilhorne put it this way, in defining a senior officer (director) who could be identified with the company, by contrast with other people within it, such as employees, however high ranking:

> A person who is in actual control of the operations of a company or of part of them and *who is not responsible to another person in the company for the manner in which he discharges his duties* in the sense of being under his orders cannot be regarded as 'another person' [separate from the company].[32]

Naturally, if I am the sole director of the firm,[33] then any act in which I engage, including a criminal act, automatically carries with it the imprimatur of corporate approval: *L'État, c'est moi*. However, what about companies with more than one director, where ethical heterogeneity means that director X may act in a way X believes best serves the company, in circumstances where this goes wholly against what director Y believes will best serve the company?[34] As Davies LJ put it, in *SFO v Barclays*, 'there is no general principle that the knowledge and approval of one director is necessarily and for all purposes to be regarded as the knowledge and approval of the board of directors (and thereby of the company)'.[35] In *Tesco v Nattrass*, the leading case on the identification doctrine at common law, this issue was simply not addressed. It is submitted that the answer to the problem lies in the use of failure-to-prevent offences that do not rely on identifying particular criminal acts with the company as the perpetrator.

Under section 7 of the Bribery Act 2010, a company may be found criminally liable for a failure to prevent bribery, if bribery is committed by someone associated with the company (whatever their status) in order to benefit the company. That, of course, is precisely what has happened in *Andrews Wetherfoil*, discussed above. Suppose, then, that someone associated with a company,[36] no matter what their status within the company, has committed bribery in order to benefit the company.

[31] As we saw in Chapter 1, this notion turned out to be unfounded, as illustrated by the decision in *SFO v Barclays PLC & ANR* [2018] EWHC 3055 (QB).

[32] *Tesco v Nattrass* [1972] AC 153, 187 G-H (my emphasis).

[33] As in the case that first established the identification doctrine in corporate criminal law: *Lennard's Carrying Co Ltd v Asiatic Petroleum Co Ltd* [1915] AC 705.

[34] For a prescient early discussion of this point, see Brent Fisse (1983).

[35] *SFO v Barclays PLC & ANR* [2018] EWHC 3055 (QB), para 86.

[36] Meaning someone over whom the company ought to exercise supervision. On this point, see the discussion in Jeremy Horder and Gabriele Watts (2021), and in ch 5.

As argued in Chapter 1, it is hard to imagine a more appropriate and fitting label for the company's involvement, on such facts, than to say that it failed to prevent the bribery, especially in circumstances in which it had taken no steps (or only ineffectual steps) to prevent such a thing happening. However, as a result of section 196 of the 2023 Act (and hence clause 196 of the 2025 Bill), the clear picture in point of labelling provided by this legal position has become obscured. We now have to accept that, in a case where the person associated with the company who committed the bribery was someone the court rules to have been engaged in (for example) 'managing a substantial part of [the company's] activities', the company itself is guilty of that self-same bribery.

Yet, the element of value judgement involved in making such a ruling inevitably means that, on identical facts, a different court could reach the conclusion that the associated person who committed the bribery, although acting in a managerial capacity, was not managing a substantial enough part of the company's business for the purposes of section 196(4)(c).[37] In that case, section 196 (and hence clause 196 of the 2025 Bill) would have no application, and the corruption offence the company may have committed (if it is a 'large' company) is failing to prevent bribery, contrary to section 7 of the 2010 Act. So, on virtually identical facts, two different corporate crimes with different labels will be applicable. Here is an example of the difficulties that may arise, using fraud as an example:

> C company operates through employees overseas. The company launches a new product, marketed world-wide. Over a period of time, C company employees in some jurisdictions engage in fraud to persuade local companies to buy the new product. C company grew rapidly over this period, and it is unclear if the timing of fraudulent conduct corresponds with the point at which it become a 'large' company. Further, as some employees in the affected jurisdictions took on new responsibilities during the marketing period, it is unclear which of them, if any, were 'senior managers' at the time the frauds were perpetrated.

If the relevant offence applicable to these facts was a generally applicable offence of failure to prevent fraud, then none of the complications involved would have any bearing on C company's liability: the company would be guilty of failing to prevent fraud in each and every instance (subject to any applicable defence). However, under the law as it now is, we must decide not only whether, at the relevant time, C company was a 'large' company, bringing into play the offence of failure to prevent fraud, but also—whether or not that offence is applicable—if any of the employees was, at the time they engaged in fraud, a 'senior manager'. That is an unsatisfactory situation, not least because only failure-to-prevent offences come with a complete

[37] See the beginning of Section 2.2 above.

defence that the company had in place at the relevant time adequate or reasonable crime-prevention procedures. No such defence applies to a company charged with an offence based on the application of section 196 (and hence clause 196 of the 2025 Bill). There is then no defence, even though the most senior people in the company may have been just as much in the dark about the commission of offences by subordinate senior managers as when a failure-to-prevent offence does apply.[38] Section 196 (and hence clause 196 of the 2025 Bill) thus creates a perverse incentive to cover up crime of all kinds committed by senior managers, so that the company will not be found to have committed the crimes itself, whilst (with the failure-to-prevent offences in mind) also enforcing procedures to prevent fraud or bribery being committed by lower-level employees. As we will now see, the problems with the extension of corporate liability in section 196 (and hence clause 196 of the 2025 Bill) do not end there.

2.3 'Senior Managers' as Company Representatives under the 2023 Act

There is an inherent vagueness in the definition of 'senior manager' under the 2023 Act (and hence under the 2025 Bill), creating unnecessary uncertainty for companies concerning the scope of their potential liability. The Law Commission acknowledged, in relation to its consultation on the issue, that 'the majority of respondents thought there was no merit in the Canadian and Australian identification principles which attribute corporate criminal liability when a member of the senior management has the requisite fault'.[39] Nonetheless, the Law Commission concluded in relation to the definition of 'senior manager' that:

> It would not usually capture someone whose role was limited to management of a discrete unit—such as an individual store—which does not represent a substantial part of the company's affairs. However, where that operation did represent a substantial part of the company's activities, it would be captured. To take one instance, if a media company's affairs consisted of the publication of two newspapers, each publication could be 'a substantial part' of the affairs of the company, and accordingly each publication's senior management would be caught by the expanded definition.[40]

[38] Celia Wells has argued that it should be possible for a company to escape conviction for an offence even when committed by a senior manager, if the commission of the offence did not 'represent the practices and procedures of the corporation': Celia Wells (2001), 159.

[39] Law Commission (2022), para 4.25. Naysayers included the Crown Prosecution Service (CPS) and the Serious Fraud Office (SFO).

[40] Law Commission (2022), paras 4.67–68.

The difficulty with such speculation is how little concrete guidance it is capable of providing. In the example given, the chief editor-manager of each of two newspapers might, as the Law Commission suggests, be regarded as in charge of a 'substantial part' of the company's affairs; would the position really be so different if the company owned a string of local newspapers, each with its own editor-manager, and if so, why? In the case of each newspaper owned by the company, the editor-manager may (ex hypothesi) have essentially the same role.

The problem lies with the fact that the definition of 'senior managers' representing the company itself in section 196 (and hence clause 196 of the 2025 Bill) goes beyond persons having what might be called 'strategic policy' responsibilities for the company or group of companies as a whole.[41] In order to avoid a reform that might be perceived as merely tinkering at the edges of the old identification doctrine, 'hands-on' managers downstream (of a substantial part of a firm's activities) are included. Such people are included, even though they may have no role whatsoever in setting the company's overall strategy and policy, and may—depending on how the company operates—rightly see themselves largely as rule-followers, perhaps in a technical capacity, rather than primarily as rule-setters: think of someone employed to manage the running of a company's IT system. In that regard, the advantage of failure-to-prevent offences over the section 196 basis for liability is that, whatever the rank of the employee or agent associated with the company who committed the relevant crime, the company knows that it will face liability unless it had robust procedures in place to prevent such crimes.

In that respect, there is an irony about section 196 (and hence clause 196 of the 2025 Bill), given its intellectual and legislative origins. As indicated above,[42] the extension is based on corporate crime legislation in Canada, where—for example—corporate bribery of a foreign public official is committed if it is engaged in by a 'senior officer' of the company.[43] However, in its report on anti-bribery compliance in Canada, the Organisation for Economic Co-operation and Development (OECD) was critical of the effectiveness of the 'senior manager' version of the identification doctrine, when compared with the potential benefits of a failure-to-prevent offence.[44] Although clause 196 of the 2025 Bill will extend the provision to all crimes in the United Kingdom,[45] section 196 was introduced mainly to cover, for most part, offences where it should be needed least: financial crimes to which failure-to-prevent offences applies or ought to apply.[46]

[41] The Canadian case law on the meaning of 'senior officer' seems in practice to have confined that notion to individuals with strategic policy responsibilities: see OECD (2023), paras 253–55.

[42] See text at n 41 above.

[43] Criminal Code (Canada), s 22.2, as applied to the Corruption of Foreign Public Officials Act (Canada) 1999.

[44] OECD (2023), paras 252–53.

[45] By virtue of the Criminal Justice Act 2023, s 14; Crime and Policing Bill 2025, cl 196.

[46] Having said that, section 196 does cover some crimes, such as export offences, to which the failure-to-prevent offence is inapplicable, and to that extent makes a difference to the scope of liability. The 2023 Act extends the new identification doctrine principles to the serious export control offence of being

2.4 Failure to Prevent Fraud: Too Small to Fail?

The introduction of an offence of failure to prevent fraud, in section 199 of the 2023 Act, should be regarded as a major step forward in the field of corporate criminal liability. For the first time, it provides a theoretically sound basis for corporate criminal responsibility for economic crime, and for fraud in particular. The background to the creation of this offence are National Crime Agency claims that there were 3.7 million incidents of fraud in England and Wales in the year ending December 2022, but also that £2.46 billion was lost by businesses and individuals alone to fraud in the financial year 2021/22.[47] Section 199 of 2023 Act now provides:

> A relevant body which is a large organisation (see sections 201 and 202) is guilty of an offence if, in a financial year of the body ('the year of the fraud offence'), a person who is associated with the body ('the associate') commits a fraud offence intending to benefit (whether directly or indirectly)—
> (a) the relevant body, or
> (b) any person to whom, or to whose subsidiary undertaking, the associate provides services on behalf of the relevant body.

The most obvious point of comparison, in analysing this new offence, is its counterpart prohibiting corporate failure to bribery: section 7 of the Bribery Act 2010.[48] In that regard, the most notable difference between the two offences is the restriction of the failure-to-prevent fraud offence to so-called large organizations, which under the 2023 Act means organizations meeting two or more of the following criteria: a turnover of more than £36M, total assets of the more than £18M, and an average of more than 250 employees.[49] By contrast, section 7 of the 2010 Act applies to all relevant commercial organizations irrespective of size. Of the 5.5 million businesses in the United Kingdom in 2022, only around 8,000 were large businesses—with 250 or more employees—representing just 0.1 per cent of the business population, even though such businesses support 39 per cent of jobs and

'knowingly' concerned in the export of goods with intent to evade a restriction or prohibition', contrary to section 68(2) of the Customs and Excise Management Act 1979, a very welcome step. Compare the position with accessorial liability in tort for human rights breaches: *Kadie Kalma & Others v African Minerals Limited & Anor* [2018] EWHC 3506 (QB).

[47] https://www.nationalcrimeagency.gov.uk/what-we-do/crime-threats/fraud-and-economic-crime#:~:text=The%20threat%20from%20fraud&text=The%20most%20robust%20figures%20currently,are%20estimated%20to%20go%20underreported (last accessed 16/11/2023).

[48] The crimes of failing to prevent the facilitation of tax evasion, contrary to the Criminal Finances Act 2017, provide a less clear analogy with the new offences under the 2023 Act, in virtue of the fact that such offences can be committed even when the predicate offence (facilitating tax evasion) was not committed in order to benefit the company. See Karl Laird (2017).

[49] 2023 Act, ss 201 and 202.

nearly half of all business turnover.[50] It follows that, in relation to many key investment decisions taken by families—such as buying a car or renovating a house—the firms such families rely on to conduct transactions ethically will be outside the scope of this offence.

The Government rejected an invitation to confine the exemption from its scope to small companies: the small company threshold being fifty employees, £10.2 million of turnover, and a £5.1 million balance sheet. In explaining this decision, Kevin Hollinrake MP said:

> We are very clear that we believe we have the right threshold. Larger companies clearly have the capacity and the human resources and risk compliance departments to mitigate these kinds of risks, whereas small and medium-sized enterprises are rightly much more focused on driving their business forward, which is very important to the economic health of our country. I think we have it right.[51]

Hollinrake also said, 'The Government are extremely mindful of the pressures on companies of all sizes, including SMEs, and therefore do not feel it is appropriate to place this new unnecessary burden on over 450,000 businesses.'[52] It is understandable that the Government would wish to ensure that the burden of complying with what is (in fact, in not in law) a requirement to have reasonable procedures in place to prevent fraud does not outweigh the benefit of having the offence. The potential for encountering fraud, both offending and becoming a victim, is widespread through many sectors of the economy and by no means confined to larger firms. That provides a contrast with bribery, which is an offence that, for example, few plumbers, window cleaners, bakers, or cab drivers will ever have to worry about (a point I come back to in due course).[53] However, two criticisms should be made of the Government's approach.

First, there is the general theoretical point made in the House of Lords that, if corporate failure to prevent fraud is (in the absence of reasonable procedures to prevent it) so wrong as to justify criminalization, then that justification applies with equal force to all firms irrespective of size.[54] The use of arbitrary line-drawing

[50] https://www.money.co.uk/business/business-statistics#:~:text=A%20total%20of%207%2C960%20businesses%20were%20considered%20%E2%80%9Clarge%E2%80%9D,up%20just%200.1%25%20of%20the%20UK%E2%80%99s%20business%20population (last accessed 18/09/2024).

[51] https://hansard.parliament.uk/Commons/2023-09-13/debates/6B54D16C-EB32-4B94-A02C-D1128422C107/EconomicCrimeAndCorporateTransparencyBill, col 947 (Kevin Hollinrake MP) (last accessed 23/09/2025).

[52] Ibid., col 938.

[53] See the discussion in Jeremy Horder and Gabriele Watts (2021).

[54] See the discussion of Lord Garnier's amendment: https://hansard.parliament.uk/commons/2023-10-25/debates/9B96F457-D7EB-4A0E-923D-6D9521659DA3/EconomicCrimeAndCorporateTransparencyBill (last accessed 23/09/2025).

between firms, based on size, to determine which firms are in scope, is to confuse the permissible kinds of limits that can be placed on criminal law with factors relevant only to regulatory intervention. It would have been open to any small firm to which the section 199 offence applied to claim the benefit of the defence in section 199(3)—considered in Section 2.6 below—that it was reasonable in all the circumstances not to have fraud prevention procedures in place. Secondly, even if an exemption for smaller firms could be justified, it needs to be justified in terms of sound economics and criminology.

In that regard, it seems probable that the firms most likely to find that their employees have engaged in fraud to benefit the company will be firms seeking or undergoing economic growth.[55] It follows, thus, that if there is a case for exempting a class of firms from the scope of the offence, it will be not *all* 'small firms' (those with, e.g., fewer than fifty employees), since many such firms will be those striving for rapid growth and thus at greatest risk of encountering the use of fraud by their employees to achieve that end. Instead, the exempted class should be so-called micro companies, with a turnover of £632,000 or less, £316,000 or less on their balance sheets, and ten employees or fewer.[56] That is because it is overwhelmingly likely that this class of firm—forming the majority of firms in the United Kingdom—will be run as a form either of 'subsistence' or of 'lifestyle entrepreneurship' rather than for the purposes of economic growth.[57] In other words, as explained in Chapter 4, they will be run solely for the purpose of providing employment (and worthwhile activity) for an individual or family. Whilst such firms may well engage in tax fiddles, health and safety violations, and sector-specific regulatory infringements,[58] they are unlikely to be involved in the commission of rapid, growth-related fraud of the kind the provisions of the 2023 Act are meant to address.

One final point should be made about the scope of the section 199 offence. By virtue of section 199(7) and (8), it is brought into play when a fraud offence is committed by an employee, agent or subsidiary (or employee of a subsidiary), or by any other person providing services for the company. In that respect, a wider range of persons are to be regarded as 'associated' with a (large) company when they commit a predicate offence than is the case with other failure-to-prevent offences.[59] Even so, there is a notable set of excluded cases, created by the requirement for the associated person committing the fraud offence to have acted with the intention (directly or indirectly) of benefiting the company itself or some other person

[55] Jennifer Schwartz et al (2021).
[56] https://www.gov.uk/annual-accounts/microentities-small-and-dormant-companies (last accessed 17/11/2023).
[57] For detailed analysis of subsistence and lifestyle entrepreneurship, see ch 4, Carlos M Jardon (2018), and Sara B Marcketti, Linda S Niehm, and Ruchita Fuloria (2006).
[58] See Hazel Croall (1989).
[59] This point is considered in more depth in ch 5.

for whom the associated person provides services for the company. Consider this example:

> D, a financial adviser working for C bank, dupes P, a customer with C bank, into investing in a firm privately owned by D, when P contacts D asking for the bank's advice on investments. D, acting for personal private gain, does not disclose to P that he owns the firm in question, and pockets P's investment.

In this example, it is a long-standing principle of private law that C bank will be vicariously liable in damages to P, assuming that D was acting in the course of his employment.[60] By contrast, however negligent it may have been, C bank will not be criminally liable under the 2023 Act for failing to prevent D's fraud. That is because, in committing the fraud, D (ex hypothesi) did not act in order to benefit the bank or another person (such as P) to whom D was legitimately providing services for the bank.

The difference in outcome does more than illustrate a principle of parsimony at work in the imposition of criminal liability. It reveals a difference in the understanding of the 'company' for the purposes respectively of tort law and of failure-to-prevent offences in criminal law. Tort law regards companies as in essence a network of contracts,[61] with the result that principles of liability centre on harmful wrongdoing in the course of performing those contracts (broadly construed, in scope[62]), in acting with actual or ostensible contractual authority, and so on. By contrast, failure-to-prevent fraud offences are limited not only by the need for an appropriate nexus with the wrongdoer but by the requirement to prove an intention on the wrongdoer's part to further the commercial objectives of the company through the wrongdoing (liability model E, as described in Section I.4). Accordingly, failure-to-prevent fraud offences (like their vicarious liability counterparts in the United States[63]) see the company in this respect as a 'real entity', an entity with overarching commercial plans and goals, alongside systems, culture, and processes.[64] On such a view, to be fairly attributable to the company, fault-based wrongdoing on the part of an associated person must intelligibly have been related to the pursuit of these plans or goals. It is not enough merely that the wrongdoing was engaged in during the course of employment. Whether such a restrictive view of the scope of failure-to-prevent fraud proves acceptable to the public, once its implications become clear, remains to be seen. It would have been a relatively straightforward matter to change to wording of section 199 to make it clear that where an associated person's fraud is intended to cause financial *detriment* to a customer, the company can be liable for failing to prevent that fraud. That would

[60] *Lloyd v Grace, Smith & Co* [1912] AC 716 (HL).
[61] See the discussion of the nexus-of-contracts theory in Eva Micheler (2021), and in ch 1.
[62] *Mohamud v WM Morrison Supermarkets* [2016] UKSC 11.
[63] See n 3 above.
[64] See Eva Micheler (2021).

have a desirable extension, even if—an issue explored in Section 2.6 below—there are reasons not to make the company liable for a failure to prevent fraud where the intended detriment is to the company itself.

2.5 Small Firms and Liability under the 2023 Act

There is an irony about the 2023 Act (and 2025 Bill) reforms to the identification doctrine. The identification doctrine at common law was widely considered to operate in a way that was unfair to very small firms. In such firms, directors are more likely to be involved in, or to have personally approved, operational decision-making, and thus likely themselves to have engaged the company itself in any wrongdoing committed to further the company's interests. By contrast, in larger firms, this is less likely to occur. That is because, in such firms, operational decision-making (and hence, potentially, offending) is more commonly engaged in by middle managers and other employees, with directors unaware of the details or of individual decisions taken. Such unawareness on the part of directors made it traditionally all but impossible to identify the wrongdoing with the company itself. Yet the 2023 (and 2025) reforms, whilst doing a small amount to remedy this injustice by extending the reach of the identification doctrine, create a new source of injustice. This is an injustice involved when the conduct of a large firm is being investigated in relation to the economic wrongdoing of senior managers. In such cases, it is possible for prosecutors to choose between prosecution for a substantive offence (say, fraud) and prosecution for a failure to prevent that offence. In such circumstances, it will be open to the large firm to seek to influence prosecutors in their course of action by pointing to (say) the robustness of procedures the company will put in place to prevent crime in future, if prosecutors are willing to offer a deferred prosecution agreement (DPA) respecting the company's failure to prevent fraud. When the wrongdoing of a small (or, indeed, a medium-sized) firm's senior managers is in issue, no such luxury is afforded to prosecutors or to firms. That is because the failure-to-prevent offences do not apply to small and medium-sized businesses, and the robustness of their crime-prevention procedures is, in law, irrelevant. Consequently, an important fair labelling possibility for wrongdoing associated with small to medium-sized businesses has been (wrongly) excluded in law.

It is worth reflecting more broadly on the implications for very small firms of the 2023 Act's (and hence the 2025 Bill's) extension of the identification doctrine to cover the wrongdoing of senior managers. As we have seen, of the 5.4 million registered businesses in the United Kingdom today, 4.1 million (74 per cent) had no employees and 3.1 million (56 per cent) were unincorporated sole proprietorships almost all of which had no employees.[65] Accordingly, the vast majority

[65] https://www.gov.uk/government/statistics/business-population-estimates-2022/business-population-estimates-for-the-uk-and-regions-2022-statistical-release-html (last accessed 11/06/2023). Only 2 per cent of UK businesses trade from more than one site.

of businesses will seemingly be unaffected by the reforms in the 2023 Act, because they do not have 'senior managers' apart from the directors themselves (and so will remain unaffected by the reformed identification doctrine) and because they are too small to fall within the scope of the failure-to-prevent fraud offence. Such figures might appear to expose a glaring omission, in the scope of liability. Consider this example from personal family history. M Horder & Co was founded in 1925. The company's directors were my grandfather and his brothers, who had a small number of men working with them on a single site, building trucks for other businesses (and for the army, during WWII). After the Second World War, my father took over when my grandfather died, and the latter's brothers retired. Seeing an opportunity with the post-war consumer boom beginning ('cars for everyone!') my father changed the business focus to the sale of second-hand cars. The business was run with three employees who worked for the company for a number of years: a personal office assistant, a car sales' person, and a cleaner—a not untypical model of operation (director, plus a small number employees) for hundreds of thousands of micro businesses in the United Kingdom today. A potentially lucrative fraud committed by second-hand motor traders is 'clocking'. This involves turning back the mileometer clock or odometer on a car to make it appear as if it has done a smaller mileage than it has in fact done, thus giving the car a false (higher) value. Although such an act amounts to a strict liability criminal offence under the law of trade descriptions,[66] it is worth considering in what circumstances such an act would also be regarded as a fraud committed by the company.

The answer, under the 2023 Act (and hence under the 2025 Bill), appears to be that if the crime was committed by ex hypothesi low-level employees (such as the Horder & Co salesperson) then, quite possibly even if the firm's directors suspected what was going on but did nothing, the company itself would seemingly not be guilty of fraud. Section 196 of the 2023 Act (and hence clause 196 of the 2025 Bill) does nothing to change that long-established position. By contrast, in such circumstances, if it were possible to charge the company with failure-to-prevent fraud, then the position would change dramatically. When cars are clocked by (low-level) employees acting in their capacity as employees, then they commit fraud, a fraud that the company fails to prevent, and—as I argued in Chapter 1—it is hard to think of a fairer or more accurate label for the company's offending. Yet, small firms are excluded from the scope of the failure-to-prevent fraud, even though some of the most significant lifetime financial decisions made by consumers are likely to be made through transactions with smaller firms. Can this anomaly be resolved? The answer lies in the interpretation of the term 'senior manager', something already examined but now considered in a small or micro-firm context. As we will see, the

[66] See the discussion at: https://hansard.parliament.uk/commons/1996-07-17/debates/5cae95bf-7047-4d7c-878a-480bef0fc83a/CarClocking (last accessed 23/09/2025).

potential 'liability gap' just described may turn out to be less significant that it appears to be, once the practical operation of small firms is better understood.

As indicated earlier, under section 196(4) of the 2023 Act (and hence under the 2025 Bill), 'senior manager' means an individual who plays a 'significant role' in 'the making of decisions about how the whole or a substantial part of the activities of the body corporate ... are to be managed' ... or '[in] the actual managing or organising of the whole or a substantial part of those activities'. In a medium to large-sized firm, it might be expected that a person having responsibilities of one of these two kinds would have been recruited or trained specifically to discharge those responsibilities, and to have them specified (in more or less detail) in their contract of employment. Such practices reflect the more *gesellschaft* understanding of employee roles within the bureaucratic administrative structure of a typical medium to large-sized firm. As is well known, a *gesellschaft* form of law:

> [e]mphasises . . . precise legal provisions and definitions and the rationality and predictability of legal administration. It is oriented to the precise definition of the rights and duties of the individual through a sharpening of the point at issue and not the day to day ad hoc maintenance of . . . community traditions and organic solidarity.[67]

When considering the status of a wrongdoer within a medium to large-sized firm, thus, we can expect that the predominant—albeit not the sole—concern will be with the rights and duties the wrongdoer was expected by contract to exercise or perform.[68] Did the possession of these rights and duties indicate that the wrongdoer can and should be described as a 'senior manager'? The importance of such a question derives from the essentially Weberian character of the identification doctrine,[69] a doctrine according to which what matters to fair labelling is the fact that there are persons—directors (or senior managers)—with (largely) unchallengeable authority to engage in or authorize corporate conduct.

By contrast, small or micro firms are far more likely to run in accordance with a *gemeinschaft* form or organization ('*ad hoc* maintenance of community'[70]), particularly when persons occupying roles that are notionally employee roles are close family members or long-serving members of the business. In such a Durkheimian form of organization, what Durkheim called 'mechanical solidarity'—mutual understanding, implicit trust, and the almost unwitting incremental development of roles—is more likely than formal contract to guide the job understandings and

67 E Kamenka and A Erh-Soon Tay (1975), 137.
68 For example, this was the key issue in *SFO v Barclays PLC & ANR* [2018] EWHC 3055 (QB).
69 See the discussion in ch 1.
70 See E Kamenka and A Erh-Soon Tay (1975), 137.

business decisions of key (long-term) employees accustomed to what is probably almost daily interaction with the director or (a small number of) directors.[71] Most importantly, in such a business, the legal form characteristic of company–employee relations, in which the director is in a position to exercise command and control with respect to decision-making, and the employee is in a position in which they are expected to follow (lawful and reasonable) directorial decisions, can over time and incrementally become replaced by a different, more communal ('share and share alike') decision-making model.

A strong analogy here is with the way in which people living together in a property may over time come to regard the property itself as communally shared, as a part of their joint lives. As Simon Gardner explains:

> [A] relationship ... may imply, more positively, that the parties have committed themselves to sharing the incidents of the relationship between them—good and bad; wealth and costs; work and enjoyment. The thrust of communality ... is that the parties ... trust and collaborate with one another for the good of both. In a nutshell, restitution is about 'mine or yours'; communality is about 'ours'.[72]

If one replaces, in this analysis, the notion of 'property' being shared with the notion that business decision-making is shared, then one can see how in a family micro business formally separate roles (director and employee) may become blurred, when it comes to the location of authority to take particular kinds of decision. To go back to the example of M Horder & Co, over time, a long-serving personal assistant or sales person, very familiar with the disposition, leanings, and beliefs of the director, may find themselves taking decisions (and being relied on to take decisions) that in effect mean that they are—perhaps without fully realizing it—playing a 'significant role' in 'the making of decisions about how the whole or a substantial part of the activities of the body corporate ... are to be managed' or '[in] the actual managing or organising of the whole or a substantial part of those activities', to use the language of section 196 of the 2023 Act (and hence clause 196 of the 2025 Bill). A broader point along such lines is made by entrepreneurship scholar, Storey, who points out:

> If you work in a relatively small firm employing, let us say, fewer than ten people, the probability is that if you have enough managerial talent, you will see the whole operation through from the beginning to the end; in other words, you will sweep the floor, you will do the accounts, you will do the buying, you will do the

[71] Carole Howorth and Martin Kemp (2019), 1: 'In some family-owned businesses, attitudes of trust, love and commitment may engender positive stewardship behaviours and reduce the need for formal controls.'

[72] Simon Gardner (1993), 286–87.

company marketing, public relations, and might even lend a hand on the production side.[73]

It follows that, in many cases involving small firm frauds such as 'clocking' by motor traders, the liability gap explained above may turn out to be more apparent than real. That is because employees who commit such crimes, even without the knowledge of directors, may be construed as having over time taken on the mantle of 'senior managers', with the result that wrongdoing they commit is ipso facto the company's wrongdoing.

Even so, the application of section 196 (and hence of clause 196 of the 2025 Bill) ought not to be the only way in which small firms can come to be regarded as committing offences through the actions of employees. The examples just discussed are ones in which decision-making responsibilities come to be shared or allocated between persons associated with a firm, without those responsibilities necessarily reflecting the formal status (director, manager, and employee) of the person taking them on. However, especially in a small, close-knit firm, it is possible that a different understanding of decision-making responsibility may develop. On this understanding, it is explicitly or implicitly accepted by directors that when employees act, they act in the name of—'as'—the firm irrespective of whether there has been a formal delegation of power: the ethos of 'all for one and one for all'. So, consider a case in which, in a firm comprised of close-knit family members, wrongdoing is committed by a family member who is undoubtedly only an employee and not a senior manager, but the firm is one in which the strong bonds of family loyalty are such that in practice each member accepts full responsibility for the acts of the others ('we succeed as a team, and fail as a team'). As indicated in Chapter 1, such a firm meets the conditions for being regarded as ethically homogenous, even in circumstances where wrongdoing by an employee was engaged in without the knowledge or consent of family members at directorial level. That being so, the wrongdoing can be identified with the firm, and a more sophisticated identification doctrine would acknowledge as much.

Having said that, we should notice how the ways in which the senior manager provisions of the 2023 Act can impact the liability of small firms, in the ways just described, create rule-of-law unfairness that is particularly acute for such firms. In a medium- to large-sized firm, it is likely that a 'senior manager' is fairly readily identifiable as such in advance of any consideration of a firm's possible criminal liability for the acts of such a person. It is in the nature of employment contracts in such firms, with more Weberian, *gesellschaft* forms of organization, that they will specify someone's duties in such a way that the (non-)application of the 'senior manager' test will be reasonably readily apparent ex ante. By contrast, in small,

[73] David J Storey (1982), 93–94.

resource-poor firms, commonly competing in highly fragmented industries—retailing, small-scale manufacturing, or wholesaling—that have many competitors which are prone to price-cutting as a way to build revenues, the owner's salary is likely to be a large element of the firm's budget, leaving little to spend on employees or managers.[74]

So, consider a case with facts similar to those in the problematic example set out at the start of the chapter:

> A window cleaning firm consists of two brothers. Their sister, D, who is not employed by the firm, has greater numeracy skills than her brothers. She always does the firm's accounts and tax returns, and keeps track of who has proved to be a reliable customer in the past (hence influencing the firm's contracting policy). As the firm is experiencing a cash flow crisis, confident that her brothers could be persuaded to agree if asked, she knowingly sends a repeat invoice to a large corporate client, in the hope that the client will pay twice without realising that it has done so.

In this instance, the liability of the firm turns on whether D is to be regarded as a senior manager of the firm, assuming that she is acting with 'apparent authority' when sending the repeat invoice.[75] Recall that a 'senior manager' under the section 196(4) of 2023 Act (and hence under the 2025 Bill) is an 'individual who plays a significant role in … the actual managing or organizing of the whole or a substantial part of those activities'. As we may now observe, this definition does not require that the person in question be an employee of the firm. So, in principle, D in the example may be a 'senior manager' of the firm. Furthermore, the definition of 'senior manager' is wholly context specific, embedded in the trading practices of the firm in question. Accordingly, the status of someone as a senior manager may have to be determined in part diachronically, looking at how their role has developed over time, rather than simply synchronically (considering what, at a particular moment in time, their responsibilities were).

Thus understood, the inherently interpretive nature of a 'senior manager' poses particularly significant problems of rule-of-law certainty for micro firms, in which it is far more likely that roles within the firm will be shifting and evolving, and may (as in my example) not even be confined to formal employees. As indicated at the outset, this is a particular problem for groups heavily represented in the micro firm sector, as compared with their representation in senior management roles within larger firms. Evidence has shown that a very substantial proportion of small business proprietors come from the 'lower-middle' sections of society,

[74] See, e.g., John A Welsh and Jerry F White (1981).

[75] On 'actual or apparent authority' and its meaning, see the text at the beginning of Section 2.2 above, and the more detailed discussion in ch 5.

including skilled manual workers (who make up about a third of working-class people overall).[76] In relatively recent history, in businesses employing between one and twenty-four employees, skilled manual and lower-middle class white-collar workers supplied over 35 per cent of the total (and over 40 per cent of the total of sole proprietorships).[77] Such groups were particularly prominent in businesses involving manual craft (artisanal) trades. Such businesses are typically what I will refer to in Chapter 4 as 'subsistence' businesses (although they may also be what I will call 'lifestyle' businesses), the aim of which is simply to provide an income sufficient to satisfy the more or less basic needs of the owner and their family.[78]

In that regard, worldwide, over two-thirds of all businesses are owned or managed by families, a figure that rises to 80 per cent in the case of Europe and the United States.[79] In a study of ethnic minority businesses in 2004, Basu found that, in businesses owned by men, the involvement of entrepreneurs' wives was very common.[80] In more business-oriented firms, wives tended to be involved as formal employees, whereas in family-oriented entrepreneurs' businesses, there was a high likelihood of wives helping out and providing support on an informal basis a pattern also found in small businesses more generally.[81] In recent decades, women have formed about 25 per cent of the self-employed small business sector of the UK workforce, as compared with 15 per cent of male population.[82] The prominent position of women in the small business sector can be explained by a number of factors, but Sara Carter and her colleagues, reviewing the research literature, found that the inability to gain access to the start-up resources necessary to develop a larger business is significant:

> There is now a growing body of evidence that suggests that a woman's pre-venture labour market experience has a profound effect on her ability to mobilise appropriate start-up resources. In comparison with men, when women enter

[76] David Goss (1991), 51.

[77] See research discussed in ibid., 51–54.

[78] Subsistence businesses are sometimes referred to as 'no growth' firms, which are 'typically . . . home-based and employ only one or two people including the owner manager': ibid., 40. They also tend to operate in well-tried areas of the economy, using traditional methods rather than innovating, serving markets that already exist in a way that simply mirrors existing businesses: ibid., 47. Many such businesses will be unincorporated sole proprietorships.

[79] INSEAD (2020), 5: 'Companies that are owned and controlled by families are the cornerstone of global economic activity, accounting for two thirds of all businesses, 70–90 percent of annual global GDP, and 50–80 percent of jobs in most countries.'

[80] Anuradha Basu (2004). In 2021, 6.1 per cent of small and medium enterprise employers were led by a majority of people from an ethnic minority (excluding white minorities): https://www.ethnicity-facts-figures.service.gov.uk/workforce-and-business/business/leadership-of-small-and-medium-enterprises/latest/ (last accessed 08/05/2024).

[81] Anuradha Basu (2004), 26.

[82] See, generally, Sara Carter et al (2000–01). In 2021, 21 per cent of all SMEs in the United Kingdom were led by women: https://www.forbes.com/uk/advisor/business/small-business-statistics/ (last accessed 22/09/2025). By contrast, in FTSE companies, only about 15 per cent were led by women in 2024.

> self-employment they do so with fewer financial assets, with less experience in management, and are under-resourced in terms of their human and social capital. Women generally lack both hard resources, such as finance and capital assets, and soft resources, such as management experience, networks and family support.[83]

It is one thing to tolerate uncertainty in relation to the conduct element of a crime. Such toleration may be necessary when the behaviour to be prohibited cannot—without weakening or over complicating provisions unduly—be specified in more detail than to say, for example, that 'unwarranted' or 'unreasonable' behaviour is prohibited. It is quite another thing to tolerate uncertainty in relation to who is subject to (such) criminal prohibitions in the first place. Yet, this kind of uncertainty is created by the 'senior manager' provisions of the 2023 Act (and hence of the 2025 Bill), in so far as it applies to the smallest (and most common) businesses, and hence in so far as it applies—disproportionately—to women, ethnic minority, and working-class entrepreneurs.

2.6 'Reasonable in the Circumstances'? The Failure to Prevent Defences

In virtue of section 199(3) and 199(4) of the 2023 Act, there is an excluded category of fraud in relation to, and there are two possible defences to, the offence of failing to prevent fraud or related offences:

> (3) [T]he relevant body is not guilty of an offence under subsection (1)(b) if the body itself was, or was intended to be, a victim of the fraud offence.
> (4) It is a defence for the relevant body to prove that, at the time the fraud offence was committed—
> (a) the body had in place such prevention procedures as it was reasonable in all the circumstances to expect the body to have in place, or
> (b) it was not reasonable in all the circumstances to expect the body to have any prevention procedures in place.

The section 199(3) exclusion is designed to avoid the prospect of effective 'double punishment' of companies, who find not only that they have been the victims of occupational fraud (fraud by an employee or manager) but also that they are then liable to prosecution for failing to prevent the fraud. Should section 199 ever be

[83] Sara Carter et al (2000–01), 78.

applied to small firms (the 2023 Act contains a power to do this), it would be an especially important provision for them. They are likely to suffer proportionately greater losses from occupational fraud when it is committed against them, and are more likely to be the victims of such fraud. That is because there are fewer systematic constraints on their directors, and because they rely to a greater extent on simply placing trust in the honesty of employees.[84] I will come back to this point in discussing section 199(4)(b).

Then there are the section 199(4) defences—that the company had in place such prevention procedures as it was reasonable in all the circumstances to expect it to have, or that it was reasonable in all the circumstances for it not to have such procedures in place. These defences are drawn from the defence to the offence of failing to prevent the facilitation of tax evasion, contrary to sections 45(2) and 46(3) of the Criminal Finances Act 2017. I will focus, first, on the 'reasonable in all the circumstances' procedures defence in section 199(4)(a). This defence embodies an intended departure, in point of wording, from the analogous provision in section 7(2) of the Bribery Act 2010. Section 7(2) of the 2010 Act makes it a defence to the offence of failing to prevent bribery that the company 'had in place *adequate* procedures designed to prevent persons associated with C from undertaking such conduct'.[85] A possibly unintended (although not necessarily always unwelcome) consequence of this change is that, in some circumstances, it might be 'reasonable in all the circumstances' to have in place clearly inadequate procedures. A relatively benign example would be where a UK-based firm, X Company, takes over or merges with a firm, Y Company, in a jurisdiction where corporate crime is rarely detected or prosecuted, but negotiations aimed at ensuring that Y Company adheres to UK standards of crime prevention prove unexpectedly difficult and prolonged. In such a case, it might be possible to argue that Y Company's inadequate anti-fraud procedures are ones that, in the circumstances, it was reasonable for X Company to leave in place, at least for a period of time.

More broadly, the replacement of 'adequate' procedures with 'reasonable in all the circumstances' procedures came about after suggestions that an 'adequate' procedures defence is no real defence at all, because if bribery is committed by someone associated with the company then—by definition—the procedures were inadequate. For example, Bean and MacGuidwin have suggested:

[84] JP Kennedy (2016); Association of Certified Fraud Examiners (2022).

[85] Inexplicably, the 2023 Act does not harmonize the defences available to failures to prevent financial crime. So, we now have different defence tests depending on whether a company is charged with failing to prevent fraud or failing to prevent bribery. It is anyone's guess why Parliament has not thought fit to use the time-honoured statutory defence commonly used in other commercial crime contexts: that the defendant 'took all reasonable procedures and exercised all due diligence'. A defence phrased in such terms is defended in Chapter 4 as the right defence of all instances of failure-to-prevent crime.

> To establish this defence the company must prove that it 'had in place adequate procedures designed to prevent persons associated with [the company] from undertaking such conduct'. However, the term 'adequate' is a curious choice here, since the procedures in place were clearly not entirely adequate, or the bribery would not have occurred in the first place.[86]

This criticism involves a category mistake. It elides the distinction explained in Chapter 1 between safeguarding in respect of act-tokens and safeguarding in respect of act-types.[87] If bribery is committed by an employee in order to benefit the company, there is a wrongdoing 'token' (the act of bribery). As indicated in Chapter 1, this is a space-time particular, respecting the occurrence of which the prevention procedures the company had in place (if any)—however sophisticated—were self-evidently inadequate. However, whilst in-principle corporate liability under section 7 of the 2010 Act is for bringing about the bribery event (bribery as an act-token), the defence of 'adequate procedures' does not relate to that act-token. It relates instead to what section 7 of the 2010 Act calls '*such* conduct', meaning conduct of that (corrupt) type. So, the company's defence is assessed in terms of whether it was doing enough by way of safeguarding to prevent or reduce the risk of bribery as a *type* of wrongdoing. A 'type' is an abstract, acausal category (by reference to which tokens can be identified as such), in itself lacking a spatio-temporal location.[88] Prevention procedures in respect of act-types, such as 'bribery', can clearly be adjudged adequate, in particular circumstances, even if they were not enough to prevent a particular act-token of bribery occurring. That is so, in much the same way that the methods I adopt to clean your office might be of a kind or type acceptable to us both, even if (as we may both be aware) some dust and dirt may escape the cleaning process.[89]

What of the provision in section 199(4)(b) that it will be a defence to show that, in all the circumstances, it was reasonable not to have crime-prevention procedures in place? Sensible though it sounds, this defence confronts firms with a difficult choice between having some crime-prevention procedures (to be judged by their reasonableness) and taking the risk of having no safeguarding in place at all. Confronting businesses with such a choice is, in effect, to hollow out the notion that companies are under a duty to prevent crime, and to make the duty uncertain in scope. Accordingly, even if for some businesses it is not appropriate

[86] Bruce W. Bean and Emma H. MacGuidwin (2012), 43. See also the evidence of Eoin O'Shea, cited by House of Lords (2019), para 204.

[87] Linda Wetzel (2018).

[88] Ibid.

[89] In that regard, act-types may have different levels of specificity. 'Bribery' is an act-type at a very general level, by way of contrast with (say) 'payment of an under-the-counter fee to secure a public service', which is a more specific kind of act-type. It should be for the jury to decide what degree of specificity should be given to the notion of 'act-type', for the purpose of deciding whether or not procedures were adequate (reasonable, in a quantitative sense) in the circumstances.

or proportionate to have safeguarding procedures in place, it should be made clear there is always a duty to consider on a regular basis whether such procedures might be desirable and should be introduced. The section 199(4)(b) defence would have made sense in a world in which the failure to prevent fraud offence applied (as it ought to have done) to all firms, large and small. Instead, the defence now applies where it is needed least—in relation to very large commercial organizations that will almost certainly already have compliance departments, whistleblowing procedures, and so on.

By contrast, the defence will not apply where (you might argue) it is needed most: in relation to the Bribery Act 2010. The 2010 Act requires all commercial organizations, irrespective of size, to have bribery prevention procedures, however rudimentary, a requirement that seems somewhat incongruous in the case (say) of a small, local plumbing firm. Having said that, the Government's own research indicates a relatively high level of knowledge and confidence about the 2010 Act amongst small- and medium-sized entities (SMEs), with 66 per cent of SMEs aware of the Act, and 72 per cent of these firms believing that they has sufficient knowledge and understanding to implement adequate prevention procedures.[90] So, it is arguable that section 199(4)(b) is neither use nor ornament, where fraud prevention is concerned. That impression is reinforced by the aforementioned exclusion of liability under section 199(3) in cases where the company is itself the victim of fraud. Whilst not free from difficulty,[91] this provision would have in effect benefited small firms the most, because it is these firms that are most likely to fall victim to occupational fraud. That being so, it might be argued that, quite apart from the protection provided by section 199(4)(b), there was already sufficient protection from regulatory burdens on small firms to make their exclusion from the scope of the section 199 offence unjust.

2.7 Conclusion on the 2023 Act

Almost all statutory reform involves missed opportunities, but there is a significant muddle at the heart of the 2023 Act. The muddle stems from uncertainty over how to approach corporate crime when committed by firms of different sizes. Given that roughly 75 per cent of UK businesses have no employees, the vast majority of businesses will be unaffected by the reforms in the 2023 Act (and hence the 2025 Bill), because they do not have 'senior managers' apart from the directors themselves (and so will remain unaffected by the reformed identification doctrine), and

[90] HM Government (2015), 4.

[91] It is not, for example, entirely clear what happens in a case where an employee fraudulently uses company resources to perpetrate a fraud against a third party. In such a case, the company's fraud victimization is bound up with that of the third party.

because they are too small to fall within the scope of the failure-to-prevent fraud offence. However, micro and small businesses that do have someone who could be described as a 'senior manager' under the 2023 Act—and hence under the 2025 Bill—are (as under the present law) exposed to the potential for harsher treatment than larger firms. That is because such businesses may be exposed to primary liability under section 196 of the 2023 Act (and hence under clause 196 of the 2025 Bill) for fraud through the actions of their senior managers, without having the benefit of the 'reasonable prevention procedures' defence that will be available to a large company charged with failing to prevent fraud.

Moreover, in virtue of section 196 of the 2023 Act (and hence clause 196 of the 2025 Bill), all firms—large and small—now face the prospect of being found liable for substantive economic crimes, even in cases where those overseeing the offending senior manager could not realistically have done more to prevent the latter's wrongdoing. It would have been simpler and fairer to have applied the failure-to-prevent offence (with a reasonable procedures defence) to all firms, so far as economic crime is concerned, and then begun the process of considering how far to extend such liability beyond economic crime (liability model D, as described in Section I.4). There is nothing new about failure-to-prevent offences outside an economic crime context. For example, under section 34(1) of the Environmental Protection Act 1990, it is an offence for a relevant person to have failed to take all applicable measures as are reasonable in the circumstances to prevent any contravention *by any other person* of one of the main waste disposal offences, in section 33(1). If corporate bodies, no matter what their size, can be liable respecting the acts of associated persons in this context, would it have been such a big step to extend the failure-to-prevent fraud offence to all companies?

Is the failure-to-prevent model thus the future for criminalization of companies? That is less clear. Failure to prevent offences perform a valuable fair labelling function by linking the company to a harmful wrong done by an associated person. By contrast, fifty years ago, the Health and Safety at Work Act 1974 relied on a different model of corporate criminality: what might be called the 'risk-management' model focused on a firm's failure to ensure (so far as reasonably practicable) that people who might be affected by a firm's operation are not exposed to *risks* to their health and safety.[92] On this model, whether or not a third party endures a consequential setback to their health and safety, in virtue of such a failure, is not relevant to the commission of the offence. Broadly speaking, it is this risk-management model (what I called in Section I.4 liability model B) that has been followed in, for example, part 5 of the Online Safety Act 2023 as it applies to major social media companies. They are now exposed to fines for systems and process failures with respect to fraudulent advertising on their platforms.[93] For example, under the Online Safety Act 2023, the largest service providers must establish proportionate processes and systems (1) to prevent users from encountering fraudulent adverts

[92] Health and Safety at Work Act 1974, s 3. This is liability model B, as described in Section I.4.
[93] Online Safety Act 2023, pt 5.

on the platform, (2) to minimize the length of time for which fraudulent adverts are present, and (3) to swiftly take fraudulent adverts down where they have become aware of them or have been alerted to their presence. The focus, thus, is on the operation of the company as a 'real entity'[94]—on systems and processes for reducing the risk that users will fall victim to fraudulent advertising—and not on liability for harm suffered by a user when falling victim to such advertising. In a similar way—but following liability model C, as described in Section I.4—in the field of human rights abuses, instead of facing liability for failing to prevent human rights abuses, large companies face now pressure to report on the systems they have put in place to ensure their business and supply chains are free from slavery and human trafficking, as required by section 54 of the Modern Slavery Act 2015.[95] This is a form of 'due diligence' obligation on large companies with respect to risk management. Backed by sanctions, in relation to large companies, such an approach has recently been extended in the European Union to cover supply-chain risks of environmental as well as human rights abuse.[96]

There may be no definitive answer to the question of which approach (harmful wrong-focused, or risk-focused) is right.[97] However, the adoption of the risk-management model in the field of health and safety, and in relation to online protection from fraudulent advertising, reflects the important fact that both these fields are governed by expert regulatory bodies, with powers or duties proactively to advise on best practice or warn about poor practice, as well as reactively to investigate and prosecute breaches of standards.[98] A risk-management offence model is well suited to that regulatory and preventative context. By contrast, outside the financial sector, there is no proactive duty on prosecutors to advise or warn companies, or to promote risk minimization generally, as opposed to reactively investigating and prosecuting (or agreeing DPAs). In that regard, unless and until the Financial Conduct Authority is given regulatory responsibility for strategizing the prevention of corporate economic crime generally, it is the failure-to-prevent model, model E,[99] that best fits the current non-regulatory context, with the commission of the predicate offence setting the reactive processes in motion.[100]

94 See the discussion in Section 2.2 above.

95 See, further, the discussion in ch 5. The pressure to report comes from the requirement to issue a formal statement marking the fact, if no due diligence with respect to human rights is to be exercised.

96 EU Corporate Due Diligence Sustainability Directive (24/05/2024): https://www.consilium.europa.eu/en/press/press-releases/2024/05/24/corporate-sustainability-due-diligence-council-gives-its-final-approval/ (last accessed 06/07/2024). Baroness Young recently sought to introduce a similar law in the United Kingdom: https://lordslibrary.parliament.uk/research-briefings/lln-2024-0021/ (last accessed 22/09/2025).

97 In Chapter 5, I argue that a risk-focused approach is appropriate in relation to supply-chain contractors, as opposed to persons and entities more closely associated with a company such as subsidiaries or special purpose vehicles.

98 The same point could be made about the Financial Conduct Authority, which also operates with a risk-management focused, as opposed to harm-based, set of principles: https://www.handbook.fca.org.uk/handbook/PRIN/2/1.html (last accessed 22/09/2025).

99 See Section I.4.

100 For strong criticism of the use of the risk-management model by prosecutors in economic crime cases, see, e.g., Karen Woody (2017).

3

FAILING TO PREVENT CRIME

HISTORY, LAW, AND MORALITY

3.1 Different Bases for a Failure-to-Prevent Crime Duty

PROBLEMATIC EXAMPLE: Company C was run by two directors, D1 and D2. D2 engaged in bribery to benefit the firm without telling D1. Company C was charged with failing to prevent bribery. It was admitted that D2 was a person 'associated' with Company C, for the purposes of section 7 of the Bribery Act 2010. Even so, D1 claims that, except in special circumstances, a company director does not act under the control of another director or directors, and without the existence of such control at the time of the offence, the section 7 offence has no application, even if the director was acting in the course of the firm's business when committing the offence.

The overarching aim of Chapters 1 and 2 was to establish the case for an approach to corporate crime in which the failure-to-prevent model plays a key role. It was argued that the model should play such a role, even if the 'identification' doctrine that fixes companies with liability for substantive offences still has an important part to play when small (family-run) businesses are in issue. The main issue addressed in this chapter is the moral basis for the failure-to-prevent model. What we will see is that, with the exception of public nuisance cases,[1] the common law adopted a classical liberal approach to corporate criminal liability.[2] On such an approach, a company was to be regarded simply as an individual (corporate) person, responsible for its own—directorial—wrongdoing, on the same basis as any other (human) individual, and hence not in principle liable for the wrongdoing of any other person: even an employee.[3] By contrast, Parliamentary intervention forced judges to accept a different approach that embodied nascent liberal-welfarism. First, criminal statutes were interpreted as making the company itself responsible for the acts or omissions of an employee (vicarious liability). Secondly, duties were imposed on companies by statute to protect the public from the potentially

[1] Se the discussion in Section 3.5 below.
[2] See the discussion of 'classical' liberalism in the Introduction.
[3] See the discussion in Section 3.5 below.

A Theory of Corporate Crime. Jeremy Horder, Oxford University Press. © Jeremy Horder 2026.
DOI: 10.1093/9780198936534.003.0004

harmful consequences of the ownership and running of their businesses, even when harm done or risky conduct was attributable to a third party.[4] Such developments effectively gave corporate failures to prevent harm or wrongdoing done by other persons—even if they were not explicitly analysed in such terms—an important role in corporate criminal responsibility. This provided a foundation for what was to become a more liberal-welfarist (as opposed to classical liberal) approach to corporate criminal liability.

On occasion, the punishment of failures to prevent crime committed by others has been justified, in classical liberal terms, simply on the basis that—through its deterrent impact—it helps to reduce the occurrence of offending overall, by encouraging preventive directorial intervention. For example, such an argument has been used to support the application to companies of the doctrine of vicarious criminal liability for the wrongdoing of employees or agents, a doctrine closely related to, even if in important ways very different from, the failure-to-prevent model of corporate criminality.[5] In affirming the applicability of vicarious criminal liability to corporate bodies respecting fault-based crimes committed by employees or agents, Justice Day has said:

> [W]e see no good reason why corporations may not be held responsible for and charged with the knowledge and purposes of their agents, acting within the authority conferred upon them . . . If it were not so, many offenses might go unpunished and acts be committed in violation of law where, as in the present case, the statute requires all persons, corporate or private, to refrain from certain practices, forbidden in the interest of public policy.[6]

In and of itself, though, such an instrumentalist, crime-reduction-focused justification falls well short of what would be sufficient to make it morally appropriate to prosecute and punish companies for the wrongdoing of associated persons. In this chapter, I explore how the failure-to-prevent model can be given a sounder theoretical explanation, an explanation capable of morally legitimating a prosecutorial and punitive response to such failures.

The normative significance of a failure to prevent crime committed by associated persons stems from the existence of a pre-existing duty to prevent it. My main focus here will be the nature of that duty when it arises. There are three possible bases for such a duty in corporate contexts, outlined as follows:

[4] For example, under the Petroleum (Hawkers) Act 1881, governing persons licensed to 'hawk' petroleum, a series of obligations were created to ensure the safe storage of petroleum. Section 2(8) of the 1881 Act required, on pain of criminal penalty for breach, that 'all due precautions shall be taken for the prevention of accidents by fire or explosion, and for preventing *unauthorised persons* having access to the vessels containing the petroleum' (my emphasis).

[5] See the discussion in Section 3.5 below, and in ch 5.

[6] *New York Central and Hudson River Railroad Company v US* 212 US 481 (1909), para 15.

1. where D has control over the person who engages in wrongdoing;
2. where D has influence over the person who engages in wrongdoing; and
3. where D has an oversight relationship with the person who engages in wrongdoing.

In this chapter, I will examine in detail (1)—'control principle' cases—and (2)—'influence principle' cases—as bases for a failure-to-prevent crime duty. I will consider the potentially more controversial case of (3) briefly in Section 3.2 below, and also in Chapter 5, when examining liability for wrongdoing engaged in by independent contractors.

As we will see in Section 3.2, the principal basis on which a failure-to-prevent crime duty arises is (1) above: control principle cases.[7] However, it is important to analyse (2), influence principle cases, because—as we saw in Chapter 2—many companies are not based on hierarchical relationships of control. Instead, they have a more horizontal structure and understanding of accountability. In that regard, I will defend the view that there can be a duty on senior company officers, in particular, to exercise influence over certain categories of persons associated with the company (peer groups), persons who are under a reciprocal duty to be open to that influence in decision-making.[8] Where, as in the problematic example at the start of this chapter, such a duty to exercise peer-to-peer influence has been neglected or inadequately discharged, and associated wrongdoing occurs, there is then a failure to prevent that wrongdoing in a normative sense. The failure comes in the form of an omission to persuade the peer group wrongdoer to treat the influence as a decisive reason not to engage in the wrongdoing. Whereas in control-failure cases, we may say, '[t]he company did not use its legitimate authority over someone to prevent their wrongdoing' (a 'command' basis for prevention), in influence-failure cases, we may say, '[t]he company did not use its legitimate sway over someone to convince them not to engage in the wrongdoing' (a 'persuasion' basis for prevention). Concentrating on control principle cases, in broad terms, the central argument is that a corporate failure to prevent crime is justifiably made subject to criminal sanctions, when that failure reflected the absence of proper safeguards designed (1) to prevent wrongdoing resulting from the use of land or premises under the company's control, or (2) to prevent wrongdoing being committed by persons under the company's control.

[7] A form of the control principle has been well developed in the tort of negligence. See, e.g., the classic case of *Home Office v Dorset Yacht Club* [1970] AC 1004 (HL).

[8] The influence principle that I develop is particularly significant in cases where we are concerned with relationships between fellow directors or business partners. The principle may also have an important application to relationships between parent companies and other bodies such as independent contractors or subsidiary companies not directly controlled by the main company. See the discussion in ch 5.

Let us step back for a moment from the construction of this analytical framework for understanding a corporate duty to prevent crime by associated persons. Once one moves beyond the sole trader model, corporate activity involves the potential for the management, direction, and control of—and the use of influence over—(potentially) hundreds or thousands of associated persons, in relation to the multiple ways through which a company's mission may be manifested nationally and internationally. It might, thus, appear to be the sheer scale of such corporate power to shape human thinking, goals, and conduct that creates a general public interest justification for the imposition of corporate crime-prevention duties. However, the case for the imposition of corporate crime-prevention duties does not depend simply on considerations of scale (the size of the business). A corporate duty not merely to avoid committing crime oneself but to prevent associated persons from doing so can be linked to a morally 'active' account of individual human well-being.[9] From the perspective of such an account of well-being, the power possessed by a company employing just one employee, to shape the working life of that employee for good or ill, or the possible effect of the (bad) behaviour of one director in a small family firm on the working lives of other family member-directors, is in itself enough to justify the imposition of such duties.

To be personally autonomous is to be part author of value-creation in one's own life. However, in a corporate context, the value of so much of what one does in one's working life depends on the control or direction set by one's employer in that respect, and on the standards observed by other employees with whom one works as part of the company as a concrete legal entity.[10] A company that fails to pay sufficient attention to how its associated persons view the importance of (say) product and employee safety, or integrity in contracting, threatens to undermine the personal investment made by ethically well-disposed and other-regarding employees seeking to create something authentically valuable in their lives when at work.[11] So, a system of corporate criminal law that takes seriously an active account of individual well-being must be seen to address corporate failures to prevent crime by associated persons. It must be seen to do this, as part of a broader legal strategy of incentivizing the creation by companies of a working environment within the concrete legal entity in which the active pursuit of sound commercial values flourishes.[12]

[9] John Gardner (1998). See also the discussion of this issue in chs 4 and 5.
[10] For an explanation of the term 'concrete legal entity', see ch 1.
[11] See the argument about the justification for punishing companies in ch 6.
[12] This point is more fully developed in ch 4.

3.2 The Control Principle Explained

What is the common law approach to the criminal liability of X, for a crime committed by an associated person, Y, in particular when X is a corporate organization? Traditionally, there have been two situations in which (company) X may be found criminally liable at common law for Y's criminal wrongdoing:

1. Company X is complicit in harm or wrong done by employee or agent Y, through knowingly failing to exercise control or authority over Y.
2. X' s employee or agent, Y, commits a public nuisance.

As we will see, other than in the very narrow circumstances of situation (2), the courts have paid precious little attention to the public interest in ensuring that common law rules governing criminal liability for the actions of associated persons are tailored to fit corporate activity. The indifference of the classically liberal common law, in that respect, will be contrasted with the position as it developed in a series of statutes enacted from the Victorian period onwards. I suggest that a third basis for criminalization of X respecting Y's wrongdoing is discernible in those statutes, namely the control principle.

I will argue that Parliament effectively developed, and the courts (through their approach to statutory interpretation) then in practice endorsed, a new principle of criminal liability, based on combination of elements in situations (1) and (2) above. Although never clearly articulated as such, the principle was designed to govern wrongdoing arising not only from the ownership of land or premises, but also from the conduct of a company's employees or agents. As indicated in Section 3.1 above, this is the 'control principle', the central case of which has the following '2 + 1' format, involving offence-focused right and duty elements (the '2'), coupled with a normally defence-focused ascriptive element (the '1'):

1. *The attributability criterion: the control-right element.* A person (the 'controller') had the right to control something or someone (the 'controlled entity')—such as land, premises, employees, or agents—in circumstances in which criminal wrongdoing occurring within the domain of control was associated with the controlled entity.
2. *The duty criterion: the control-duty element.* In cases where the attributability criterion is satisfied, the controller breached what was in the circumstances a duty to use their control to prevent the occurrence of the criminal wrongdoing associated with the controlled entity.

And in the central case, but not in all cases:

3. *The ascriptive question: the control-evaluation question.* In cases where both the attributability and duty criteria are satisfied, did the controller

nonetheless take adequate safeguarding steps, if there was an expectation that such steps be taken, to prevent the occurrence of the relevant type of criminal wrongdoing?[13]

The 'attributability' criterion, involving ownership of land or employment of persons, determines when a company (the 'controlling entity') may legitimately be called to answer for wrongdoing associated with something occurring on the land or something done by the employees or agents ('controlled entities'). The attributability criterion is a normatively 'thin' notion that identifies only when wrongdoing is attribut*able* to someone, and not when wrongdoing can be attribut*ed* to that person. So, for example, suppose that wrongdoing was committed by a trespasser on company land. That may make the wrongdoing attribut*able* to the company, because the land was an entity ex hypothesi under the control of the company: the company had a control-right over the entity associated with the wrongdoing. However, to establish that the attributability criterion has been satisfied is not to have established that the wrongdoing can in fact be attributed to the company. That depends on the satisfaction of the second element to the control principle: the duty criterion.

As the term 'duty' criterion implies, this element concerns the nature and scope of the company's safeguarding duties (if any) respecting the wrongdoing, which have come into focus in virtue of its control-right. In many instances, what I call a control-duty will follow naturally from the possession of a control-right.[14] For example, if pollution seeps from land I occupy into a river, I have 'failed to prevent' that event, having had at the relevant time both the right of pollution control over the land and (ordinarily) a control-duty to intervene to prevent pollution coming from the land.[15] However, control-duties have normative limits. So, a control-duty in relation to pollution coming from my land is unlikely to extend to guarding against possible meteorite strikes on (say) the tank on my land storing the pollutant. In such a case, whilst the control-right holder certainly has the right to try to protect the tank from meteorite strikes if they so wish, there is ordinarily no duty to do so.[16] Broadly speaking, the attributability and duty criteria together give shape to the offence element in a failure-to-prevent crime. Together, these criteria explain how a person who was in control can—if they did not intervene to prevent wrongdoing—be regarded as thereby 'blame*worthy*' as that term is helpfully explained by Mitch Berman.[17]

[13] See, further, the discussion of these three elements in Jeremy Horder (2024).

[14] For discussion of some instances in which the duty does not follow from the right, see ibid.

[15] *Empress Car Company (Abertillery) Ltd v National Rivers Authority* [1999] 2 AC 22 (HL). For more detailed discussion in a pollution context, see Jeremy Horder (2024).

[16] See the discussion in the speech of Lord Hoffmann in *Empress Car Company (Abertillery) Ltd v National Rivers Authority* [1999] 2 AC 22, 33E, and Jeremy Horder (2024), 242–43.

[17] Mitchell N Berman (2021), 9–10.

The possession of a control-right and a control-duty, respecting property or a person associated with wrongdoing, makes one blameworthy in a normative sense: suitable or apt for blame respecting that wrongdoing. So, being blameworthy for a failure to prevent crime does not mean that one ipso facto deserves blame for the failure (an ascriptive matter). Instead, being blame*worthy* means that, in short, one is in a position to be blamed. Berman gives the analogy of someone who is trustworthy. Being 'trustworthy' does not mean that the trustworthy person ought, in fact, to be trusted by someone else, any more than a ship being seaworthy means that it ought to be put to sea. It means simply that, respectively, the person can be or is in a position to be (safely) trusted, and that the ship can be or is in a position to be (safely) be put to sea. Similarly, that someone in breach of a duty to act in certain way is blameworthy means no more than that they are fit for blame, or in a condition such that blame may legitimately (but not must) be laid at their door. That blameworthy condition is the position in which a person—including a company—will find themselves if (1) they had a control-right over land that was the source of harm, or over the actions of persons who engaged in wrongdoing; (2) they were under a safeguarding control-duty to exercise that control-right to intervene; and (3) they did not use their control-right to prevent the harm or wrongdoing occurring.

However, in what I am calling the central cases of the control (and influence) principles, there is a third element to liability alongside the control-right and control-duty elements. This is what I call the ascriptive (blame) question: (3) above. This question is concerned with whether, if the company was admittedly in breach of its control-duty to prevent wrongdoing through the exercise of a control-right, it had nonetheless tried hard enough to prevent wrongdoing of that type occurring. If, but only if, the company had tried sufficiently hard in general to perform its safeguarding control-duty, then a complete defence to the failure-to-prevent crime should apply, because the company is not sufficiently (or at all) to blame for the failure in question.[18] We are now in a better position to understand what makes the 2 + 1 case of the control principle, morally speaking, a central case of that principle. It is that the incorporation into the test of liability of the ascriptive question makes it clear that there is a route to acquittal only for companies living up to the ideal-typical commercial standards endorsed by liberal-welfarism. These are the standards of a company concerned not just to conform its conduct to the law, but beyond that to embrace a commitment to finding intrinsic value in striving consistently and creatively to safeguard against wrongdoing.[19] On the

[18] This 'due diligence' criterion is examined in detail in ch 4.

[19] The point here about the intrinsic value to be found in 'striving' to safeguard properly is discussed in detail in ch 4. By contrast, it is obvious that instances of strict liability require the prosecution to establish only that the first two elements of the control principle have been satisfied—the attributability criterion and duty criterion—without the need additionally to address the ascriptive question (so, in

liberal-welfarist approach, the way in which criminal law and sanctions are devised and implemented is meant to encourage responsible corporate attitudes and practical commitment to harm-prevention and risk-reduction ('safeguarding'). The aim is not merely to use the (hoped-for) deterrent impact of retributive punishment of individual instances of misconduct, after the event, as a means of producing more compliant behaviour through fear of future sanctioning.[20] In that regard, the failure-to-prevent model bridges the gap between the two approaches (classical liberal and liberal-welfarist). It places classical liberal emphasis on individual—directorial—corporate responsibility (for failing to prevent wrongdoing), whilst also offering a liberal-welfarist-inspired excuse to companies that can demonstrate their sense of civic responsibility by pointing to the robustness of safeguarding efforts that they made.

As we will see in Chapter 4, in the post-war period, and in particular during the period of Labour Government from 1997 to 2009, the number of control-principle-based offences aimed at businesses (and hence the hegemony of liberal-welfarism) grew exponentially. Many such offences embodied the central case of the control principle. For example, whilst a defence to a criminal wrong that one had exercised 'all due diligence' to prevent harm or wrong is to be found in under 100 pieces of legislation prior to 1972, it is to be found in well over 1,000 pieces of legislation or regulations enacted between 1972 and 2023.[21] Modern instances in which liability is imposed for failures to prevent financial crime provide an example of the control principle in operation. In such cases, even when the control-right and control-duty criteria have been satisfied by the prosecution, criminal liability will not follow if D can show either (other than in bribery cases) that it was not reasonable for D to have taken any steps in advance to safeguard against a breach of duty, or if such steps should have been taken, that adequate or reasonable safeguarding procedures were in place at the relevant time.[22] Let me take failure to prevent bribery (contrary to section 7 of the Bribery Act 2010) as an example. A commercial organization, C, will be criminally liable for failing to prevent bribery, contrary to section 7(1), if someone 'associated with' C commits bribery, 'intending—(a) to

effect, a '2' formula). The 'strictness' of strict liability cases, thus, is that they treat proof of blameworthiness (breach of a control-duty) as sufficient by itself to justify criminal liability, without proof that D, the controller, was in fact to blame.

[20] See the discussion in the Introduction.

[21] A significant proportion of such offences were created as part of the legislative response to the foot and mouth crisis, and the ensuing reorganization of what was to become the Department for the Environment, Food and Rural Affairs. Some thirty-eight of the offences under the Environmental Protection Act 1990 ('the 1990 Act') are phrased in terms of a 'failure to' ensure that the prohibited conduct does not occur: https://www.gov.uk/government/publications/offence-response-options-environment-agency/waste-offences (last accessed 26/11/2022). See, further, the discussion in ch 4.

[22] See, e.g., the Bribery Act 2010, s 7 and the Economic Crime and Corporate Transparency Act 2023, s 199.

obtain or retain business for C, or (b) to obtain or retain an advantage in the conduct of business for C'. Someone 'associated with' C is defined in section 8 of the 2010 Act as someone who 'performs services for or on behalf of C'. The implication is, I suggest, that a person 'associated with' C is someone who is—in a broad sense—under C's control and direction:[23] the attributability criterion of the control principle.

What about the duty criterion and the ascriptive question of the control principle? The notion of a 'failure to prevent bribery' carries with it an implication that there is a duty on the company to safeguard against the commission of bribery by employees, agents, or subsidiaries. Whilst it is an offence of strict liability, the offence created by section 7 is not a merely regulatory contravention. Even if the offence has a regulatory element, conviction carries significant stigma. Accordingly, liability is not to be imposed on C for failure in the duty to prevent the bribery, if C can establish that there were 'adequate procedures' in place to prevent acts of that kind (section 7(2)). This is the ascriptive question, a liberal-welfarist question at the heart of the central case of the control principle. In this offence under section 7, as in other failure-to-prevent offences, Ds may be acquitted, notwithstanding a safeguarding control-duty failure, if they came up to the relevant standards of adequacy *in trying* to discharge that duty.

In cases where wrongdoing is committed by an employee or agent, the attributability criterion of the control principle has a superficial resemblance to vicarious liability, as a basis for criminalization.[24] However, there is a crucial theoretical difference, best illustrated by cases in which the 'controlled entity' is an employee. This crucial difference is not (merely) that, under the control principle, liability may turn on an answer to the ascriptive question, a question that has no bearing on vicarious criminal liability. The crucial difference is that when wrongdoing is associated with the conduct of an employee, as the controlled entity, the key focus in point of vicarious liability are the actions of the controlled entity, and not the failures of the controlling company. Vicarious liability means that if the controlled entity commits the offence when under the controller's control, then so (automatically and vicariously) does the controlling corporate entity. Vicarious criminal liability is thus controversial precisely because the focus is not on D's (the controller's) role in events, even though D stands to be convicted, but on the role of the controlled entity: the employee or agent.[25] The principle of fair labelling is compromised by this kind of criminal liability 'by proxy', as one might (albeit somewhat misleadingly) call it, even though—as we saw in Chapter 1—it is possible to discern a glimmer of justification for such liability by conceiving of the

[23] Subject to what I will say in due course about relationships of influence, as opposed to control.

[24] I will consider the relationship between the control principle and vicarious criminal liability in more detail in Section 3.5 below, and in ch 5.

[25] For an instructive discussion, in a private law context, see the judgment of Lord Burrows in *Trustees of the Barry Congregation of Jehovah's Witnesses v BXB* [2023] UKSC 15.

company as a concrete legal entity. By contrast, offences based on the control principle, whether or not they involve a requirement to consider the ascriptive question, are focused in point of liability squarely on the inaction—or the failure—of the (corporate) controller, even if the controller's liability is brought into play only by the commission of a different, predicate offence by another person (the controlled entity). This could be called 'contingent' liability, as opposed to vicarious liability.[26]

I have said that in a central ('2 + 1') case of the control principle, the key ascriptive focus is whether or not enough effort was put in by the controller to safeguarding against the *type* of harm done. This focus becomes legally significant when there has been a breach of the control-duty: when the occurrence of a wrongdoing token of the relevant type can be associated with the controller through, say, a harmful action by a controlled entity that the controller ought to have prevented.[27] Crucially, though, the ascriptive focus comes into play, in such circumstances, whether or not there was any causal link between the occurrence of the wrongdoing that should have been prevented and (any deficiencies in) the controller's safeguarding practices:[28]

> Company C, dealing with the disposal of confidential waste, has neglected to update its employee vetting policy that no longer reflects modern vetting practices. Subsequently, Company C unwittingly employs someone (X) who, although having no personal connection to organized crime, has close family members involved in such activities. A close family member of X, under the influence of an organized crime group, pressures X into paying a bribe from company funds to a company owned by the crime group to supply services to Company C. However, it turns out that even had modern vetting practices been in place, X's family connections to organized crime would not necessarily have come to light.

In this example, Company C has failed in its control-duty to prevent X paying a bribe to secure a business advantage for Company C. Company C also had (ex hypothesi) inadequate procedures in place to prevent bribery being committed by persons with an undisclosed ethical vulnerability or purpose of their own to serve, albeit when acting to benefit the company. It follows that Company C is guilty of failing to prevent bribery contrary to section 7 of the Bribery Act 2010. That is so, even though it cannot be shown that, had Company C's anti-bribery policies been modern 'industry standard' policies, they would have made it less likely that

[26] Instances of contingent liability may also be instances of strict liability, but there is no necessary connection between these forms of liability. Contingent liability may equally be fault-based, and we will come across a number of instances of this in the course of this chapter.

[27] On the importance of the distinction between act-tokens and act-types, see the discussion in ch 1.

[28] This point about the difference between control and causation is pursued further in Jeremy Horder (2024).

X was employed at all, or was entrusted to engage unsupervised in contracting on the company's behalf.[29] That outcome might seem unfair or illogical, even though it is highly likely in most cases that in practice there will be a link between the occurrence of the wrong and deficiencies in safeguarding efforts. However, in this respect, failure-to-prevent liability plots a course between two alternative, better-known bases for liability that have their own important weaknesses.

It is possible to justify corporate criminalization of purely negligent breaches of duty unconnected to any harm done, as when a company maintains an unsafe system of work but without having caused harm.[30] In some circumstances, it is also possible to justify corporate criminalization for faultless wrongdoing (strict liability).[31] The advantage of the central case of the control principle is that it is capable of ameliorating some of the difficulties associated with criminalization in both of these instances. On the one hand, the insistence on proof of the occurrence of wrongdoing associated with an entity controlled by the company (the attributability criterion) mitigates what is otherwise a significant risk associated with criminalization. This is the risk of retrospective criminalization, based on nothing more than a mistaken or controversial ex post facto judgement by regulators or prosecutors that D has failed to put in place effective safeguards.[32] In the example given above, this risk would be raised by the possibility that Company C could be found criminally liable simply for having had in place 'inadequate' vetting procedures, whether or not these procedures had been highlighted by some wrongdoing engaged in on company business. On the other hand, the insistence on proof of a generic failure in point of safeguarding (the ascriptive question) at least adds a liberal-welfarist moral dimension to the justification for liability in cases such as Company C's, liability that might otherwise be based largely on the brute fact of Company C's control-right and (breach of) control-duty[33] respecting the activities of the errant employee, X. So, the central case of the control principle adds some rule-of-law moral credibility to the basis of a controller's liability, even when the controller's deficiencies in point of safeguarding are not (causally) connected to their control-duty failures. These advantages come in addition to the fair labelling advantages of the failure-to-prevent model, discussed in Chapter 1.

There is a final, initial point to make about the control principle, and that concerns its relationship with the 'oversight' of conduct and activity. Control rights and duties may involve control over individual pieces of conduct, over a course of conduct as a whole, or over the values that another person is meant to embody in

[29] See, further, the discussion of this point in Section 4.7.

[30] See the Health and Safety at Work Act 1974, s 1, and the discussion at the end of ch 2.

[31] See, e.g., AP Simester (2005).

[32] For an excellent critical discussion of this problem in corporate contexts, see Karen E Woody (2017), and the analysis in Section 1.8.

[33] The conditions of Company C's 'blameworthiness' (as opposed to being in fact to blame): see the discussion earlier in this section.

their conduct. Here are some examples of each of these instances in which control is exercised:

1. D instructs X, an employee, on the use of a piece of machinery. This involves giving instructions to X about each action to be taken in sequence (control over individual pieces of conduct).
2. D instructs X, an employee, on what output X is expected to achieve each day through the use of a company machine (control over a course of conduct).
3. D requires X, an agent, to abide by certain standards of integrity, transparency, and fairness, in agreeing contracts for the company (control over the values to which X is expected to adhere).

In each of these instances, what it means for D to be in 'control' is that D has the right—and commonly, the duty—to intervene in what X is doing, if need be, to ensure that instructions and requirements are followed, whether these relate to individual pieces of conduct, to courses of conduct, or to the values to be reflected in conduct. For that to happen in an efficient and effective way, X must clearly be supervised in the way that they carry out their work, albeit perhaps in a relatively 'hands-off' manner in cases (2) and (3) above. Supervision, in turn, requires that someone has what can be called 'oversight' of the activity in question.

However, an element of oversight is separate from the elements of control-right or control-duty, and the supervision that the latter involve directly (or through a delegate). That is because an oversight role may not in itself be accompanied by any right to intervene. Here is a simple example. D—the controller—may ask Z to 'oversee' X—the controlled entity—in situations (1) to (3) above, without Z themselves having any supervisory control-right or control-duty to intervene to ensure that X behaves as expected. Z's oversight duties may extend only to (say) reporting to D on X's performance, so that D then has a basis on which to consider whether to intervene in the exercise of their supervisory control-right. It is easy to miss this point, because D will often have both a control-right and duty, and an oversight right and duty that fit closely together. However, that (supervisory) control, on the one hand, and oversight, on the other hand, are separate phenomena can be illustrated by some instances of arms-length relationships between companies and their independent contractors. It may be that a company (D) establishes a relationship with an independent contractor such that D only has a right to keep a 'watching brief' over (to oversee) the activities of the contractor, respecting either or both of its conduct and its values. In such a case, D may have no control-right or duty to intervene in relation to these matters. In that regard, a relationship of oversight is also different from a formal relationship of 'influence', as I will in due course define it. As we will see, central to a formal influence relationship is D's right and duty to seek to influence an associated person, and reciprocally, the duty of the associated person to be open to that influence. Whilst a formal influence relationship may sometimes characterize the relationship between one company and another, just as one company may control another, a relationship of oversight between companies (a watching brief) may be as far as it goes. Is the existence of a mere oversight relationship, as opposed to a (supervisory) control or influence relationship, sufficient to give rise to a failure-to-prevent crime duty on a company?

It is a truism that knowing one's behaviour is being watched is liable to change the behaviour. So, a company's well-known practice of exercising a right to check if its independent contractors comply with (say) standards of integrity, is likely to have some positive ethical impact on the behaviour of those contractors. Contrariwise, a company's consistent failure to exercise a right of oversight in this respect may lead to a decline in, or to inconsistency in, the observance of ethical standards by its contractors. However, in the latter case, even if a contracting party consequently commits an economic crime, the parent company may legitimately argue that without a (supervisory) control or influence right, it could not have been expected to intervene to prevent the commission of the crime. In practice, most rights of oversight are set in a context in which a company also has a supervisory control or influence right over another company's—typically, a subsidiary's—course of conduct, or over the values it embodies in its conduct. Even so, as we will see in Chapter 5, new duties of 'due diligence', imposed on large companies respecting the observance of human rights obligations by independent contractors, are best analysed in terms of a pure oversight right and duty. This is a duty without an accompanying (supervisory) control or influence right and duty, of a kind that would entail intervention by the large company in the affairs of the contractor.

3.3 The Control Principle, Safeguarding, and Omissions Liability

A (corporate) failure to prevent crime involves a safeguarding omission. So, in this section, I will discuss the relationship between safeguarding omissions or failures and 'simple' omissions. Safeguarding omissions are a narrower and more specific species of omission. A simple omission is in law 'simple' when what matters is no less, but no more, than that D breached a duty by failing to do something D ought to have done at the relevant time.[34] The precise explanation for the omission—stupidity, laziness, confusion, forgetting orders, and not following established protocol—is not critical to the characterization of the omission as a breach of duty.[35] By contrast, safeguarding failures involve a particular kind of omission. This is the failure of a system, process, or procedure to guard against

[34] A simple omission, in that it *does* involve a breach of duty, is thus different from a so-called mere omission, when one does not do something one is under no obligation to do or to consider doing. For a general discussion, see Andrew Ashworth (2013).

[35] Other than when the circumstances giving rise to the omission amount to a 'reasonable excuse' for the omission.

a type of event or outcome occurring, including a failure to have such a system, process, or procedure at all when one should have been in place. To define omissions in terms of safeguarding failures makes such failures appear by nature bureaucratic ones, and most of the safeguarding failures we will encounter have that quality; but in fact, the idea of a 'procedure' or 'system' that ought to be followed is not by its nature bureaucratic. For example, if one thinks of parents' safeguarding duties respecting their children's need for proper nourishment, the 'procedure' or 'system' might be nothing more sophisticated than (say) a practice of regular mealtimes underpinned by budgeting for shopping trips and checking the nutritional content of food. That point is significant, because in smaller or one-person firms, safeguarding procedures may also legitimately be relatively informal and non-bureaucratic. An important feature of examples from commercial life, though, is that (unlike the parent and child example) they do not presuppose a one-way safeguarding relationship of control or direction. In, say, a two-director company with no employees, it could be that each of the directors has a responsibility to ensure that certain procedures are followed by the other (as in the problematic example given at the start of the chapter). The important point to note is that, in all such cases, when we focus on an omission, we are focused on the special sense of that term as a safeguarding failure.

To understand the contrast between types of omission, consider the case of *Webster*.[36] In this case, the question was whether the owner of a car could be found complicit, as a passenger, in dangerous driving on the part of the driver, simply on the basis he—the owner—knew of the circumstances making the driving dangerous and failed to intervene. Although D's conviction in that case was quashed due to a misdirection, the Court of Appeal held that:

> [T]he prosecution had to prove that [D] knew that [P] was, by virtue of the speed the vehicle was travelling, driving dangerously at a time when there was an opportunity to intervene. It was [D's] failure to take that opportunity and, exercise his right as owner of the vehicle, which would lead to the inference that he was associating himself with the dangerous driving.[37]

The court is here applying a version of the control principle to justify D's conviction: D was under a duty to prevent the dangerous driving and failed in that duty.[38] However, bearing in mind that D is an individual and not an organization, it is the encouragement provided by D's (simple) omission to intervene and stop P driving dangerously that is the key issue. On the facts, it would have involved a misleading

[36] [2006] EWCA Crim 415. See also *Story v United States*, 16 F 2d 342, 344 (DC Cir 1926).

[37] [2006] EWCA Crim 415, para 29. See also *R v Martin* [2010] EWCA Crim 1450. For further discussion of the fault element in such cases, see Brent Fisse (1968).

[38] Dennis Baker (2021), 16.38–41.

distraction to seek to judge D by reference to the 'procedures' or 'safeguards' that might have been put in place by D to prevent P driving dangerously. It is not in the nature of relations between friends that they can be expected to set down in advance and then to follow set processes and procedures in such circumstances, in the discharge of the duties they owe to one another, important and stringent though those duties might be.

By contrast, a driving instruction company might well be expected to have such procedures or safeguards in place, prior to any driving being done by learner-drivers under the supervision of instructors in the car with them. Such a company would hence be appropriately judged in accordance with the central case of the control principle, which involves making judgements of safeguarding sufficiency. My concern will be with this kind of case. In such cases, the yardstick by which D is judged is the adequacy of safeguarding processes and procedures in place at the time when the relevant wrong or harm was done. Consider an analogous example. Even the most conscientious care home company cannot hope to prevent every individual instance in which an employee-carer abuses a patient. Nonetheless, such a company should have adequate safeguards in place to deter or prevent behaviour of this type (such as panic buttons, covert surveillance, employment vetting, training courses, etc.). Accordingly, in relation to incidents of patient abuse, the company should be judged by the adequacy, in all the circumstances, of those safeguards. Safeguarding failures have a special relevance to both public and private institutions, and hence to companies. The bureaucratic or systematic nature—however rudimentary it may be—of institutions makes any unjustified inaction on their part, or on the part of those working in and for them, well suited to analysis in terms of safeguarding failure as I have explained that notion.

Care home examples are a good way in which to illustrate how, under the control principle,[39] safeguarding may have different dimensions to it:

1. When safeguarding is provided through the simple expedient of locked doors and windows, and the like, it can be described as *preventative* in character.
2. When safeguarding is provided through systems such as covert surveillance, patient-operated panic buttons, and the like, it can be described as *deterrent* in character.
3. When safeguarding is provided through effective education and training, through advisory guidance that is non-binding but nonetheless taken into account, or simply through informed commitment to the value of safeguarding, it can be described as *fully autonomous* in character. That is because, when working properly, it is self-governing, in that the controlled entity themselves takes responsibility for compliance throughout.

[39] Or in some instances involving (3) below, as a manifestation of the influence principle as well.

4. When safeguarding is provided through the supervision of the controlled entity, it can be described as *semi-autonomous* in character. That is because, although the controlled entity themselves takes the relevant decisions and engages in the relevant actions, they are obliged to do so in accordance with orders, policies, or other requirements set down by the controller-supervisor.

It is noticeable how the courts do not generally judge individual Ds who were *not* in institutional safeguarding positions, in terms of (particular) safeguarding procedures they ought to have been following to prevent wrongdoing. For example, in the famous case of *Sweet v Parsley*,[40] 'hobby landlady' Stephanie Sweet was found not guilty of being concerned in the management of premises (her farm) that had been used for the purpose of smoking cannabis or cannabis resin, contrary to section 5(b) of the Dangerous Drugs Act 1965. The House of Lords read into section 5(b) a requirement for the prosecution to prove that the 'purpose' was that of the landlord, not the tenant. It is clear that this generous construction stems in part from their Lordships' desire not to place the 'hobby landlord' effectively under the same strict safeguarding obligations, with regard to the prevention of crime, as—to give the examples used by Sweet's Counsel—'the master of a college or the warden of a hostel, or the governor of a prison'.[41] As Lord Reid put it, in departing from the stricter approach adopted in the Court below:

> If this section means what the Divisional Court have held that it means, then hundreds of thousands of people who sublet part of their premises or take in lodgers or are concerned in the management of residential premises or institutions are daily incurring a risk of being convicted of a serious offence in circumstances where they are in no way to blame.[42]

It is hard to imagine that the same landlord-friendly approach would have been taken by their Lordships had D been a large commercial landlord profiting from renting flats to (say) vulnerable individuals. Such a person would surely have been treated as, in effect, a safeguarder, and hence obligated to have systems or processes in place to ensure that drugs were not used by tenants on their premises.

3.4 Corporate Complicity at Common Law: The '*Alford*' Principles

At the beginning of Section 3.2, I explained how, at common law, the doctrine of complicity was one way in which (company) X could be found liable for

[40] [1970] AC 132 (HL).
[41] Ibid., 140.
[42] Ibid., 150.

wrongdoing engaged in by (an associated person) Y. I will begin my analysis of corporate responsibility for the actions of individuals associated with companies by discussing corporate complicity in crime.[43] Following the decision of the Supreme Court in *R v Jogee*,[44] D may be found complicit in (and hence liable for) a crime committed by P, if D 'intended to encourage or assist [P] to commit the crime, acting with whatever mental element the offence requires of [P]'.[45] The position of companies as potentially complicit parties was not considered by the Supreme Court in *Jogee*. Understandable though that is, it is unfortunate.

First, the failure to consider this issue widens the gap between the rules governing the test for a company's complicity in a crime committed by a senior company officer (when such a person is not representing the board itself[46]) and the rules governing the converse situation, in which it is alleged that a senior company officer is complicit in a crime committed by the company. In the former situation, the company—and, in particular, its directors or senior managers—will have to be shown to have possessed the fault element set down in *Jogee*, if the company is to be found complicit in the crime committed by the senior company officer. By contrast, in the latter situation (an allegation of individual company officer complicity in their company's crime), the prosecution is required to satisfy a much less demanding fault element. Typically, all that needs to be shown is that the senior company officer 'consented to' or 'connived at' the commission of the crime by the company.[47] That will be enough to make the company officer themselves guilty of the offence in question, whether or not the officer had the intention required to be proved in cases governed by *Jogee*. For example, where a company has engaged in false accounting, by virtue of section 18 of the Theft Act 1968:

> Where an offence committed by a body corporate under section . . . 17 of this Act is proved to have been committed *with the consent or connivance* of any director, manager, secretary or other similar officer of the body corporate, or any person who was purporting to act in any such capacity, he as well as the body corporate shall be guilty of that offence, and shall be liable to be proceeded against and punished accordingly. (my emphasis)

[43] Complicity is the main basis of Gobert and Punch's analysis of corporate involvement in wrongdoing committed by employees or agents: see James Gobert and Maurice Punch (2003). However, their analysis requires a very broad understanding of 'complicit' that includes, for example, instances in which a culture of tolerance of employee wrongdoing has developed in a company, even when this is in fact unknown to the board. It is submitted that this stretches the meaning of 'complicit' beyond breaking point. It would be more accurate, as argued in this book, to describe such situations as ones on which, more or less culpably, the company has failed to prevent employee wrongdoing.

[44] [2016] UKSC 8.

[45] Ibid., para 90 (Lord Toulson).

[46] See, e.g., *SFO v Barclays* (2018) EWHC 3055.

[47] For a general discussion of such provisions, see Jeremy Horder and Gabriele Watts (2024).

The fact is that the question of how complicity in crime should be addressed, as between companies and their senior officers, has received almost no attention whatsoever at common law, in over 170 years since the passing of the Joint Stock Companies Act 1844. Secondly, *Jogee* leaves unresolved the position when it is alleged that a company is complicit in a crime committed by an employee. That brings me to the case of *JF Alford Transport*.[48]

In *JF Alford Transport*, a transport company's drivers had, contrary to section 99(5) of the Transport Act 1968, falsified tachograph records recording the amount of driving they had been doing. The company and its directors were charged with and (initially) convicted of the offence, as complicit parties, on the basis that they had known about the drivers' offending but had done nothing to prevent it. The Court of Appeal was asked to consider whether the company and its directors could, in law, be found complicit in the drivers' offences on such a basis. Although it quashed the convictions, in the light of a misdirection by the trial judge, the Court of Appeal nonetheless said that there could be corporate criminal liability in such circumstances, if:

1. the company had the right to control the actions of those engaged in the offending, and
2. the company knew about the offending, but
3. the company intentionally took no steps to prevent the offending.

It is submitted that, underlying the decision in *JF Alford Transport*, is an application of the control principle. The attributability and duty criteria are satisfied, in that the company ('the controller') had control over the conduct of controlled entities—the drivers—in circumstances in which there was a duty to prevent criminal wrongdoing of the kind in question attributable to a controlled entity. The ascriptive question is clearly answered in the negative, in that, in the circumstances, the controller (knowingly) failed to put in place adequate safeguards to prevent the criminal wrongdoing. In Chapter 5, I suggest that the '*Alford* principles' provide a potentially sound basis for the creation of a failure-to-prevent offence, applicable to crimes intentionally committed by an associated person, even in the absence of an intention to benefit the company thereby.[49]

JF Alford Transport is, of course, a case about the alleged complicity of the company and its senior officers in wrongdoing. So, the application of the control principle had superimposed on it a requirement to prove knowledge (of the offending) and intent (to do nothing about the offending). In that respect, the approach of the court in *JF Alford Transport* is similar to cases in which the control principle has

[48] [1997] EWCA Crim 654.

[49] See the discussion of liability model D: 'liability for ailing to prevent a free, deliberate, and informed criminal act (not Intended to Benefit the Company) of an associated person' in Section I.4.

been drawn on implicitly by courts to explain and justify criminal liability for 'permitting' environmental pollution, when a state of affairs controlled by a company has given rise to such pollution. For example, in *Alphacell v Woodward*,[50] Lord Salmon suggested that

> [t]he creation of an offence in relation to 'permitting' pollution was probably included so as to deal . . . with the type of case in which a man knows that contaminated effluent is escaping over his land into a river, and does nothing at all to prevent it.[51]

This understanding of 'permitting' can be straightforwardly explained in terms of the control principle. In Lord Salmon's example, there is the attributability criterion of the control principle: D, as owner, controls the land (the controlled entity), and the occurrence of the pollution is associated with the controlled entity. Moreover, the duty criterion of the control principle is also satisfied: as owner, D was, ex hypothesi, under a duty to contain the escape of noxious substances, and hence under a duty to put in place safeguards aimed at preventing escape, but did not.

What should we make of Lord Salmon's understanding that proof of pollution being 'permitted' to occur involves proof of knowledge, as was also required in *JF Alford Transport*? It is submitted that we should think of a requirement to prove knowledge as, in this context, akin to the civil law doctrine of actual 'notice'.[52] In other words, its legal significance is not, or not simply, that it satisfies a requirement for (subjective) fault. Under the control principle, what may in some key cases make knowledge or awareness of a (illegal, unduly risky, etc.) state of affairs under one's control *guilty* knowledge is that one was alerted to the fact that inadequate (or no) safeguards against harm or wrong being done were in place, but then one did nothing—or had no procedures in place—to remedy that state of affairs.[53] As we will see in Chapter 5, this provides an alternative normative foundation—liability model D, as explained in Section I.4—for convicting a company of failing to prevent fault-based wrongdoing, when the alternative normative foundation—the associated person's intention to benefit the company—is absent.[54] Having said that, as indicated in the discussion of the elements of the control principle,[55] a requirement to prove guilty knowledge is not a necessary part of the application of the control principle. When interpreting statutory phrases to establish criminal

[50] [1972] AC 824 (HL).
[51] Ibid., 849.
[52] *Hunt v Luck* [1902] 1 Ch 428.
[53] See, by comparison, *R v Miller* [1983] 2 AC 161 (HL), and *Warner v MPC* (1968) 2 All ER 356 (HL).
[54] As in cases, for example, where the associated person engages in sexual offending in the course of employment: see the discussion in the Introduction and in ch 5.
[55] See Section 3.2 above.

offences that involve no fault element at all, such as 'causing' environmental pollution, the courts have also explained liability in terms of control principle.[56]

JF Alford Transport has the merit that it seeks to develop common law rules (here the rules of complicity) with a view specifically to tailoring them to fit a corporate context. There is self-evidently a socio-economic imperative to develop principles of criminal liability capable of (1) accommodating the distinction between companies and their individual officers, and capable of (2) navigating divisions of labour directed or managed through hierarchy,[57] not least because there are now some 5.5 million businesses in the United Kingdom (albeit many of them sole proprietorships).[58] By applying the control principle to assess the complicity of a company and its directors in the acts or omissions of company employees, *JF Alford Transport* does something to meet that challenge. However, the case has obvious limitations in that regard. Whilst the case involves an application of the control principle, the principle is not adopted as a common law principle of *primary* liability. Instead, the control principle is serving merely as a justificatory pillar supporting a finding of derivative, secondary liability. *JF Alford Transport* can, thus, be contrasted with *Alphacell v Woodward*,[59] and other cases involving statutory interpretation considered in Section 3.5 below, where the control principle has been used to justify primary liability.

Moreover, seen in terms of the post-*Jogee*[60] common law elements of complicity, *JF Alford Transport* is perhaps now of doubtful authority, in so far it purports to apply the control principle (with the fault elements described above) to determine liability. That is because the case does not make clear the post-*Jogee* requirement, in the law governing complicity, that the relevant act or omission—here, encouraging the offender by taking no steps to safeguard against offending—would have to be accompanied by an intent that the offence itself be committed: mere knowledge that it would be committed no longer suffices.[61] Nonetheless, the '*Alford* principles', as we may call them, could be of enduring significance. As already indicated and explained further in Chapter 5, they could provide a convincing basis for

[56] See the discussion in ch 4.

[57] This economic model is commonly adopted by all but the very smallest corporate enterprises, to benefit from the efficiency gain involved when a company does not have to go to market to secure every service it requires. Why, for example, incur the transaction costs involving in bidding for contracts with transport firms to carry my goods to their customers, when I can simply employ drivers myself? See Ronald Coase (1937).

[58] https://www.gov.uk/government/statistics/business-population-estimates-2022/business-population-estimates-for-the-uk-and-regions-2022-statistical-release-html (last accessed 05/04/2023).

[59] [1972] AC 824 (HL).

[60] *R v Jogee* [2016] UKSC 8.

[61] For example, *JF Alford Transport* relies on the (now) erroneous claim by Devlin J in *NCB v Gamble* [1959] 1 QB 11, 23: 'if one man deliberately sells to another a gun to be used for murdering a third, he may be indifferent whether the third man dies and interested only in the cash profit to be made out of the sale, but he can still be an aider and abettor'. Post-*Jogee*, in this example, to be complicit in the murder, the gun seller would have to be shown to have intended the gun purchaser to act with the intent to murder someone.

convicting companies of failure to prevent crime, committed by associated persons in the course of their employment, when the crime was not intended to benefit the company (model D, as explained in Section I.4).

3.5 Vicarious Liability at Common Law and Under Statute

In analysing corporate criminal liability for the acts of individuals associated with companies, I now turn to the second instance in which the common law traditionally permitted X to be found criminal liable for an offence committed by Y.[62] This is where X' s employee or agent, Y, commits a public nuisance in the course of employment. In *R v Medley*,[63] employees of the Equitable Gas Company (created by statute prior to the Joint Stock Companies Act 1844) had allowed by-products of gas production—'filthy, noxious, unwholesome and deleterious liquids, matters, scum, and refuse'—to enter the Thames. This poisoned the water, killing a large number of fish, thereby damaging the livelihoods of those dependent on fishing in the Thames. The decision to dump the by-products into the river was an expedient to which the workmen resorted when machinery designed to dispose of the refuse by process of evaporation failed. The gas company chairman, deputy chairman, and directors, together with the gas engineer and the superintendent in the company's employment, were indicted for public nuisance.

The chairman, deputy chairman, and directors claimed ignorance of what had happened and how it had occurred. Moreover, following their discovery of what had happened, they claimed to have had no repetition of the offending conduct since a better system was put in place to stop discharges. Even so, they were convicted,[64] following a direction to jury from Denham CJ as follows:

> It is said that the directors were ignorant of what had been done. In my judgment that makes no difference; provided you think that they gave authority to [the superintendent] to conduct the works, they will be answerable. It seems to me both common sense and law, that, if persons for their own advantage employ servants to conduct works, they must be answerable for what is done by those servants.[65]

We will consider in due course the precise kind of reasoning used here, according to which D must accept responsibility vicariously for P's criminal act.

[62] See the beginning of Section 3.3 above.
[63] (1834) 172 ER 1246.
[64] When a later hearing was conducted to determine the punishment, a reduced fine was imposed, in the light of the (successful) measures taken after the offence was discovered to abate the nuisance.
[65] (1834) 172 ER 1246, 1250.

An important point to note is that *Medley* is regarded by some US scholars as one of the foundation stones underpinning the later US Federal adoption of a vicarious liability approach to corporate criminal liability across the board.[66] By contrast with the position in the United States, though, English courts turned their backs on a broader development of that kind. This meant that the common law was woefully ill-equipped to address the need for an appropriate basis for a key element of corporate criminal liability: taking responsibility for the wrongdoing of an associated person. *Medley* came to be regarded as an outlier case, and the employer-friendly common law[67] extended vicarious criminal liability no further. The well-known dictum of Cave J in *Chisholm v Doulton*[68] provides an example of classical liberal opposition to vicarious criminal liability in principle:

> A master is not criminally responsible for a death caused by his servant's negligence, and still less for an offence depending on the servant's malice; nor can a master be held liable for the guilt of his servant in receiving goods knowing them to have been stolen.[69]

A notable feature of this passage from *Chisholm v Doulton* is that it withholds criminal responsibility from the employer not only when a servant commits an offence with 'malice' or knowingly (and hence, ex hypothesi, through a free, deliberate, and informed act), but also when a death is caused by a servant's 'negligence': when the servant's act—whilst possibly deliberate and free—will not have been informed.[70] Adopting an individualist, classical liberal approach to the scope of corporate criminal liability,[71] *Chisholm v Doulton* effectively sets up a kind of qualified immunity for (corporate) employers respecting criminal acts committed or harm done by their servants.

Cave J took a similar approach not long afterwards, in *Massey v Morris*.[72] In this case, the question was whether a shipowner could be said to have 'allowed' the overloading of a vessel, when it was one of their ships' masters who had allowed the overloading to occur. Cave J overturned the shipowner's conviction, on the grounds that 'the mere fact that he appointed the master who allowed [the overloading] to be done [did not] amount to an "allowing" of it'.[73] In the court's view, liability could be sustained only if 'the owner appointed a particular master

[66] Kathleen F Brickey (1982), 419.
[67] On this, see, e.g., Hugh Collins (1982), chs 2 and 3.
[68] (1889) 22 QBD 736.
[69] *Chisholm v Doulton* (1889) 22 QBD 736, 741, cited by the Court of Appeal in *R v St Regis Paper Company Ltd* [2011] EWCA Crim 2527, para 25. See also the judgment of Cave J in *Massey v Morriss* [1894] 2 QB 412.
[70] See, further, *R v Cory Brothers and Company Limited* (1927) 1 KB 810 (KB).
[71] For an outline of such an approach, see the Introduction.
[72] [1894] 2 QB 412.
[73] Ibid., 413.

knowing that he would overload the ship, and intending that he should do so' (complicity-based reasoning).[74] Economically, the decision fails to acknowledge the increasing welfarist need for the criminal law to address neglect or inattention on the part of employers, in supervising the huge army of people working—often in trades that posed significant risks to the public—in the private sector.[75] Whereas, in 1844, only 720 companies were listed by the Stock Exchange, by 1884 there were 9,300 companies registered as engaging in business, a figure that was to rise to 64,692 by 1914.[76] What is more, it would have been possible to continue to treat pure vicarious criminal liability of the kind imposed in *Medley* as an atypical feature of the common law, by adopting the central case of the control principle (focused on D's own safeguarding failures) to govern a wider range of cases.

However, in interpreting statutes, as opposed to developing common law principles, the courts proved more amenable to the application of vicarious liability. In *Chuter v Freeth & Pocock*,[77] a company was convicted of providing a false warranty concerning the nature and quality of milk for sale, contrary to section 20(6) of the Sale of Food and Drugs Act 1899, in the absence of proof of a reason to believe that the warranty was true. In *Chuter*, it was agents of the company, and not the company itself, who were responsible for giving the warranties (in the absence of such a belief). The company was nonetheless convicted, Lord Alverstone CJ deciding that:

> There is no reason why a warranty should not be given by a corporation. It can give a warranty through its agents, and through its agents it can believe or not believe, as the case may be, that the statements in the warranty are true.[78]

Chuter v Freeth & Pocock was followed in the leading case of *Mousell Bros Ltd v London and North-Western Railway Co.*[79] In *Mousell*, a company was convicted of giving a false account of the number or quantity of goods conveyed by railway, with intent to avoid the payment of any tolls payable in respect of the goods. In this case, the false account had been given by regional manager, but the company

[74] Ibid., 414.

[75] Private sector employment constituted well over 90 per cent of all employment in the second half of the nineteenth century. At that time, some 90 per cent of employed people worked in agriculture, mining, manufacturing, or construction (and only 10 per cent in the service industry): see Office for National Statistics (2019). Once the benefits of separate legal personality and limited liability had been extended to smaller companies, by the Joint Stock Companies Act 1856, there followed more than half a century of rapid corporate expansion into almost every field of trade.

[76] See PW Ireland (1984), 244–45. Of course, company registrations are not simplistically to be equated with economic activity. For example, of the 26,000 companies registered between 1856 and 1886, only 9,300 were reported as still making returns in 1884. Overall, business proprietors increased from around 1 million in 1850 to around 2 million in 1911: Robert J Bennett, Harry Smith, Piero Montebruno, and Carry van Lieshout (2021).

[77] [1911] 2 KB 832.

[78] Ibid., 836.

[79] [1917] 2 KB 836.

was itself convicted, because the manager had been 'entrusted with the performance of this class of acts, and [was] therefore acting within the scope of his employment'.[80] The importance of these cases is, in part, simply that they firmly establish the acceptance by the courts, in the early twentieth century (and possibly before), that Parliament intended to apply the principle of vicarious liability in corporate criminal law.[81] A classic example of a case reflecting this development is *Pearkes, Gunston & Tee v Ward*.[82]

In *Pearkes*, the appellant company was a grocer and provision merchant registered in the City of London, but with sales outlets in other locations, including Richmond, London.[83] It was at this outlet in Richmond that, contrary to section 6 of the Sale of Food and Drugs Act 1875, one of the appellant's shop workers sold, 'to the prejudice of the purchaser', butter that was not of 'the nature, substance, and quality . . . demanded by such purchaser'.[84] The appellants claimed that a company could not be convicted of the offence, but the conviction was upheld. For Lord Alverstone CJ:

> This question, in my opinion, depends upon very much the same considerations as those which arise in an ordinary civil action when it is sought to make a person responsible for the acts of his servants . . . the protective object of the section and the necessary ingredients of the offence all seem to point to the conclusion that a corporation is placed in the same position as an individual, provided the sale is made on its behalf.[85]

A classical liberal system of liability that allows companies to hide behind the harmful or wrongful actions of their employees and agents, on the basis that the companies did not themselves—through their directors—perform or authorize the actions, substantially reduces the deterrent power of the criminal law, and damages its integrity as a system.[86] Judicial acceptance of (corporate) vicarious liability under statute simply reflected the emerging reality of the intensification of the division and specialization of labour, brought about by the emergence of widescale

[80] Ibid., 842 (per Viscount Reading CJ).

[81] For a useful discussion, see KJM Smith (1998), ch 6. *Mousell* has been relied on in recent cases such as *Shah v Harrow BC* [2000] 1 WLR 83, 90.

[82] [1902] 2 KB 1.

[83] See Charles Wilson (1965), 190: 'The importance of the retail stores was not simply as a commercial improvement. They were in many instances unavoidably necessary if the industries whose products they were designed to sell were to work economically. Perishable goods like margarine, imported meat, milk, eggs needed the swift put-through of the multiple . . . at every point the retailing changes were closely connected with new or reorganised systems of mass manufacture; each indeed was a function of the other. Each called for capital, labour, enterprise, ingenuity to supply the needs of an urban people living at standards which most believed were higher and all agreed were different.'

[84] *Pearkes, Gunston & Tee v Ward* [1902] 2 KB 1, 2.

[85] Ibid., 9.

[86] In that a criminal law focus solely on the employees or agents who committed the crime would be disproportionate and unfair.

corporate activity, and encapsulated by distinctions between owners, producers, distributors, and sellers.[87] Such developments meant that no one person could reasonably be expected to know of defects occurring in any single mass produced or distributed item: say, the adulteration of food occurring at some point in the supply chain from farm to fork.[88] In Chapter 5, I give as one basis for distinguishing between vicarious criminal liability and criminal liability under the control principle, that vicarious criminal liability reflects no less but (crucially) no more than an inward-looking concern with the reality of more-or-less formalized divisions of labour internal to companies. By contrast, the right and duty element of the control principle may be as much outward as it is inward-looking. The control principle has the potential to be concerned not just with control over employees, but with (say) a corporate landowner's control over the conditions facing visitors on the land, or a parent company's control over its contractual agents and subsidiaries: persons well outside the scope of vicarious liability.

3.6 Vicarious Liability and the Control Principle

Whatever the socio-economic benefits of a system of vicarious liability may be, we need to scrutinize the basis on which it was explained and justified. As KJM Smith has argued, by the end of the nineteenth century, 'even the most fundamental basis of the doctrine [of vicarious responsibility] had not been settled'.[89] On the one hand, the employee or agent might artificially be regarded simply as the *alter ego* of the company, as in *Shah* or in the earlier case of *Pearkes, Gunston & Tee v Ward*. Such an analysis involves some smoke and mirrors, by eliminating the need for any consideration of the company's independent role vis-à-vis the employee or agent. On the other hand, a defendant company might be regarded as having—in a more-or-less formal sense—delegated responsibility for the conduct of some aspect of company business to an agent or employee, whilst accepting the risk that any liability that fell on the employee or agent (acting in that capacity[90])

[87] As Wilson describes it, 'Joseph Lyons' new mechanical bakery and its rivals demanded the turnover only a multiple shop system could provide. The manufacturers of machine-made boots and shoes also needed swift mass distribution of their output at the lowest cost. Hence the 500 specialised retailers of 1875 became the 5000 of 1900. Behind the new multiple tailors was a new industrial organisation replacing the bespoke tailor sitting cross-legged on his board with needle and thread in the back room of a cottage': Charles Wilson (1965), 190.

[88] A further relevant issue was the increasing regionalization of mass production, in order to bring economies of scale through—for example, the replacement after 1880 of smaller rural flour mills with much larger mills based at the ports. This meant that local knowledge of individual traders' practices, and awareness amongst town officials of those traders' likely (dis)honesty, disappeared along with the craft-based, producer-seller model itself, making the locally run market courts of pie powder that revolved around such knowledge an increasing irrelevance to the criminal law governance of trade: Charles Gross (1906).

[89] KJM Smith (1998), 331.

[90] In that regard, in imposing vicarious liability, the courts laid emphasis on the need for an employee who engaged in wrongdoing to be acting in the course of their employment: *Budd v Lucas* [1891] 1 QB

would simultaneously fall on the company (*Medley*, *Chuter v Freeth & Pocock*, and *Mousell Bros Ltd v London and North-Western Railway Co*). On this basis, as Lord Burrows has recently observed, D's liability 'does not rest on the defendant having owed a duty, whether strict or of reasonable care, to the claimant. It was the third party ... [the employee] who owed that duty'.[91]

The latter analysis fits with sophisticated explanations of vicarious liability in private law, such as that of Jason Neyers.[92] Neyers argues that vicarious liability in tort is justified, in virtue of 'an employer's implied promise in the contract of employment to indemnify the employee for harms (including legal liability) suffered by the employee in the conduct of the employer's business'.[93] I suggested in Chapter 1 that one justification for imposing liability on a company, rather than on the offending associated person (especially someone at a low level in the hierarchy), was a similar argument. Even so, as Neyers rightly observes, this explanation succeeds only by eliminating from the moral picture the relationship between the employer and the harm or wrong done, and concentrating on the contractual relationship between the employer and the employee. In a criminal law context, such an explanation simply will not do the necessary justificatory work, for much the same reason that, for example, if D is caught drink-driving, D could not seek to escape criminal liability by pointing to a pre-existing contract with X under which X agreed to accept the penalty imposed on D.[94] The control principle is not open to this objection, because each party involved (employer-company, employee, agent, and subsidiary) can be made liable for their own conduct: for the criminal act, in the case of corporate representatives, and for the failure to prevent that act through a safeguarding failure, in the case of the company.

However, it is possible to discern in the case law on vicarious liability under statute the glimmer of a rationale based on the control principle, and hence on the moral and legal significance of safeguarding failures. In justifying liability, courts sometimes laid emphasis on the opportunity that the control over an employee's or agent's conduct gives the employer (the control-right criterion), to put in place procedures to prevent wrongdoing by the employee in the discharge of statutory duties (the control-duty criterion). As we have seen, even in *Medley*, where the defendants were held vicariously liable for pollution caused by employees, the

408; *Boyle v Smith* [1906] 1 KB 432. See also *Coppen v Moore* (No 2) [1898] 2 QB 306. See, further, the discussion of this point in ch 5.

[91] *Trustees of the Barry Congregation of Jehovah's Witnesses (Appellant) v BXB (Respondent)* [2023] UKSC 15, para 1.

[92] JW Neyers (2005).

[93] Ibid., 301.

[94] See *Burrows v Rhodes* [1899] 1 QB 816, 828: 'It has, I think, long been settled law that if an act is manifestly unlawful, or the doer of it knows it to be unlawful, as constituting either a civil wrong or a criminal offence, he cannot maintain an action for contribution or for indemnity against the liability which results to him therefrom. An express promise of indemnity to him for the commission of such an act is void.' See also *Lancashire County Council v Municipal Mutual Insurance* [1997] QB 897.

defendants were given reduced fines when they swore that 'the nuisance had been wholly abated by the establishment of an adequate system of evaporation'.[95] An example of the invocation of the duty criterion to the control principle to justify the imposition of vicarious liability as such is *Bond v Evans*.[96] In this case, the appellant was a licensed victualler, charged under section 17 of the Licensing Act 1872 with 'suffering' gaming to be carried on, on his premises. The gaming took place when an employee permitted it to go ahead, at a time when the employer was present but unaware of the gaming going on. The court held that the employer could be convicted, if and in so far as the gaming was 'suffered' to occur by an employee, as opposed to the employer, because:

> It was intended by s. 17 absolutely to prohibit gaming on licensed premises, and that the substantial effect is that the responsibility is thrown upon any person who keeps a licensed house *to take proper precautions* to prevent all gaming on his premises.[97]

In *Fitzpatrick v Kelly*,[98] a shop owner was found vicariously liable for the act of his shopman, in selling adulterated butter. In answer to the submission that knowledge of the adulteration ought to be proved by the prosecution, Blackburn J said:

> The sale of an adulterated article as unadulterated may well be made punishable without knowledge on the part of the seller, for a very little trouble would enable a tradesman to ascertain, if he wishes to avoid all danger, that the articles he sells are not adulterated.[99]

A rationale for vicarious liability in terms of safeguarding failures can also be found in the judgment of Devlin J in *Reynolds v GH Austin & Sons*,[100] where he said:

> A man may be made responsible for the acts of his servants, *or even for defects in his business arrangements* because it can fairly be said that by such sanctions citizens are induced to keep themselves and their organisations up to the mark. Although in one sense the citizen is being punished for the sins of others, it can be said that, if he had been more alert to see that the law was observed, the sin might not have been committed.[101]

95 (1834) 2 C & P 292, 300.
96 (1888) 21 QB 249.
97 Ibid., 252, per Manisty J (my emphasis).
98 (1873) LR 8 QB 337.
99 Ibid., 341–42.
100 [1951] 2 KB 135.
101 Ibid., 148–49 (my emphasis).

In justifying liability in these cases, the courts are effectively applying elements of the control principle. Moreover, they are applying the control principle to circumstances in which the wrong is done through a free, deliberate, and informed act, and not simply (as in *Alphacell*[102]) by accident. That provides us with a different way of analysing such cases in theoretical terms.

3.7 The Influence Principle and Collective Directorial Failures

Most theories of corporate criminal law focus on the vertical 'top-down' relationship between an employer or directors and employees: the one-way projection of authority (to use Lon Fuller's pejorative notion).[103] That focus is linked to the hierarchical model of the firm in which it is employees who do most of the work, and whose conduct is accordingly most commonly at issue in criminal cases; but the majority of companies have no employees. As indicated in Chapter 1, of the 5.4 million registered businesses in the United Kingdom, 4.1 million (74 per cent) had no employees, and 3.1 million (56 per cent) were unincorporated sole proprietorships almost all of which had no employees.[104] So, we should address the many examples in which a company is comprised of a number of directors, but has no employees, a situation consistently neglected in the academic literature on corporate crime.[105] *Lennard's Carrying Company, Ltd v Asiatic Petroleum Company, Ltd*[106] equates the (in)actions of a company with the (in)actions of directors. However, as indicated in Chapter 1, perhaps because the case involved only a single director company, the case does not tell us what is to happen if, say, a director commits a crime about which the other directors know nothing, or where a minority of directors defy the will of the majority by committing a crime.[107] In such examples, is the crime committed by the company, or only by the individual directors in question? On my account, whilst the crime itself is committed by the individual directors, the failure to prevent it (in the absence of adequate or reasonable crime-prevention procedures) is the crime committed by the company. It is a corporate crime, in virtue of the

[102] [1972] AC 824 (HL).

[103] Lon Fuller (1969), 209–10.

[104] https://www.gov.uk/government/statistics/business-population-estimates-2022/business-population-estimates-for-the-uk-and-regions-2022-statistical-release-html (last accessed 11/06/2023). Only 2 per cent of UK businesses trade from more than one site.

[105] In the case of a company comprised of a sole director, when the crime in question is committed by the proprietor or director themselves, an issue of 'failure to prevent' the commission of the crime is unlikely to arise, although it is not impossible. Suppose that a sole director (D) becomes aware that their accountant has in error submitted a tax return to HMRC that understates the company's income. If D does nothing to correct the error, then we may say that the company—through D's inaction qua director—has failed to prevent the evasion of tax. In practice, D's company would, of course, be treated as simply having evaded or attempted to evade tax, given that there is no offence of failing to prevent the evasion of tax.

[106] [1915] AC 705 (HL).

[107] An issue long ago noted by Brent Fisse (1983).

collective failure to prevent it on the part of the directors, whatever their precise role of each director within the company.

This proposition accords with economic theories that place the greatest emphasis on the part played by directors, rather than shareholders, within the company. For example, Blair and Stout have argued that the legal requirement for companies to be managed by a board of directors has evolved not to minimize agency costs, but to encourage the firm-specific investment essential to certain forms of production by the corporate 'team' as a whole.[108] On their account, boards exist not to protect the interests of shareholders as such, but to protect the enterprise-specific investments of all the members of the corporate team. So, as they argue in relation to a company's assets:

> Within the corporation, control over those assets is exercised by an internal hierarchy whose job is to coordinate the activities of the team members, allocate the resulting production, and mediate disputes among team members over that allocation. At the peak of this hierarchy sits a board of directors whose authority over the use of corporate assets is virtually absolute and whose independence from individual team members . . . is protected by law.[109]

Accordingly, we need to look more closely at the justification for regarding directorial failures to prevent crime as collective failures, before turning to the conceptual foundations of that idea.

It is important to bear in mind that the modern distinction commonly drawn between 'executive' and 'non-executive' directors (the functions of each being regarded as different) is not recognized or acknowledged in company law. Broadly speaking, constitutionally, all directors are equal. As the explanatory notes to section 278 of the Company Act 2006 indicate:

> The Act does not attempt a more detailed definition of a director because it is important to ensure that the term is applied to anybody who exercises real power within the company, particularly in relation to decision taking. The term 'director' therefore includes: an executive director who has been properly appointed by the company; a non-executive director who has been properly appointed by the company; a de facto director (that is, a person who has assumed the status and functions of a company director even though he has not been properly appointed).

An illustrative case to consider, in this regard, is *Powers v Greymountain Management Ltd*.[110]

[108] Margaret M Blair and Lynn A Stout (1999).
[109] Ibid., 253.
[110] [2022] IEHC 599.

In *Greymountain*, the defendant, an Irish registered company, Greymountain Management Ltd, was under the directorship of two Irish directors, Liam Grainger and Ryan Coates, with brothers David and Jonathan Cartu acting as shadow directors. All four directors were sued by American investor William Powers as the lead plaintiff among thirty-five others who were suing the directors for more than $4.5 million in losses. The investors believed they were trading in binary options. However, no legitimate trades were carried out, the binary options were never purchased, and the investors' money was syphoned off for the use of the shadow directors and others. The plaintiff sought orders against the directors and the shadow directors making them personally liable for the funds that were lost as a result of the alleged fraud. Twomey J concluded that Greymountain was used as an instrument of fraud and that the sole purpose of Greymountain was to defraud unsuspecting individuals of their money. Twomey J noted that, while lifting the corporate veil should not be taken lightly, there are certain circumstances where an Irish court would be justified in piercing the corporate veil, and this was such a case. More important, though, for our purposes, is Twomey J's finding that the Irish directors, and in particular Ryan Coates, would face personal liability along with all the other directors.

Coates was a college student at the time that he became a paid director of Greymountain, at his mother's suggestion, to help with his college fees. Coates claimed that he was a director in name only, that he had no role whatsoever in the running of the company, and that he knew nothing about the fraudulent conduct of the company. Even so, he was found personally liable, because—however inexperienced, ignorant, peripheral, and uninvolved he may have been—he was under the same duty as all directors, namely under a duty, 'to acquire and maintain a sufficient knowledge and understanding of the company's business to enable them properly to discharge their duties as directors'.[111] In that regard, most importantly, on the basis of what they have learned about the company, every director is then under a duty, 'to exercise appropriate supervision or oversight at board level in respect of the execution or discharge of whatever tasks or functions have properly and appropriately been delegated to others'.[112] With that legal background in mind, we can understand how it might be that a failure on the part of directors to prevent a crime can be regarded as a collective failure, whatever the status of any given individual director. When a crime has been committed by someone associated with the company, and both the attributability and duty criteria are satisfied, then, however peripheral and insignificant a director may believe themselves to have been, they—in common with other directors—did not succeed in using their

[111] *Kavanagh v Delaney* [2005] 1 IRLM 34, para 40, quoting *Re Barings PLC & Others* (No. 5) [1999] 1 BCLC 433 (see the discussion in ch 1).
[112] *Re Laragh Civils Ltd* [2016] IEHC 533, para 26 (Keane J).

powers of 'appropriate supervision or oversight'[113] to prevent the crime; and so, they are all guilty of a collective failure to prevent its occurrence.

I will now look in more detail at this key notion of 'appropriate supervision or oversight'.[114] Under the control principle, the foundation for criminal liability is the existence of a control-right and correlative control-duty in D (the company) concerning the controlled entity associated with the commission of the offence. It might be easy to see how a piece of land, business premises, an employee, an agent, or a subsidiary company might be a company's 'controlled entity', and hence how the attributability criterion of the control principle might be established with respect to such an entity; but how does the control principle account for cases in which the commission of the crime is associated with a company director themselves? Is such a person a 'controlled entity', respecting whom the directors collectively (and hence the company) have a control-right and correlative control-duty to safeguard against the commission of offences? Whilst there may be some cases in which the answer to that is 'yes',[115] there will be as many or more cases in which the answer is 'no'. Directors may not have control over one another in the same sense that they have control over (say) employees or agents. The relationship between directors is more typically horizontal (peer-to-peer) than it is vertical (chain of command), and so it must be analysed in a different way.[116] Such an analysis may be found in the notion of what can be called an 'influence-right' and a correlative 'openness-duty' with regard to that influence.

The existence of a control relationship, of the kind with which we have so far been concerned, is properly described as a vertical or hierarchical relationship of authority. It is a relationship in which the controlling entity can either permit the controlled entity to engage in conduct of a certain type, or insist that the controlled entity engage in or refrain from certain conduct, irrespective of the merits of doing so (as the controlled entity sees it). How, though, should one characterize peer-to-peer relationships, such as relationships between directors in companies (and arms-length relationships between a main company and an independent subsidiary[117]), where one person does not necessarily enjoy the right authoritatively to give permission for, determine, or direct the conduct of another? How can one director—or a group of directors—properly be found liable for the acts of another director (D) who engages in wrongdoing, even though it will not normally be right to say that D is under the authority of fellow directors?[118] I argue that the liability of a director for failing to prevent crime committed by a fellow

[113] To use the language of *Re Barings PLC & Others* (No 5) [1999] 1 BCLC 433, discussed in ch 1.

[114] It will be recalled that, earlier in the chapter, I distinguished the concepts of supervision and oversight, but these differences are not significant in this context.

[115] See, e.g., *SFO v Barclays* (2018) EWHC 3055.

[116] The 'problematic example' at the start of this chapter is meant to raise this issue.

[117] An issue addressed in ch 5.

[118] Of course, in some instances, one director may be under the authority of other directors: see, e.g., *SFO v Barclays* (2018) EWHC 3055.

director should be analysed (whether the directors are directors in law, in fact, or shadow directors) in terms of what can be called influence 'correlatives'. The importance of *Greymountain*, and of the cases on which it relies, is that they illustrate the centrality to the role of a director (be they never so insignificant in the practical running of the company) of using the information and understanding they are under a duty to acquire to seek to *influence* those performing executive roles to behave in a certain way. What Keane J refers to in *Re Laragh Civils Ltd*[119] as the exercise by a director of 'appropriate supervision or oversight' over another director or directors—whether or not at board meetings—simply cannot take on normative significance unless, in relation to a given policy or decision, one director sees it as their role to exercise influence over an executive director or directors, and most importantly, the latter regard themselves as open to that influence.

In Hohfeld's classic scheme of fundamental legal conceptions, jural correlatives covered right/duty, privilege/no-right, power/liability, and immunity/disability.[120] However, it can be argued that another such correlative commonly to be found in legal systems, but unaccounted for by Hohfeld, is 'having influence',[121] and its jural correlative, 'openness to such influence'.[122] The relationship between jural correlatives is normative, as opposed to causal, even though one can clearly make a causal impact through influence. I can influence the flow of water into a bowl by turning the tap one way or another, and if I do this, then in causal terms, it can be said that I 'had influence' over the flow of water. However, it makes no sense to say that, normatively, I (like some latter-day Moses facing the Red Sea) 'had influence' over the water flow. What, then, constitutes having influence, normatively speaking? In this context, normative influence involves the provision of reasons to think and act in a certain way that the person-to-be-influenced should find (at least) worthy of consideration in practical reasoning, because those reasons have been suggested in good faith by the would-be influencer. To say, 'I have (some) influence with the official in charge' is to suggest precisely that: namely to suggest that, when I speak to the official, they will find what I say worthy of consideration as a guide to thought and action.[123] So, on the other side of the normative relationship with 'having influence' is its correlative: 'openness to influence'. This means—as the phrase suggests—a receptiveness to reasons for thinking and acting in a certain way, at the would-be influencer's suggestion.[124] A very general willingness of this kind is

[119] [2016] IEHC 533.

[120] Wesley Newcomb Hohfeld (1917), 710.

[121] The jural opposite of that, in Hohfeldian terms, being 'having no influence'.

[122] The jural opposite of that, in Hohfeldian terms, being 'imperviousness to influence'.

[123] Naturally, the nature and degree of my influence may vary. I could be very influential with the official, such that any suggestion of mine is bound to be acted on. At the other end of the scale, perhaps my 'influence' extends little further than getting a hearing.

[124] The importance for decision-makers of the maxim, 'hear the other side', can be attributed to the significance of the influence correlatives: someone with a certain sort of stake in the outcome of a decision ought to be able to give reasons to the decision-maker for thinking and acting in a certain way, and importantly, the decision-maker should be open to the influence of those reasons.

what is commonly referred to as 'open-mindedness', but open-mindedness in that general sense is not in issue here. We are concerned with a narrower phenomenon, in which X has the power or duty to seek to exercise influence over Y, and correspondingly, Y has the power or duty to be receptive to X's influence—even if to no other's—whilst retaining the ability to think and act independently.

In that regard, in the typical relationship of influence, its normative basis will not simply be power-based but will also be duty-based. That relationship may nonetheless be asymmetrical, in that whilst X may have the power, but no duty, to seek to influence Y, Y may very well be under a duty to be receptive to X's influence. That is the position, for example, when, as a householder affected by a prospective building development, I make representations about it to the local authority. I have the power to (seek to) influence the local authority, but no duty to (try to) do so. By contrast, the local authority has not only the power but also in many instances the duty to be—at least to some extent—receptive in its thinking to my influence. In some instances, though, there may be duty involved on both sides. I suggest that a company director has not only a power but also a duty to seek to influence fellow directors concerning the running of the company, and the other directors have not only a power but also a duty to be receptive to such influence. When not only is X in a position to influence Y's conduct, but Y is also meant to be receptive to X's influence in that respect (albeit that Y has the power to think and act independently), then we may say that X is normatively connected to the possible direction of Y's conduct. What makes it appropriate to analyse the relationship in this way is the presence of the 'openness to influence' correlative.

I can make a causal difference to someone's conduct—even a complete stranger's conduct—by influencing them, as by encouraging them to engage in a course of conduct that they then undertake. A simple example would be where I, forming part of a crowd-watching sport, shout encouragement to a player to make a particular move. However, in such a case, it would not be right to describe my influence as normative in any way, at the time when the encouragement is offered. In the example, whilst the player might conceivably be influenced (causally) by my encouragement, the player is under no obligation in that respect; indeed, it seems likely that, in game management terms, players should ordinarily not respond to such fan-based encouragement. By contrast, when, in virtue of the nature of our relationship, you are already meant to be receptive to my influence, at the time when it is given—whether by (dis)encouragement or otherwise—then it is right to say that I have a normative connection to an outcome you bring about in consequence. So, contrast the example of fan encouragement with one in which it is the team manager who shouts encouragement to one of the players to make a particular move. The player is under some obligation to be open to the manager's influence, and so it would be right to say that the manager's position to influence the player (unlike the crowd's) has normative significance. The relationship between directors can be described as normative in broadly this sense. It is a relationship in which each director may and should—*qua* director—seek to influence a co-director in relation to the way the company is run, and (crucially) each director—*qua* director—ought to be open to such influence. That is so even if, naturally enough, the power dynamic in any given company may be such that some directors—such as CEOs—are the ones doing most of the influencing with their fellow directors, whilst the latter must settle largely for being open or receptive to such influence.

That raises a further important point about the normative relationship between 'having influence' and 'openness to influence'. The way I have described that relationship might make it seem as if it involves a 'one-way projection' of influence from the person having it to the person meant to be receptive to it, not so very different from the one-way projection of authority more typical of relationships of control. In fact, this is not a structural element of the influence relationship. For example, it may be a feature of that relationship that it is reciprocal, in a way that control relationships are not; indeed, that element of reciprocity is commonly at the heart of influence-based director-to-director relationships.[125] Periodically, or at key moments, persons in a reciprocal relationship of influence may be obliged to seek each other out to determine whose influence should be followed. Whilst not every influence relationship will have this feature, it is and ought to be a feature of the relationship between directors.[126] The 'openness to influence' correlate must thus be understood to include, at least in some cases, an active as well as a passive component. Whilst the passive component entails taking advice or guidance seriously (and in some cases, as definitive), the active component involves seeking it out at the right time.

The ability to analyse the relationship between directors in terms of influence correlates helps us, because it enables us to explain the in-principle responsibility of co-directors for failing to prevent wrongdoing by another director. At any given time, directors are in a position to influence each other, and—crucially—ought correspondingly to be open to fellow directorial influence. As we have seen, directors are, for example, under a duty 'to acquire and maintain a sufficient knowledge and understanding of the company's business to enable them properly to discharge their duties as directors'.[127] On the basis of what they have learned about the company, every director is then under a duty, 'to exercise appropriate supervision or oversight at board level in respect of the execution or discharge of whatever tasks or functions have properly and appropriately been delegated to others'.[128] Such

[125] See, e.g., the discussion in John Roberts, Terry McNulty, and Philip Styles (2005), 12: 'Drawing from our research we argued that, in practice . . . accountability [of senior managers] is realized through a wide range of behaviours—challenging, questioning, probing, discussing, testing, informing, debating and exploring—that draws upon non-executive experience in support of executive performance. Through such conduct, non-executives are constantly seeking to establish and maintain their own confidence in the conduct of the company.'

[126] Ibid.

[127] *Kavanagh v Delaney* [2005] 1 IRLM 34, para 40, quoting *Re Barings PLC & Others* (No 5) [1999] 1 BCLC 433.

[128] *Re Laragh Civils Ltd* [2016] IEHC 533, para 26 (Keane J).

tasks or functions will of course include the institution of compliance procedures aimed at deterring breaches of the criminal law.[129] The reference here to supervision and oversight 'at board level' has been understood theoretically to cover both strategy and executive performance, through 'challenging, questioning, probing, discussing, testing, informing, debating, exploring, [and] encouraging'.[130] This is, in my terms, a duty to exercise influence on fellow directors, who are under a correlative duty to be responsive to that influence.

As with the control principle, the influence principle can be set out in terms of the attributability, duty, and ascriptive criteria:

> *The attributability criterion—the influence-right element.* A person (the 'influencer') had the right to influence someone (the 'influenceable person') in circumstances in which criminal wrongdoing, within the domain of the influence, was associated with the influenceable person.
>
> *The duty criterion—the influence-duty element.* In cases where the attributability criterion is satisfied, the influencer breached what was in the circumstances a duty to use their influence to give decisive reasons to the influenceable person to avoid engaging in criminal wrongdoing, at a time when the influenceable person would have had a duty to be open to the influence.

And in the central case, but not all cases:

> *The ascriptive question—the influence-evaluation question.* In cases where both the attributability and duty criteria are satisfied, did the influencer nonetheless take adequate safeguarding steps to prevent criminal wrongdoing of the relevant type occurring through disregard of legitimate influence?

In one important respect, the influence principle is like the control principle. When potential wrongdoing is in issue, the influence—like control—is meant to be decisive, and my description of the duty criterion reflects this point. It is just that its decisive character comes about in a different way. It comes through the effect it has on an influenced person's own assessment of their priorities, rather than through the generation of an authoritative command that a controlled person is bound to follow.

Now consider the facts of *SFO v Barclays*.[131] In this case, fraud charges were laid against Barclays and certain high-ranking individuals within the bank. The fraud allegations concerned the £3.95-billion investment secured by Barclays in

[129] See, further, in the US context, *In re Caremark International Inc Derivative Litigation*, 698 A 2d 959, 970 (Delaware Chancery 1996), and the discussion in Eric J Pan (2010).

[130] John Roberts, Terry McNulty, and Philip Stiles (2005), 6.

[131] *SFO v Barclays* (2018) EWHC 3055.

June and October 2008 from two Qatari investors. Barclays also entered into an advisory services agreement (ASA) with one of the investors in June 2008, which was extended in October 2008, pursuant to which fees of £322 million were payable. The SFO's case was that the sums payable under the ASA were disguised commissions, which rendered the statements as to the fees and commissions in the prospectuses and subscription agreements for the capital raisings false or misleading (in effect, fraudulent). Crucially, as the law stood at that time, the ASA was drawn up and agreed by Barclays CEO (JV) and the group finance director (CL), without—so it was assumed—the knowledge of the Barclays board. These individuals had been given only a limited mandate to negotiate and deal by the board, rather than wholesale delegated power to act as if they were the board. Accordingly, Barclays successfully applied to dismiss all charges brought against them, with Mr Justice Jay in the Crown Court ruling that that the alleged criminal dishonesty of senior officers could not be attributed to the bank. In spite of the fact that JV and CL were themselves directors, it was held that the fraud (if any were proved) was not committed by Barclays but by these individuals *qua* individuals. However, there was no doubt in this case that the bank had both a right and a duty to oversee and to influence the conduct of JV and CL; indeed, the bank had appointed a subcommittee to do just that. These individuals were under a corresponding duty to be open to the influence of the board and its committee. The failure to use that influence to give JV and CL decisive reasons not to enter into the 'advisory service agreements' means that Barclays would most certainly have committed the offence of failing to prevent fraud (if fraud was committed), assuming that its procedures for fraud-prevention were in all the circumstances lax.

As we will see in Chapter 5, beyond the case of relationship between directors as between themselves, it may also make sense to analyse the relationship between companies and independent subsidiaries in terms of influence correlates. The puzzle about holding main companies liable for the wrongdoing of subsidiaries has always been that whilst some subsidiaries are effectively controlled entities, other are more fully independent companies with no majority representation of the parent company on the board. So, a focus solely on 'control' as the important nexus between a parent and its subsidiary, in relation to wrongdoing engaged in by the subsidiary, risks confusion and difficult line-drawing exercises between different subsidiaries set up by a parent.[132] However, this difficulty can be avoided by expanding the reach of failure-to-prevent offences to include influence, alongside control, as a normative theoretical basis. As one commentator puts it:

> [P]arent companies often have considerable influence over their subsidiaries. They—along with other subsidiary shareholders, if any—vote to elect a subsidiary

[132] See the discussion of this issue in ch 5.

company's board of directors, and there may often be a board-member overlap between a subsidiary and its parent company.[133]

To be sure, in some instances, a parent company may have (vertical) control over a subsidiary company. However, even when that is not so, and the relationship is more horizontal in character, it seems plausible to suggest that parent companies may not only have the power but also the duty to seek to influence some aspects of the operation of a subsidiary in a decisive way.[134] The other side of that coin is that even a largely independent subsidiary may be under an obligation to be open to the influence of the main company, in some instances, even if the subsidiary has the power to take decisions independently. Accordingly, normatively speaking, there can be a sufficient nexus between the parent and the subsidiary (an influence-based nexus) to justify liability for a failure-to-prevent offence applicable to the parent, even when the subsidiary is not controlled by the parent.

[133] James Chen (2023).
[134] See the discussion in ch 5.

4
CORPORATE SAFEGUARDING AGAINST WRONGDOING

4.1 Sufficient Safeguarding Efforts as a Form of Excuse

PROBLEMATIC EXAMPLE: D, who is eighteen years old and has no business experience, is left as the sole owner-director of a cosmetic surgery firm when his father (the former owner) dies. D's mother, a long-standing employee of the firm, subsequently administers a subcutaneous injection of a filler into a person under eighteen years of age, contrary to section 1 of the Botulinum Toxin and Cosmetic Fillers (Children) Act 2021. D is charged, contrary to section 2 of the 2021 Act, with having failed to take all reasonable precautions and exercise all due diligence, having been the business owner at the time, to prevent the commission of the offence. D says that, in all the circumstances, he fulfilled this duty by reasonably placing trust in his mother not to engage in offending contrary to section 2.

In Chapter 1, I explained how failure-to-prevent offences place at the heart of the enquiry into liability the efforts that companies have made to avoid offending by associated persons. Politico-economically, this focus represents the state's liberal-welfarist ambitions for companies: to incentivize them to develop a commitment to use their knowledge of the relevant industry to shoulder some of the burden of what would otherwise be an unacceptably costly, impractical, intrusive, and inefficient system of proactive safeguarding intervention by the state into millions of UK firms.[1] Analytically, this focus comes about because of the '2 + 1' structure (offence and defence elements, respectively) of the central case version of the control and influence principles that underlies failure-to-prevent offences.[2]

It will be recalled that the '2' are the offence elements of (1) possession of a control or influence right to prevent the wrongdoer committing the wrong and (2) possession of a control or influence duty to prevent the wrongdoer committing the wrong. In-principle criminal liability arises when a company is in breach

[1] See the discussion in the Introduction.
[2] See the discussion of these concepts in ch 3.

A Theory of Corporate Crime. Jeremy Horder, Oxford University Press. © Jeremy Horder 2026.
DOI: 10.1093/9780198936534.003.0005

of its control-duty to prevent wrong done by the wrongdoer. However, the right and duty-holding (corporate) person may nonetheless avoid liability for their breach of duty by showing, in answer to what I called the ascriptive question (the '1' element), that sufficient efforts were made to safeguard against wrongdoing of the relevant type. In this chapter, I will examine in detail the ascriptive question as an element of the control and influence principles. I will defend the view that, rather than expressing the notion of corporate effort-sufficiency solely in terms such as 'adequate procedures' or 'reasonable procedures',[3] the law should build on the long-standing, tried and trusted concept of having taken 'all reasonable precautions, and exercised all due diligence'.[4] This concept embodies, in a way that other forms of words fail unequivocally to do, the idea of a corporate *commitment* to safeguarding against wrongdoing through measures adopted to that end. This is a commitment capable of transcending or going beyond the mere presence in the workplace of safeguarding procedures. It reflects the overall approach to compliance of the entrepreneur who is a 'positive responder' or a 'proactive learner'.[5] This is a commercial operator who adopts what I call an 'active striving' approach to compliance: someone who regards a committed and creative approach to compliance as a civic and not just a legal duty.[6]

Another advantage of employing the concept of taking all reasonable precautions, and exercising all due diligence, is that it can readily be made to fit different corporate contexts. There are three different kinds of corporate context, not commonly distinguished in legislation or commentary, to which the concept can be applied. First, there are instances of one-person businesses. Clearly, in such cases, what is going to matter are the individual efforts that the sole director has themselves made to take precautions and exercise due diligence. Secondly, there are cases of micro firms where relations between (family) members of the firm are governed mainly by close personal bonds, on a *gemeinschaft* model.[7] To accommodate the *gemeinschaft* model on which so many firms are based, it should be arguable

[3] Although I will for convenience sake refer to a 'reasonable procedures' requirement, in fact—where it speaks in terms of reasonableness—the law requires such procedures as are reasonable in all the circumstances, a subtly different notion.

[4] On the tried and trusted status of this term, see Section 4.4 below.

[5] For detailed discussion of these concepts, see Section 4.3 below. The ideal of cultivating a corporate commitment is not new. In 1891, a leading Medical Health Officer said, in relation to sanitation standards, 'It was far better that people should be taught by inspectors the reasons why different work had to be done, and to persuade them to carry out the principles necessary for the removal of nuisances and infectious disease. It was far better for them to do the work willingly, and look upon the sanitary inspector as their friend rather than as a prying, intolerant autocrat who would force down their throats the principles of sanitation whether they liked it or not': Alfred Carpenter (1891), 144.

[6] As we will see, so far as a commitment to safeguarding is concerned, the concepts of taking 'all reasonable precautions' and exercising 'all due diligence' may draw on different ideal-types of the responsible, regulated corporate citizen. Two such ideal-types that we will encounter are the risk-averse, perfectionist safety officer and the risk-embracing, but nonetheless ethical CEO: see the discussion in Section 4.6 below.

[7] See further the discussion in ch 2.

that for a director simply to have placed their trust in another member of the firm to fulfil a particular compliance obligation (as in the problematic example given at the start) is, given their knowledge of that person, itself a manifestation of taking all reasonable precautions and exercising all due diligence. This may well not be true in relation to all compliance obligations, or respecting all (or even most) instances in which a close relationship of trust exists between the relevant members of a small firm. Nonetheless, it is important to recognize the possibility that such circumstances may arise, and that—a point pursued later in this chapter—the taking of all reasonable precautions and the exercising all due diligence need not and should not be understood solely as a bureaucratic, rule-based phenomenon.

Finally, there are (larger) firms in which relations between persons associated with it are governed first and foremost by a mixture of bureaucratic-administrative and *gesellschaft* principles,[8] even if it is inevitable that personal trust must also be placed by members of the business in each other to perform their roles. In such cases, and in particular where compliance obligations are discharged through relations of authority, there will and should be a greater emphasis on the robustness of formal process and procedure (including appropriate AI-driven automated compliance management systems[9]), in assessing whether all reasonable precautions have been taken and all due diligence exercised. Even so, as part of their responsibility for the development of the company as a real entity, the company's senior management should be regarded as obliged to establish, maintain, and enforce a particular kind of safeguarding framework: a framework within which striving for compliance is valued intrinsically (for its own sake) by associated persons. This is a framework oriented towards making the employees responsible for the firm's criminal law and regulatory compliance people who are committed to, who find intrinsic value in, the safeguarding enterprise, just as the sole entrepreneur who fits the ideal-type of the positive responder or proactive learner is committed to and finds such value in safeguarding in the running of their business.

Liability for failure-to-prevent crime, based on the central case version of the control or influence principles, can be justified instrumentally in terms of providing incentives for businesses to engage pro-actively in risk-reduction, to prevent or minimize the chance of wrongdoing in their commercial operations. However, the creation of 'best endeavours' defences[10] can also be understood to reflect the liberal state's desire to engage with those running and working in the company as moral agents. The creation of such defences—defences that reflect D's efforts to prevent wrongdoing—is a way of seeking to ensure that the risk of compliance failure in a regulated activity, and consequent penalization, will not deter

[8] See the discussion in ch 2.

[9] See José-Miguel Bello Y Villarino and Simon Bronitt (2024).

[10] Defences such as 'due diligence' undertaken, 'reasonable precautions' exercised, or 'adequate procedures' put in place.

ethically well-disposed participants from attempting successful engagement in it. As Gardner puts it, 'morally speaking, even a criminal wrong which is not a moral wrong should be defined in such a way that both committing it and *avoiding committing it* could, in principle, be actions of moral agents *qua* moral agents'.[11] The existence of 'best endeavours' defences is thus an appropriate acknowledgement of the desirability of reflecting, in the structures of liability, the development by ethically well-disposed corporate agents of their company into a real entity proactively orientated towards compliance. In that regard, the existence of such defences is an essential part of what it means to show adequate moral sensitivity to what is at stake for the individuals running and working for ethically well-disposed companies: their personal investment in the reputational as well as financial success of such companies.[12] These considerations are what makes the central case of a failure-to-prevent offence based on the control or influence principles, morally speaking, a central case in the liberal-welfarist state.

It is important to bear in mind some key differences between a defence focussed on corporate compliance efforts, and more traditional defences focused on (say) the reasonableness of D's conduct in an emergency, or under more or less sudden and severe emotional pressure. First, a defence focused on corporate compliance measures is a defence where Ds assert responsibility in full measure for their safeguarding actions. The claim is 'I did everything that could reasonably have been expected in safeguarding terms', a claim largely—albeit not wholly—inconsistent with reliance on individual cognitive or emotional defect or other impairment common to more familiar excuse claims. In that regard, in the latter kinds of case (such as duress or loss of self-control), the reasonableness of D's conduct at the time of the offence can usually be perfectly adequately assessed by a lay tribunal of fact, applying its common sense ethical judgement.[13] By way of contrast, a defence focused on corporate efforts to avoid wrongdoing may commonly turn on expert—regulatory or prosecutorial—assessment of a company's planning, preparation, and procedure engaged in prior to (as well as at the time of) the occurrence of the wrongdoing.[14]

Secondly, whereas excuses such as duress or loss of self-control are commonly subject to a synchronic judgement of an isolated and exceptional incident, corporate efforts to secure compliance are and ought to be assessed diachronically. The issue is: what was being done and what could reasonably have been done, in relation to a company's attitude to and capacity to implement safeguarding measures, in the period leading up to (and immediately following) the relevant incident? In answering such a question, what will be needed is understanding of the

[11] John Gardner (1998), 48 (my emphasis).
[12] See the discussion on this point in chs 1 and 6.
[13] See *R v Turner* [1975] 1 QB 835.
[14] See the discussion in Jeremy Horder (2004), ch 6.

relationship between both corporate and enforcer (regulatory or criminal) attitudes towards safeguarding values, an issue that has no analogy in 'exceptional circumstances' defences. In that sense, defences such as 'adequate (or reasonable) procedures or of 'due diligence' are best thought of not as trump cards D can play to escape liability, so much as bargaining chips in negotiations with prosecutors or regulators over the appropriate way not only to dispose of the case fairly but to plan for the future.[15]

In a theoretical sense, defences of 'adequate (or reasonable) precautions' or 'due diligence' are unusual defences, and have not received the attention from theorists that they might have done.[16] A safeguarding (control or influence-based) failure to prevent wrongdoing is what might be called a first-order normative failure: an 'outcome' failure. By contrast, a 'best endeavours' failure, such as a failure to take all reasonable precautions or to exercise all due diligence, is a second-order normative failure: an 'effort sufficiency' failure in relation to safeguarding obligations. It is an example of the wrongdoing involved in failing to try hard enough (or in the right way) to prevent or reduce the risk of a first-order failure.[17] It is tempting to think that this distinction between first- and second-order failures is essentially the same distinction as the distinction between the conduct element of a crime and its fault element, but things are not quite so simple. In '2 + 1' failure-to-prevent cases, the focus is not the question of whether D committed the wrongdoing token due to—say—negligence or recklessness (the classic question of fault-based responsibility). Instead, it is the question of whether it was reasonable to expect D to have had stricter safeguards, or to have monitored existing safeguards more closely, making wrongdoing of the relevant type—whether or not it occurred through someone's fault—less likely to occur.[18]

Further, there is a key difference in point of culpability. Suppose that a company fails catastrophically to prevent the abuse of someone in its care, contrary to section 21 of the Criminal Justice and Courts Act 2015, or badly neglects health and safety standards, leading to the death of an employee, contrary to section 1 of the Corporate Manslaughter and Corporate Homicide Act 2007. In such cases, the Crown bears the burden of showing that D's failures were in the relevant sense 'gross' failures. What that means is that the focus is only evidentially on D's (ex hypothesi) feeble efforts to succeed in safeguarding, and hence on the extent of

[15] With the fall-back position that D can appeal at trial to a jury that a prosecution should fail given the adequacy or reasonableness of procedures that were in place at the relevant time.

[16] See Jeremy Horder (2004), ch 6.

[17] On the significance to liability of the distinction between failures to succeed and failures to try, see John Gardner (1998).

[18] As I pointed out in ch 3, a conviction for a failure-to-prevent offence is possible even if deficiencies in safeguarding processes were not causally related to the likelihood of the offence occurring. See further Section 4.2 below.

any measurable departure from industry standards.[19] The focus in point of legal liability is on the 'vice' displayed in what is an instance of first-order wrongdoing, the evidence of blatant disregard (the opposite of due diligence) for safeguarding that led causally to the harm.[20] By contrast, when the question is whether or not D has taken sufficient precautions and exercised all due diligence, the question of legal liability is whether D has shown sufficient 'virtue', in pursuing a second-order goal: the goal of trying hard enough to prevent the possible occurrence of first-order wrongdoing. That 'virtue' question is, of course, then answered against a background in which regulators' values jostle with competing commercial priorities in shaping diachronic judgments of whether enough was done to secure compliance over time.

4.2 Wrongdoing, Causation, and Safeguarding Against Wrongdoing

In Chapters 1 and 2, we saw how safeguarding defences governed by the ascriptive element of the control principle, such as demonstrating 'adequate' or 'reasonable' procedures, or 'all due diligence', involve an assessment of whether a company was doing enough by way of safeguarding to prevent or reduce the risk of a *type* of wrongdoing occurring ('bribery', 'fraud', and 'the facilitation of tax evasion'). 'Types' of wrongdoing are abstract, acausal categories by reference to which tokens of wrongdoing can be identified as such, but the types themselves (unlike the tokens) lack a spatio-temporal location.[21] In this, safeguarding defences differ from some other kinds of excuse. Consider, for example, the new summary offence created by section 102(3) of the Economic Crime and Corporate Transparency Act 2023 Act. Section 102(3) reads:

> It is an offence for a person, without reasonable excuse, to—
> (a) deliver or cause to be delivered to the registrar, for any purpose of the Companies Acts, a document that is misleading, false or deceptive in a material particular, or
> (b) make to the registrar, for any purpose of the Companies Acts, a statement that is misleading, false or deceptive in a material particular.

In relation to this offence, if the excuse offered by D for offending—the ex hypothesi 'reasonable excuse'—is to do its excusatory work, it must play a causal role

[19] So, for example, in relation to corporate manslaughter, the jury must be invited merely to consider the extent to which D's conduct involved a breach of health and safety standards: Corporate Manslaughter and Corporate Homicide Act 2007, s 8(2).
[20] See Victor Tadros (2002), ch 10; Findlay Stark (2016); and Jeremy Horder (1997).
[21] Linda Wetzel (2006), s 3, discussed in ch 2.

in the commission of the offence. The (reasonable) excuse must be (part of) the explanation for the offending.[22] By contrast, as we saw in Chapter 3, when a safeguarding defence is in play, the causal role of the defence is not in issue. So, for example, in relation to an 'adequate procedures' defence, the prosecution can seek to defeat the defence by showing that the defendant's safeguarding procedures were inadequate in relation to the type of wrongdoing in issue (say, 'bribery'). The prosecution will not need to go on to show that the inadequacy of the procedures in some respect was what in fact led to the wrongdoing 'token' (the bribery that occurred as an event in space and time). It is enough to show that the company was simply not doing enough by way of safeguarding to prevent or reduce the risk of wrongdoing of the relevant type.

A useful illustration of this point is *Alphacell v Woodward*.[23] D was charged with 'causing' effluent to enter a river.[24] The effluent was discharged into the river from D's land, when vegetation blocked the operation of a mechanism, installed by D on his land, to ensure that effluent did not discharge into the river. The relevant mechanism had been inspected by D the weekend before the discharge took place, and found to be clear and in working order. D's claim was that the diligence exercised in checking for blockages meant D did not 'cause' the effluent to be discharged into the river: the discharge could (conveniently for D) be put down to an unaccountable 'act of God'. As we can now see, the defence argument sought to turn an abstract, acausal safeguarding claim, to the effect that adequate procedures were in place to prevent a particular *type* of harm ('pollution'), into a concrete, causal safeguarding claim that the adequacy of those procedures meant that the actual pollution—the polluting event, in space and time—was not caused by D at all. That argument was rightly rejected by the House of Lords. It would have been enough, in that regard, simply to observe that the offence with which D was charged was not subject to a safeguarding defence based on adequate procedures or due diligence. However, in justifying conviction, Lord Cross adopted a line of argument that in fact evaluates D's conduct in terms of safeguarding adequacy, in relation to pollution as a *type* of prohibited outcome. He said:

> All that the evidence shows is that, despite the false sense of security into which the appellants had been lulled by their experience over the last twelve months, vegetable matter was in fact liable to collect quite quickly . . . and although it may not be fair to blame them for not inspecting . . . more often than once a week, *if they did not have more frequent inspections, they were running the risk* of 'causing' polluting effluent to enter the river.[25]

[22] Following the principle in *R v Dadson* (1850) 3 C & K 148.
[23] [1972] AC 824.
[24] Contrary to the Rivers (Prevention of Pollution) Act 1951, s 2.
[25] [1972] AC 824, 846 (my emphasis).

We find a similar effort to justify conviction by turning an act-token-based causation argument into an act-type safeguarding failure argument, in *Empress Car Company (Abertillery) Ltd v National Rivers Authority*.[26]

In *Empress Car*, pollution was caused when an unknown third party gained access to D's site, and intentionally turned on a tap that released diesel oil into a river. In spite of the fact that the proximate cause of the pollution was the free, deliberate, and informed act of the third party, D was charged contrary to section 85(1) of the Water Resources Act 1991with 'causing poisonous, noxious or polluting matter or solid waste to enter controlled waters'. Accordingly, it was necessary for the court to explain D's liability for the offence, contrary to section 85(1), in terms of 'causation'.[27] Lord Hoffmann purported to do so by holding that, in the circumstances, the intervention of the third party was something within the range of normal events, rather than something wholly abnormal such a terrorist attack.[28] By contrast, though, Lord Clyde finds the element of causation in D's failure to fulfil (in my terms) a safeguarding control duty.[29] He said:

> The maintaining of a system, the carrying on of an enterprise, and the management of a going concern may each constitute causative factors . . . In many cases an omission may be analysed as the provision or operation of an inadequate or deficient system. Thus a failure to take precautions in relation to a risk of the escape of a pollutant in the course of the management of premises such as those which the appellants were occupying in the present case may be seen as an active operation for the purposes of causation.[30]

For Lord Clyde, thus, it is evaluation in terms of corporate (landowner) safeguarding failure, respecting a control duty, that provides the best justification for conviction in such cases. That is so, even if—for the purposes of statutory interpretation—such an argument must be distorted into intelligibility as an argument about 'causation'.

More generally, a duty-based safeguarding analysis is much better suited than ordinary causation enquiries to assessments of the role of organizations in relation to wrongdoing occurring under their control or influence. For example, it is in the nature of food manufacture and retailing, as business activities, that there is a risk of unfit food being put into circulation thereby.[31] Suppose, then, that there is a food poisoning incident traceable to a controlled entity within a food manufacturing

[26] [1998] UKHL 5.
[27] See the fuller discussion of this case in Jeremy Horder (2024).
[28] For criticism of this line of argument, see ibid.
[29] On control rights and duties, see ch 3. See also Dennis Baker (2021), 440: '[Empress Car] failed to take sufficient steps to prevent strangers from causing the oil to be released.'
[30] [1998] UKHL 5, 24.
[31] See the discussion in *Smedleys v Breed* [1974] AC 839 (HL).

firm or retail outlet. It makes perfect sense to judge the controlling food manufacturer or retailer by the yardstick of safeguarding measures that were—or could have been—taken in advance to eliminate or reduce the risks of food poisoning generally, as a type of wrongdoing, rather than by seeking to determine whether or not the particular poisoning can causally be traced to a given (faulty) action or omission on the controller's part.[32] The same point can be made about control or influence principle–based liability for the free, deliberate, and informed actions of third parties. When an employee or subsidiary company commits bribery in order to benefit the parent firm, there may be no causal link between the commission of that act and a particular safeguarding omission on the part of the firm. Nonetheless, it may still be true that, had bribery-prevention procedures been better, there would have been a smaller chance of bribery (as a type of wrongdoing) occurring. Morally speaking, under a liberal-welfarist approach, the failure to put in place better safeguarding procedures respecting bribery as a kind of wrongdoing (the second-order failure) may be more than sufficient to justify associating the firm with the occurrence of the bribery act-token (the first-order failure), as something for which it must take responsibility in criminal law for having failed to prevent.[33]

4.3 Welfare Capitalism and Compliance Obligations

Almost unnoticed, the creation of offences closely modelled on the central case ('2 + 1') version of the control principle has become one of the most significant post-war (and in particular post–EU membership) developments in UK criminal law. I will briefly track this development. A Westlaw search for the phrase 'commits an offence' reveals that in the twenty-seven years between 1945 and 1972 (the year of UK entry into the European Union), this phrase appeared in new legislation over 250 times, with fourteen appearances in statutory instruments. By contrast, in the forty-one years between 1972 and 2023, this phrase appears over 10,000 times, with over 4,300 such appearances being in statutory instruments. Whilst commentators have noted this huge growth in criminalization,[34] less well documented has been the parallel rise of defences to such crimes, defences often created in regulatory contexts applicable to businesses.

For example, consider Parliament's use of the term 'take all reasonable precautions and exercise all due diligence', as part of a criminal law defence, or as a way of

[32] Criminal liability may, of course, be imposed for safeguarding failures in this respect, whether or not any harm occurred. That is, of course, the approach to the creation of unacceptable risk under the Health and Safety at Work Act 1974. But—to repeat an important point—my concern is with a distinct form of criminal liability, the contingent form of liability known as failure to prevent crime. Such liability requires satisfaction of both the attributability and duty elements of the control principle.

[33] See Section 4.1 above for a discussion of the distinction between first- and second-order failures.

[34] For further discussion of the growth of criminalization, see James Chalmers and Fiona Leverick (2013).

defining the scope of a primary criminal law duty. There are over 1,000 instances in which Parliament has used this phrase in such a way since 1945, over 500 of them in statutory instruments. Even so, there were merely twenty-five such occasions on which this phrase was so used between 1900 and 1972 (with no uses of the phrase in statutory instruments in that period).[35] By way of contrast, between 1972 and 2023 there were over 1,000 uses of the phrase (with over 500 uses appearing in statutory instruments).[36] Perhaps significantly, the Blair–Brown years of Labour Government between 1997 and 2010 accounted for not far short of half these post-1972 instances (over 400 instances, including over 200 in statutory instruments).[37] One may surmise that the increasingly common use of the defence from 1972 onwards was, at least in part, a dimension of the Government's response to the need to bind businesses to observe an array of common European standards in a variety of fields, such as food standards.[38] Certainly, the exponential growth of offences in the post-1972 period to which the defence of 'all reasonable precautions and all due diligence' applies is a testament to the influence of the European Union's liberal-welfarist ideology on English corporate criminal law,[39] a far cry from the authoritarian populism to which the growth of criminal laws targeted at individuals is usually attributed.[40]

A historically significant example, considered in Chapter 3, is section 24(11) of the Trade Descriptions Act 1968, which provides in relation to trade descriptions offences:

[35] Possibly the earliest example of the use of the defence is in the Children and Young Persons Act 1933. Section 12(C) provided that: 'If—(a) a person sells on any premises any tobacco [, cigarette papers, or nicotine product] in contravention of a restricted premises order, and (b) the person knew, or ought reasonably to have known, that the sale was in contravention of the order, the person commits an offence . . . (3) It is a defence for a person charged with an offence under subsection (2) to prove that the person took all reasonable precautions and exercised all due diligence to avoid the commission of the offence.' Bearing in mind that a tobacconist would be found vicariously liable for a sale made by an employee, in contravention of the 1933 Act, this is in effect a use of the defence as a defence for a retailer's failure to prevent crime by another person. See the discussion of *Chuter v Freeth & Pocock* [1911] 2 KB 832, discussed in ch 1.

[36] To give a post-war example that was doubtless of concern to many right-thinking people, under section 23 of the Artificial Insemination of Cattle (Animal Health) (England and Wales) Regulations 1985, if D—including by oversight—caused P to supply semen from a semen shop other than in compliance with a semen shop licence, D committed an offence unless, by virtue of section 10 of the Animal Health and Welfare Act 1984, D had taken 'all reasonable steps and exercised all due diligence to avoid committing the offence.'

[37] Although the matter is not entirely clear, many of these offences were created as a result of the reorganization of legislation governing agricultural businesses following the Foot-and-Mouth outbreak in 2001 and the creation of the Department for the Environment, Food and Rural Affairs (DEFRA) that year.

[38] Some 231 statutes and 4,283 statutory instruments implemented EU obligations between 1993 and 2014, although clearly far from all of these would involve criminalization: https://www.bbc.co.uk/news/uk-politics-eu-referendum-36473105 (last accessed 28/08/2025).

[39] European Union (2018), 1: 'An extensive body of EU-wide law covers the entire food production and processing chain within the EU, as well as imported and exported goods.'

[40] See, e.g., John Pratt and Michelle Miao (2019).

> In any proceedings for an offence under this Act it shall . . . be a defence for the person charged to prove—
> (a) that the commission of the offence was due to a mistake or to reliance on information supplied to him or to the act or default of another person, an accident or some other cause beyond his control; and
> (b) that he took all reasonable precautions and exercised all due diligence to avoid the commission of such an offence by himself or any person under his control.[41]

A more recent example from secondary legislation—discussed in the Introduction—is the Consumer Protection from Unfair Trading Regulations 2008, which largely replaced the 1968 Act.[42] Amongst other things, the regulations create offences of making misleading statements or omissions, or engaging in aggressive trading practices, and section 13 provides for a two-year maximum penalty upon conviction. However, it is a defence under section 17 to show that an offence was due to the act or default of another person and that D 'took all reasonable precautions and exercised all due diligence to avoid the commission of such an offence by himself or any person under his control'.[43] In effect, so far as the offence of making false or misleading statements is concerned, section 17 turns the offence into one covering failures to prevent species of fraud, based on the control principle. The use of these phrases—'taking all reasonable precautions'; exercising all due diligence'—in conjunction with one another, is a classic example of the 'boiler plate' drafting technique that has characterized much of regulatory criminal law creation by Parliament in the late twentieth and twenty-first centuries.

Peter Ramsay has pointed to the twentieth century rise of regulatory criminal law (and in particular of strict liability offences), and of 'best endeavours' defences to such offences, as a feature of liberal-welfarist concern for risk-reduction. Rather than placing the burden of ensuring their safety solely on the individual consumer or workers (a common feature of individualist, classical liberal approaches[44]), or placing the burden wholly on state officials (the dirigiste social-democratic approach), liberal-welfarism carves out a domain of welfare responsibility for companies themselves. It places on them the responsibility for developing systems and attitudes conducive to preventing or reducing the risks from, say, adulterated food, or from unsafe working conditions.[45] As Ramsay puts it:

[41] See CJ Miller, Brian W Harvey, and Deborah L Parry (1998), ch 15.
[42] See also the General Product Safety Regulations 2005, s 29.
[43] See, to similar effect, Consumer Credit Act 1974, s 168; Weights and Measures Act 1985, s 34; and Consumer Protection Act 1987, s 39.
[44] See the classic discussion in Hugh Collins (1984).
[45] Peter Ramsay (2006), 49. See also Tom Crook (2007).

> If [the entrepreneur or company] causes, or in respect of some offences fails to prevent, the harm then she is liable . . . Where liability allows for a defence of due diligence, a given industry standard is enforced. Where liability is absolute, even meeting a given industry standard would be insufficient, and the law implicitly demands that participants seek continually to improve their safety standards.[46]

As indicated in the Introduction, under liberal-welfare capitalism (as under dirigiste social democracy[47]), it is recognized that Government has a role in regulating businesses in order to try to guarantee that, for example, 'goods and services do not have an adverse effect on the current well-being of the public at large, future generations, or the environment'.[48] However, in liberal-welfarist jurisdictions, states typically seek to co-opt firms themselves into doing more to deliver on the 'welfare' element of welfare capitalism, especially larger firms. For example, whereas all firms—large or small—are required to ensure that their own staff understand and follow safeguarding requirements in relation to food safety, larger firms must also be able to show:

(a) that they use reliable suppliers who follow accepted Codes of Practice and have effective quality and quantity control procedures [and]
(b) that they require suppliers to provide written confirmation that food meets the quality required, (a warranty).[49]

In effect, this is a trading standards obligation compliance with which the state devolves to larger firms, in the expectation that they will use the power given to them by their market position to influence other firms to observe welfare-driven food safety standards.[50] By contrast, small retailers (including farm shops) are only likely to be prosecuted when they themselves are responsible for breaching food safety legislation, as by operating dirty premises or applying misleading descriptions to foods.[51] Even in the latter case, smaller firms will not necessarily be under obligations to check that, say, imported wine accurately states alcohol strength, because it would be disproportionate to expect them to set up an independent testing

[46] Ibid. To some extent, there is an oversimplification here. The law employs different 'industry' standards, sometimes applying what I called the 'ethical CEO's perspective' to judge compliance, and sometimes applying the 'stereotypically risk-averse compliance officer's perspective' to judge compliance, as well as imposing absolute liability in some cases. See the discussion in Section 4.5 below.

[47] See Gøsta Esping-Andersen (1990), and the discussion in the Introduction.

[48] Dennis R Cooley (2009), 354.

[49] Humber Authorities Food Liaison Group (1991), 12. The warranty needs to be as specific as possible as the courts have criticized 'blanket' assurances in warranties.

[50] In recent times, the same approach has led to obligations being placed on large firms to use their market position to disadvantage potential contracting partners overseas engaged in human rights abuses. See the discussion in ch 5.

[51] Humber Authorities Food Liaison Group (1991), 11.

system when selling small volumes of the goods in question.[52] This kind of differentiated regulatory 'steering' approach is anathema to classical liberalism, with its strict emphasis on the need for rules to be general in application: to each person alike.[53] However, it is submitted that liberal-welfarism rightly acknowledges the importance of a differentiated approach, one that acknowledges the special compliance challenges faced by small traders, by way of contrast with the power possessed by larger firms to demand compliance not only from their own employees but from other firms with which they deal.[54]

4.4 Compliance Approaches in Small and Large Firms

In analysing the attitudes of enforcers as well as businesses to compliance, the Local Better Regulation Office has observed:

> Given that business regulations have often been designed to reduce the risk of harm, regulatory culture has evolved in a way that focuses on prevention and protection. In the past, this has sometimes led to regulatory delivery being viewed solely as a way to stop negative behaviour, rather than a mechanism to support a more positive approach towards compliance. In turn, this has meant that regulatory reform has tended to focus on the costs of regulatory interactions, rather than acknowledgement of their potential benefits.[55]

In this passage, we see the Regulation Office in effect endorsing the theory of liberal-welfarism, according to which it is realistic to think that companies can be incentivized to become positive responders or proactive learners in relation to compliance obligations, an ambition embedded in the notion of a requirement to take all reasonable precautions and exercise all due diligence. The Regulation Office is implicitly criticizing the dirigiste social-democratic approach to corporate criminal liability. As indicated earlier, according to that approach, corporate regulatory or criminal wrongdoing must be met predominantly with a retributive and deterrent approach. That is because it is supposed that companies cannot by and large be trusted themselves to become motivated to be positive responders or proactive learners, in interpreting and applying obligations to take all reasonable precautions and exercise all due diligence.[56] I shall now suggest that this supposition

[52] See, e.g., *Hurley v Mlartinez & Co* (1990) 154 JP 821. There has been heavy criticism of cases that effectively impose on small retailers obligations to check with overseas manufacturers that UK regulations have been complied with: see, e.g., *Riley v Webb* (1987) 151 JP 372.
[53] See, e.g., FE Hayek (2007), 44 and FE Hayek (1960), discussed in the Introduction.
[54] This point is pursued further in relation to obligations to deter human rights abuses in ch 5.
[55] Local Better Regulation Office (2012), 6.
[56] Se the discussion in the Introduction.

is mistaken, and that there is sound evidence to believe that a liberal-welfarist approach to compliance can be effective.

Vickers et al have distinguished different types of small-firm attitude towards regulatory compliance.[57] Vickers et al identify:

1. 'Avoider-Outsiders', whose knowledge of legal requirements is very limited, and whose presence in the marketplace may be ephemeral, transient, and episodic, leading them to prioritize short-term benefit and avoid contact with officialdom, especially in enterprises operating in the grey or shadow economy;[58]
2. 'Minimalist Reactors', who are quite similar to avoider-outsiders, but because they have a more stable presence in the marketplace, may to some extent engage in (reluctant) regulatory compliance;
3. 'Positive Responders', a significant proportion of UK businesses, who are generally tolerant of and responsive to regulatory intervention, seeing compliance as important to the interests of staff and customers, and regarding enforcement as important to prevent unfair competition; and
4. 'Proactive Learners', who embed law requirements and good practice in organizational activity, and then go beyond this by treating regulatory intervention as an opportunity to learn and improve. Proactive learners are likely to be larger firms, perhaps in industries where commercial activity is generally more hazardous.

Vickers et al suggest that most small firms are likely to fall into categories (3) and (3), with larger firms being the biggest proportion in category (4). As indicated in Section 4.1, I will take categories (3) and (4) as the ideal-types in relation to which companies' safeguarding procedures should be assessed.

With that background in mind, it is important to highlight evidence showing that businesses predominantly seek to comply with applicable criminal legislation and regulation, rather than to evade it. The maintenance of a good reputation for law abidingness and for business integrity, more broadly, can be 'mission critical' for many businesses: a key dimension of their own active well-being.[59] The National Audit Office has estimated the annual cost of regulatory compliance for UK businesses generally to be between £70 and £100 billion (the cost of compliance in the United States between 1970 and 2018 was $1 trillion[60]): 3–4

[57] Ian Vickers et al (2005), 160–65.

[58] See, further, Hazel Croall (1989).

[59] The idea that, when an obligation is 'mission-critical'—central to the raison d'être of a business—this justifies additional or enhanced obligations is drawn from US case law: see, e.g., *In re the Boeing Company Derivative Litig No 2019-0907* (Delaware Chancery 7 September 2021).

[60] Shikhar Singla (2023). In the United States, a study has shown that from 1980 to 2020, 292 billion hours were spent by firm on preparing and filling 2.24 trillion forms to comply with 36,702 regulations, accounting for 3 per cent of the average company's wage bill: Joseph Kalmenovitz (2023).

per cent of GDP.[61] These figures reflect the fact that, more broadly, as Department for Business, Energy and Industrial Strategy concluded in 2020, '[r]egulation was seen [by businesses] as a process that needed to be followed and, for some, often medium and large sized businesses, this was very much part of the day-to-day running of the business'.[62]

There is also more sector-specific evidence that businesses take legal compliance seriously.[63] For the Food Standard Agency, writing in 2021, 'food business compliance with food safety regulation has remained high with slight increases in all four countries of the UK in the past six years'.[64] In 2017–18, of the 14,000 industrial permits the Environment Agency regulates in England, there were non-compliance issues in fewer than 3 per cent of those permits.[65] In the financial services sector, the Financial Conduct Authority's survey of regulated firms showed that the overwhelming majority (89 per cent of fixed firms) regarded the launching of a criminal investigation or the withdrawing of authorized status as being effective in reducing further harm to the industry, and—most importantly—67 per cent of such firms reviewed the robustness of their own compliance processes and procedures, after hearing of an investigation.[66] According to 2022–23 figures from the Health and Safety at Work Executive, in relation to over 16,800 inspections conducted in that year, in 79 per cent cases businesses said they had taken action as a result of a visit,[67] and (a significant point bearing on legitimacy) 89 per cent stated the outcome of the visit was proportionate to the risks identified.[68]

A broader 2020 study of business attitudes towards regulatory compliance has concluded:

> For many medium and large businesses, regardless of sector, complying with regulation was perceived as a series of processes to be followed. These processes

[61] National Audit Office (2017), 4. The House of Commons Regulatory Policy Committee has estimated that the increase, alone, in the cost of regulatory compliance for UK business between 2019 and 2023 was £17.2 billion: https://rpc.blog.gov.uk/2023/09/15/the-increase-in-the-cost-of-regulation-on-business-and-the-end-of-the-bit/ (last accessed 10/05/2024). See also New approach to ensure regulators and regulation support growth (HTML)—GOV.UK (last accessed 28/03/2025). It has been estimated that the regulated financial sector in the United Kingdom spends £34.2 billion each year on compliance with applicable criminal laws: https://www.thebanker.com/Video/The-cost-of-financial-crime-compliance-in-the-UK2#:~:text=%C2%A334.2%20billion%20is%20the,financial%20crime%20compliance%20(FCC (last accessed 08/06/2023). See also Oxford Economics (2024).

[62] Department for Business, Energy and Industrial Strategy (2020), introduction.

[63] See Ian Ayers and John Braithwaite (1992), 22: 'Corporate actors are not just value maximizers—of profits or of reputation. They are also often concerned to do what is right, to be faithful to their identity as a law-abiding citizen, and to sustain a self-concept of social responsibility.'

[64] https://www.gov.uk/government/statistics/united-kingdom-food-security-report-2021/united-kingdom-food-security-report-2021-theme-5-food-safety-and-consumer-confidence (last accessed 10/06/2023).

[65] See the discussion in Peter Kellett (2020), 190.

[66] Financial Conduct Authority (2023), 54.

[67] Research clearly indicated that in-person visits are more likely to lead to action taken to secure compliance, in the field of health and safety: Frank Peck et al (2012), 20.

[68] Health and Safety Executive (2022–23), 11.

> were the result of businesses striving to implement regulations consistently across organisations. As a result, these processes were often perceived to be part of core operations . . . Overall, medium and large businesses were more likely to feel sanguine about the need to comply with regulations, and accepted that by doing so they demonstrated that the business was abiding by the law . . . small and micro businesses also perceived regulations as processes to be followed and legal requirements.[69]

Almost needless to say, behind such overall figures lies a more complex story, in part stemming from the wide variation in types of (criminal) regulation. On the one hand, the bigger the business, the greater its capacity is likely to be to absorb the cost of compliance with additional regulation, whatever the business's attitude to that regulation. Moreover, evidence suggests that big businesses may sometimes favour certain types of regulation, if its introduction is likely to make it more difficult for their less well-resourced competitors to continue to compete in the market place while remaining compliant.[70] For example, an increase in the minimum wage will make little medium-term difference to firms that can afford to slim down their workforce numbers over time, and perhaps replace some workers with automated processes. Contrariwise, such an increase may threaten the economic viability of much smaller competitors, for whom such a response does not make business sense (even if it were affordable). On the other hand, compliance with some regulatory requirements, such as General Data Protection Regulation requirements, may be extremely challenging for big firms storing large amounts of potentially confidential data in different forms over a number of sites, but relatively straightforward for smaller firms holding little material of this type on a single site.[71]

More generally, though, the development of compliance policy and strategy may be more challenging for smaller businesses. Evidence shows that, in smaller businesses, the costs of compliance take up far more of the time of senior management than in larger enterprises. In smaller firms, senior managers themselves may have to take personal responsibility for criminal and regulatory compliance, as well as for leading the firm's revenue-earning activities.[72] Small businesses frequently cannot afford more than the minimum in terms of, for example, accounting and bookkeeping services. Unsurprisingly, thus, there is far less likely to be a documented and systematic compliance programme in a small business. In the United

[69] Department for Business, Energy and Industrial Strategy (2020), 13. On small business attitudes, see further Better Regulation Executive (2010), 1.

[70] See the discussion in Shikhar Singla (2023).

[71] Department for Business, Energy and Industrial Strategy (2020), 6. Out of the 2.768 million VAT and/or PAYE-registered UK businesses, only 58,000 operated from more than one site in 2022: https://www.ons.gov.uk/businessindustryandtrade/business/activitysizeandlocation/bulletins/ukbusinessactivitysizeandlocation/2022 (last accessed 20/05/2024).

[72] Frank Peck et al (2012), 9.

States, 90 per cent of the 5,000 (mainly, small- to medium-sized) firms sentenced for federal crimes between 1991 and 2023 lacked such a programme.[73] As Welsh and White explain:

> [T]he very size of small businesses creates a special condition—which can be referred to as resource poverty—that distinguishes them from their larger counterparts and requires some very different management approaches. Resource poverty results because of various conditions unique to smaller companies. For one thing, small businesses tend to be clustered in highly fragmented industries . . . that have many competitors which are prone to price-cutting as a way to build revenues.[74]

Small businesses are more likely to perceive the need to comply with regulations as separate to supposedly 'core' operations. Such businesses tend to distinguish between business processes implemented by themselves, for their own benefit, and business processes that need to be implemented as a result of regulatory requirements, but which are not necessarily perceived to be for their benefit.[75] The contrast being drawn here is one that can be explained as a contrast between an understanding of the values underpinning regulation as values to be simply acknowledged and so (at best) 'honoured', as compared with an understanding of those values as ones to be positively embraced and so 'promoted' for their own sake.[76]

Where a corporate culture develops in which regulatory values—and their associated obligations—are understood as merely to be acknowledged (and so, at best, honoured), they will be more vulnerable to neglect or disregard when economic hard choices must be made.[77] That this is a particular risk for smaller firms is borne out in Croall's valuable study of regulatory enforcement against trading companies, which was populated largely by 'restaurants, food stores, grocers, bakers, butchers, and garages'.[78] By contrast, for many medium-sized and larger businesses, with greater financial and organizational room for manoeuvre, complying

[73] https://www.complianceandethics.org/5-reasons-why-small-and-mid-size-companies-need-compliance-programs/ (last accessed 14/05/2024).

[74] John A Welsh and Jerry F White (1981). See also David Smallbone et al (2012), who refers to 'more limited internal resources compared with larger firms; a typically narrower base of customers and product lines across which to spread risk; and less bargaining power with a variety of external actors, including customers, suppliers and finance providers'.

[75] See, further, the discussion in Frank Peck et al (2012).

[76] See, on the distinction between honouring and promoting values, David McNaughton and Piers Rawling (1992).

[77] For example, an EU-wide study found that it is in small- to medium-sized enterprises that around 82 per cent of all work-related injuries and up to 90 per cent of fatal accidents take place: F Salguero-Caparrós et al (2020).

[78] Hazel Croall (1989), 162. It must be kept in mind, in that respect, that most business-focused regulatory crimes are crimes of strict liability, and hence the risk of committing them is part of the inherent risk of engaging in business at all.

with regulation is perceived (regardless of sector) as something to be incorporated into normal business processes; and hence, compliance comes to be perceived as a part of core operations.[79] In that regard, it is unclear whether the introduction and spread of AI-driven automated compliance management systems will create or reduce disparities in point of capacity to implement robust compliance procedures, as between small and large firms.[80]

For example, providers of such systems tend to assume that a firm will have a compliance department devoted to matching the AI compliance system with the needs of the firm:

> Best practices for AI integration involve a collaborative approach, where compliance teams work closely with IT departments. This collaboration ensures that AI tools are tailored to the specific needs of the compliance department, maximising their effectiveness. Training staff to work with AI tools is crucial, as it ensures that employees understand how to interpret AI-generated insights and apply them in their compliance tasks. Ensuring AI strategies align with regulatory standards and requirements is another critical aspect of integration. Compliance teams must ensure that AI tools comply with existing regulatory frameworks, particularly regarding data handling and privacy. Regular reviews and updates of AI tools are necessary to keep pace with evolving regulatory landscapes and technological advancements.[81]

How realistic is it to suppose that a small firm will be able to adapt their business processes to match such a large firm-biased understanding of 'best practice' in relation to AI-generated compliance?

A purist or hard-line approach to these issues might be to say that small-scale entrepreneurs, who cannot afford to run consistently regulation-compliant businesses, should simply exit the marketplace. However, such an approach is simplistic and undesirable. As discussed in Chapter 2, it would disproportionately impact ethnic-minority businesses and businesses run by women, who are to be found proportionately in greater numbers at leadership level (as compared with white men) in the small business sector.[82] In that regard, any assessment of the adequacy of safeguarding attitudes, processes, and procedures ought to encompass evidence of reliable practices and good habits, and not just more formal 'systems', if it is to be a test capable of fair application to (say) a close-knit family firm. The notion of 'procedure' or 'system' may lend itself to interpretation in terms of the formal, bureaucratic requirements characteristic of larger firms that, if they are not to lose a sense

[79] Department for Business, Energy and Industrial Strategy (2020), 13.
[80] See José-Miguel Bello Y Villarino and Simon Bronitt (2024).
[81] https://gradient-ascent.com/ai-in-compliance/ (last accessed 06/06/2025.
[82] Anuradha Basu and Eser Altinay (2002); Anuradha Basu (2004). See the discussion of this point in ch 2.

of corporate direction, must govern employees, outlets, and subsidiaries through such means. What, though, of the sole proprietor or small family firm, for which such a mode of governance is either superfluous or an inferior substitute for personal guidance, because personal example and charismatic authority may—in that business context—be as or more important than rule-governance?[83] Family firms characterized by a *gemeinschaft* mode of operation may often embrace paternalistic forms of leadership, in which 'a dominant leader . . . treats followers as if they were part of the family, whilst relying on hierarchy and expecting loyalty and obedience in return.'[84] What is needed, thus, is an approach to the interpretation of 'reasonable precautions', 'adequate procedures', and due diligence that accounts for small (family) firm modes of operation, and does not seek to drive such firms out of the market by enforcement of an over-bureaucratized conception of these ideals.

4.5 Different Dimensions to Stringency in Safeguarding Obligations

In pure strict liability cases, analysed in terms of the control principle, the controller is regarded as having been under an obligation to take steps, however costly or difficult, that—in counterfactual terms—would have made a decisive difference to the outcome. This can be called an 'outcome-stringent' obligation.[85] Such obligations are considered further below. In some cases, though, in the application of the control principle's ascriptive question, the counterfactual analysis will not be outcome-stringent. Instead, the counterfactual safeguarding question will be 'risk-stringent': might the taking of certain steps have reduced to an acceptable level the *risk* of a prohibited outcome of the relevant type occurring?[86] For example, if I am going directly to sell to consumers food that may contain nuts, it is possible that at some point a consumer will have an allergic reaction to something I sold them; but that does not necessarily mean I have to put measures in place to guarantee that this will not happen to any given consumer (outcome-stringency). Broadly speaking, I may simply need to reduce to an acceptable level the risk that my customers may unwittingly come into contact with allergy-provoking elements in their food, by focusing on generic safeguarding in relation to the outcome-type. This could be done by (say) implementing proper staff training, paying attention to the sourcing and preparation of ingredients, and providing a clear warning to consumers.[87] In

[83] Alexander Fries, Nadine Kammerlander, and Max Leitterstorf (2021), s 4.

[84] Ibid.

[85] See, further, Jeremy Horder (2024). The classic case illustrating such outcome-stringent reasoning is *Smedleys v Breed* [1974] AC 839 (HL).

[86] What I am calling 'counterfactual' analysis is sometimes referred to in the law-and-economics literature as the focus on a 'causal link' as opposed to 'causation': see Mark F Grady (1983), 804–05.

[87] See, further, https://www.food.gov.uk/business-guidance/allergen-guidance-for-food-businesses (last accessed 27/07/2023).

such cases, the seller's obligations are being guided by a risk-stringent obligation, as opposed to an outcome-stringent obligation. Obligations to have in place adequate (or reasonable) safeguarding procedures, or to take all reasonable steps and exercise all due diligence are risk-stringent forms of safeguarding obligation.

The obligations relating to risk-stringency, and hence the basis for applying the ascriptive element to the control and influence principles, have different dimensions to them. First, there may be more or less stringency as it relates to the *nature* of the risk. Safeguarding against severe allergic reactions to food products clearly needs in principle to be more stringent than safeguarding against a risk that a food product may stain someone's clothes. Secondly, more or less stringency may be demanded depending on *degree* of risk involved in an activity, before safeguarding steps of any kind must be taken (or before existing measures must be strengthened). There will be a less stringent approach to the degree of risk, if controllers are obligated to put in place some kind of safeguarding procedures—or strengthen them—only if the risk that certain outcomes will occur is high.[88] Obviously, the more serious or widespread a harm may be, if it results from business activity, the lower the degree of risk of its occurrence that will trigger the need for safeguarding steps to be taken. In that regard, related to both the nature and the degree of risk will be what is demanded of the safeguarder in terms of the intensity of risk-prevention procedures.

For example, in *Alphacell v Woodward*,[89] Lord Cross justified the company's conviction for a strict liability pollution offence, by pointing to the fact that the company could have implemented more intensive kinds of safeguarding (such as more frequent checks), even if these would not necessarily have guaranteed that the pollution incident was avoided. Risk-based obligations may also be more or less stringent in relation to the *range* of risks that must be addressed through safeguarding. In this sense, safeguarding analysis is risk-stringent when it requires controllers to anticipate different types of risk of a prohibited outcome or outcomes occurring, and put in place procedures to deal with each risk. It is arguable that when the House of Lords applied the duty criterion of the control principle in the *Empress Car* case, it applied a risk-stringent obligation in this range-focused sense.[90] The company in that case was obliged to safeguard not only against reasonably obvious risks that (say) a mechanical malfunction or flood would lead to effluent seeping from the storage tank, but also to safeguard against trespass by malign actors bent on sabotaging the tank to release effluent.[91]

[88] Contrariwise, an approach to the degree of risk is more stringent when there is an obligation to put safeguarding procedures in place—or enhance them—even if the risk of the occurrence of the prohibited outcome is merely realistically possible, or slightly enhanced.

[89] [1972] AC 824.

[90] *Empress Car Company (Abertillery) Ltd v National Rivers Authority* [1998] UKHL 5.

[91] See the analysis in Jeremy Horder (2024).

The UK Government's 2010 guidance on 'adequate procedures' for corporate bribery-prevention provides a useful illustration of these distinctions in action. Consider paragraph 6 of the Introduction to the guidance:

> Commercial organisations should adopt a risk-based approach to managing bribery risks. Procedures should be proportionate to the risks faced by an organisation. No policies or procedures are capable of detecting and preventing all bribery. A risk-based approach will, however, serve to focus the effort where it is needed and will have most impact. A risk-based approach recognises that the bribery threat to organisations varies across jurisdictions, business sectors, business partners and transactions.[92]

In stating that 'no policies or procedures are capable of detecting and preventing all bribery', the Government acknowledges that its approach to commercial bribery is not outcome-stringent, but risk-stringent. The possible occurrence of bribery in the course of running a business need not be treated in the same way as (say) the possible occurrence of a nuclear explosion. In general terms, under a risk-stringent approach, safeguarding against bribery (or fraud) may legitimately be addressed as part of a broader set of questions about how much time, effort, and expense can reasonably be justified in managing each and every business risk during a relevant period, such as fiscal year or for the duration of, say, a five-year development strategy. This is what I will refer to as the approach to the risk of wrongdoing adopted by the 'ethical, risk-embracing Chief Executive Officer'.

The passage cited does not say anything specifically about what I referred to above as the 'nature' of the bribery risk firms should be considering. In this context, the nature of the bribery risk means, for example, the risk of encountering demands for unlawful payments for routine administrative actions, for excessive hospitality, or (more seriously) payments for the award of contracts or for favourable exercises of official discretion. However, turning to the Government's avowedly 'risk-based approach', the approach appears to endorse a stringent approach to risks for which the company must account, with regard to the *range* of risks of bribery (whatever its nature) being committed. So, the passage makes it clear that firms must be alert to the possibility of bribery occurring in different jurisdictions, in different business sectors, in different types of transaction, and with different business partners. By contrast, there is seemingly a more flexible approach to the *degree* of risk that bribery may be committed in each of these contexts, and hence to the intensity of safeguarding that may be needed. The passage anticipates that anti-bribery measures may not be necessary in relation to at least some business sectors, transactions, and business partners, if the risk is very low. As we saw in

[92] Ministry of Justice (2010), para 6.

Chapter 2, this issue was the subject of a specific legislative provision where the risk of fraud is concerned.[93] There cannot be a 'one size fits all' approach to bribery prevention, even when such prevention is needed. For example, there might a significant risk for a UK company trading in Blueland that its employees will be asked to make small 'administrative payments' on the rare occasions when they will need to have documents officially stamped. That risk will need to be addressed with appropriate guidance, but with nothing like the intensity required if there is also a significant risk of a company's agents asking for large payments to be made into secret bank accounts, if access is to be granted to officials in charge of multimillion-dollar procurement contracts.

Returning to the issue of outcome-stringent safeguarding obligations, cases of strict liability pose problems of fairness when the costs and burdens of discharging the obligations are out of all proportion to the harmfulness or riskiness of the outcome.[94] Whatever one's general view of strict liability, though, outcome-stringent obligations are clearly appropriate at least in some cases: for example, when the stakes are very high, if safeguarding goes wrong.[95] If an incident at a nuclear installation leads to an explosion, then the controlling entity would rightly be judged by the yardstick of whether it has failed to take steps, however costly or difficult to implement, that would have guaranteed the prevention of explosions. Under section 13 of the Radioactive Substances Act 1993, the following offence is made punishable by up to five years' imprisonment:

> [N]o person shall, except in accordance with an authorisation granted in that behalf under this subsection, dispose of any radioactive waste on or from any premises which are used for the purposes of any undertaking carried on by him, or cause or permit any radioactive waste to be so disposed of, if (in any such case) he knows or has reasonable grounds for believing it to be radioactive waste.

No provision was made by Parliament under the 1993 Act for any defence of due diligence, or of 'act of default of another'. In this kind of case, an insistence on nothing less than a successful safeguarding strategy—whatever the effort and cost—may be both necessary and proportionate.[96]

As is well-known, in *AG for Hong Kong v Gammon*,[97] the Privy Council adopted just such an approach when interpreting ordinances concerned with building

[93] Section 199(4) of the 2023 Act created the following defence to an alleged failure to prevent fraud: 'It is a defence for the relevant body to prove that, at the time the fraud offence was committed . . . (b) it was not reasonable in all the circumstances to expect the body to have any prevention procedures in place.'

[94] A classic example is that of *Smedleys v Breed* [1974] AC 839 (HL).

[95] Jeremy Horder (2024).

[96] After all, a company bidding for contracts to transport hazardous waste can build the cost of such a safeguarding strategy into its contract price.

[97] [1985] AC 1 (PC).

safety, and a risk of injury or damage. The facts were that a lateral support for a building had been removed by a subcontractor on site, in breach of one of the ordinances. Strict liability was imposed on the subcontractor (making the main contractor liable vicariously), in circumstances in which it was said that the risk of injury or damage might 'frequently be enormous', if the statutory requirements were not followed.[98] Accordingly, so far as safeguarding was concerned, the Privy Council took the view that:

> criminal liability and punishment were needed as a deterrent against slipshod or incompetent supervision, control or execution of the building works. The imposition of strict liability . . . clearly would emphasise to those concerned the need for high standards of care in the supervision and execution of the work.[99]

This is an example of the use of an outcome-stringent evaluation of D's conduct ('more could have been done'), without it following from that evaluation that any blame should be attached to D, if the incident occurred in spite of high safeguarding standards being observed. That may sound paradoxical. One might ask how it can be right to criticize a company for applying a broadly satisfactory safeguarding solution, simply on the grounds that an optimal—safety maximizing—approach would have done more to reduce the risk.[100] One way of supporting the outcome-stringent application of the ascriptive question under the control or influence principles, in cases such as *Gammon*, is to draw a distinction between different ethical corporate-professional perspectives on adequate safeguarding.

Making safeguarding compliance a top priority might be wholly appropriate (indeed, essential) in some cases. For some organizations, a stringent safeguarding obligation of some kind is their raison d'être (as in the case of prisons) or is in some respect 'mission critical', as in the cases of aircraft safety or the operation of nuclear reactors. In such cases, the ethically appropriate perspective from which to assess the adequacy of D's compliance processes is what can be called the risk specialist perspective of the 'risk-averse, perfectionist compliance officer'. This is a person focused solely on securing the robustness of compliance processes and, relatively speaking, indifferent to competing calls on time and resources within their company. In effect, it is the perspective on safeguarding of such a hypothetical person that is adopted by the Privy Council in *Gammon*. However, the adoption of such a perspective in determining the nature and scope of safeguarding obligations may not be appropriate in all fields of corporate activity, or for all kinds of compliance within a given field. So, for example, whilst a demolition firm should doubtless

[98] Ibid., 8 (per Lord Scarman).

[99] Ibid.

[100] For example, in *Alphacell v Woodward* [1972] AC 824 (considered earlier), the magistrates trying the case had accepted expert evidence that the appellants had taken all 'reasonable' steps to ensure that polluted water did not enter the river.

try to safeguard against noise generated by its activities, noise reduction (whilst important, in general) need be seen as neither its raison d'être nor—one might plausibly argue—even as a mission critical element of its business. In such a case, the right perspective on safeguarding against noise pollution is the 'risk-generalist' perspective of what can be called the ethical but risk-embracing Chief Executive Officer (CEO).

From a risk generalist (as opposed to risk specialist) perspective, all relevant business and commercial risks must be managed responsibly within a relevant period, such as the fiscal year or (say) a corporate five-year plan. So, the question for the risk-embracing, but ethical CEO is: how much time, effort, and expense can reasonably be justified in managing each and every business risk during that period? In that regard, the hypothetical, ethical CEO will be 'risk-embracing', meaning that they will actively seek properly to assess and address all relevant risks rather than ignoring them, 'kicking the can down the road', and so on. So, answering the question just asked may very well involve the ethical CEO in balancing the risk of—say—a safety breach, against the gain from pursuing some other conflicting (and perhaps incommensurable) but important goal, such as increasing salaries for the lowest paid employees. That may lead the ethical CEO to look for and adopt what is commonly known as a 'satisficing' solution to a problem of risk: a solution that addresses a risk by reaching an 'acceptability' threshold, even if the solution may not be optimal.[101] Broadly speaking, obligations to establish 'adequate' or 'reasonable' procedures to guard against harm or wrongdoing, of a kind familiar in failure-to-prevent financial crimes, are informed by this risk-stringent perspective on safeguarding. Few, if any, firms are expected to adopt a 'safety at any cost' approach to (say) bribery or fraud prevention. The right approach is one that balances risk-reduction in an ethical way against the other legitimate demands on a firm's time and resources.

Most importantly, the 'active striving' account of safeguarding defended in this chapter should be regarded as compatible with the adoption of either of the perspectives on safeguarding just outlined. Accordingly, what legitimately counts as 'active striving' will differ, depending on which perspective is being employed to determine a company's safeguarding attitudes, processes, and practices. In that regard, we should keep in mind that over-safeguarding increases rather that reduces social costs. Speaking of corporate liability in tort for the acts of a third party, in terms of 'expected accident cost', as Posner J put it (in explaining the negligence standard):

[101] On 'satisficing', see Herbert A Simon (1956). Commonly, where the law provides a defence of 'reasonable excuse', or where the obligation is do no more than what is 'reasonably practicable' (as under the Health and Safety at Work Act 1974), then what is envisaged in general is that the adoption of a 'satisficing' solution is enough to warrant an excuse.

> The analytically, not necessarily the operationally, most precise [expression of the standard] . . . is that it involves determining whether the burden of precautions is less than the magnitude of the accident, if it occurs, multiplied by the probability of occurrence . . . If the burden is less, the precaution should be taken.[102]

Courts have held that where (additional) risks involved in failing to take a precautionary step are small, but the costs of taking that step are large, D will not be required to take those steps.[103] In Dov Weisman's helpful analysis,[104] companies are morally obligated to invest in safety precautions until the lesser of the following two points is reached: (1) the point at which further expenditure on safety would threaten the long-term survival of the activity or (2) the point at which further expenditure would reduce the well-being of each person responsible for bearing precaution costs by more than it would increase the expected well-being of each person exposed to the risk. Such a safeguarding policy can be called an 'ethically efficient' approach.

4.6 Reasonable Precautions and Due Diligence: Whose Responsibility?

A question may arise, in relation to any defence focused on efforts undertaken to prevent wrongdoing, concerning whose efforts are in law to count, for the purposes of establishing the defence. For example, it is perfectly possible that senior management may have instituted robust safeguarding procedures, but that an employee has in a given instance failed to abide by those procedures; or contrariwise, it could be that whilst senior management have done nothing to ensure safeguarding, employees themselves take as much care as possible to prevent wrongdoing. The existence of these—and other—possibilities is a product of the (very commonly) ethically heterogenous nature of firms with two or more associated persons.[105] Consistent with the theory developed in Chapter 3, on my account, what matters is whether or not the directors (the supreme executive authority within a firm) have done enough collectively—as by instituting appropriate processes and procedures to be followed by employees—to safeguard against wrongdoing. If there is a concern about such an approach, it is that, remote as they may frequently be from the place in which offences are committed, directors seem to be in a weak position to secure compliance, as compared with employees (and their immediate line managers) 'at the coalface'. So, the argument runs, the obligation to try hard enough to

[102] *McCarty v Pheasant Run Inc* 826 F 2d 1554 (2nd Cir 1987), 1556.
[103] *Berkshire CC v Olympic Holidays Ltd* (1994) 158 JP 421.
[104] Dov Weisman (2014).
[105] See the discussion of this notion in ch 1.

avoid wrongdoing should be binding on everyone associated with the firm, and a failure in that obligation by any such person should be regarded as a failure of and by the firm itself.[106]

In evaluating this important argument (the 'comprehensive safeguarding obligation' argument), it is important to keep in mind that employees, like directors, are commonly under a personal obligation not to commit the offences with which a company can also be charged. So, employees do not lack motivation provided by law to engage in appropriate safeguarding. Putting that point on one side, though, when it is a company's liability that is in question, a key consideration is that, as argued in Chapter 3, directors—the embodiment of the company—relate to associated persons within the company either through (authoritative) control or through (normatively significant) influence. Accordingly, what matters, in understanding whether or not 'all due diligence' has been exercised and 'all reasonable precautions' taken, is whether directors—through properly supervised delegation where appropriate—have striven actively to use their control or influence (as the case may be) to ensure proper safeguarding. The comprehensive safeguarding argument overlooks this point. It does so by suggesting implicitly that the adequacy of safeguarding can only be judged by an evaluation of someone's personal efforts towards that end; and given that directors cannot be expected themselves to check price labels, don hazmat suits to make work areas safe, and so on, the evaluation in law should be focused on the relevant employee's personal efforts. Whilst not wrong, such an argument fails to take seriously the labelling argument made in Chapter 1: that a company's liability should turn on an evaluation of the (in)action of its supreme executive authorities, the director or directors. Accordingly, the *company's* efforts to safeguard should be judged, in ethically heterogenous companies, by the extent to which directors have adequately striven to ensure that their authority respecting adequate safeguarding measures is accepted by those under their control, or (in appropriate cases) that their influence is heeded by those subject to it.

For example, in making his case for what I am calling a comprehensive safeguarding obligation, Mark D'Souza was scathing about the Law Commission's suggestion that the responsibility for establishing an adequate procedures or due diligence defence rests on the firm's directors. He says:

> The Law Commission plumped for disjunctive identification, but undermined its position by blithely suggesting that when corporations relied on its proposed due diligence defence to strict liability offences, reference should be made to 'the due diligence of directors (or equivalent persons)'. Effectively, it employed the same

[106] See Law Commission (2010), appendix A (John Cartwright) and Mark D'Souza (2020).

Nattrass style generalisation as to which officers could be identified with the company, that it was recommending against.[107]

It is unclear why D'Souza assumes that the same approach, in terms of responsibility, needs to be taken for corporate defences as it is for corporate offences. It is perfectly intelligible that a company might be fixed with in-principle liability when someone below board level commits a fault-based offence, but that the responsibility for establishing a due diligence defence to that offence is that of the board. For example, suppose that, in the face of directorial hostility and indifference, middle managers themselves devise a reasonably robust system to safeguard against the commission of offences by employees or agents; but an offence is nonetheless committed by an employee. Should the company be able to rely on the actions of the middle managers to claim that it had exercised 'all due diligence'? It should not. Unless adequate action was taken at board level, such as proper supervision of the middle managers' actions in setting up and running the safeguarding system, the defence should fail.

[107] Mark D'Souza (2020), 205, considering Law Commission (2010).

5
THE REACH OF CORPORATE CRIMINALITY

5.1 Understanding the 'Reach' of Corporate Crime

PROBLEMATIC EXAMPLE: C company sets up a corporate special purpose vehicle (SPV), unconnected to C company in law, to conduct business in Redland. Someone associated with the SPV engages in bribery in Redland, to benefit C company. C company also employs a UK independent contractor, X company, to find the best IT equipment for C company. Dependent on C company's business for its own financial viability, X company gives in to C company pressure to abide by C company's model standards for contracting and hiring. X company later engages in fraud to benefit C company.

As indicated in Chapter 1, questions of corporate criminal liability are inevitably relational, because the company as an abstract legal entity can only act through the persons—such as employees, agents, or subsidiary companies—forming part of it as a concrete legal entity. An understanding of whose crimes are the responsibility of the company (whether vicariously, or through failing to prevent them), and in what circumstances, is what I mean here by the 'reach' of corporate criminal liability. The mere fact that (say) an employee or subsidiary forms part of a company as a concrete legal entity may or may not be sufficient to fix that company with liability for a crime committed by such a person. For example, in virtue of section 8(5) of the Bribery Act 2010 ('the 2010 Act'), there is only a presumption that an employee 'is a person who performs services for or on behalf of C [the company]', making them someone in the relevant sense 'associated with' the company. Even where the presumption is not rebutted, an employee must, under section 7(1)(a) and (b) of the 2010 Act, still act with the intention 'to obtain or retain business for C, or to obtain or retain an advantage in the conduct of business for C' if their payment of a bribe is to trigger corporate liability for failing to prevent bribery. Similarly, in the case of failure-to-prevent fraud offences, section 199 of the Economic Crime and Corporate Transparency Act 2023 ('the 2023 Act') requires a legally associated person to have committed the predicate offence 'intending to benefit' the (parent) company, before the company may be found liable for failing to prevent that

A Theory of Corporate Crime. Jeremy Horder, Oxford University Press. © Jeremy Horder 2026.
DOI: 10.1093/9780198936534.003.0006

offence.[1] This requirement is also a key element in vicarious liability for fault-based crimes in the United States.[2]

A key concern of this chapter is with the legal consequences of the rise in the use of subsidiary companies, corporate 'special purpose vehicles (SPVs)', and of non-employed agents doing business (and perhaps committing offences) to benefit parent companies.[3] The language of 'course of employment' has appeared inapposite to describe the relationship between such persons and the company with which they are associated, and so different terms have been used to describe that relationship. In the case of bribes paid by subsidiaries or agents, section 8(1) of the 2010 Act says that, if the parent company is to be found liable for failing to prevent such bribes, the subsidiary or agent must have been 'performing services for or on behalf of' the parent company at the relevant time. However, the 2023 Act now appears to have dispensed with the idea, embodied in the 2010 Act, that the need for a subsidiary or agent to have been 'providing services for or on behalf of' a parent company is an appropriate limitation on a parent company's liability for failing to prevent frauds committed by its subsidiaries or agents. Under the 2023 Act, it is enough (other things being equal) that the offender simply *was* a subsidiary or agent at the relevant time, when committing fraud to benefit the company. The 2023 Act also extends the potential scope of parent company failure-to-prevent liability to frauds committed by employees of subsidiaries, even if the subsidiary itself (as an authoritatively led entity) was innocent of wrongdoing. These important changes are critically analysed in Section 5.7 below.

Finally, I will consider a key modern liberal-welfarist concern in corporate criminal liability. This is whether the reach of corporate criminality, and failure-to-prevent liability in particular, is appropriately extended in some instances to cases in which a contracting party (as opposed to a subsidiary) engages in wrongdoing, a key example being a human rights abuse committed by such a party.[4] I argue that it is going too far to insist that a company has a direct obligation to prevent wrongdoing by the independent contracting party. In such cases, it would be fairer and more proportionate to demand only that a company abide by an 'auxiliary' welfarist obligation, an obligation to ensure that the contracting party itself has

[1] Failing to prevent bribery and failing to prevent fraud, thus, fall into the category of corporate liability cases set out in model E in Section I.4. By contrast, no 'intention to benefit' requirement is involved in the offences of failing to prevent the facilitation of tax evasion, which therefore fall into the category of cases set out in model D in Section I.4. On this point about the absence of an intention to benefit a company in the offence of failing to prevent the facilitation of tax evasion, see the discussion in Karl Laird (2017).

[2] *Sun-Diamond Growers of California* 138 F 3d at 970, aff'd, 526 US 398 (1999).

[3] See further Sections 5.5 and 5.6 below. Globally, over 370,000 subsidiary companies have been created by the world's largest companies: https://www.investmentmonitor.ai/features/where-do-the-worlds-top-companies-have-subsidiaries/ (last accessed 04/10/2024).

[4] From the scheme set out in the Introduction, this is 'model C', as a basis for corporate liability: 'Liability for a Failure Respecting a Dangerous External State of Affairs Open to Company Control or Influence'.

appropriate prevention procedures in place. This is an indirect duty of vigilance or of 'oversight' (as I called it in Chapter 3), as opposed to a direct duty of prevention. Before turning to these issues, though, we should consider a preliminary question about the relationship between what I am calling the reach of corporate criminality and the jurisdiction to try companies for offences.

5.2 Questions of Reach and Questions of International Jurisdiction

Jurisdictional questions about corporate criminal liability raise some of the same issues that affect analysis of the reach of corporate criminal liability. Here is an example:

> X company, registered in Delaware, has a UK-based subsidiary, Y company, and a Lichtenstein subsidiary, Z company. Unbeknownst to X company, Z company has committed a bribery offence in Lichtenstein.

Bearing in mind that subsidiaries are separate entities in law from parent companies, should it be possible to say that UK prosecution authorities can claim jurisdiction over X company respecting Z company's commission of the crime? The 2010 Act permits such jurisdiction to be claimed in respect of the offence of failure to prevent bribery, because (1) X company is a company 'doing business in the United Kingdom'—through Y company[5]—and (2) the 2010 Act stipulates that it is of no legal concern where in the world the bribery offence itself takes place.[6] The justification for this, although not made clear in the 'travaux préparatoires' leading up to the relevant UK statutes, is presumably some kind of benefit-and-burden theory. Under such theories, if a parent company takes the benefit of being permitted to establish a subsidiary in a particular jurisdiction, it must accept the burden of that jurisdiction's understanding of the extent of civil and criminal liability attaching to the parent company arising from the establishment of that subsidiary.[7] Be that as it may, whilst questions of what I am calling the 'reach' of corporate criminality are clearly interlinked with questions of criminal jurisdiction, they are separate, and my focus is the former and not the latter.

[5] For the sake of argument, I assume here that establishing a commercially active subsidiary company in country X necessarily involves 'doing business' in country X, but clearly there is room for argument that this is not always so.

[6] Bribery Act 2010, s 7(5)(b) and section 12(5). In these respects, the 2010 Act follows, in a very broad sense, the approach of US law under the Foreign Corrupt Practices Act 1977.

[7] In 2021, there were 12,475 overseas companies incorporated outside of the United Kingdom but having a physical presence in the United Kingdom (such as a place of business or branch) through which they carried out their business: https://www.gov.uk/government/statistics/companies-register-activities-statistical-release-2020-to-2021/companies-register-activities-2020-to-2021 (last accessed 29/07/2024). On jurisdiction more generally, see Micheál Ó Floinn et al (2023).

To illustrate the separateness of the issues, suppose that X company has a subsidiary, Y company, and—unknown to X company—Y company pays a bribe or commits fraud to win a contract. An important question, central to the discussion in this chapter, is whether X company can (or should) in such circumstances be found guilty of failing to prevent bribery or fraud. The answer to that question depends on what we take to be of salient moral significance, for the purposes of criminal responsibility, in the relationship between X company and Y company (the 'corporate relationship' question). Is it enough, as under section 196 of the 2023 Act merely, that Y company is in law a subsidiary of X company, or is something more required (as under US Federal prosecution practice[8]) such as a relationship of agency or effective control of the subsidiary by the parent company? In that regard, we should note that the corporate relationship question to be answered remains in principle the same, wherever the subsidiary is located. So, suppose that a UK parent company has a subsidiary in Manchester and another subsidiary in a foreign jurisdiction.[9] If each subsidiary engages in (say) bribery or fraud, it is quite plausible to suppose that we will wish to answer the corporate relationship question in the same way, irrespective of whether what is in issue is the offence committed in the United Kingdom, or the offence committed in the overseas jurisdiction. It will be a separate, albeit clearly interlinked, question—a jurisdictional question—whether the parent company's failure to prevent the offence committed overseas by the overseas-based subsidiary is triable in the United Kingdom.[10]

The same point can be made in relation to 'individual relationship' questions, as opposed to 'corporate relationship' questions. For example, suppose that the issue is whether a company is guilty of a criminal offence committed by one of its senior managers, in virtue of section 196 of the 2023 Act (clause 196 of the 2025 Bill). Then, the question of whether the senior manager was acting within 'the actual or apparent scope of their authority' (as required by section 196 and clause 196) must be settled wherever in the world the offence took place, and whatever the connection between the company and the prosecuting jurisdiction.

5.3 Vicarious and Control-based Liability for Another's Crime

When an employee commits a fault-based crime, the act in question will commonly be a free, deliberate, and informed act. Orthodox analysis suggests that such an act is not directly 'caused' in law by another person,[11] such as the company that

[8] For a good general discussion, see Marcela E Schaefer (2019).

[9] Even in countries where companies do a significant amount of overseas trade, it tends to be as—or more—common for a large company to set up subsidiaries within the jurisdiction rather than outside it.

[10] The resolution of the jurisdictional question will also turn on the nature of the parent company's connection to England and Wales.

[11] See, e.g., *R v Kennedy* (No 2) (2007) UKHL 38.

employed the wrongdoer acting in the course of their employment. However, for the reasons given in Chapter 3, the fact that the employee's crime involved a free, deliberate, and informed act will not by itself necessarily serve to relieve the company completely of in-principle responsibility for that crime. As we saw, in failure-to-prevent cases, that is because liability is control or influence principle–based and not based on causation.[12] It is the controller's or influencer's duty-failure, respecting the person under control or influence, that is the focus of liability, and not the controller's or influencer's causal role in events. In that respect, in spite of very important theoretical differences between the doctrines (explored in Chapter 3), there is a similarity with vicarious criminal liability. That doctrine, too, is not concerned with the causal role of a corporate employer in the course of events leading to employee wrongdoing. In the case of vicarious liability, of course, that is because what matters in such cases is only the proof of employee wrongdoing in the course of their work, wrongdoing that is then automatically attributed to the corporate employer.[13]

For simplicity's sake, I will put aside the influence principle, and use the control principle as my analytical focus here. To summarize the argument in Chapter 3, in relation to fault-based wrongdoing, in-principle liability is incurred under the control principle when (2) a person (the 'controlling entity') had the right to control someone (the 'controlled entity') in circumstances in which the fault-based wrongdoing occurred within the domain of control associated with the controlled entity, and (2) the controlling entity was under a duty to exercise that control-right to prevent the wrongdoing. In addition, (3) the blame, if any, to be attached to a controlling entity for a breach of such a duty depends on whether or not safeguarding procedures could have been expected to have been adopted in advance to prevent the type of wrongdoing in question, and if there were such procedures (as expected), whether they were adequate or reasonable. In this respect, there is another link here with vicarious liability. In Chapter 3, we saw that vicarious criminal liability has historically sometimes been justified through a control principle–inspired focus on the safeguarding failures of the controlling entity, alongside the traditional focus on the wrongdoing of the controlled entity. The courts have sometime justified vicarious criminal liability by answering affirmatively the ascriptive question: 'Was there something that the company-employer could realistically have been expected to do to prevent wrongdoing of the kind in which the employee engaged?'[14] Whether in relation to the duty question ((2) above), or in relation to the ascriptive question ((3) above), both the control principle and vicarious criminal liability can thus be said to be in some sense concerned with an

[12] See, further, Jeremy Horder (2024).

[13] The differences are well explained in the private law case of *Trustees of the Barry Congregation of Jehovah's Witnesses (Appellant) v BXB (Respondent)* [2023] UKSC 15, but I say more about them in due course.

[14] *Bond v Evans* (1888) 21 QB 249.

employer-controller's authority over employees. I return to this point in Section 5.4 below.

Nonetheless, employees—and by extension, formal agents—are a key focus in vicarious liability cases, in a way that they are not under the control principle. The conduct of employees is ex hypothesi a manifestation of the internal division of labour in companies, whereby different persons within the firm are entrusted with powers or duties to carry out different tasks associated with the firm's purposes.[15] In *Cox v Ministry of Justice*,[16] Lord Reed said about persons within the scope of vicarious liability:

> [A] relationship . . . is in principle capable of giving rise to vicarious liability where harm is wrongfully done by *an individual who carries on activities as an integral part of the business activities carried on by a defendant* and for its benefit (rather than his activities being entirely attributable to the conduct of a recognisably independent business of his own or of a third party), and where the commission of the wrongful act is a risk created by the defendant by assigning those activities to the individual in question.[17]

When the Law Commission, amongst others, suggested that in vicarious liability cases the law treats the employee's acts as the acts 'of the company itself',[18] that suggestion should be understood in this light. Clearly, an employee's act is not to be identified with 'the company itself' in the sense employed when the identification doctrine is in issue.[19] That is because the identification doctrine can be applied—and indeed, works best—when there is no division of labour within a firm because it is comprised of a sole director.[20] Instead, as explained in Section 1.2, in vicarious liability cases, a dimension of the company as a concrete legal entity is in play, in relation to employee misconduct. This is the dimension of such an entity that is constituted by the network of 'internal' contracts binding persons together as company representatives in the discharge of corporate powers and duties. The theoretical plausibility of vicarious liability for employee (and by extension, agent) wrongdoing turns on this point about the existence of an internal division of labour—founded on contract—manifesting corporate activity. For, by way of contrast, when wrongdoing is committed by an independent contractor or subsidiary

[15] See the discussion of Ronald Coase's theory of the firm in Section 1.6.

[16] [2016] UKSC 10.

[17] [2016] UKSC 10, para 24 (my emphasis).

[18] See Law Commission (2022), para 5.7.

[19] When then latter doctrine is in issue, the conception of the company involved is of the company as an authoritatively led entity. See Section 1.2 for this understanding of a company.

[20] See the discussion in ch 1. In this, I disagree with Mark D'Souza's suggestion that the acts of employees can be identified with the company without drawing any distinction between a vicarious liability basis for doing so and an identification doctrine basis for doing so: see Mark D'Souza (2020), and the discussion in ch 1.

company (unless, perhaps, it is wholly controlled by an agent of the parent),[21] even if the company entrusted the contractor or subsidiary to perform certain tasks in much the way that it might have entrusted an employee, the actions of the independent contractor or subsidiary do not reflect an internal division of labour within the (parent) company. Instead, those actions reflect an ex hypothesi independent decision on the part of the contractor or subsidiary to agree to perform some task or tasks to benefit the company, an independence inconsistent with the application of vicarious liability in respect of wrongdoing engaged in when performing such tasks.

By contrast, under the control principle, the question of whether a company was under a duty to prevent the commission of an offence by another person does not depend on whether that other person's role stemmed from their role in the company's internal division of labour. Instead, the answer to that question depends (in part) on consideration of a broader issue: whether the person—even if external to the company—fell within the company's 'domain of control' ((1) above). Whether a person falls within a company's domain of control, triggering a duty to prevent crime, is a question that can be answered in the affirmative in cases going well beyond relationships internal to the division of labour. Here is an example:

> C company sets up a subsidiary company (X company) overseas, with powers to take its own commercial decisions. However, a majority of the members of the subsidiary's board of directors are also directors of the parent company.[22]

We consider the issue in more detail in Section 5.5 below, but in this example, it cannot conceivably be supposed that X company is part of C company's internal division of labour and hence equivalent in status to an employee or agent: X company has been established, in law, as an independent body. Even so, the fact that X company has a majority of its directors from the C company board is an indication that X company is within the domain of C company's control, in spite of the fact that X company is formally free to take its own independent decisions.

The 'domain of control' basis for a relationship of responsibility is more extensive and flexible than the doctrine of vicarious liability, and hence better equipped to give substantive, policy-based answers (as opposed to purely formal, technical answers) to the question of whether a subsidiary's wrongdoing is something respecting which the parent must bear responsibility through having failing to prevent it.[23] In that respect, the duty-based nature of the supervisory and safeguarding

[21] A subsidiary company is part of the main company, conceived as a concrete legal entity (see Section 1.2), but not in that respect part of its internal division of labour, and so not governed by the doctrine of vicarious liability.

[22] A company's creation of subsidiaries is an aspect of its development as a real entity. See the discussion in Section 1.2.

[23] See also the discussion in Section 5.5 below, and in Robert Luskin (2020).

role occupied by a controlling entity means that this role may encompass not only the conduct of subsidiaries but the conduct of other persons well outside the scope of vicarious liability, such as (say) corporate SPVs, or even trespassers on land.[24] This flexibility stems from the fact that, by way of contrast with vicarious liability, the duty-based control principle involves a simultaneous focus on the different, active roles of persons associated with a firm: one person (the controlled entity) working for the firm, and the other (the controlling entity) in a supervisory or safe-guarding position with respect to the controlled entity.

To compare and contrast the two doctrines further, let us consider the principles governing when an employer can be held vicariously liable in tort for intentional criminal wrongdoing engaged in by an employee, an extension of the reach of vicarious liability disavowed by English criminal law.[25] English tort law has moved away from what was for a long time an essentially normative focus on whether the employee's criminal act was an unauthorized *mode* of doing something previously authorized by the employer as an aspect of the division of labour.[26] Replacing, or overlaying, this older ex ante conduct rule has been an ex post facto decision rule, involving a broader evaluative approach. The new focus of this decision rule is the extent to which there was (in the court's view) a sufficiently 'close connection' between the powers or duties granted to or imposed on the employee by the employer and the employee's unauthorized criminal acts.[27] In *Mohamud v WM Morrison Supermarkets*,[28] the employee, who worked at one of Morrison's petrol pump kiosks, initiated an unprovoked and violent confrontation with a customer, which started in the kiosk and continued while the customer was in his car, as a result of which the customer was injured.

The supermarket company was held vicariously liable to compensate the injured customer. Lord Toulson said of the employee's assault: '[H]e was purporting to act about his employer's business. It was a gross abuse of his position, but it was in connection with the business in which he was employed to serve customers.'[29] In such a case, the foundation for imposing vicarious liability is still partly normative: the employee was on duty at the employer's premises, and thus bound ex ante to carry out his customer-related duties in a way that respected customers. However, the ultimate basis for imposing liability to pay damages on the employer is an ex post evaluation.[30] It involves the judgement that a state of affairs existed in which the

[24] See the discussion in Jeremy Horder (2024).
[25] See the discussion in ch 1.
[26] The so-called Salmond test: see the discussion in *Lister v Hesley Hall Ltd* [2002] 1 AC 215, para 36.
[27] See, e.g., *The Catholic Child Welfare Society & Ors v Various Claimants & Ors* [2012] UKSC 56 and *Lister v Hesley Hall Ltd* [2002] 1 AC 215.
[28] [2016] UKSC 11.
[29] [2016] UKSC 11, para 47.
[30] See, e.g., the observations of Lord Nicholls in *Dubai Aluminium Co Ltd v Salaam* [2002] UKHL 48, para 26: 'Essentially the court makes an evaluative judgment in each case, having regard to all the circumstances and, importantly, having regard also to the assistance provided by previous court decisions.'

employee's status as an employee still loomed sufficiently large (as one might say) when he acted, even though the act was ex hypothesi wholly unauthorized. Had the offending employee in *Morrison Supermarkets* followed the customer home after his shift ended, and the confrontation then occurred at the customer's home, no doubt the necessary close connection would not have been found.

My concern here is obviously not with whether the 'close connection' test provides a sound basis for determining when harm tortiously done by an employee must be compensated for by an employer, through an application of the doctrine of vicarious liability. How, though, should *Morrison Supermarkets* be understood in terms of the control principle, which does apply to intentional wrongdoing? Recall that, by way of contrast with vicarious liability, the focus of the control principle is not principally the wrongdoing of the employee *qua* employee[31] but the supervisory and safeguarding role of the controlling entity: the corporate employer. In *Morrison Supermarkets*, the employer was doubtless under a control-duty to ensure that customers were treated by employees with appropriate respect. Further, it is reasonable to think that, if a senior manager had happened to be there in person when the incident occurred, they would have been expected to use—would have been under a duty to use—their control-right to intervene to prevent the attack. So, unprovoked and unexpected though the attack may have been, employee attacks of this kind on customers are wrongs that the corporate employers can conceivably be under a control-duty to prevent.

However, in terms of the ascriptive, blame element of the control principle ((3) above), it would be going too far to say that the corporate employer should ex ante have had safeguarding *procedures* in place addressing the risks of wholly unprovoked attacks by employees on customers. That would be going too far, in terms of the range of risks for which safeguarding measures should have been provided in advance,[32] even though the employer clearly had the control-right to introduce such measures.[33] Contrast the *Morrison Supermarkets* case with a case in which an employee is a residential manager in charge of children's home, and misuses his position to abuse children in his care.[34] In such a case, the intentional wrongdoing, even though it is obviously unauthorized conduct, is wrongdoing of a kind that children's home owners (the controlling entities) clearly have not only a control-right but a duty to prevent. However, crucially in this instance, it is also

[31] Under the control and influence principles, the employee wrongdoing is a predicate offence, in relation to which the company's failure-to-prevent offence is defined.

[32] For a discussion of the significance of the 'range' of risks to safeguarding obligations, see the discussion in ch 4.

[33] The crime committed by the employee in *Morrison Supermarkets* was not intended to benefit the employer. That is why, if a company is to be held criminally liable for the wrongdoing in such a case, it should be on a different normative basis, as an instance of model D in the scheme outlined in Section I.4. Such a basis requires proof of corporate knowledge of the specific wrongdoing, or proof of awareness on the company's part about the possibility that wrongdoing of that kind might take place, without proper procedures being in place to prevent it. See further the discussion in Section 5.7 below.

[34] See the tort case of *Lister v Hesley Hall* [2001] UKHL 22.

wrongdoing respecting which the home owners must be aware requires the creation and enforcement ex ante of adequate safeguarding measures to prevent its occurrence.[35]

5.4 Subsidiary Company Wrongdoing: Weaknesses in Vicarious Liability

In English private law, a relatively clear separation is acknowledged, as between parent companies and their subsidiaries. In *Adams v Cape Industries PLC*,[36] Slade LJ put the point this way:

> Our law for better or worse, recognises the creation of subsidiary companies which though in one sense the creatures of their parent companies, will nevertheless under the general law fall to be treated as separate legal entities with all the rights and liabilities which would normally attach to separate legal entities.[37]

Given its commitment to supporting the values of efficiency and legal certainty in transacting and property-holding, it is understandable that private law takes such an approach. What would be the consequences for the criminal law of unconditionally accepting the position set out by Slade LJ?

It would follow that the ultimate duty to safeguard against crime committed by a subsidiary company is solely that of directors within the subsidiary, and not that of the parent company. A failure in that duty would then expose the subsidiary, but not the parent, to prosecution for a substantive or failure-to-prevent offence (as applicable). However, the subsidiary might not be within the jurisdiction, and might hence not be subject to UK law. Indeed, it might have been established overseas precisely in order to free its operation from the governance of UK law. So, if Slade LJ's approach to the status of subsidiary companies were to be imported wholesale into the criminal law, the reach of the criminal law would be too limited. The law could be out-manoeuvred by the simple expedient of setting up a subsidiary company in a jurisdiction with weak law enforcement, that then goes on to commit wrongdoing in order to benefit the main company.[38] In this section, I consider different ways in which the law can be understood and developed to encompass

[35] Ibid. Section 21 of the Criminal Justice and Courts Act 2015 imposes liability through a separate offence on a (grossly negligent) care provider, when there has been ill-treatment or wilful neglect of a patient by someone working under the aegis of the care provider. It is, of course, possible that sexual abuse by someone in a position of authority will not occur in the course of their employment, and will hence not be wrongdoing over which an employer had a control-right or duty: see *Trustees of the Barry Congregation of Jehovah's Witnesses (Appellant) v BXB (Respondent)* [2023] UKSC 1.

[36] [1990] 1 Ch 433.

[37] *Adams v Cape Industries Plc* [1990] 1 Ch 433 at 536 per Slade LJ.

[38] See the discussion of the *BAE* case in ch 6.

wrongdoing engaged in by subsidiary companies, so as to mitigate or avoid this problem.

Under US federal law, a parent company may be found vicariously criminally liable for fault-based wrongdoing engaged in by a subsidiary company;[39] but that means that the relationship between the parent and the subsidiary in any given case must meet the strict criteria (considered in Section 5.3 above) making the doctrine of vicarious liability applicable. Under federal law, a parent company may be found vicariously liable for criminal wrongdoing—and for bribery in particular—engaged in by a subsidiary, if (inter alia) the subsidiary was in effect acting as an agent for the parent as principal.[40] For example, under the Foreign Corrupt Practices Act 1977, an individual or body based overseas (and having no presence in the United States) will be subject to the 1977 Act if that person was an 'agent of a foreign concern'. In interpreting that phrase, it has been held that ordinary common law agency principles must be applied, meaning that the prosecution must establish the three elements involved in a principal–agency relationship:

> The three elements necessary to an agency relationship are (1) a manifestation by the principal that the agent will act for him; (2) acceptance by the agent of the undertaking; and (3) an understanding between the parties that the principal will be in control of the undertaking.[41]

Accordingly, in relation to the enforcement of the 1977 Act, the US Department of Justice has stated that:

> A parent may be liable for its subsidiary's conduct under traditional agency principles. The fundamental characteristic of agency is control. Accordingly, DOJ and SEC[42] evaluate the parent's control - including the parent's knowledge and direction of the subsidiary's actions, both generally and in the context of the specific transaction—when evaluating whether a subsidiary is an agent of the parent. Although the formal relationship between the parent and subsidiary is important in this analysis, so are the practical realities of how the parent and subsidiary actually interact.[43]

Indications of control that may suffice to establish the necessary agency relationship might include the following: a major proprietary interest in the subsidiary,

[39] See US Department of Justice (2020), 28, and the discussion of vicarious liability in ch 3.

[40] Marcela E Schaefer (2019), 1664. See *Pacific Can Co v Hewes* 95 F 2d 42 (9th Cir 1938), 46: 'Where one corporation is controlled by another, the former acts not for itself but as directed by the latter, the same as an agent, and the principal is liable for the acts of its agent within the scope of the agent's authority.'

[41] *United States v Hoskins* No 20-842 (2d Cir 12 August 2022), 17.

[42] The Securities and Exchange Commission.

[43] US Department of Justice (2020), 28.

majority representation at board or senior management level, veto rights, commercial arrangements impacting control (such as operating agreements or the consolidation of accounts), or mutual assent and control over the details of the person and agency involved in the wrongdoing, such that the principal controls the details over any assignment.[44] The significance of this can be appreciated when one considers that, of the leading 6,000 companies worldwide—operating through more than 370,000 subsidiaries—27.5 per cent of the parent multinational companies are based in the United States and responsible for the creation of over 101,000 subsidiaries.[45]

By way of comparison, under the Companies Act 2006, section 1159(1) defines a subsidiary in the following terms:

> (1) A company is a 'subsidiary' of another company, its 'holding company', if that other company—
>   (a) holds a majority of the voting rights in it, or
>   (b) is a member of it and has the right to appoint or remove a majority of its board of directors, or
>   (c) is a member of it and controls alone, pursuant to an agreement with other members, a majority of the voting rights in it, or if it is a subsidiary of a company that is itself a subsidiary of that other company.
>
> (2) A company is a 'wholly-owned subsidiary' of another company if it has no members except that other and that other's wholly-owned subsidiaries or persons acting on behalf of that other or its wholly-owned subsidiaries.

In the cases addressed by section 1159(1), the domination of the parent—and hence the subservience of the subsidiary—is expressed through the untrammelled power of the parent to exercise constitutional direction over the subsidiary. So far as the crucial element of executive control or direction is concerned, in *Smith, Stone and Knight v City of Birmingham*,[46] Atkinson J set down the following test to determine whether a subsidiary could be regarded as in effect the agent of the parent:

1. Were profits of the business treated as profits of the parent?
2. Did the parent appoint persons to carry on the business?
3. Was the parent the 'head and brain' of the trading venture?
4. Did the parent govern the adventure?

[44] Ibid.; https://www.linklaters.com/en/knowledge/publications/alerts-newsletters-and-guides/2022/may/19/reflections-on-abc-liability-for-parent-companies-and-jvs-a-usuk-comparison (last accessed 10/10/2023).

[45] https://www.investmentmonitor.ai/features/where-do-the-worlds-top-companies-have-subsidiaries/?cf-view (last accessed 29/07/2024).

[46] (1939) 4 All ER 116.

5. Did the parent make profits via that direction?
6. Was the parent in effectual and constant control?[47]

Clearly, answering these questions may not be a straightforward issue, but as we will see in the next section, in English law that will not be a matter of great concern in failure-to-prevent cases. That is because the principal–agent relationship is only one kind of relationship capable of turning (corporate) wrongdoers into 'associated persons': the key concept in failure-to-prevent offences. A corporate body engaged in wrongdoing might fail to meet one or more of the criteria set out in section 1159(1), or one or more of the criteria set down by Atkinson J above, and still clearly be an 'associated person' of another (parent) company.[48]

By contrast, the precise contours of the principal–agent relationship in corporate contexts matter much more to US corporate criminal law, even though commentators agree that the contours are unclear and contested.[49] They matter much more because as we saw in Section 5.3 above, under the doctrine of vicarious liability, only a narrow and relatively formal set of relations between the wrongdoer and the (parent) company will serve to trigger such liability. Accordingly, a parent company's vicarious responsibility for the wrongdoing of its subsidiaries must be understood in relatively formal (principal–agent) terms, even though corporate criminal law must address the ever-changing, dynamic relationship between a parent and its subsidiaries, in addition to other investment bodies like SPVs, considered in the next section. When it comes to the 'reach' of corporate criminal liability, the doctrine of vicarious liability is almost inevitably going to be relatively narrow and inflexible, even if—as in US law—it is interpreted creatively by prosecutors to cover a wide variety of parent–subsidiary relations.[50] That is because liability is still premised on an assumption that the parties are in a relatively formal 'top down' or 'command and control' relationship, with regard to executive matters, even if the wrongdoer was granted more or less wide powers of executive discretion in acting by the (parent) company. However, subsidiaries may over time become real entities, with a culture and ethos of their own. As separate corporate entities, they may make their own independent decisions on the hiring of employees and the making of contracts (factors that may have a key bearing on crimes committed by the subsidiary), whether or not these decisions are intended to benefit the parent company.

[47] Ibid., 120. See the discussion in US Department of Justice (2020), 28.
[48] I pursue this point further in the next section.
[49] Marcela E Schaefer (2019); Christian R Martinez (2020).
[50] In practice, of course, the Department of Justice disregards the kind of legal niceties being discussed here, and in effect coerces US-based firms into agreeing settlements even when it may be unclear whether a foreign subsidiary company was in fact an 'agent' of US-based parent company: see generally Karen Woody (2017).

Consider the example of WPP PLC, a British multinational communications, advertising, public relations, technology, and commerce holding company.[51] In the 1970s, it was a firm that specialized in making wire baskets for supermarkets. No doubt, it was sufficient at that time that offences that the firm was regarded as capable of committing were confined to offences committed by directors themselves, or—through the doctrine of vicarious liability—by its employees. However, WPP has not only grown to be a firm with revenues of £14.8 billion and 115,000 employees but, most significantly in this context, it has the third largest number of subsidiary companies of any multinational worldwide: 2,153.[52] The doctrine of vicarious liability is simply ill-suited to the task of determining when, if ever, offences committed by any one of such a vast number of subsidiaries should be regarded as also committed by WPP. Accordingly, a different path has been pursued by the UK legislature, in determining the reach of failure-to-prevent offences.

5.5 Failing to Prevent Crime: Bodies 'Associated' with a Company

Larger UK companies were operating through no less than 28,707 subsidiary companies in 2022, about half of which were based overseas.[53] It is essential to be able to determine when these parent companies will be liable for the wrongdoing of their subsidiaries. Failure-to-prevent offences seek to answer this question through an examination of the relationship between the parent company and what is called an 'associated person'. Such offences thus subtly change the emphasis, in terms of the reach of corporate crime, from a primary focus on the status of the criminal act ('in the course of employment') to the status of the person when they engaged in such an act ('associated person'). According to now well-established principles, when an associated person commits a relevant crime, that will—subject to any available defence—trigger liability in the corporate person with whom the offender is associated: liability for the separate offence of failing to prevent the associated person's crime.[54]

In that regard, there is no assumption underlying the notion of an 'associated' person that such a person is integrated into the (parent) company's internal division of labour, in a way that might make vicarious liability a possible route to

[51] https://www.wpp.com/media (last accessed 20/08/2025).

[52] https://www.investmentmonitor.ai/features/where-do-the-worlds-top-companies-have-subsidiaries/?cf-view (last accessed 29/07/2024).

[53] https://www.investmentmonitor.ai/features/where-do-the-worlds-top-companies-have-subsidiaries/?cf-view (last accessed 29/07/2024). Large UK companies owned 14,762 domestic subsidiaries and 13,945 foreign subsidiaries. Subsidiaries are established for various reasons, including brand recognition, financial considerations, the ability to raise capital, and the capacity to deal with reporting and disclosure issues.

[54] See, generally, the discussion of the relationship between failure-to-prevent offences and vicarious liability in ch 3.

conviction. On the contrary, suppose that a parent company creates a 'satellite' company, which is not in law a subsidiary because (say) the parent company does not have majority voting rights, or the right to remove a majority of the directors. Even though such a satellite company does not meet the formal criteria in section 1159(1) of the Companies Act 2006 necessary for it to be classed as a 'subsidiary' company—in that it is not under the constitutional domination of the parent company—it can and should nonetheless be regarded as an 'associated person', having been intentionally created (or taken over) for some purpose by the parent company.[55] This is a point of some significance, in that companies have also created other bodies at greater arms-length through which to do business: as a way, say, of separating assets or liabilities from the main company. An example is the so-called orphan SPV.

Acting as a kind of affiliate of a parent company, an SPV can itself be a company, or it may be a partnership or a purpose trust. It is commonly set up as an indirect source of financing for the original parent company. Establishing an SPV allows a company to isolate assets, liabilities, and risks related to a particular project, but SPVs are useful for large credit risk items, like subprime mortgage loans. In 2015, some 600 SPVs in the Republic of Ireland held 150 billion Euros in assets, many of these vehicles having been established according to English law.[56] The 'orphan' status of an SPV means that its assets and liabilities are not those of the main company, and will not appear on the main company's balance sheet. There is a particular risk of fraud being associated with the use of SPVs. An example is when firms seek to attract investment on the basis of claims about anticipated financial growth, in circumstances in which the establishment of an SPV enables the claims to be detached from a complete record of the main company's past and current financial performance, and its overall financial health.[57] An SPV is manifestly outside the possible scope of vicarious liability. Accordingly, in such cases, a key issue will be whether an SPV is a person (assuming it has 'person' status, in law) 'associated with' the company that created it, and hence whether the offence of failing to prevent fraud applies. It is submitted that, as an entity intentionally created by a (parent) company to serve a purpose of the company, such an entity ought in principle to fall within the scope of an 'associated person'.

In looking in more detail at these issues, I will start with the original failure-to-prevent offence, the offence of failure-to-prevent bribery created by section 7 of the 2010 Act. This offence is committed when an 'associated person' commits

[55] Even in the absence of parental control, such bodies may well in law or in practice be subject to what I described in Chapter 3 as the 'influence' principle, according to which they are obliged to listen to advice or instruction given, even if they are not necessarily obliged to follow such advice or instruction.

[56] Brian Godfrey, Neil Killeen, and Kitty Moloney (2015).

[57] See, e.g., https://www.latimes.com/business/story/2022-10-14/head-of-zero-emission-truck-venture-found-guilty-of-fraud (last accessed 01/08/2024).

bribery intending to obtain or retain business (or an advantage in the conduct of business) for the company. In that regard, section 8(5) of the 2010 Act creates only a 'presumption' that an employee is an associated person. That illustrates that the 'associated person' doctrine was not meant simply to be an outgrowth of traditional vicarious liability, but a separate basis for determining the reach of corporate crime. More broadly, as we saw earlier, an 'associated person' is described in section 8(1) as follows:

> (1) A person ('A') is associated with C if (disregarding any bribe under consideration) A is a person who performs services for or on behalf of C.
> (2) The capacity in which A performs services for or on behalf of C does not matter.
> (3) Accordingly, A may (for example) be C's employee, agent or subsidiary.

Section 8(4) goes on to say that whether or not A is a person who performs services for or on behalf of C is to be determined by reference to all the relevant circumstances, and not merely by reference to the nature of the relationship between A and C.[58] The test set down in section 8 is thus substantive rather than formal, eschewing reliance on the 'capacity' in which someone acts, by way of contrast with the test applicable to employees.[59] The key issue is whether the person is—apart from the 'service' constituted by the bribe—performing services for or on behalf of the (parent) company.

How wide is the notion of 'performing services for or on behalf of' a company? In its report on bribery,[60] the Law Commission said:

> [T]he test of whether a subsidiary company is providing services 'on behalf of' a main company should be a substantive rather than a formal test. In other words, the question of whether the test has been satisfied will depend on all the circumstances. It should not depend simply on whether, for example, the subsidiary company does business with foreign officials using papers that all say, 'none of the (subsidiary) company's actions are done on behalf of the main company'. It could be that, in such a case, there is clear evidence that the official sought, and received, an assurance that an advantage was to be conferred on behalf of the

[58] This provision has its parallel in section 199(9) of the 2023 Act, in relation to failures to prevent fraud, which reads: 'Whether or not a particular person performs services for or on behalf of a relevant body is to be determined by reference to all the relevant circumstances and not merely by reference to the nature of the relationship between that person and the body.'

[59] The offence of failing to prevent the facilitation of tax evasion, contrary to section 45(1) of the Criminal Finances Act 2017, requires the associated person to be acting in their capacity as a service provider when the facilitation offence is committed, making the test under the 2017 Act more formal than that under the 2020 Act. Section 45(1) says that, 'a relevant body (B) is guilty of an offence if a person commits a UK tax evasion facilitation offence when acting in the capacity of a person associated with B'.

[60] Law Commission (2008).

main company. If that were the case, then the advantage would be one to be conferred 'on behalf of' the main company, notwithstanding the contrary indication on the paperwork.[61]

There is an ambiguity about this guidance. The first part of the passage is clear enough. The test of whether S (the subsidiary) is providing services for or on behalf of C (the parent) is not one to be governed by looking at matters of form. It is an evaluative question, a matter of judgement on the facts and in the circumstances, as under the US Department of Justice guidance (cited in Section 5.4 above). However, the second part of the passage appears to suggest that what matters is whether the subsidiary claimed authority to act for the parent company in offering the bribe itself.[62] That suggestion is in tension with the terms of section 8(1), which makes it clear that what matters is whether S is providing services 'for or on behalf of' C, *apart from* the 'service' constituted by the bribe itself.

In fairness, the Law Commission made it clear that the full circumstances in which a parent company should be held liable for bribery committed by a subsidiary should be dealt with in a review of corporate criminal liability more generally; but when the Law Commission later conducted such a review, no clear opinion was offered on this question.[63] Ultimately, it will be for the courts to determine whether a body such as an orphan SPV is a body providing services for or on behalf of the main company. In that regard, Government guidance on the scope of providing services 'for or on behalf of' a large company, for the purposes of the 2023 Act, says this:

The term 'providing services' does not include providing goods. It is also important to note that 'providing services *for* or on behalf of the relevant body' does not include providing services *to* the relevant body. Thus, persons providing services to an organisation (for example, external lawyers, valuers, accountants or engineers) are not acting 'for or on behalf' of the organisation. This means they would not be associated persons for the purposes of the offence.[64]

One advantage of the 'associated person' test used in both the 2010 Act and the 2023 Act (considered in Section 5.7 below)—the test of whether a body is providing

[61] Ibid, para 6.120.

[62] This suggestion is confirmed by an earlier passage in which the Commission said that, in contrast with the example in which S acts with real or apparent authority in paying the bribe, 'This kind of situation is different from the situation in which a question arises whether liability should be imposed on a company for a failure adequately to supervise a subsidiary, when that subsidiary has committed bribery on its own account, and not specifically on behalf of the main company. It is this difficult question that we believe is best left to the general review of corporate liability': ibid., para 6.110.

[63] See Law Commission (2022).

[64] Home Office (2024), 9 (emphasis in the original). In Section 5.9 below, I will criticize the distinction between providing services 'for' and providing them 'to' a main company.

services for or on behalf of a company—is that it cuts through a legalistic approach to 'quasi-subsidiaries' (not controlled by the parent) and orphan SPVs. In all such cases, the key question will be the substantive question of whether the body in question is providing services for or on behalf of the (parent) company—giving rise to control or influence duties—and not a formal question about the legal or equitable relationship between them.[65]

A provision that takes such an approach and focuses on the supervisory and control duty of the parent company is section 5 of the Criminal Justice (Theft and Fraud Offences) (Amendment) Act 2021, governing the Republic of Ireland. This creates an offence in the following circumstances, designed to punish corporate fraud against EU institutions:

> Where a relevant offence is committed for the benefit of a body corporate by a relevant person and the commission of the relevant offence is attributable to the failure, by a director, manager, secretary or other officer of the body corporate ... to exercise, at the time of the commission of the relevant offence and in all the circumstances of the case, *the requisite degree of supervision or control of the relevant person*, the body corporate shall be guilty of an offence.[66] (my emphasis)

Although section 5 of the 2021 Act artificially confines the scope of 'relevant person' to employees, agents, and subsidiaries, there is no reason why the model that it provides could not equally be applicable to other entities, such as (orphan) SPVs, in appropriate circumstances.

5.6 The 2025 Bill: The Liability Role of an 'Intention to Benefit' the Firm

The case for regarding companies as duty-bound to oversee (albeit, in some cases, with a light touch) the observance of ethical compliance obligations by associated persons fits well with an important requirement in section 7 of the 2010 Act (mentioned in Section 5.5 above), a requirement included in a modified form in section 199 of the 2023 Act in relation to failure to prevent fraud. This is the requirement that, if a company is to be held responsible for failing to prevent bribery, the bribe must have been intended to benefit the company commercially.[67] Section 7 of the 2010 Act says that 'a relevant commercial organisation ("C") is guilty of an offence under this section if a person ("A") associated with C bribes another person

[65] For the detail of this argument, see Jeremy Horder and Gabriele Watts (2021).
[66] It will be a defence for the company to show that it 'took all reasonable steps and exercised all due diligence to avoid the commission of the offence'.
[67] The 2023 Act extends this notion to cover an intention to benefit someone (such as a customer) to whom the associated person provides services.

intending (a) to obtain or retain business for C, or (b) to obtain or retain an advantage in the conduct of business for C'.

A requirement that the associated person's criminal act be intended to benefit the firm commercially connects with an ethically significant feature of the safeguarding procedures C should adopt. A business may—like any institution or household—have to safeguard against 'extrinsic' risks, such as risks posed by ransom-seeking computer hackers. It may—again, like any other institution, public or private—also have to safeguard in relation to 'intrinsically human' risks, such as the risk that a director or employee may act wholly self-interestedly, using their position to benefit only themselves, as when 'skimming the take' or when making recommendations for promotion dependent on the provision of sexual favours.[68] I consider such cases below. However, it is 'commercially intrinsic' risks with which a business is most closely associated, in virtue of its raison d'être. These are the risks that arise from conduct *aimed at* making the company commercially successful, such as the risk that an employee might pay a bribe or engage in fraud to win a contract of potential value to the firm. In such a case, the employee may naturally also be hoping to benefit themselves, by proving a success in securing the contract (which may even have been their main intention); but in this instance, that intention to benefit personally comes accompanied by an intention to benefit the firm commercially.[69] The presence of the latter intention, when someone commits an offence in the capacity of an associated person, provides a fair and appropriate normative foundation for convicting the company for failing to prevent the offence.

Corporate criminal liability for fault-based offences should be especially, even if not solely, concerned with providing a structure within which companies can be held accountable when commercially intrinsic risks of criminal activity turn into reality: model E, as a basis for liability, from Section I.4. The associated person's intention to benefit the firm, by committing the crime, is an intention they would not have formed and acted on, were it not for their role in the company as a (would-be) going concern. Although taking the form of a free, deliberate, and informed act on the associated person's part, the crime they commit is thus a role-based act related to the company's pursuit of its commercial objectives. It thus provides an appropriate normative foundation for a company's conviction for a failure to prevent its occurrence (subject to a procedures-based defence), irrespective of the company's state of mind. Consider, by contrast, the offence of failing to prevent the facilitation

[68] See the private law case of *Lister v Hesley Hall Ltd* [2002] 1 AC 215.

[69] Government guidance on the failure-to-prevent-fraud offence under the 2023 Act makes it clear that even if an associated person's principal intent is to benefit themselves, the possession of a (subsidiary) intent to benefit the company is sufficient: Home Office (2024), 11: 'The intention to benefit the organisation does not have to be the sole or dominant motivation for the fraud. The offence can apply where a fraudster's primary motivation was to benefit themselves, but where their actions will also benefit the organisation.'

of tax evasion, contrary to the Criminal Finances Act 2017. Section 45(1) of the 2017 Act, which creates the UK-based version of the offence, provides that 'a relevant body (B) is guilty of an offence if a person commits a UK tax evasion facilitation offence when acting in the capacity of a person associated with B'. What should we make of this offence? A controversial element of offences based purely on the capacity in which the associated person acts is that they do not rule out holding the company liable when the offence committed by the associated person is entirely self-serving.[70] As Karl Laird points out in his commentary on the 2017 Act, a company might be held liable for failing to prevent the facilitation of tax evasion, contrary to section 45, when the associated person uses the capacity granted by the firm to facilitate the evasion of their own personal tax liability.[71] In such circumstances, the case for incriminating the firm—if it did not have reasonable procedures in place to prevent such offending—seems weak, in the absence of the normative foundation provided by an associated person's intention to benefit the firm by offending. In such cases, it is submitted that a different normative foundation for conviction must be found, in the form of an element of culpability on the firm's (meaning the directors') part.

This brings me directly to the distinction, set out in the Introduction,[72] between two species of failure-to-prevent crime. First, there is the (now) quite commonly encountered variety—my main focus—in which the associated person's intention to benefit the firm plays a crucial role in establishing corporate liability (model E from Section I.4). Secondly, there is a putative variety, in which no such intention on the part of the associated person is required (model D from Section I.4). The need to consider the latter is raised by the drafting of clause 196 of the Crime and Policing 2025 Bill. The 2025 Bill will make it possible to convict companies of any offence in English law, including (say) murder, rape, or bigamy. As we saw in the Introduction, that clause will make companies liable for any crime committed by a senior manager, if the manager committed it when acting within the scope of their actual or apparent authority. It follows that a company is exposed to liability, when that test is met, even when a senior manager acts purely self-interestedly and for non-commercial purposes. To recall the example from the Introduction, a private medical company is now exposed to liability for rape, if one of its senior doctor-managers deceives a patient into believing the sexual intercourse is actually a kind of invasive medical examination,[73] in circumstances where had a lower-ranking employee-doctor done the same thing, no corporate liability would arise.

One way of avoiding that kind of counter-intuitive and arbitrary result would be to create a presumption that, if the company is to be convicted under clause

[70] See the discussion of this point in the Introduction.
[71] Karl Laird (2017).
[72] See Section 5.4 above.
[73] See *Flattery* (1877) 2 QB 410.

196 for an offence requiring an intentional element, that offence must have been engaged in by the senior manager in order to benefit the company commercially. That would allow the courts to use their common sense in deciding which offences require proof of an intention to provide a (commercial) benefit through offending. However, an alternative approach would be to apply the failure-to-prevent regime to all offences involving an intentional element, but in cases where there was no intention—whether or not a subsidiary intent—to benefit the firm, to require proof of fault at directorial level on the part of the company. In the Introduction, I suggested that this fault element should broadly follow what I called the '*Alford* principles',[74] taking the form of either (1) knowledge at the highest level of the company that the offending was going on or (2) awareness at the highest level that offending of this kind might be taking place, coupled with an absence of appropriate procedures in place to prevent it taking place. As argued in Chapter 3, in both these cases, the nature of the fault element is chosen for qualitative rather than quantitative reasons.

Building on the decision in *Hunt v Luck*,[75] knowledge or awareness (coupled with inadequate preventative procedures) of a state of affairs or course of conduct can be regarded as having the transformative quality or potential to change someone's normative position with regard to responsibility for the occurrence of that state of affairs or course of conduct. So, the possession of one or other of these states of mind at the highest level, in relation to an associated person's wrongdoing, means that the company cannot now disassociate itself from the commission of that wrongdoing, given that the company ex hypothesi had control or influence over the associated person's conduct,[76] even though the wrongdoing was not intended to benefit the company. The analogy here is the decision in *Gaunt*.[77] In *Gaunt*, an employee with learning difficulties had been subjected to persistent racial and physical harassment at the hands of other employees. The manager at the site admitted that he was aware that the complainant was forced into a grab device, and that objects were thrown at the complainant by other members of the staff. In admitting guilt, the manager's Counsel said of him that, 'by reason of his inaction he accepts that those responsible for those incidents may have taken the inaction as an encouragement of the conduct'.[78] The manager was found to be complicit in the offences and sentenced to imprisonment.[79] As indicated in the Introduction, there is clearly an irony about the application of the *Alford* principles to the failure-to-prevent model, in that this model was first designed to avoid the need for proof of (subjective) fault at the highest level. However, the introduction of such a

[74] See the discussion of *JF Alford Transport* [1997] EWCA Crim 654 in Section 3.4.
[75] [1902] 1 Ch 428.
[76] In accordance with the principles discussed in ch 3.
[77] [2003] EWCA Crim 3925.
[78] Ibid., para 10.
[79] See the discussion in ch 3.

requirement is the price that must be paid to establish a proper normative basis for convicting the company, when the free, deliberate, and informed wrongdoing of an associated person is not intended to benefit the company.

In cases involving commercially intrinsic risks, where the normative foundation for conviction is the associated person's 'intention to benefit' the company, an issue arises over the meaning of this term. For directors, statute provides that they should see the success of the company in terms of 'the benefit [to] its members as a whole',[80] a strategic conception of the intention to benefit. However, there is no reason to insist that associated persons must have acted with such an intention, when engaging in wrongdoing, if the firm is to be implicated. For example, employees or agents may seek to promote financial gain for the company, even though their acts will involve (unacceptable) reputational risks. In such instances, they should be regarded as acting in order to benefit the company even when they are aware that the company 'as a whole' may not benefit from their actions. In a discussion of vicarious liability, in *Standard Oil Company of Texas v US*,[81] the court explained the concept of intention to benefit in this way:

> If [the act] is done with a view of furthering the master's business, of doing something for the master, then the expectation or hope of a benefit, whether direct or indirect, makes the act that of the principal. The act is no less the principal's if from such intended conduct either no benefit accrues, a benefit is undiscernible, or, for that matter, the result turns out to be adverse.[82]

On this (rightly) broad account, an intention to benefit reflects, what I referred to in Chapter 1 as, the heterogenous nature of many companies, where different individuals within the firm may have different conceptions of where its interests lie, even if it is ultimately the directors who are responsible for the delivery of overall benefit to the company.

A related point about the meaning of an 'intention to benefit', raised briefly in Chapter 1, concerns the different conceptions of the company that may be involved in understanding that idea. On one view, companies are concrete legal entities involving a network of contracts.[83] On that view, to intend to benefit the company is to intend to pursue one's obligations under contract (such as meeting a sales target), even though the means one has chosen may involve criminal wrongdoing such as bribery or fraud. The wording of the 2010 Act (cited in Section 5.5 above), in setting out the failure-to-prevent offence—using the Organisation for Economic Co-operation and Development's (OECD) language of seeking to obtain or retain

80 Companies Act 2006, s 172.
81 307 F 2d 120 (5th Cir 1962).
82 Ibid., 128–29.
83 See the discussion in Eva Micheler (2021), ch 1, and in Section 1.2.

a business advantage—perhaps owes something to this understanding of benefitting a company. However, the 2023 Act uses the broader and simpler term 'intention to benefit', and that wording is marginally to be preferred. As indicated in Chapter 1, one can seek to benefit a company by treating it as an evolving real entity, helping it in terms (for example) of its evolving philosophy, goals, and self-image. A fraud can be committed to further such a real entity-based concern, such as a 'greenwashing' fraud that seeks to dupe customers or investors into believing that a company's overall ethos and outlook is environmentally responsible. Of course, such a fraud seeks in a sense to secure a 'business advantage'; but it is better to speak in terms of the broader notion of 'benefit', to avoid arguments that there was no intention to secure a specific (monetary) advantage through a fraud.[84]

5.7 'Associated Persons' and Failure-to-Prevent Crimes: The 2023 Act

As discussed in Chapter 2, the offence of failure to prevent fraud, contrary to section 199 of the 2023 Act, can be committed only by a 'large' organization, and not by a small- or medium-sized company.[85] Large companies may, though, have many people and satellite organizations attached to them. We considered the case of WPP in Section 5.4 above, but a more typical case involving a major banking firm would be that of Barclays, which listed over seventy 'entities' through which it was doing business in countries around the world in 2019,[86] and had no less than 85,000 people working in those entities.[87] The approach taken in the 2023 Act to the issue of who is associated with a large company, for the purposes of the failure-to-prevent fraud offence, is broader than the approach taken to that issue in the 2010 Act.[88] Section 199(7)–(8) of the 2023 Act reads as follows:

> (7) For the purposes of this section a person is associated with a relevant body if—
> (a) the person is an employee, agent or subsidiary undertaking of the relevant body, or
> (b) the person otherwise performs services for or on behalf of the body.

[84] Government guidance on this issue states: 'The [intended] benefit may be financial or non-financial. For example, a fraud intended to confer an unfair business advantage would be in scope, as this would constitute an indirect benefit. Equally, a fraud that disadvantaged a competitor would be in scope': Home Office (2024), 12.

[85] Unless the small company is a subsidiary of a larger company.

[86] https://home.barclays/content/dam/home-barclays/documents/investor-relations/reports-and-events/annual-reports/2019/Barclays%20PLC%202019%20Country%20Snapshot%20-%20LE%20Listing.pdf (last accessed 23/08/2025).

[87] https://www.barclays.ae/home/why-barclays/#:~:text=With%20over%20325%20years%20of,for%20customers%20and%20clients%20worldwide (last accessed 22/11/2023).

[88] Surprisingly, the approaches were not harmonized.

(8) For the purposes of this section a person is also associated with a relevant body if the person is an employee of a subsidiary undertaking of the relevant body [if and only if such a person intended, directly or indirectly, to benefit the main company when committing the offence].

Section 199(7)(a) thus makes it clear that all employees, agents, and subsidiaries are 'associated persons', whereas under the 2010 Act this issue must be resolved by showing that such a person was at the relevant time providing services 'for or on behalf of' the main company. So, the 2023 Act imposes what is in effect a duty on parent companies to intervene in the management and business activities of subsidiaries (however many they have), to ensure that they are doing enough to safeguard against fraud.[89]

In that regard, whilst there may not be big differences between the tests under the 2010 and 2023 Acts respectively, it is certainly possible that important differences could emerge as between the 2010 and 2023 Acts, in terms of the circumstances in which control or influence duties arise relating to subsidiaries. Here is a possible example:

Y company, based in Redland, is a subsidiary of a large UK company, X company. Redland suspends Y company's licence to trade while officials investigate its activities. After some months of suspension and hence inactivity, Y company directors bribe a Redland official to allow Y company to resume trading, and then engage in fraud to smuggle assets back to the United Kingdom.

In this example, assuming that the intention of the fraud was to benefit X company,[90] X company will be guilty of a failure to prevent fraud (unless it can establish a defence), simply in virtue of the fact that Y company was a subsidiary company at the time the offence is committed. By contrast, it is at least arguable that X company is not guilty of a failure to prevent bribery, because at the time of the offence Y company—putting aside the paying of the bribe, as the 2010 Act requires us to

[89] There is in effect (if not in law) a duty, because a failure to put in place reasonable safeguards against fraud will expose a company to strict liability for an offence. As indicated in the last section, the courts may also find that, unless it is merely a purpose trust, (orphan) SPVs are also in the circumstances 'persons' performing services for a company under section 199(7)(b), and are thus within the scope of the failure-to-prevent duty.

[90] Section 199(1)(b) of the 2023 Act makes it clear that a large company can commit the failure to prevent fraud offence not only when the intention of the fraudulent employee, agent, or subsidiary was to benefit the main company but also when the intention was to benefit 'any person to whom, or to whose subsidiary undertaking, the associate provides services on behalf of the relevant body'. By contrast, the 2010 Act requires simply an intention to benefit the main company. However, section 199(1)(b) should be regarded as largely clarificatory rather than an extension of the law. When (say) an X company subsidiary engages in bribery to benefit a different X company subsidiary, whilst more broadly engaged in providing services for X company, it ought to be easy to infer that such an act was—albeit indirectly—intended to benefit X company, thus fulfilling the terms of section 7 of the 2010 Act.

do—was not in fact providing services for or on behalf of X company. It would have been helpful had the 2023 Act made amendments to the 2010 Act to clarify how such a point should be decided.

Section 199 doubles down on its broader approach to 'associated' persons, by extending the liability of a parent company for failure-to-prevent when fraud is committed by an employee of a subsidiary,[91] and not just by the corporate subsidiary itself. Section 199(8) says: 'For the purposes of this section a person is also associated with a relevant body if the person is an employee of a subsidiary undertaking of the relevant body', although in such a case the associate must intend the fraud offence to benefit the parent company itself. Here is an example:

> C company sets up a subsidiary in Blueland, and gives one of its Redland subsidiaries the task of ensuring that the Blueland subsidiary builds up its business successfully. Some months later, with the Blueland subsidiary struggling financially, an accounts clerk working for the Redland subsidiary commits fraud in order to keep the Blueland subsidiary afloat and hence benefit C company.

It might seem obvious that if C company can be guilty of a failure to prevent fraud when the Redland subsidiary itself commits a fraud (indirectly) to benefit C company, then C company should equally be guilty of failing to prevent fraud when an employee of the Redland subsidiary commits fraud with same end in view; but it is in fact far from obvious.

An employee employed by a subsidiary is typically in law a further step removed from the parent company than the subsidiary itself, and—in the absence of contractual conditions, or some other state of affairs indicating otherwise[92]—will owe their duties entirely to the subsidiary company. It will thus ordinarily be the responsibility of the subsidiary to secure the ethical conduct of the employee, not the responsibility of the parent company. Other things being equal, a subsidiary employee is a legal 'stranger' to the parent company. So, the mere fact that a subsidiary company employee commits fraud to benefit the parent company does no normative work, vis-à-vis the establishment of the parent company's responsibility for that act. There are probably only two sets of circumstances in which such a normative connection could be established. First, the parent company would rightly be regarded as bearing responsibility if it was aware that employees of the subsidiary might commit a fraud offence to benefit the company, but stood by and did nothing. Secondly, the relevant duty to prevent might arise when the relevant *Chandler v Cape*[93] conditions have been established in relation to particular

[91] Non-employee agents working for a subsidiary are for some reason not included within scope.

[92] Such as the sharing between management and subsidiary of management responsibility for hiring employees: see, generally, *Okpabi & Others v Royal Dutch Shell Plc & Another* [2021] UKSC 3.

[93] [2012] EWCA Civ 525. See the discussion of *Chandler v Cape* in Section 5.8 below.

(groups of) employees. The Supreme Court has expressed these conditions to include circumstances in which a parent company was:

(a) taking steps to adopt and implement group-wide policies,[94] or
(b) holding out that it exercises a particular degree of supervision and control through a subsidiary.[95]

As things stand under section 199, though, to go back to my example of Barclays, it seems that the parent banking company's unconditional supervisory duties respecting the prevention of fraud extend not only to the seventy entities working on its behalf in over forty countries worldwide, but also to the 85,000 employees working for those entities. The difficulty of establishing adequate procedures in such circumstances is a recipe for the development of the classic perverse incentive of unrestrained strict liability: the incentive to cover up offending rather than prevent it occurring.[96]

5.8 Liability for the Crimes of Independent Companies

In relation to the potential liability of large companies for failing to prevent fraud committed by organizations in a 'supply chain' Government guidance says this:

> Companies within an organisation's supply chain are not associated persons unless they are providing services for or on behalf of the relevant body. Where they are providing services for or on behalf of the relevant body, they are associated persons, even if they do not contract directly with the relevant organisation.[97]

An arms-length commercial relationship does not necessarily imply or require an arms-length ethical relationship. Can or should an independent company be an 'associated person', for the purposes of the failure-to-prevent offences under 2010 and the 2023 Acts? In answer to this question, I suggest that in some circumstances, an independent company can be an associated person. That relationship between companies can come about if the main company exercises de facto control or influence over the independent company, in such a manner as to give rise to

[94] In that regard, it is notable that Government guidance on parent company liability states: 'Depending on the organisation's structure, there are steps that can be taken by parent undertakings to prevent fraud by subsidiaries. For example, implementing group level policies or training and ensuring that there is a nominated person responsible for fraud prevention in each subsidiary': Home Office (2024), 13.
[95] *Okpabi & Others v Royal Dutch Shell Plc & Another* [2021] UKSC 3, paras 26–27.
[96] On perverse incentives in corporate criminal law, see Jennifer Arlen (1994).
[97] I considered the meaning of 'providing services for or in behalf of' a relevant body in Section 5.7 above.

a duty of ethical supervision and intervention. If that is accepted, then in some circumstances, a company can be liable for failing to prevent economic crimes committed by its independent contractors. However, the courts should not too readily find that such circumstances exist, because there will otherwise be a risk that an over-extensive and disproportionate burden of crime (or human rights abuse) prevention will be placed on companies. The right way to capture the normal ethical relationship between companies in (say) a supply chain is to describe it as one in which—to go back to a distinction drawn in Chapter 3—the main company has oversight duties but not (supervisory) control-based crime-prevention duties with respect to other companies in the chain.

Suppose, as in the problematic example given at the start of this chapter, that it is alleged that X company failed to prevent bribery committed for its benefit by a fully independent contractor (Z company), contrary to section 7 of the Bribery Act 2010:

> X company sets up a subsidiary, Y company, to source from overseas the latest software programmes for X company's computers. X company also hires an external consulting firm, Z company, to advise on the right software programmes. Unknown to X company, Y company pays a bribe to secure an important software programme, and Z company pays a bribe to secure the services of an expert whose advice is needed.

This example exposes some arbitrariness in the Government's assumption that there is a clear distinction between companies providing services 'for' the main company (within scope) and companies providing services 'to' the main company (outside scope).[98] In the example, both Y and Z can equally be described as either providing services 'for' X company or 'to' X company. However, it seems likely that, for the purpose of determining the scope of the failure-to-prevent bribery offence, only Y company—in virtue of being a subsidiary—would be regarded as in law an 'associated person'. By contrast, it seems probable that Z company would not be so regarded, because Z company is a wholly independent contractor.

However, it is important not to fall into the trap, which the 2010 Act clearly seeks to avoid, of being too formalistic in analysing such situations. Consider, by way of example, supermarkets' use of the so-called buyer power to dictate terms of business to their suppliers (especially those involved in agricultural produce).[99] In some instances, supermarkets have been known to use their dominant market position to demand retrospective payments, extra discounts, after-sale rebates, and retrospective changes to agreed terms, amongst other forms of market coercion.[100]

98 See the Government guidance cited in Section 5.6 above.
99 Catherine Nicholson and Bob Young (2012).
100 Ibid., 6.

What should be the position when a main company is able to use its position to interfere in such ways, to its benefit, in its business partner's terms of trade, even if the relationship may have begun as an arms-length contract between independent contractors? In such circumstances, there is a case for saying that the business partner is now an 'associated person' over whose terms of business the main company has a crime prevention–related duty of ethical supervision (not just an oversight duty), whether or not it can be determined that the business partner is providing services 'for' and not 'to' the supermarket. So, if, for example, the business partner engages in bribery with a third party in order to help it to fulfil its contract with the main company, the bribery may be regarded an offence that, in law, the main company failed to prevent for the purposes of section 7.

In that regard, there is an analogy here with the way in which private law treats the relationship between companies and third parties injured by the (in)action of one of their subsidiaries, In *Chandler v Cape*,[101] Chandler had contracted asbestosis as a result of working for a Cape Ltd subsidiary, Cape Building Products Ltd, some fifty years before. The subsidiary was no longer trading, and so Chandler brought an action in tort against Cape Ltd. The Court of Appeal upheld his claim that Cape Ltd had itself assumed a responsibility for protecting his health from the risks of asbestos, and breached their duty of care to him through negligence. The court did not set down an exclusive list of circumstances in which a parent company would be found to have assumed a responsibility towards third parties dealing with one of its subsidiaries.[102] However, the court said, amongst other things:

> The court will look at the relationship between the companies more widely. The court may find that . . . [a duty] is established where the evidence shows that the parent has a practice of intervening in the trading operations of the subsidiary.[103]

Of particular relevance to this context is the Court of Appeal's later explanation of the *Chandler v Cape* duty as capable of arising where the parent company has given relevant advice to the subsidiary about how it should manage a particular risk (which might be a risk of financial crime).[104] The giving of such advice is something that could equally happen in the course of a relationship between a company and a (long-term) contractual partner. It is always possible to argue that cases determining the scope of private law duties have no relevance or application to the criminal law. However, that argument is a double-edged sword, so far as determining the scope of a duty is concerned. In some instances, the duty of care may be

[101] [2012] EWCA Civ 525. See also *Lungowe v Vandata and KCM* (2017) EWCA Civ 1528.
[102] [2012] EWCA Civ 525, para 80.
[103] Ibid.
[104] *Unilever PLC and Unilever Tea Kenya Limited* [2018] EWCA Civ 1532.

wider in criminal law than it is in private law.[105] It is thus arguable, by analogy with *Cape*, that if a parent adopts a practice of intervening in the trading operations of a contractual partner (not just a subsidiary), that may make the partner an 'associated person'. Accordingly, the company will then be responsible, albeit perhaps only at a high level, for the ethical standards observed by that partner when it is acting to benefit the company.

To reflect further on this point, let us go back to some of the criteria set out in Section 5.4 above in *Smith, Stone and Knight v City of Birmingham*[106] to determine when a subsidiary is acting as the agent of its parent: such as whether the parent governed the activities of the subsidiary, and whether the parent is in effectual and constant control. We can see here the implicit influence of a restricted Hohfeldian model of correlative relations between the companies, in which what matters is a control-based notion that the parent has the right to determine the subsidiary's conduct, and the subsidiary has the duty to follow the directions of the parent in that regard.[107] By contrast, the model of relations between parent and subsidiary relied on in *Cape* is different. In *Cape*, the question was, had the parent, inter alia:

1. given relevant advice to the subsidiary about how it should manage a particular risk?
2. had a practice of intervening in the trading operations of the subsidiary?
3. provided high-level strategy guidance to the subsidiary?

A different model of jural relations, governed by the influence principle, lies behind this conceptualization of the relationship between a parent and its subsidiary. As we saw in Chapter 3 (concerning the relations between company directors), another correlative relationship to be found in legal systems, but unaccounted for by Hohfeld, is 'having a right to influence',[108] and its jural correlative, 'a duty to be receptive to such influence'.[109] Suppose that, either through practice (such as exercise of market dominance) or through agreement, the relationship between a parent company and a contracting partner dependent on trading with the company is such that the parent has assumed a right to influence the partner's trading policy and conduct, and the partner has correlatively submitted to a duty to be receptive to such influence. Then, it can be argued that the requisite degree of connection between the company and the partner has been established, making the latter an 'associated person' providing services under the 2010 and 2023 Acts.

[105] An example is provided by *Willoughby* [2004] EWCA Crim 3365, in which the Court of Appeal refused to apply the private law doctrine of *ex turpi causa* to limit the scope of a duty of care.
[106] (1939) 4 All ER 116.
[107] Wesley Newcomb Hohfeld (1917), 710. See also the discussion of this issue in ch 3.
[108] The jural opposite of that, in Hohfeldian terms, being 'having no influence-right'.
[109] The jural opposite of that, in Hohfeldian terms, being 'no duty to be receptive to influence'.

Having said that, it is not clear that the courts should be too readily disposed to find that independent contractors are persons associated with a company, for the purposes of failure-to-prevent offences. In that regard, the metaphor of 'supply chain' can be misleading. Such chains may be more or less tightly bound together, with some (parts of) chains involving close collaboration and direction, and other (parts of) chains involving a much lower degree of interdependency.[110] Accordingly, a finding that an independent contractor is an 'associated person' ought to be highly fact-specific, and not a matter for presumption. A less unwieldy and uncertain solution would be to place companies under a 'duty of vigilance' (discussed in detail in the next section) with regard to economic crime procedures adopted by their contracting and subcontracting partners, backed by administrative penalties or criminal sanctions for breach of the duty: model C from Section I.4. On this model of corporate crime, a company would not be under an obligation itself to prevent economic crime committed by an independent contractor. Instead, it would be under a duty—an oversight duty—to satisfy itself that the contractor themselves has robust procedures in place for economic crime prevention. That is also a model that could be adopted in relation to human rights abuses in the supply chain.

5.9 Liability for the Human Rights Abuses of Independent Contractors

The International Labour Organisation estimates that, worldwide, the profits from forced labour in the private sector are \$236 billion.[111] The majority of these profits come from sexual exploitation,[112] but (heavy) industry and service provision account for the largest share of these profits outside of that context. Some 70 per cent of international trade involves production in global supply chains, with goods and services exchanged across frontiers before being developed into a consumer-ready product.[113] Almost inevitably, thus, knowingly or unwittingly, otherwise legitimate UK-based companies are at risk of making profits from trade with organizations involved in forced labour. To what extent does the criminal law already impose liability on companies engaging in 'at risk' transactions? Knowledge or suspicion that a contracting organization may be involved in human rights abuses, such as forced labour, already exposes companies to liability for proceeds of crime

[110] Indeed, a company may sometimes outsource the management of the supply chain to a third party, rather than seek to deal with such issues itself.

[111] International Labour Organisation (2024), 15.

[112] Commercial sexual exploitation accounts for more than two-thirds (73 per cent) of the total illegal profits from forced labour, despite accounting for only 27 per cent of the total number of victims in privately imposed labour: ibid.

[113] https://www.chathamhouse.org/2021/09/us-and-european-strategies-resilient-supply-chains/02-global-supply-chains-definition (last accessed 12/08/2024).

offences, even when they have paid a market price to a supplier for goods and services received.[114] Moreover, even in the absence of such knowledge or suspicion, a UK-based company could conceivably face liability for failing to prevent the facilitation of tax evasion in such cases, as tax evasion is a crime embedded in the practice of forced labour.[115] On this point, the UK Government's message to businesses is that they are obliged to check, 'your suppliers' tax and legal compliance, for example, submitting their tax returns and payments on time, complying with legal and social responsibilities, and having reasonable procedures to prevent the criminal facilitation of UK and foreign tax evasion'.[116]

However, in labelling terms, a facilitation of tax evasion offence is not a substitute for an offence of failure-to-prevent human rights abuses as such: an offence advocated by a number of influential organizations,[117] and carefully considered—although not endorsed—by the Law Commission.[118] In that regard, the point was made in the last section that an independent contractor can be regarded as an associated person, in virtue of a relationship of influence that may have been established between a company and one or more of its contractors in the supply chain. In the *Vedanta* case,[119] which concerned liability in tort for harm done by health and environmental damage at the hands of a subsidiary company, Lord Briggs said of the liability of the main company:

> Even where group-wide policies do not of themselves give rise to such a duty of care to third parties, they may do so if the parent does not merely proclaim them, but takes active steps, by training, supervision and enforcement, to see that they are implemented by relevant subsidiaries. Similarly, it seems to me that the parent may incur the relevant responsibility to third parties if, in published materials, it holds itself out as exercising that degree of supervision and control of its subsidiaries.[120]

The *Vedanta* case, unlike the *Cape* case, appears to place greater emphasis on the element of main company 'control', rather than main company 'influence', but it is nonetheless submitted that where a relationship of influence along proto-Hohfeldian lines[121] has been established between a main company and any other

[114] The nature of such exposure is explained by the Court of Appeal in *R (World Uyghur Conference) V NCA* [2024] EWCA Civ 715.
[115] See the discussion in International Labour Organisation (2024).
[116] https://www.gov.uk/government/publications/use-of-labour-providers/advice-on-applying-supply-chain-due-diligence-principles-to-assure-your-labour-supply-chains (last accessed 21/03/2025).
[117] See, e.g., UK Joint Committee on Human Rights (2016–17).
[118] See the discussion in Law Commission (2022), ch 8. See the comprehensive discussion in Nick Friedman (2021).
[119] *Vedanta Resources PLC and another (Appellants) v Lungowe and others (Respondents)* [2019] UKSC 20.
[120] Ibid., para 53.
[121] See the discussion in Section 5.9 above.

body, that relationship may be sufficient to make the other body an 'associated person'.

Even so, as indicated at the end of the last section, it would be possible to adopt a different approach to human rights abuses in the supply chain. This would involve placing companies under a regulatory or criminal law–backed duty of vigilance: an oversight duty to check whether independent contractors have robust procedures in place to prevent human rights abuses being committed by their own managers or employees, or by subcontractors: liability model C from Section I.4. Such a duty is what I referred to in Chapter 3 as an oversight duty, as compared with the supervisory-interventionist control or influence duties.

The Office of the High Commissioner for Human Rights has defined human rights due diligence as follows:

> [H]uman rights due diligence comprises an ongoing management process that a reasonable and prudent enterprise needs to undertake, in light of its circumstances (including sector, operating context, size and similar factors) to meet its responsibility to respect human rights.[122]

An unanswered question arises from this definition, which is central to a discussion of the limits of corporate liability. Can a company fully discharge by *indirect* means what is called by the Office of the High Commissioner 'its [the company's] responsibility to respect human rights', by simply checking on whether another (independent) person has procedures in place to respect human rights? Thus understood, a duty of human rights vigilance is what might be called an 'auxiliary' human rights obligation. As the term implies, an auxiliary obligation buttresses or supports (the discharge of) a primary obligation. Just as the practice of installing CCTV cameras in public places can be intended to buttress and support prohibitions on public order offences, so a (secondary) duty of human rights vigilance on the part of a main company can provide auxiliary support for a (primary) duty on a contracting partner not to engage in human rights violations.

A duty of prevention involves a primary duty to ensure that someone—or a class of persons—come to no harm either from some conduct on my part or from some activity in which persons under my supervision or control are involved.[123] Failure-to-prevent offences are, of course, primary duties of that type. Following the *Cape* line of authority,[124] private law sometimes finds that a primary duty of prevention has arisen between a main company and persons who have suffered human rights abuses at the hands of a subsidiary company: where the subsidiary's conduct was

[122] Office of the UN High Commissioner for Human Rights (2012), 4.

[123] See the discussion of *Home Office v Dorset Yacht Club* [1970] AC 1004, in *Vedanta Resources PLC and another (Appellants) v Lungowe and others (Respondents)* [2019] UKSC 20.

[124] See the discussion in Section 5.8 above.

in some relevant respect subject to the control of the main company.[125] What gives rise to the primary duty of prevention is the main company's control over the conduct or policies that led to the breaches of human rights committed or permitted by the subsidiary.[126] So, the key duty-based relationship is thus a direct one between the main company and the very individuals who suffered harm.

With the distinction between primary and auxiliary duties in mind, what is the nature of the obligation imposed on UK-based large companies by section 54 of the Modern Slavery Act 2015?

> Large companies with a UK base are obliged by section 54(4) to:
>
> prepare a slavery and human trafficking statement for each financial year of the organisation …
>
> (a) a statement of the steps the organisation has taken during the financial year to ensure that slavery and human trafficking is not taking place—
>
> (i) in any of its supply chains, and
>
> (ii) in any part of its own business, or
>
> (b) a statement that the organisation has taken no such steps.

We can now see that, in so far as it is concerned with the active prevention of human rights abuses, section 54 is not concerned with merely being vigilant but with the primary duty of prevention. To be sure, in virtue of section 54(4)(b), a large company can opt simply to declare that it has taken no steps with regard to respect for human rights in the supply chain. However, if the large company does decide to issue a declaratory statement, that statement must concern, as section 54(4)(a) puts it, 'the steps the organisation has taken during the financial year to ensure that slavery and human trafficking *is not taking place*' (my emphasis). In other words, the statement must concern the large company's attempts to prevent actual human rights abuses in the supply chain (and not just the risk of such abuses occurring), period. The statement must therefore concern the relationship between the large company and those who have suffered the abuses, even if the steps taken come in the form of pressure placed on the abusing contracting party.

By contrast, an oversight duty of vigilance is focused solely on the relationship between the large company and its contracting party. The key question is what, if anything, was the large company doing to check whether the relevant contracting parties have robust and active policies in place to prevent human rights abuses in

[125] *Vedanta Resources PLC and another (Appellants) v Lungowe and others (Respondents)* [2019] UKSC 20.

[126] The language of 'control', in relation to subsidiaries, is also the language used in the French 'duty of vigilance' law: 'Art L225-102-4—1, "The controlled subsidiaries or companies that exceed the thresholds mentioned in the first paragraph are deemed to satisfy the obligations laid down in this Article from the moment that the company which controls them, within the meaning of Article L. 233-3, establishes and implements a vigilance plan for the company's operations, as well as the operations of all the subsidiaries or companies that it controls." '

the workplace? This is an auxiliary duty, a duty meant to support or underpin the primary duty on the contracting parties not to engage in human rights abuses. As the *Chandler v Cape* line of authority makes clear, it is always possible that a large company might engage in this (auxiliary) duty in such a way as to be regarded as having accepted a (primary) duty of prevention respecting persons who went on to suffer human rights abuses at the hands of a contracting party. Even so, it is not inherent in the nature of the discharge of an auxiliary vigilance obligation of oversight that it will have this consequence. Had there been a better understanding in 2015 of the distinction between auxiliary oversight duties of vigilance (liability model C from Section I.4), and primary duties of preventive control or influence (liability models D and E from Section I.4), perhaps the Government would not have felt it necessary to include section 45(4)(b) permitting companies to 'opt out' of seeking to ensure respect for human rights in the supply chain, because the duties on companies were confined to auxiliary vigilance duties.

We find a similar conflation of the auxiliary oversight duty of vigilance and the primary duty of prevention in the French 'duty of vigilance' law relating to human rights abuses and environmental harms in a supply chain involving a large France-based company.[127] The law requires:

> reasonable vigilance measures . . . [that] allow for risk identification and for the prevention of severe violations of human rights and fundamental freedoms, serious bodily injury or environmental damage or health risks resulting directly or indirectly from the operations of the company and of the companies it controls within the meaning of Article L.233-16, II, as well as from the operations of the subcontractors or suppliers with whom it maintains an established commercial relationship, when such operations derive from this relationship.[128]

Under this provision, thus, the duty of 'risk identification' (auxiliary vigilance duty) is treated pari passu with the duty of 'prevention' (primary care duty) of serious human rights or environmental violations.[129] Even so, when it comes to the

[127] The law applies to French companies with more than 5,000 employees in the company's direct or indirect French-based subsidiaries and with more than 10,000 employees if including direct and indirect subsidiaries globally.

[128] Article L225-102-4—I.

[129] The law provides for a formal notice mechanism to order the company to comply with its vigilance obligations. In case of non-compliance, a court can order the company to comply with its vigilance obligations. This includes ordering the company to develop a vigilance plan when such a plan is missing, or to improve its vigilance measures when these are inadequate. A court may impose a penalty for each day of non-compliance.

The law also provides for civil liability. Under the law, harmed individuals can bring a civil lawsuit (based on French tort law) to seek damages resulting from a company's failure to comply with its vigilance obligations, where compliance would have prevented the harm: see https://www.business-humanrights.org/en/big-issues/corporate-legal-accountability/frances-duty-of-vigilance-law/ (last accessed 15/08/2024).

detail of what must be in a large company's strategic plan for tackling such violations, the emphasis is clearly on vigilance (risk identification and evaluation) rather than on prevention. Article L225-102-4—I goes on to say:

The plan . . . shall include the following measures:

1. A mapping that identifies, analyses and ranks risks;
2. Procedures to regularly assess, in accordance with the risk mapping, the situation of subsidiaries, subcontractors or suppliers with whom the company maintains an established commercial relationship;
3. Appropriate action to mitigate risks or prevent serious violations;
4. An alert mechanism that collects reporting of existing or actual risks, developed in working partnership with the trade union organizations representatives of the company concerned;
5. (new) A monitoring scheme to follow up on the measures implemented and assess their efficiency.

The emphasis here is clearly on the oversight of risk identification, evaluation, and mitigation, rather than on prevention as such. In relation to independent contractors, as opposed to bodies under the direct control or influence of a large company, that may be a fairer and more proportionate approach. Placing an emphasis on a duty of vigilance and oversight (liability model C from Section I.4), as opposed to a far more—perhaps impossibly—demanding duty of prevention (liability model D or E from Section I.4), makes it perhaps more likely that large companies will be willing to take a broader and more open approach to risk, working with external agencies such as NGOs and, for example, the Gangmasters Licensing Authority. Such an approach can be coupled with, for example, the inclusion of indemnity or penalty clauses with contractors requiring them to compensate a large company in respect of any damages the company must pay out following human rights abuse or environmental harm done by the contractor.

6
THE AFTERMATH OF CORPORATE WRONGDOING

6.1 Corporate Crime and Penitential Punishments

PROBLEMATIC EXAMPLE: D company, a UK-based multinational IT company, is negotiating a deferred prosecution agreement with the Serious Fraud Office (SFO), following the discovery of evidence implicating the company in bribery worldwide over two decades. As part of the settlement, the SFO proposes a fine of £250 million, in line with previous fines for offending on a similar scale. The company instead proposes to spend £150 million over ten years on establishing a division of the firm devoted to increasing IT capacity and innovation in jurisdictions where the bribery offending took place.

In this chapter, I seek to explain and justify the place of 'intrinsic value–generating' forms of punishment, amongst the possible responses of the state to corporate wrongdoing, especially—even if not solely—serious wrongdoing in the form of a failure to prevent economic crime.[1] Intrinsic value–generating forms of punishment principally involve what I call victim- or community-focused penitential commitments, when undertaken as part of a broader, integrated penitential response to wrongdoing on the part of the offender.[2] At the behest of the state, victim- or community-focused penitential commitments involve hard treatment in the form of compelled investment of resources, time, and effort in 'common good' projects or enterprises. A common good project is a project or enterprise in which everyone (albeit in practice, perhaps, those living in a certain area), or a key defined group such as victims of a particular crime, stands to benefit through non-exclusive use of the good.[3] Illustrations of penal use of common good projects are:

[1] The account I provide draws inspiration from John Gardner's work on the 'activity condition' in English criminal law: John Gardner (1998).

[2] The idea of penitential activity is in some ways similar to John Braithwaite's notion of 'reintegrative shaming': see John Braithwaite (2016) and John Braithwaite (2020). However, it seems contentious that 'shaming' needs to be an enforced element of penitential activity, and so I avoid use of that notion here.

[3] So defined, a common good is provided in 'common', even if access to it may in some instances be rivalrous, as when not all victims qualify for access to the benefit.

A Theory of Corporate Crime. Jeremy Horder, Oxford University Press. © Jeremy Horder 2026.
DOI: 10.1093/9780198936534.003.0007

1. compelling polluters to become involved in making environmental improvements and contributing to urban regeneration (community-focused projects) and
2. requiring fraudulent companies to provide training and skills programmes in IT fraud resilience for vulnerable people, especially those affected by the companies' fraud (a victim-focused project).

A key element of the intrinsic value–generation in the establishment and running of a common good project is the commitment shown by the offender to the project over its duration, as part of their penitential response to wrongdoing. Accordingly, as a response to corporate wrongdoing, the hard treatment involved has a morally active dimension. It is a process engaged in *by* the offender, and not a one-off (financial) impact *on* the offender. In consequence, the success of the punishment is measured over time—diachronically—and depends in part on what creative energy and imagination the wrongdoer has consistently brought to bear in discharging their penitential obligations to develop the relevant common good.[4] My defence of intrinsic value–generating penitential commitments to the development of common goods, as the morally soundest form of corporate punishment, is a dimension of the liberal-welfarist approach to corporate liability. This is an approach in which private companies prove their responsible citizenship by demonstrating their willingness to become involved in developing (or restoring) some of the conditions of human flourishing.[5]

Thus understood, an intrinsic value–generating common good project is to be contrasted with two alternative kinds of punitive response. First, there is the grant of individual private goods, such as compensation payments; and secondly, there are contributions (such as fines) to common pool resources that increase aggregate state wealth. Both of these are wealth redistributive kinds of punishment that in many cases may be permitted or required in the interests of justice. However, as we will see, the conceptions of justice to which these kinds of redistributive punishment are linked—*restitutio in integrum* in the case of compensation, and just deserts in the case of fines[6]—have proved to be deeply problematic in the most

[4] In a way, this idea represents a development and expansion of Brent Fisse's theory that companies should be judged by reference to their reaction to the discovery of wrongdoing: 'Reactive corporate fault may be broadly defined as unreasonable corporate failure to devise and undertake satisfactory preventive or corrective measures in response to the commission, by personnel acting on behalf of the organization, of the actus reus of the offence': Brent Fisse (1990), 253.

[5] Section I.2.

[6] Backward-looking punishment theories, such as just deserts theories focused on fines and compensation orders, are aimed (in a rough-and-ready way) at re-establishing a supposed moral status quo upset by the offending. So, for John Finnis, punishment 'characteristically seeks to restore the distributively just balance of advantages between the criminal and the law-abiding': John Finnis (1980), 263. See https://www.sentencingcouncil.org.uk/offences/magistrates-court/item/organisations-illegal-discharges-to-air-land-and-water-unauthorised-or-harmful-deposit-treatment-or-disposal-etc-of-waste/ (last accessed 29/10/2024). For criticism of backward-looking theories of punishment, see Victor Tadros (2011), Victor Tadros (2017), and the discussion in Section 6.6 below.

serious cases.[7] For example, just deserts–based constraints of proportionality may mean that a fine should not exceed a certain level, even when it is known that the offender will treat a fine at that level as merely a tolerable cost of doing business. Further, the value generated where either compensation orders are made or fines are imposed is extrinsic in character. What matters is simply that the outcome of *restitutio in integrum* or just deserts is achieved synchronically, at the moment when D pays the compensation or the fine when ordered to do so. D's attitude towards the payment or D's intentions regarding future behaviour, in the light of the punishment imposed, are punitively quite irrelevant.

Consider this example:

> A company is ordered to pay £1 million in fines and £10 million in compensation for bribery-related offences. A majority of directors resolve to refuse to make any payments and to defy the court's rulings. However, the Finance Director privately disagrees with the directors' decision, and pays the fines and compensation.

In this example, the company will be regarded as having fulfilled its punitive obligations when the money is paid. The hostile attitude and the collective decision of the directors to defy the court ruling makes no difference. There need be, thus, no penitential attitude—or, indeed, any attitude at all on the offender's part—involved in the making of the payments themselves, which are valued purely as a means to the wealth redistributive ends of compensatory *restitutio* and just deserts.

It is essential to note that the employment of fines (or compensation orders) may be fully justified in many—perhaps in most—cases (I say more about this in due course). Further, given the commonplace nature of low-level offending, it is also justified to systematize their use. Even so, such practices should not blind us to the fact that the justification for using fines—whether or not systematically—must always be considered a 'second-best' justification: the opposite of the current position under which fines are regarded as presumptively the best (just deserts–based) option.[8] Fines should be regarded as justifiable only as a second-best option, however widely they must be used in practice, because they are morally inferior to intrinsic value–generating forms of punishment. They are little more than a mechanism for opportunistic wealth redistribution between an offending company and the state, which in transnational cases may not even be the state in which the offending company's HQ was located or where the offending itself took place.[9] Even so, we should acknowledge that second-best justifications for

[7] Many commentators have viewed the utility of fines in corporate contexts unfavourably: see, e.g., Brent Fisse (1990), 214ff.

[8] For a good discussion of the weakness of fines as a form of corporate punishment, see ibid. By contrast, whilst compensation orders are not a 'second-best' option in all instances—far from it—their use is nonetheless morally problematic in many instances, as we will see.

[9] See the discussion in Section 6.2 below.

particular forms of punishments are still justifications for the use of such punishments. So, in minor- to medium-level cases of corporate wrongdoing, it may be that the use of fines is justified. This will, in part, be simply because seeking a victim- or community-focused response from the wrongdoer would be disproportionately time-consuming for the wrongdoer and for the supervising authority, or because (given the low level of seriousness) any such response would be purely a token one. Accordingly, in many cases, resort to calculation of cardinal and ordinal proportionality in relation to fining may be the right (second-best) approach.

However, the more serious the corporate wrongdoing, the greater the potential for the moral inferiority of using fines as a punishment to manifest itself, and hence the greater the need for an approach with superior moral integrity. Such an approach may be found in requiring corporate offenders to give their wholehearted (penitential) commitment to developing and sustaining appropriate victim- or community-focused common good projects. When a corporate wrongdoer has badly failed in their role as a worthwhile member of a local, national, or—in some instances—international community, a principal aim of punishment ought to be to build the company back up as a credible performer of that role. Penitential responses to wrongdoing of the kind I advocate, offered to one or more of these communities, can involve an authentic reaffirmation of a company's status as a worthwhile member of the community. This is something that purely redistributive (retributive or compensatory) demands made by the state will be increasingly unable to do, the more serious the offence in issue. That brings me to a consideration of the intrinsic value–generating element of penitential punishment when a company has offended.

When an individual offender engages in ex hypothesi valuable forms of community service, they must obviously engage in such service personally.[10] In corporate cases, matters are not so simple. In some cases, there may be a good match between the nature of the offender's business and an appropriate community-focussed penitential commitment to the creation of a common good. An example is the *Danilow Pastry* case, in which a bakery company involved in price fixing was ordered to bake for charitable organizations.[11] However, in many cases, the nature of an appropriate community-focussed penitential commitment may be such that it is better to ask the company to secure the fulfilment of the commitment through another agency, rather than to fulfil the commitment itself. To give a simple example, a transport firm guilty of pollution may have neither the knowledge nor the expertise needed to restore the damaged environment. Even so, the firm may nonetheless have the resources to see to it that the environment is restored by an

[10] https://www.sentencingcouncil.org.uk/overarching-guides/magistrates-court/item/imposition-of-community-and-custodial-sentences/ (last accessed 06/11/2024).

[11] *US v Danilow Pastry Co Inc*, 563 F Supp 1159 (SDNY 1983). See the discussion in Brent Fisse (1990), 245.

expert body appointed to perform that task. In such cases, though, the intrinsic value–creating element in the company's penitential response will be absent unless—monitored by an appropriate state agency—the guilty party educates itself to play (over time) a creative, involved, and fully engaged part in overseeing and evaluating the work of the appointed body.[12] In that respect, in the most serious cases, it is possible to envisage a requirement of corporate commitment to victim- or community-focused penitential activity that is enduring: an intrinsic value–generating form of corporate 'life sentence'. An example would be an obligation to maintain a biodiverse environment, in an area affected by a firm's activities, for as long as the firm (or its successors in any form) continues to exist.

Apart from their allure as a deterrent, what is the reason for the predominance in the criminal justice system more generally of second-best punishments (such as fines) that are valued only for their redistributive consequences? It is that it can be hard to find a way adequately to engage sufficient numbers of individuals in intrinsic value–generating forms of punishment. Many (vulnerable) offenders, or those with chaotic lifestyles, may struggle individually to engage properly with a value-generating form of punishment. Even for those who could engage properly, the logistical problems involved in setting up and monitoring adequate programmes are daunting, and likely to be prohibitively expensive to develop in a systematic, meaningful, and accountable way.[13] However, this is not true of corporate offenders to anything like the same extent. Corporate wrongdoers in the regulated sector are already commonly subjected to external assessment and reporting obligations by the Financial Conduct Authority,[14] and the expectation is that those who enter into deferred prosecution agreements (DPAs) with the prosecution authorities will be subject to similar requirements.[15] For example, in the DPA agreed with Airbus, the company was subject to the monitorship of the Agence Française Anticorruption (the French Anti-corruption Agency), and required to review and modify its compliance programme, updating the SFO on relevant developments.[16] It is a short step from here to extending official monitoring to cover the engagement in intrinsic value–generating penitential activity by the relatively small number of companies facing criminal prosecution for serious wrongdoing.

[12] See Brent Fisse (1990), 247: '[C]ommunity service orders offer a means of affecting nonfinancial, as well as financial, motivations. Whereas cash fines or penalties require only the payment of money, personally performed community service requires the expenditure of time and effort.'

[13] The criminal justice system dealt with 1.4 million offenders in the year to June 2023: https://www.gov.uk/government/statistics/criminal-justice-system-statistics-quarterly-june-2023/criminal-justice-statistics-quarterly-june-2023-html (last accessed 01/07/2024).

[14] https://www.fca.org.uk/about/how-we-regulate/supervision/skilled-persons-reviews (last accessed 03/07/2024).

[15] See https://www.sfo.gov.uk/publications/guidance-policy-and-protocols/guidance-for-corporates/deferred-prosecution-agreements/ (last accessed 03/07/2024).

[16] https://www.sfo.gov.uk/2020/01/31/sfo-enters-into-e991m-deferred-prosecution-agreement-with-airbus-as-part-of-a-e3-6bn-global-resolution/ (last accessed 03/07/2024).

Victim- or community-focused penitential commitments to the creation of common good projects fit well into what I referred to as the necessary broader penitential response on the part of the offender. The carrying out of such commitments (activity impact) should be regarded as one side of a penitence 'coin', the other side of which involves reforming attitudes and conduct regarding compliance, guided by the values underlying the laws breached (attitude impact).[17] In that regard, it is clear that an essential part of prosecutorial engagement with corporate offenders in cases of economic crime is securing impact on moral attitudes. The goal is putting in place measures that will transform compliance-focused attitudes and ethical frameworks for decision-making in the future. For example, in seeking to obtain a DPA, Rolls-Royce spent over £15 million devising more stringent anti-bribery measures, revising its ethics and compliance procedures, re-examining its due diligence processes, and reviewing its collaboration with third parties.[18] In consequence, the DPA settlement noted that Rolls-Royce is 'no longer the company that once it was': a key aim forming part of the required penitential response.[19]

The importance of attitude impact, in determining the state's penal response, is apparent in other DPAs that have been reached since the introduction of those measures in 2013. For example, in the *Serco Geografix* case, William Davies J said:

> Since 2013 Serco Group PLC has undergone a complete change of senior management. It has subjected itself to numerous forms of internal and external review and audit. It has set up a continuing corporate renewal programme designed to strengthen and improve the operating practices of all companies within the group structure . . . I am satisfied that these matters amount to significant remedial measures.[20]

So far as this subjective side of the penitence coin is concerned, the approach is clearly linked to the ideal-type or model of the liberal-welfarist company explained in Chapter 4. This is the 'proactive learning' or 'positively responding' company[21] that takes its compliance obligations seriously in pursuit of its commercial objectives, acknowledging that those objectives should be shaped by those obligations.

[17] See, e.g., Brent Fisse (1990), 248: 'The major limitation on community service as a sanction against corporations is that community service in itself hardly guarantees adequate organizational reform. This limitation, however, can be overcome by a combination of community service and probation that requires the defendant to develop innovative compliance controls and to prepare instructions and follow-up reports with a view to their use by similarly situated corporations.'

[18] https://www.judiciary.uk/wp-content/uploads/2017/01/sfo-v-rolls-royce.pdf (last accessed 16/08/2025), para 47 (Sir Brian Leveson).

[19] *SFO v Rolly Royce* (2017), https://www.judiciary.uk/wp-content/uploads/2017/01/sfo-v-rolls-royce.pdf (last accessed 16/08/2025).

[20] *SFO v Serco Geografix Ltd* (2019), https://www.judiciary.uk/wp-content/uploads/2019/07/serco-dpa-4.07.19-2.pdf (last accessed 20/08/2025), para 25.

[21] For discussion of these ideal-types of the company, see Section 4.3.

The broader, integrated penitential approach endorsed here makes it possible to carry over the liberal-welfarist emphasis I placed in Chapter 4 on a commitment to compliance, into what the state may require of corporate wrongdoers in the aftermath of wrongdoing.

Highlighting the importance of punishment in the form of penitential commitments to the development of common good projects—commitments developed, implemented, and monitored over time—takes us back to a point explained in Chapter 1. This is that the larger the company, the greater the importance of punishing the company itself, as compared with individual wrongdoers within the company (although the latter remains important). John Coffee Jr has powerfully argued that, given the well-known difficulties with holding high-level individuals within companies to account, the justification for a punitive focus on the company is that only such a focus will provide systematic support for employee monitoring, self-reporting, and whistle-blowing.[22] However, correct though that suggestion may be, it makes the punitive focus on the company too narrowly concerned with deterrence and law enforcement, vital though these aims are. Corporate punishment should aspire to do more, through an equal punitive focus on incentivizing commitment to morally valuable activity and impact.

In that respect, it is equally true that only a punishment imposed on the company can make it the collective, fiduciary responsibility of the directors as a body (and of any employees and agents involved in implementing punitive demands) to deliver a response to offending that has genuine and lasting moral significance: such as long-term institutional commitment to structural reform, to ongoing reparation, and to victim- or community-focused common goods. In the case of medium- to large-sized firms, this kind of systematic and possibly long-term penitential response simply cannot be generated merely by convicting and punishing individuals associated with the company for their role in wrongdoing. To begin with, the larger the firm, the less significant the influence of any given individual convicted director (assuming they still work at the firm) is likely to be on the future attitudes or conduct of the firm as a whole. More importantly, no matter how many individuals are punished, and no matter how severely, no collective and integrated firm-wide penitential response can emerge from an individualized approach to punishment.[23] Accordingly, for the purposes of this chapter, I will assume that, with the adoption of a theory of punishment focused on morally active, victim- or community-focused penitential commitment, a punitive focus on punishing medium- to large-sized companies themselves comes to have moral significance and

[22] John C Coffee Jr (2022).

[23] By contrast, in the case of a very small firm, a draconian punishment imposed on an individual director is more likely to be the catalyst for change to the way the company itself is run henceforth, given the dominating role of a director in every aspect of the running of such a firm.

importance. This chapter will be chiefly concerned with the explanation and justification of this penitential theory in corporate cases.

It is an implicit part of what I have said that a requirement for victim- and community-focused penitential commitment to common good creation will not necessarily be the only, the best, or even a feasible punishment in all cases of corporate wrongdoing; far from it. John Gardner has rightly drawn attention to the fact that there may be various justifications for punishment, each of which (and some together) may come to the fore in different types of case.[24] For example, on the so-called economic model of corporate punishment, the kind of penitential commitments advocated here are regarded as involving 'heavy administrative and supervisory costs, attenuated connection to profit incentives, less accurate measuring of monetary harm, and interference with the competitive process'.[25] Such considerations certainly have weight in cases where the overall level of appropriate punishment is (relatively) low. Consider a case in which a shop on a single occasion criminally mis-labelled a low-value product on sale.[26] In such a case, a requirement for victim- or community-focused penitential commitment to the development of a common good enterprise—however beneficial—seems disproportionate, quite apart from the fact that the costs of imposing such a punishment may outweigh any appreciable benefits. According to the economic model, the principal punishment for corporate offending should always be the fine, because the advantage of fines is that—if sufficiently high—they provide a deterrent, compensate society and punish offenders, at a relatively low overall cost.[27] In cases of medium- to low-level offending, especially in regulatory contexts such as the shop example just given, it will certainly be important to investigate and prosecute companies with a view to imposing some kind of low-cost punishment, such as a fine, even if the eventual penalty imposed in particular cases should be little more than nominal. That is because upholding the credibility and integrity of the regulatory scheme in question may depend on a willingness consistently to take rapid, easily understood, and applied punitive action against such offenders.[28]

Now consider some other examples that also illustrate the need for flexibility of response in relation to corporate wrongdoing. First, suppose that a major company guilty of large-scale fraud becomes insolvent after its assets are stripped by company officers who then flee the jurisdiction.[29] In such a case, the company may possibly have some remaining assets that could be used to extract (perhaps, largely symbolic) fines. However, there would be little punitive point in requiring

[24] John Gardner (2007), ch 11.
[25] Christopher A Wray (2017), 2019.
[26] *Tesco Supermarkets Ltd v Nattrass* [1971] UKHL 1.
[27] Christopher A Wray (2017), 2019. For criticism of the use of fines, see Brent Fisse (1990).
[28] I will say more about this in due course, in discussing the 'membership' rule-breaking justification for punishment in Section 6.4 below.
[29] For comparison, see the analogous 'Wirecard' case: https://www.ft.com/content/4901a824-f862-4b7c-8b16-7e1ae088e729 (last accessed 29/10/2024).

the company to engage in medium- to long-term penitential commitments, if it is in effect no longer a going commercial concern. Secondly, even when a corporate wrongdoer is still a going concern, it may be that other pressing issues simply eclipse in importance penitential commitments (or other kinds of punishment). An illustration is where wrongdoing has damaged or destroyed victims' vital interests, and giving proper priority to restoring the integrity of those interests will effectively exhaust corporate assets reasonably regarded as available to use in satisfaction of that process. In such a case, the aim of making of adequate compensatory provision for victims might be largely frustrated by a demand that the offender also be subject to just deserts–based financial or other cost-incurring measures, including the cost of penitential commitments.[30]

Here is an example:

> Despite lacking an appropriate qualification, a manager at F company gives (misleading) pensions advice to a group of workers, who in consequence lose their pension funds in speculative investments. F company has set aside sums to restore the funds lost in their entirety, dismissed staff responsible for supervising the manager in question, and has adopted new safeguarding and ethics procedures. However, any significant fine (or punitive damages) added to the firm's costs will place in jeopardy the existence of the firm, and the jobs of its 150 employees.

In this kind of example, it may seem obvious that securing full individual compensation for the workers, to implement *restitutio in integrum*, should take precedence over other penal measures.[31] However, these kinds of examples may be limited. In some instances, *restitutio in integrum* is no punishment at all, as when it involves no more than the reversal of unjust enrichment. If you steal my car, and the police compel you to return it to me, then the compelled return is not properly regarded as a punishment.[32] By contrast, in other instances, seeking to secure *restitutio in integrum* would involve punitively disproportionate treatment. Consider an analogy with the private law action taken by no less than 202,600 claimants against BHP Group (UK) Ltd, relating to losses incurred as a result of the Fundão dam disaster in 2015.[33] If such a case came before a criminal court, involving (say)

[30] The Powers of Criminal Courts (Sentencing) Act 2000, s 130, requires judges to give 'priority' to the compensation of victims over the payment of financial penalties. See also Stéphane Bonnifassi et al (2024), Alison Cronin (2024), and Corruption Watch (2019).

[31] For a classical private law statement of *restitutio in integrum*, see *Livingstone v Rawyards Coal Co* (1880) 5 App Cas 25, 39, per Lord Blackburn, characterizing the general measure of damages as 'that sum of money which will put the party who has been injured, or who has suffered, in the same position as he would have been if he had not sustained the wrong for which he is now getting his compensation or reparation'.

[32] It follows that where there is more involved than merely reversing unjust enrichment, as (to vary my example) when the offender is made to pay to have the car returned from an overseas jurisdiction, this could be regarded as punitive impact.

[33] *Municipio de Mariana v BHP Group (UK) Ltd* [2022] EWCA Civ 951.

one or more small corporate defendants with limited resources, it could not sensibly be a primary punitive aim of the proceedings to do something to secure *restitutio in integrum* for such a vast number of victims. Whatever the position might be in private law, the wholly unrealistic nature of such a goal ought to lead the criminal justice process to prioritize an alternative approach to penal justice. That approach should involve a focus on (long-term) penitential commitment to common good creation in the affected jurisdiction. This point will now be developed in more detail.

6.2 Corporate Financial Activity and Penitential Commitment

The importance of developing a punitive theory focused on medium- to long-term penitential commitment to common good creation stems in part from the recent exposure of two potential weaknesses in the stock response of the criminal justice system to corporate wrongdoing. Let us consider these weaknesses in turn. First, there can be problems with the hallowed principle of full individual compensation for loss (*restitutio in integrum*) as a penal goal. It is, of course, now a penological commonplace that a high priority should be given to the compensation of individual victims when considering an appropriate sentence.[34] Section 67 of the Criminal Justice Act 1982 made it possible to make compensation orders as the sole penalty against an offender, and where the offender had limited means, section 67 required that payment of compensation should take priority over the fine.[35] Further, English law now starts with the assumption that full compensation (*restitutio in integrum*) should, unless other factors intervene, be the starting point when considering a compensation order.[36] However, idealizing full compensation can lead to what Jeremy Waldron aptly described (in relation to tort cases) as the problem of addressing 'moments of carelessness and massive loss', by insisting on what he describes as the 'macabre appropriateness' of wrongdoers meeting the costs of *restitutio in integrum*.[37]

[34] US Sentencing Commission Federal Sentencing Guidelines Manual (2023), 8.1: 'As a general principle, the court should require that the organization take all appropriate steps to provide compensation to victims and otherwise remedy the harm caused or threatened by the offense.' A more nuanced view can be found in the guidance provided by the Sentencing Council: https://www.sentencingcouncil.org.uk/explanatory-material/magistrates-court/item/fines-and-financial-orders/compensation/1-introduction-to-compensation/ (last accessed 06/11/2024).

[35] See the excellent discussion in Lucia Zedner (1994), 235.

[36] https://www.sentencingcouncil.org.uk/explanatory-material/magistrates-court/item/fines-and-financial-orders/compensation/1-introduction-to-compensation/ (last accessed 10/11/2024), para 7: 'In cases where it is difficult to ascertain the full amount of the loss suffered by the victim, consideration should be given to making a compensation order for an amount representing the agreed or likely loss. Where relevant information is not immediately available, it may be appropriate to grant an adjournment if it would enable it to be obtained.'

[37] Jeremy Waldron (1997), 406.

For example, a minor trade descriptions offence engaged in by a company with millions of customers may lead to those customers collectively losing billions of pounds over a number of years. In such a case, each consumer's individual loss may in fact be small and (from the victim's perspective) relatively insignificant: something they would ordinarily regard it as rational to write off once the costs and effort of recovery have been taken into account.[38] If the company is required by a criminal court to meet the demands of *restitutio in integrum* in such a case, then a punishment is being imposed that may be out of all proportion to the gravity of the initial offence. Yet, if the company is unable to meet these financial demands, then a penal system guided ideologically by the ideal of compensation in the form of *restitutio in integrum* will inevitably be adjudged a failure by its own criteria, and the imposition of a lesser amount nothing but an unfortunate but necessary compromise. The idea of victim-focused penitential commitment to the creation of common goods is designed to realign expectations of what can and should be achieved by the penal system in such cases. A focus on such commitments is not inconsistent with a simultaneous award of an element of compensation; but it is designed to place the penal emphasis on intrinsically valuable, ongoing corporate engagement with (potential) victims as a group. This might come about in many different ways in (say) the trade descriptions example just given: as in the form of medium- to long-term development of consumer education programmes run by the Citizens' Advice Bureau,[39] or through systematic support for voluntary organizations involved in exposing commercial malpractice. Whatever the nature of an individual programme, the aim is to move the emphasis away from an exclusive and simplistic focus on the redistribution of wealth.

Different kinds of flaws in the stock response of the criminal justice system have also been exposed in relation to financial penalties. Flaws have been exposed by the entry of the United States and the United Kingdom, along with other industrialized nations, into what might be called the era of the 'mega fine'. In the United States, agreed financial penalties for economic crime can now run into the billions of dollars. For example, in 2016, Brazil-based Odebrecht SA (Odebrecht) and Braskem SA (Braskem) agreed to pay a combined total penalty of at least $3.5 billion to resolve charges with authorities in the United States, Brazil, and Switzerland arising out of their schemes to pay hundreds of millions of dollars in bribes to Government officials around the world.[40] Similarly, when Volkswagen pleaded guilty in 2017 to criminal charges relating to fraudulent evasion of emissions tests on a huge scale,

[38] For comparison, see *Hopcraft v Close Brothers Ltd* [2025] UKSC 33.

[39] https://www.citizensadvice.org.uk/wales/about-us/information/consumer-education-resources/ (last accessed 06/11/2024).

[40] https://www.justice.gov/opa/pr/odebrecht-and-braskem-plead-guilty-and-agree-pay-least-35-billion-global-penalties-resolve (last accessed 03/11/2024). See the discussion in Kevin E Davies (2019).

a US federal judge ordered Volkswagen to pay a $2.8 billion fine,[41] to go with the $14.7 billion to be paid to settle civil actions.[42] In the United Kingdom, in cases arising in the pre-'mega fine' era, fines for corporate manslaughter averaged under £1 million. By contrast, according to the Serious Fraud Office (SFO), since their introduction in 2014, payments from DPAs with corporates have exceeded £710 million, and the SFO's net contribution to HM Treasury as of December 2019 was £461 million.[43] That figure, relating to a relatively small number of settlements, compares with a figure of around £1 billion a year (before deductions) collected in fines by HM Courts and Tribunals Service from the administration of the rest of the *entire* criminal justice system.[44] When such large sums are being extracted from individual corporate wrongdoers simply in order to fatten the common purse, the moral passivity of the fine becomes problematic. That, at least in part, explains why I earlier referred to a system of punishment based on fines as a second-best system.

Consider what happens to fines as a common pool resource. In the United Kingdom, corporate fines, minus enforcement costs, are transferred directly to the Government's consolidated fund. Fine income entering the consolidated fund is not earmarked for any specific purpose, but instead becomes part of the Government's total revenues, used to pay for all Government spending on public services (such as the 17 million over three years paid to subsidize bars and restaurants in the Houses of Parliament[45]).[46] In other words, despite the obvious conceptual differences between taxes and fines from the perspective of the payor,[47] the payee—the state—has come to treat them in an identical way: as a common pool resource available for Government expenditure.[48] Yet, the dramatic increase in the level of fines that has come about in the wake of the introduction of DPAs warrants a rethink of the point and purpose of such punishments. As a form of 'just desert' or even as a deterrent, serious question marks hover over the corporate fine. As Lund and Sarin put it:

> It might not be politically feasible or legally possible to levy a sufficiently high fine to deter future incidents of corporate crime. Put differently, for large companies, criminal penalties may be just another cost of doing business—and quite a reasonable cost at that. We posit that those who embraced entity-level liability and large financial penalties as the most efficient means of securing deterrence

[41] https://www.wsj.com/articles/judge-slaps-vw-with-2-8-billion-criminal-fine-in-emissions-fraud-1492789096 (last accessed 12/11/2024).
[42] https://money.cnn.com/2016/06/28/news/companies/volkswagen-fine/ (last accessed 12/11/2024).
[43] https://www.sfo.gov.uk/about-us/ (last accessed 16/08/2023).
[44] HM Courts and Tribunals Service (2016–17), 12.
[45] https://www.opendemocracy.net/en/food-poverty-parliament-mps-taxpayers-cost-of-living-subsidies/ (last accessed 16/08/2023).
[46] https://questions-statements.parliament.uk/written-questions/detail/2019-07-18/HL17307.
[47] See, e.g., the discussion in Vince Morabito (1999).
[48] For a critical examination, see Samuel J Hickey (2021).

> neglected the practical realities of enforcement. In theory, a large fine will cause the people at the top to take steps to prevent future instances of harm across the entity. But the size of the fine necessary to lead to adequate deterrence might not be possible to calculate (What is the social cost of 86 lives?) or politically feasible (What if the optimal fine puts the firm into bankruptcy? What if the optimal fine for a large company is tens of billions of dollars?).[49]

There is an answer to these questions, in that there is now far more scope than there has been at any point in the history of the fine, as a response to corporate wrongdoing, to change the nature of its point and purpose. The way to achieve this is through a more systematic focus on the broader penitential approach, described in Section 6.1, involving properly resourced activity impact (common good creation) in which the offending company is creatively engaged, alongside compliance-focused attitude impact. The overall aim should be to require companies to use sums of money that would otherwise be devoted purely to wealth redistribution, in the form of fines and full *restitution in integrum*, to engage wholeheartedly in morally active common good–focused forms of penitential commitment to victims and to their communities, engagement that may have a genuinely redemptive quality.

We can see the potentially broader significance of this if we consider the difference that might be made by the use of company resources in the context of the common good constituted by UK charitable work. What would otherwise be simply fines imposed by the SFO (and kept by UK PLC) running into the hundreds of millions of pounds could make a transformational difference to charitable work in almost every field in which charities operate. In the United Kingdom, small or micro charities comprise some 96 per cent of the sector, yet 80 per cent of charities bring in under £100,000 annually. Around 5,000 new charities register with the Charity Commission each year in the United Kingdom; but a similar number also close down, which has left industry growth fairly static over the past decade.[50] Targeted financial assistance and business advice, replacing simple financial contributions to the public purse, could clearly make an enormous difference to such charities. Having said that, as suggested earlier, truly penitential activity does not involve simply making donations to charities. Activity impact should involve positive and creative engagement with charities' development and sustainability, helping them to devise and follow through on a business plan. That assistance would then become visible as part of each charity's report to the Charity Commission. If need be, funds could initially be used to set up an umbrella organization to assist and advise charities and corporate offenders on how best to work together.

[49] Dorothy S Lund and Natasha Sarin (2021), 299; Brent Fisse (1990).
[50] https://www.policybee.co.uk/blog/uk-charity-statistics (last accessed 16/08/2023).

It would be helpful to consider a case, *Serious Fraud Office v Glencore Energy UK Ltd*,[51] that illustrates the moral importance of making victim- or community-focused penitential commitment to common good creation central to the state's response to serious corporate wrongdoing. In this case, the appropriate state response was wrongly understood solely in terms of a (morally passive) fine, together with the award of financial compensation only to those who have suffered quantifiable loss stemming from the wrongdoing. In *SFO v Glencore*, the mining commodities giant, Glencore, was fined £183 million for using bribery to secure access to oil in operations in South Sudan, Equatorial Guinea, Cameroon, Nigeria, and Ivory Coast. The Federal Republic of Nigeria claimed compensation as a victim of Glencore's offence, in that Glencore had in effect sought to control the Nigerian oil market through bribes, thereby creating a less competitive environment, which then led to reduced prices and economic damage to the Federal Republic of Nigeria's developing economy. However, Fraser J endorsed the view of the SFO that:

(i) the nature of the offences is not such that the amount of compensation can be readily and easily ascertained.
(ii) Identifying third parties that have suffered quantifiable loss is also very difficult.
(iii) Potential victims are entitled to pursue claims for compensation in the civil courts, and those courts are more suitable as a forum for assessing the correct measure of compensation. Such claims can still be advanced in those courts, which are more suited to such an exercise than the Crown Court.[52]

It is certainly true that some questions of compensation in corruption cases are best addressed in civil litigation. More broadly, though, there is something close to moral absurdity involved in the result reached in *Glencore*. On the one hand, the UK Government pockets £183 million in unearned common pool resources resulting from Glencore's wrongdoing (an amount one of its own agencies, the SFO, was involved in determining), even though no harm was done in the United Kingdom. On the other hand, a country directly affected by the crime is denied the benefit of any atoning act, and denied any other role in influencing the outcome of the criminal proceedings.[53] It is not hard to see why some critics of overseas bribery prosecutions have accused the United States and the United Kingdom of financially benefiting from a kind of legally enforced 'imperialism', respecting the activities of companies with US or UK connections committing crimes in less

[51] [2022] EWCR 2, discussed in Stéphane Bonnifassi et al (2024).
[52] [2022] EWCR 2, para 13.
[53] For an examination of the role of the victim in corporate wrongdoing cases, see Stéphane Bonnifassi et al (2024).

prosperous countries.[54] Sam Hickey points out that since the introduction of DPAs in 2014, the SFO has fined corporations more than £1.5 billion for offences against sections 1 and 7 of the Bribery Act 2010, and yet only 1.4 per cent of that sum has been given to the citizens of developing countries who actually suffered the consequences of corruption.[55]

An equally egregious case illustrating the distorted nature of the current approach to financial sanctioning is that of *US v Boeing*.[56] In *Boeing*, Boeing entered into an agreement with the Department of Justice to resolve a criminal charge related to a conspiracy to defraud the Federal Aviation Administration's Aircraft Evaluation Group. The background to the agreement was that, in October 2018, 189 people were killed when a Boeing 737 MAX aircraft crashed into the sea off Indonesia, and in March 2019, a Boeing 737 MAX aircraft crashed after take-off from Addis Ababa airport, killing 157 people. In 2021, federal prosecutors alleged that Boeing conspired to defraud the Government by misleading regulators about a flight-control system that was implicated in the crashes. An agreement was ultimately reached not to prosecute if the company paid a penalty and successfully completed a three-year period of increased monitoring and reporting.[57] Under the terms of the 2021 DPA, Boeing paid a total criminal monetary amount of over $2.5 billion, composed of a criminal monetary penalty of $243.6 million, compensation payments to Boeing's 737 MAX airline customers of $1.77 billion, and the establishment of a $500 million crash-victim beneficiaries' fund to compensate the heirs, relatives, and legal beneficiaries of the 346 passengers who died in the Boeing 737 MAX crashes. In terms of the analysis provided here, putting aside the issue of individual compensation (important though it is), it is quite wrong that the United States profited by $243.6 million in monetary penalty, whereas there is no requirement for the company to engage in the penitential creation of any common good of a victim- or community-focused kind. For example, the sum of $243.6 million could have been devoted to projects to improve airline safety procedures around the world, or to conduct research into improved safety design for aircraft, projects in which Boeing could have been required to be actively and creatively involved. Instead, under the fine system, there is nothing to stop some of the $243.6 million penalty being ultimately used to, say, increase the amount available to defray legislators' business expenses.[58]

[54] See, e.g., Kevin E Davies (2019).

[55] Sam J Hickey (2021).

[56] *The Boeing Company*, Deferred Prosecution Agreement (DPA) 2024, Court Docket No 4:21-CR-005-O (ND Texas).

[57] In 2024, after a panel blew off a Boeing Max jetliner during an Alaska Airlines flight, the Department of Justice alleged that Boeing had violated the 2021 deal, by failing to design, implement, and enforce a compliance and ethics programme to prevent and detect violations of the US fraud laws throughout its operations: https://www.justice.gov/criminal/criminal-fraud/case/united-states-v-boeing-company (last accessed 17/07/2024).

[58] https://www.thoughtco.com/allowances-to-members-of-congress-3322261 (last accessed 17/07/2024).

As suggested above, it is arguably the sheer vastness of the sums paid by individual companies, in the most serious cases, that places in sharp relief the question of how such sums should be used, and casts doubt on the unthinking adoption of the morally passive approach of 'revenue collection' to corporate wrongdoing, even if the latter approach is in practical terms the only feasible ('second-best') option where less serious offences are in issue. For example, in *Glencore*, the company could have been required to negotiate a deal with the Nigerian Government under which the company would (say) pay for a substantial review, overhaul, and upgrade of Nigeria's Independent Corrupt Practices and Related Offences Commission,[59] the Economic and Financial Crimes Commission, the Code of Conduct Bureau, the Bureau of Public Procurement, the Nigerian Extractive Industries Transparency Initiative, the Public Complaints Commission, the Office of the Auditor-General of the Federation, and the Technical Unit on Governance and Anti-Corruption Reforms.[60] This would give proper moral meaning to the United Kingdom's guidance for agreeing to defer a prosecution, which states that the agreement should reflect any 'significant level of harm caused directly or indirectly to the victims of the wrongdoing *or a substantial adverse impact to the integrity or confidence of markets, local or national governments*'.[61]

6.3 Problems with Traditional Punitive Approaches to Corporate Crime

Understandably influenced by large-scale wrongdoing perpetrated by major companies, some theorists of corporate crime have employed a diametrically opposed model of the company to the one influencing this book.[62] According to such theories—what, in the Introduction, I called dirigiste social-democratic theories—the typical company is an amoral profit-seeker, governed by 'structures of irresponsibility' and having a 'calculative orientation'.[63] This orientation leads companies to adopt a more general political strategy of 'block[ing] the use the law to hold them to account'.[64] Accordingly, there is no space in such theories for the liberal-welfarist approach in which the law seeks to engage with companies as real entities to develop better attitudes and practices towards compliance. Dirigiste

[59] https://icpc.gov.ng/#:~:text=ICPC%20%E2%80%93%20Independent%20Corrupt%20Practices%20and%20Other%20Related%20Offences%20Commission&text=Investigation%2C%20Prosecution%2C%20and%20Prevention%20of%20offences%20of%20corruption (last accessed 01/07/2024).

[60] https://www.unodc.org/documents/corruption/WG-Prevention/Art_6_Preventive_anti-corruption_bodies/Nigeria.pdf (last accessed 01/07/2024).

[61] Serious Fraud Office, *Deferred Prosecution Agreement Code of Practice*, s 7(9), my emphasis.

[62] See, e.g., Steve Tombs and David Whyte (2015).

[63] Ibid., 128.

[64] Ibid., 121–23.

social-democratic theories take it that, in this respect, companies simply do not engage in good faith with the law. Further, in theories developed on such assumptions, the 'moral capital of capital'[65]—the view that participation in business has a moral value in itself—is simply a card that businesses play in order to secure less intensive scrutiny of their activities.[66] Something that remains unclear in such theories is how to account for the shared element of organizational failure (and cover-up) that may lead to offending in non-profit-making public or charitable bodies.[67] Nonetheless, the primary emphasis in dirigiste social-democratic theories, in terms of the appropriate state response to wrongdoing, tends to be on what can be achieved through the deterrent effect of punishment (appealing to the protective self-interests of executives) and on stigmatization and retribution, satisfying the public's desire for 'something to be done' when egregious corporate wrongdoing makes an impact on the public mind.[68]

When it comes to compliance policy, dirigiste social-democratic theories incline to the view that only state officials can be trusted to secure compliance on the part of with welfarist goals, through (the threat of) rigorous investigation and enforcement of standards. In Steve Tombs view, for example:

(i) in the area of corporate offending, the law retains some deterrent potential, since it is aimed at organisations that claim rationality for themselves and operate on the basis of calculability, as well as being managed by individuals with careers, prestige and status to protect;
(ii) criminal law retains a symbolism as a means of marking out socially unacceptable forms of behaviour and outcomes, a quality important given the fact that many companies, regulators, academics and, to some extent, members of the public, cling to the ideological assumption that corporate crimes are not 'real' crimes; and
(iii) for all its failings, it is clear that the use of the criminal law is that to which the victims of corporate violence turn as a means of achieving accountability and justice—not least because of the law's own claims.[69]

Point (ii) above is an important one, of relevance to well-disposed as well as ill-disposed companies in relation to what I explain in the next section as the 'membership rules' justification for punishment. By contrast, points (i) and (iii) embody the 'bad citizen' view of a company characteristic of dirigiste social-democratic

[65] Tombs' helpful phrase. See Steve Tombs (2004), 278.

[66] Consequently, such theories waste little time on, for example, the merits of safeguarding defences such as 'adequate' or 'reasonable' procedures, viewing these as simply convenient shields behind which corporate bodies can cynically avoid responsibility for engagement in offending altogether. See further, in the environmental context, Angus Nurse (2022).

[67] See, e.g., the discussion in Jeremy Horder (2012), ch 4.

[68] Steve Tombs (1995), 60.

[69] Ibid.

theory, according to which it cares self-protectively only about avoiding sanctions and about the stigmatizing effects of retribution on public demand.[70]

There are a number of problems with theories focused on points (i) and (iii) in this passage. In relation to (iii), for example, does the mere fact that victims themselves typically turn to a traditional and highly contentious version of criminal law and punishment, in search of justice and accountability, itself justify the deployment of that version?[71] That seems unlikely, to say the least, because it prevents us adequately questioning the moral justification for that version of criminal law and punishment. In relation to (i), the theoretical difficulty is that an emphasis solely on the effects of fear of punitive consequences on a purely self-interested company cannot hope to distinguish between the incentives such fear provides to comply with the law, and the incentives it provides simply to find ever-more sophisticated means of remaining undetected in the future. Yet, as John Finnis famously observed about a theory of law, including a theory of punishment:

> [T]he social importance of law . . . derives not only from its ability to mould the 'bad man's' practical reasoning, but also from its capacity to give all those citizens who are willing to advance the common good precise directions about what they must do if they are to follow the way authoritatively chosen as the common way to that good.[72]

The point made by Finnis about the capacity of the law to further the common good by giving 'precise directions' is significant in this context in that, as we saw in Chapter 4, many businesses by and large take seriously their compliance—and hence safeguarding—obligations.[73] A liberal-welfarist focus on corporate safeguarding develops and builds on what HLA Hart rightly claimed should be the key concern of a theory of law more generally. This is not the ill-disposed would-be lawbreaker, an excessive concern with whom distorts analysis by over-emphasizing the supposed deterrent effects of punitive sanctions, but the 'puzzled [business] man or ignorant man [*sic*] who is willing to do what is required, if only he can be told what it is'.[74] To this point, we can add that the importance attached by rule-abiding companies to compliance on the part of other companies is what links Tombs' point (ii)—the marking out of unacceptable forms or behaviour and outcomes—with the 'membership rules' justification for punishment in cases of breach, explored in the next section.

70 Ibid. See the discussion in the Introduction.

71 For a helpful discussion, see John Gardner (2007), ch 11.

72 See the classic discussion in John Finnis (1980), 325 (emphasis in original), and also the discussion of this point in the Introduction.

73 See the discussion in Section 4.3.

74 HLA Hart (1961), 40. The 'puzzled man' is equivalent to John Finnis' '[citizen] who is willing to advance the common good', and so needs precise direction.

A theory of state response to corporate wrongdoing must also reckon with the barrier to a purely retributive approach to wrongdoing constituted by the extent of 'social capital' possessed by large firms, capital that no individual or micro business offender can ever possess to anything like the same extent.[75] For example, a 2017 DPA (avoiding prosecution) between the SFO and Rolls Royce was approved by Sir Brian Leveson, in spite of criminal wrongdoing involving extensive, systemic bribery of public officials in a number of jurisdictions over many years. It was approved in part because of (as Leveson LJ put it) the:

i) adverse effect to the UK defence industry, where Rolls-Royce has a critical role in supplying engines for UK military and naval vessels, nuclear propulsion technology for nuclear submarines, and aftermarket services;
ii) consequential financial effects on the supply chain;
iii) impairment of competition in highly concentrated markets, where there are limited alternative sources of supply and significant barriers to entry;
iv) a potentially significant fall in share price, which is likely to be made more dramatic by the debarment consequences of a conviction;
iv) possible group-wide redundancies and/or restructuring; and potential weakening of Rolls-Royce's financial covenant for pensions.[76]

The dilemma posed for retributive or just deserts–based theories by such cases is obviously that the imposition of the penalty that is justly deserved may have adverse economic and social consequences far greater and more wide-ranging than any benefit gained. That may be true even if, as argued by some defenders of the corporate fine, it will not make sense for a firm to pass on the costs of fine to consumers because of the loss of competitive advantage that will result.[77] By contrast, not being tied to the achievement of 'just deserts', the requirement for an integrated (and potentially long-term) penitential response on the part of a company guilty of such wrongdoing—involving both moral attitude impact and moral activity impact—may meet demands for deterrence, reform, and reparation without (to the same extent) generating these adverse consequences.

It is true, of course, that when the conduct of the largest firms is in issue, such firms have the power themselves to set the agenda for what are regarded as socially and politically acceptable risks and harms, putting those risks and harms beyond the reach of criminal law and sanctions.[78] As Tombs and Whyte put it:

[75] See the discussion of this point, in a US context, in Richard Gruner (1988).
[76] *SFO v Rolls Royce* (2017), https://www.judiciary.uk/wp-content/uploads/2017/01/sfo-v-rolls-royce.pdf, para 56. See, in a US context, Richard Gruner (1988), 30–31.
[77] See, e.g., Christopher A Wray (2017), 2021, citing Jeffrey S Parker (1989), 573: '[T]he pass-through problem can exist only if one believes that a firm, having received a criminal fine, will then proceed to shoot itself in the foot by impairing its own ability to pay the fine and generate future profits.'
[78] The so-called Enron effect: see Federico Mazzacuva (2014), 250.

> Corporations have access to law makers through political 'representatives' . . . or, in the case of the largest companies, in their own right . . . Thus corporations and their representative organisations . . . can and do influence definitions of harm, crime, processes of criminalisation and the nature of regulation.[79]

While no one is above the (criminal) law, ensuring the systematic accountability of the largest companies, and for that matter the biggest state institutions, is likely to be predominantly a political or socio-economic task, rather than a prosecution-led one. However, the proportion or number of firms for which this is true is a tiny fraction of the number engaged in beneficial economic activity in modern states, activity centred on the pursuit of authentic commercial values. The power structures and influence of the largest companies thus provide a potentially misleading basis for shaping corporate criminal law and prosecution policy generally. Putting aside, thus, the special problems posed by the very largest companies, most companies will accept the right of the state to criminalize and regulate wrongdoing on welfarist lines. For such firms, the focus will be on establishing a successful, documented, and welfare-promoting compliance strategy, because that is what is likely to inspire employee and consumer trust and loyalty, and hence provide a way to establish with integrity a more secure basis for commercial success.[80]

Some evidence for corporate acceptance of the state's right to regulate can be found in the fact that, following the United Kingdom's entry into the European Union, there was a steady growth in the creation of small- to medium-sized enterprises (particularly during the 1980s),[81] in spite of the fact that the level of criminal law regulation of businesses rose dramatically during the same period. The number of enterprises in the United Kingdom grew from 2.4 million in 1980 to 3.7 million in 2002, and the United Kingdom saw average annual GDP growth of 2.3 per cent between 1990 and 2008,[82] placing it third in the G7, with UK GDP per capita rising by 43 per cent over the same period (faster than any other G7 economy).[83] Yet, this period coincided with a time of completely unprecedented growth in criminal regulation targeted at businesses. One sign of such growth, rough-and-ready though it may be in relation to the regulation of business (as opposed to individual human) activity, is the creation of a crime through statutory instrument rather than through primary legislation.[84] A basic Westlaw search reveals that whereas the phrase 'commits an offence', used to create or extend an offence,

[79] Steve Tombs and David Whyte (2015), 126.

[80] See, e.g., John Kitching (2007) and Robert C Bird and Stephen Kim Park (2017); https://www.investorschronicle.co.uk/ideas/2024/02/01/three-companies-benefiting-from-more-regulation/ (last accessed 14/05/2024).

[81] Robert Blackburn (2002), 4.

[82] A period that saw particularly intensive regulatory intervention during the period of Labour Government after 1997.

[83] Department for Business, Innovation and Skills (2011b), 6.

[84] See the discussion of examples in Law Commission (2010).

appears in a statutory instrument only 17 times between 1945 and 1972 (10 per cent of all instances), between 1972 and 2023 it appears no less than 4,146 times (36 per cent of all instances) in such instruments.[85] An even clearer marker of the increasing criminal regulation of businesses, in support of the authentic values of commerce, is the appearance of the following now well-known basis for convicting individual directors of offences committed by their companies:

Offences by bodies corporate:

> If an offence under these Regulations committed by a body corporate is proved—
> (a) to have been committed with the consent or connivance of an officer, or
> (b) to be attributable to any neglect on the part of an officer,
> the officer, as well as the body corporate, is guilty of the offence and liable to be proceeded against and punished accordingly.[86]

This basis for liability was to be found in only 89 pieces of legislation between 1945 and 1972, but—after the United Kingdom's entry into the European Union—in 1,106 pieces of legislation (485 in statutory instruments) between 1972 and 2023.[87] Yet, in spite of this explosion of legislative activity in the field of criminal law creation aimed at ensuring that businesses honour authentic commercial values and promote welfare, what we learn from the steady growth of (small) business activity at the same time is that most businesses were broadly content to embrace these values in the pursuit of their livelihoods. No doubt, that is because, as John Kitching puts it, 'by contributing to the creation of behavioural norms, regulation . . . stabilise[s] trading conditions that facilitate market exchange and long-term business investment'.[88] What are the implications for the way in which the state should respond to corporate offending, from a shift of focus away from the stereotype of the company as amoral, serially offending behemoth towards the ideal-type of a well-meaning small- to medium-sized company which by and large endorses the welfarist values of commerce and is willing—even if not always able—to comply with regulation in support of those values?

[85] Somewhat ironically, in 1932, the Committee on Ministers' Powers had stated: 'We doubt . . . whether Parliament itself has fully realised how extensive the practice of delegation has become, or the extent to which it has surrendered its own functions in the process, or how easily the practice might be abused': 'Delegated legislation and Parliament', HL Select Comm 2015–16.

[86] As it appears in, e.g., regulation 36 of the African Horse Sickness (England) Regulations 2012/2629.

[87] So far as the role of the European Union is concerned, as R Daniel Kelemen and Anand Menon suggest: 'EC policy makers had to craft regulatory frameworks suited to markets with a great diversity of players (including foreign firms) and little trust between the regulators and the regulated. They could not adopt the sorts of informal, flexible (and often opaque) approaches to regulation that many governments had relied on at the national level . . . thus EC regulation often relied on a rather formal, legalistic approach to regulation': R Daniel Kelemen and Anand Menon (2007), 178.

[88] John Kitching (2007), 158.

One implication is that corporate punishment theorists have more to learn from theories of regulatory responses to welfarist corporate wrongdoing, than from more traditionally punitive theories focused on non-regulatory crimes. Rather than seeking to stigmatize and shame businesses with respect to their wrongdoing, a regulatory response involves communicating disapproval in a more reintegrative way, in part by encouraging or cajoling deviant companies into reassessing their values and priorities, and conducting their business practices in a more law-abiding manner.[89] In a broad sense, there is thus a link between the justification for punishment and the rationale of (corporate) regulation. Leading regulation theorist, Julia Black has defined regulation in the following terms:

> [R]egulation is the sustained and focused attempt to alter the behaviour of others according to defined standards or purposes with the intention of producing a broadly identified outcome or outcomes, which may involve mechanisms of standard-setting, information gathering and behaviour modification.[90]

As we will see in due course, this definition has the virtue that it reaches beyond reaffirming the formal importance of law-abidingness (considered in the next section) as what Black calls a 'broadly identified outcome' of regulation. Her definition is capable of encompassing incentivization of the pursuit of substantive welfarist goals amongst such outcomes, such as more reliable product and services, or greater integrity in trading standards and methods (considered in Section 6.5 below).

As Braithwaite puts it, implicitly drawing on the 'good company' ideal-type just described, it is likely to be more productive in most cases to label corporate criminal conduct as 'a bad deed done by an essentially good person, discussing why it caused harm and how this harm might be repaired'.[91] The Food Standards Agency, for example, has said of its enforcement policy: 'We believe that prevention of non-compliance is better than cure. To that end we work proactively with business to help them understand and to comply with the rules in the first place.'[92] In pursuit of the same policy, in 2021–22, the Health and Safety Executive completed only 290 prosecutions, but issued over 6,900 'improvement' or 'prohibition' notices.[93] Similarly, the number of prosecutions conducted by the Environment Agency fell from an average of 710 per year between 2000 and 2010 to an average of 167 per year, following the introduction of 'enforcement undertakings'. These are measures

[89] See, e.g., Keith Hawkins (2003), 198, on the negotiated character of compliance.
[90] Julia Black (2002), 26.
[91] John Braithwaite (2020), 292.
[92] http://www.foodlaw.rdg.ac.uk/pdf/2019.-FSA-Board-paper-sanctions.pdf, 4.1.
[93] https://www.hse.gov.uk/aboutus/assets/docs/the-annual-report-and-accounts.pdf.

analogous to DPAs, in which the offender offers to put right the effects of their offending, compensate for the impact on third parties, and make sure the offence cannot happen again.[94]

The aim of such regulatory strategies is not compliance motivated by fear of the detrimental effect of sanctions or of having to endure retribution following conviction. Instead, the aim is compliance generated by what I call in Chapter 3 the 'fully autonomous' (self-generated), or at least 'semi-autonomous', adoption of sound business standards.[95] In Section 6.6 below, I consider further the justification for adopting a purely forward-looking strategy in the case of corporate wrongdoing, before turning in Sections 6.7 and 6.8 below to consider the role in a forward-looking strategy of requiring penitential activity on the part of the offender, as an important dimension of the state's response.

6.4 Corporate Punishment and 'Membership' Rule-Breaking

There is an understandable tendency to suppose that if corporate criminal wrongdoing is to be met with state sanctions, then the imposition of these sanctions must be capable of justification by the same theory (retributive, deterrent, and rehabilitative) that applies in cases of individual criminal wrongdoing.[96] At a time when the only serious crimes applicable to companies were crimes also applicable to individuals (bribery, fraud, manslaughter, etc.), this 'classical liberal' approach made sense.[97] However, starting in the nineteenth century with the creation of vicarious corporate liability at common law, for statutory crimes committed by employees acting 'in the course of their employment',[98] UK criminal law has developed a range of crimes targeted specifically at companies, whether or not they can also be committed by individuals. These now include not only, for example, an ever-increasing number of crimes relating to the running of companies (over 150 offences in the Companies Act 2006 alone),[99] but also corporate manslaughter and failures to prevent an array of economic crimes.[100] These developments raise the

[94] https://www.endsreport.com/article/1803690/76-drop-environment-agency-prosecutions-last-decade-ends-analysis-shows (last accessed 10/06/2023). If the Environment Agency accepts the offer, it becomes legally binding: https://www.gov.uk/government/publications/environment-agencys-use-of-civil-sanctions/enforcement-undertakings-accepted-by-the-environment-agency-1-june-2022-to-30-september-2022 (last accessed 10/06/2023). The Environment Agency makes it clear that an offender's offer should only be accepted if it is not in the public interest to prosecute, if the offer itself addresses the cause and effect of the offending, and if the offer protects, restores, or enhances the natural capital of England.

[95] See the discussion in ch 3.

[96] See, e.g., the discussion in VS Khanna (1996).

[97] On classical liberalism, see the Introduction.

[98] Considered in detail in chs 3 and 5.

[99] See, e.g., some of the offences mentioned in ch 1.

[100] See the discussion in ch 2.

question of whether there is now a justification for punishing companies for the commission of such crimes that is not available in the case of individuals.

An important theoretical impediment to justifying state punishment of individuals is that ordinary citizens do not voluntarily enter into a social contract with the state under which they explicitly or implicitly agree, on pain of penalty for breach, to abide by whatever norms are (reasonably) set down to further the common good.[101] So, an age-old-problem for would-be justifiers of punishment of individuals is that it seems inescapably unfair to use hard treatment of individual wrongdoers to reinforce a commitment to a social contract more generally, when those individuals were never morally obliged to be part of that contract.[102] By contrast, corporate activity is activity voluntarily undertaken in two interlinked institutional contexts: (1) the bureaucratic context of the legitimate creation of a legal person through registration (at Companies House) and (2) the trading context of a marketplace governed by rules designed to ensure adequate 'fair play' between persons engaged in trade. In broad terms, a rule-governed marketplace is what economists call a 'public good', a good that may be enjoyed non-rivalrously by almost anyone—in this instance—seeking to buy or sell goods or services tradeable by law. However, in the case of companies, non-rivalrous participation in a marketplace is mediated by (1) above. The institutional context of the facility to create a legal person more closely resembles what economists call a 'club good',[103] as opposed to a public good, but which I will refer to as a 'membership' good. Understanding corporate marketplace activity through the prism of voluntary membership in the good constituted by legal personhood has important implications for the possible justification of corporate punishment when membership rules have been broken. This justification centres on upholding the virtue and value of compliance with the corporate membership rules, in the eyes of law-abiding member-companies, through adverse treatment of the lawbreakers amongst member-companies.[104]

[101] See, e.g., Joseph Raz (1986), 99: 'Those who consent to the authority of reasonably just governments or respect their laws are subject to their authority and have an obligation to obey their laws. But not everyone does consent, nor do all have this attitude. Those who do not, are not necessarily guilty of any wrongdoing.' In part, this point explains attempts to provide theories of punishment that are not based on consent or benefit-and-burden, as in the case of Victor Tadros (2011) self-defence based theory of punishment.

[102] For a modern discussion of Rousseau's consent-based theory of the justification for punishment, see Corey Brettschneider (2011). See also Clare Finkelstein (2011). A version of such theories, which seeks to avoid the need to find 'consent' to punishment, is the 'fair play' (benefit-and-burden) argument that if one accepts the benefits conferred by society one must also accept the burdens (including law-abidingness), and coercion can justifiably be used to uphold this principle. See, e.g., Richard Dagger (2011). However, given that personal, social, and economic life would be all-but impossible unless one used some benefits (as by simply walking along a road maintained by the local authority), it is hard to see the 'fairness' of imposing burdens such as exposure to forced incarceration.

[103] On club goods, see, e.g., James M Buchanan (1965).

[104] Studies of small- to medium-sized enterprises have often shown a managerial preference for well-enforced rules to deter 'cowboy' behaviour: see Ian Vickers et al (2005).

I will treat membership goods as a species of club good. A club good is a 'quasi-public' good.[105] It is a public good in the sense that (1) it can be enjoyed non-rivalrously by as many people as have access to it, but (2) access to it is restricted. As S Niggol Seo explains:

> Let us consider a country club membership. The members of the club will enjoy all the benefits that the club offers. The consumption is non-rivalrous in the club to some degree. However, as the number of its members becomes larger beyond a certain size, the members will start to enjoy less than the full benefits that the club offers because of crowding by its members. In the club membership, the consumption becomes rivalrous as the club membership increases. The goods of this sort are called club goods.[106]

My focus here is on a what I take to be a subdivision of club goods that are not subject in this way to diminution in their value, as the number of club members increases. As indicated above, I will call such goods 'membership' goods. What are important examples of membership goods? One example is the travel freedom granted by being a passport-holder. This good can be enjoyed non-rivalrously by as many people as are granted passports, even though it is only available to those who meet certain impartially established membership criteria and agree (expressly or implicitly) to abide by the membership rules relating to passport-holding. As this example indicates, a membership good is comprised of two elements: a 'certification' element (I meet the criteria for entitlement) and a 'process' element (my conduct continues to be that of someone worthy of passport-holding). To give a different example of a membership good, whereas the freedom to walk on pavements is a pure public good, the freedom to drive unsupervised on public roads is only a quasi-public, membership good. The latter good can be enjoyed non-rivalrously by as many people as have access to it; but it is open only to those who (1) meet the certification element (passing a driving test, etc.) and (2) comply with the process element, through abiding by the membership rules, concerning vehicle maintenance, responsible driving, and so on.

Some quasi-public goods taking the form of membership goods meet with relatively minimal state intervention: free access to National Trust property for subscribers is an example.[107] Other such goods are the subject of frequent state intervention. A grant of legal personhood is a membership good of this latter type. To trade lawfully as a company, a company must not only meet the certification element, by registering as a legal entity with Companies House, but also comply

105 For further discussion of the significance of public goods in a criminal law context, see Jeremy Horder (2022), ch 3.

106 S Niggol Seo (2020), 2.6.

107 The trust is established under statute National Trust Act 1907, but exists as a charity.

with the process element: abiding by membership rules concerning (amongst other things) transparency about ownership, observance of directors' fiduciary obligations, proper accounting standards, and crucially, fair competition in the marketplace.[108] A departure from those norms by a voluntary corporate participant (a member) is a breach of membership rules, to which the participant is reasonably deemed to be aware that they must conform. Accordingly, just as a company can be compulsorily liquidated if found guilty of fraud or other kinds of misconduct,[109] so it can also be prosecuted—or made subject to regulatory intervention—for such a breach of membership rules.

The idea that how one conducts oneself (the process element of membership goods) can be a matter governed by membership rules relating to a quasi-public good is not controversial. Consider membership rules governing the right, mentioned above, to drive unsupervised on public roads. These rules extend to the manner in which someone drives, as well as to the certification element: their status as a driver (holding a valid licence and insurance certificate). It has been strongly argued by Sally Cunningham that, in terms of how to approach punishment for road traffic offences, deaths caused by bad driving should be understood in their road traffic context (in my terms, as breaches of membership process rules). They should not be treated as if they were simply isolated instances of *mala in se*.[110] A similar approach should be taken to the issue of justification for corporate punishment, offences—however serious—tied by law to the discharge of company business, including breaches of prohibitions on the failure to prevent *mala in se*. These should be regarded as breaches of membership rules governing process: corporate participation in the marketplace. The domain of membership rules governing corporate participation in the marketplace should be regarded as extending to market conduct (e.g. did a company try to steal a march on competitors through bribery or fraud?), beyond questions merely about market status (e.g. has the company filed annual accounts in the proper form?). It can be argued that a statutory basis for such an extension exists in virtue of section 172 of the Companies Act 2006, which says that:

> A director of a company must act in the way he [*sic*] considers, in good faith, would be most likely to promote the success of the company for the benefit of its members as a whole, and in doing so have regard (amongst other matters) to . . .

[108] See, e.g., John Kitching (2007).

[109] https://www.gov.uk/government/publications/reporting-misconduct-by-companies-directors-and-bankrupts-to-the-insolvency-service/reporting-misconduct-by-companies-directors-and-bankrupts-to-the-insolvency-service#:~:text=the%2Dinsolvency%2Dservice-,1.,reuse%20of%20prohibited%20company%20names (last accessed 24/10/2024). Under Colorado law, for example, it is possible for the Attorney General to seek the involuntary dissolution of a company if, amongst other things, '[t]he directors or those in control of the corporation have acted, are acting, or will act in a manner that is illegal, oppressive, or fraudulent': Colo Rev Stat, s 7-114-301, 2(b).

[110] See Sally Cunningham (2007).

> (d) the impact of the company's operations on the community and the environment, [and] . . . (e) the desirability of the company maintaining a reputation for high standards of business conduct.[111]

Does this argument add anything to the classical liberal view that companies, as individual persons, are bound to observe the rules of 'fair play' when trading, such as rules prohibiting bribery and fraud?[112] It does. The liberal-welfarist justification for punishing companies for offending of different kinds is understood in terms of the overarching aim of regulating the activities and attitudes of companies such that they are incentivized—through hard treatment, if necessary—to become more responsible (corporate) citizens. So, under a liberal-welfarist theory, the sharp distinction drawn by classical liberals between the criminalization of *mala in se* (required) and the criminalization of *mala prohibita* (inherently problematic) is of scant normative significance. A firm guilty of (failure to prevent) fraud may be as much in need of state measures demanding an integrated penitential response—and for the same reasons—as a firm guilty of trade descriptions offences.

6.5 Deontological and Teleological Aspects of the Membership Theory

It is important to stress that arguing in favour of regarding corporate offending in terms of breaches of membership rules is not to argue that such offending should be regarded as less serious than the commission of equivalent offences by individuals; far from it. To regard corporate offending as a breach of membership rules governing the activity of companies in the marketplace is to provide little more than a distinctive basis for justifying the punishment of corporate offending. This is the deontological foundation described in Section 6.4, based on implied consent, consent that is conclusively evidenced by informed and voluntary adoption of legal personhood as a means of participating in markets. Even so, the corporate membership rules justification for the punishment of rule-breakers would be a relatively 'thin' theory, morally, if it turned on no more than the likely attitudes to law-breaking of those whose willingness to conform depends (whatever the merits of the rules themselves) simply on the willingness of other members to do likewise. Further, the membership rules justification would remain an impoverished

[111] As we will see in Section 6.5, whereas (d) broadly represents what I will call 'workplace values', (e) broadly represents what I will call 'trading values', in commercial activity, although there is overlap between them.

[112] See the discussion in the Introduction and Milton Friedman 1970, 17: '[T]here is one and only one social responsibility of business—to use its resources and engage in activities designed to increase its profits so long as it stays within the rules of the game, which is to say, engages in open and free competition without deception or fraud.'

theory, morally, if it was tied solely to a purely subjective 'members' perspective' on what counts as a punishment liable to sustain a commitment to rule-following. No doubt, for many member-companies, what is needed might seem to be simply shaming or hard treatment of the corporate wrongdoer in the form of fines (alongside compensation and restitution, and sometimes imprisonment for individual wrongdoers), as a symbolic affirmation of the importance attached by members to compliance with the rules broken.[113] To enrich a theory of corporate punishment, morally, we must turn to the teleological dimension to the justification for punishing corporate wrongdoers, a dimension embedded in and emerging from the deontological account. The teleological dimension to punishment encompasses but goes beyond its deontological basis. It does so by reimagining, in terms of the intrinsic value-generating, integrated penitential response described in Section 6.1 above, the 'hard treatment' of wrongdoers valued by law-abiding corporate members.

An understanding of the significance of welfarist goals of punishment underpins the attitudes of law-abiding corporate members towards the importance of law-abidingness, and towards the need in some cases to support law-abidingness through requiring lawbreakers to undergo punishment. In this context, these goals centre on the authentic commercial values that corporate membership rules are designed to protect or promote. First, there are what in Chapter 4 I called 'workplace' values. These are values such as employee health, safety and flourishing, the minimization of the environmental impact of premises and working conditions, sensitivity to the concerns of one's neighbours, and so on. Secondly, there are what I called 'trading values'. These are values such as product or service safety, reliability, quality, and environmental friendliness, along with honesty and integrity in contracting and accounting practices. It is in relation to the pursuit of these welfarist commercial values that an ideal-type of a business person emerges who, as small business scholar David Goss puts it, 'takes satisfaction at producing a quality product [or service]': a demonstration of the true moral capital of capital.[114] It is from the perspective of such a person *qua* corporate member—the 'positive responder' or 'proactive learner'[115]—that punitively reinforcing the importance of corporate membership rules comes to have a teleological dimension as well as a deontological basis. What matters is not just that the wrongdoer has broken rules by which they impliedly agreed to be bound, although that is (deontologically) foundational. It is that punishment reinforces the practical and moral significance of these rules, in promoting sound welfarist commercial values of the kind just

[113] See, e.g., Ian Vickers et al (2005).
[114] David Goss (1991), 57.
[115] See the discussion of these ideal-types in ch 4.

mentioned, values of great importance to the ideal-typical, compliance-focused business person (the positive responder or proactive learner).

This teleological element to justifying the punishment of corporate offenders is clearly connected to the element of a penitence-based theory concerned with what I earlier called moral 'attitude impact', the impact on a company's attitude towards compliance. The teleological element gives substance to what it means to make D a better corporate law-abider, in terms of welfarist philosophy and attitudes as well as practice, beyond simple acknowledgement (important though this deontological element is) that members must abide by whatever membership rules exist at a given time.[116] In terms of attitude impact, reintegration as a legitimate market 'player' can be achieved through authentic and committed reform of compliance attitudes and practices, of the kind discussed in Chapter 4. However, in pursuing that goal, it will be important not to neglect the other side of the penitence coin in relation to intrinsic value–generating punishments. This is what I earlier called 'activity impact', in the form of victim- or community-focused penitential activity: the state's involvement in promoting reform of an offender's attitudes and commitments, in rehabilitating them as a trustworthy member and market participant, may lack adequate moral meaning and legitimacy (in the eyes of other members) without an additional requirement for hard treatment.[117] Yet, 'hard treatment' should not be too easily equated merely with morally passive wealth redistribution in the form of (say) fines, even if wealth redistribution can be justified as a second-best punitive option in many cases. That is because, even when victim- or community-focused penitential activity is wholeheartedly endorsed by the offender undertaking it, this cannot negate the 'hard' nature of the way in which the offender is treated by the state in such a case: compelled to put time, effort, and creative resources into a medium- to long-term project not of their own choosing. So, whilst also intended to encourage individual wrongdoers to become more committed 'welfarists', as law-abiding members of the corporate community and marketplace, an integrated penitential response to wrongdoing also has the capacity to do any necessary deterrent work, as a contribution to maintaining the faith of corporate members more broadly in the law's support for its welfarist goals. I address this point in more detail in the next section.

[116] Much of the discussion in Chapter 4 concerning 'best endeavours' defences to corporate crime was devoted to showing how corporate criminal law is shaped by this welfarist agenda, through the provision of such defences.

[117] For that reason, for example, under US sentencing guidelines, making reparation, paying a fine, and performing community service are all said to be a mandatory 'condition of' making a company subject to a probation order, and not just something that may accompany such an order on a discretionary basis: US Sentencing Commission Federal Sentencing Guidelines Manual (2023) 8D1.3(b), discussed in Christopher A Wray (1992), in relation to the 1991 version of the guidelines.

6.6 No Fear? Purely Forward-looking Approaches to Corporate Crime

It is the central case of failure-to-prevent offences,[118] with its welfarist emphasis on a company's efforts to guard against criminal wrongdoing, that provides the best background structure for accommodating the emphasis placed on attitude impact in a penitential theory of punishment. That is because the other side of such an emphasis, when it comes to responding to a company's failure to make sufficient safeguarding efforts, is a primary focus on the cultivation of attitudes characteristic of a corporate citizen—the 'positive responder' or 'pro-active [safeguarding] learner'[119]—committed to furthering the common good through such efforts. So, this work wholeheartedly endorses the supposedly contentious paradigm on corporate criminal liability under which, as Angus Nurse puts it (speaking of environmental enforcement policy), there is:

> societal and policy acceptance of corporations as positive actors who generally provide benefits to society. This paradigm suggests that harm caused by corporations is an aberration in otherwise lawful activity. This perspective also suggests that when corporations cause environmental harm, the corporation may be as much victim as perpetrator, suffering harm to its reputation and the smooth running of its operations.[120]

Such a paradigm, rather than being of limited use or naïve in character, is in fact better suited to understanding the 'small firm' commercial environment of the United Kingdom.

The influence of the 'good citizen' company ideal-type or paradigm, criticized by Nurse, has in fact been central to the development of post-war (regulatory) criminal law. As we saw in Chapter 4, there was a dramatic increase after 1972 in the number of business-focused offences in the United Kingdom to which a defence of having taken all reasonable precautions and exercised all due diligence has been applied. This is a defence whose primary purpose is to benefit the ideal-typical 'good citizen' entrepreneur described by Nurse in the passage above, who is committed to the lawful realization of authentic commercial values, but who on the occasion in question failed in that endeavour.[121] In a similar vein, regulators' policy with regard to sanctions respecting corporate wrongdoing has become predominantly concerned with what has been

[118] See the discussion in ch 2.
[119] Ian Vickers et al (2005). See also the discussion in Korkka-Knuts (2024).
[120] Angus Nurse (2022), 330.
[121] The analogous defence of 'adequate' or 'reasonable' procedures has also been central to Parliament's attempt to curb corporate involvement in serious crimes such as bribery and fraud.

called the 'just culture' approach to compliance. As the Law Commission has explained that concept:

> Under the 'just culture' approach, sanctions are aimed at encouraging safety and compliance with applicable regulation rather than punishing breaches of it. This is to promote openness and encourage operators . . . to engage with the regulator when they find themselves in breach of their obligations. This in turn promotes safety by allowing issues to be brought to the regulator's attention and rectified.[122]

Research has shown that reputational damage to a firm from criminal or regulatory intervention is a far more important concern to company managers of large firms than sanctions for wrongdoing in themselves. Share prices may plummet upon the mere public announcement of investigations taking place, whatever the eventual outcome of those investigations.[123] This suggests that the primary focus should be—as argued in Chapter 4—on the need for 'law, legal institutions and regulators to link the internal capacity for corporate self-regulation with the internal *commitment* to self-regulate, so as to build up companies' identification with, as well as their capacities for, self-regulation'.[124] As Baldwin argues, this involves 'an accountability approach which . . . require[s] or encourage[s] a company to implement a self-regulatory system when a breach has been alleged or has occurred'.[125] The aim of the state's response to wrongdoing, under such an approach, is to incentivize businesses and entrepreneurs to regard appropriate risk-minimization and risk-elimination as morally desirable features of doing business.[126] Notably absent from Baldwin's approach is the need either to incorporate, in any regulatory response, punishments for wrongdoing that 'fit' the crime, or to satisfy a public desire for revenge. By contrast, the focus is largely forward-looking: bearing in mind what the regulated entity was proved to have done, what measures would appropriately change their behaviour and attitudes in a such a way that they will henceforth meet—and be disposed to meet—ethical and legal (membership) standards?

We can see the influence of this more forward-looking reformative, non-retributive approach to punishment in the justification for DPAs, which are becoming such a key measure in responding to serious economic corporate crime.[127] By virtue of schedule 17 of the Crime and Courts Act 2013, in exchange for a

[122] Law Commission (2024), para 9.11. This passage is taken from a consultation paper concerned with the aviation industry. See also Office of Communication's (OFCOM) approach to breaches of broadcasting rules, OFCOM (2022), para 5.8: 'We generally expect the subject of an investigation to take steps to bring itself into compliance and remedy the consequences of any contravention to the fullest extent possible.'

[123] Robert Baldwin (2004), 368 and 372; Ian Ayers and John Braithwaite (1992), 22.

[124] Robert Baldwin (2004), 375 (my emphasis).

[125] Ibid., 376.

[126] This function of the criminal law is referred to in the economic literature as the 'preference shaping' function of criminal law: see, e.g., Kenneth G Dan-Schmidt (1990).

[127] See the discussion in Bastian Hertstein, Matthew Berry, and Sam C Brown (2024).

prosecutor's agreement to defer a criminal prosecution, a company suspected of such offences may be asked to take a range of steps:

(a) to pay to the prosecutor a financial penalty;
(b) to compensate victims of the alleged offence;
(c) to donate money to a charity or other third party;
(d) to disgorge any profits made from the alleged offence;
(e) to implement a compliance programme or make changes to an existing compliance programme relating to P's policies or to the training of P's employees or both;
(f) to co-operate in any investigation related to the alleged offence;
(g) to pay any reasonable costs of the prosecutor in relation to the alleged offence or the deferred prosecution agreement.[128]

These factors are very similar to those submitted to the US Sentencing Commission in 1988, as part of a proposal for the introduction of 'corporate probation'.[129] Of the six aims of a DPA, only the first could be clearly associated with the demands of retribution and deterrence, and I will come back to it in the next section. The other (in part overlapping) aims are very broadly concerned with reparative justice (b and d), with acceptance of wrongdoing and hence with a preparedness to meet the costs it has imposed (b and g), with demonstrating a determination to reform and guard against repetition (e) and with a demonstration of the willingness to atone for one's wrong (c and f).

In that regard, it is worth noting that, in approving the very first DPA, involving an offence of failing to prevent bribery committed by Standard Bank, Leveson LJ said:

> For my part, I have no doubt that Standard Bank has far better served its shareholders, its customers and its employees (as well as all those with whom it deals) by demonstrating its recognition of its serious failings and its determination in the future to adhere to the highest standards of banking. Such an approach can itself go a long way to repairing and, ultimately, enhancing its reputation and, in consequence, its business.[130]

UK prosecutors are not (formally) regulators. Even so, we should note the impact on their role of the introduction of DPAs and the involvement of prosecution services in overseeing the carrying out of such agreements.[131] The impact has been

[128] Crime and Courts Act 2013, sch 17, para 5.
[129] Richard Gruner (1988), 8–9.
[130] *SFO v Standard Bank* (2015), https://www.judiciary.uk/wp-content/uploads/2015/11/sfo-v-standard-bank_Final_1.pdf, para 22.
[131] SFO, 'Evaluating a Compliance Programme', https://www.sfo.gov.uk/publications/guidance-policy-and-protocols/guidance-for-corporates/evaluating-a-compliance-programme/ (last accessed 20/03/2024).

that the line between criminal law and regulatory governance of corporate wrongdoing has become blurred, even when the most serious crimes are in issue.[132] In the context of the liberal-welfarist argument of this work, that is no bad thing.

A decisive move towards a forward-looking emphasis on securing individual reformation and behaviour change, through the punishment system, has recently been articulated in a sophisticated new theory of state response to offending by Nicola Lacey and Hanna Pickard.[133] Whilst retaining the notions of responsibility and blameworthiness for wrongdoing, their theory seeks to detach these fundamentals of criminal law (and regulation) from what they term the commonly associated elements of 'affective blame'. The latter are, for example, the 'hostile, negative attitudes and emotions that are typical human responses to blameworthiness . . . [such as] hatred, anger, resentment, indignation, disgust, disapproval, contempt and scorn'.[134] Such reactive attitudes commonly find expression in the theory and practice of elements of the criminal justice system that are focused on seeking 'retaliation, retribution, and vengeance, rejection and banishment from the community'.[135] For Lacey and Pickard, it is important not to suppose that acknowledging someone's responsibility and blameworthiness for wrongdoing entails experiencing and acting on one of these 'affective blame' states. Indeed, sometimes, it would be highly inappropriate were that to happen.

For example, it would be decidedly unprofessional for a doctor asked to investigate an offender's responsibility and blameworthiness to allow their understanding of the offender's behaviour to be influenced by an affective blame state. Where a clinician is managing an offender on an ongoing basis, 'the clinical aim is, at least in part, to motivate, encourage and support the patient to do things differently by choosing to alter entrenched maladaptive patterns, and effecting this choice even in the face of inclinations to revert to old habits'.[136] In some instances, it may be appropriate to visit adverse consequences on the patient, but solely to reinforce the message to the patient about the importance of working to change their attitudes, beliefs, and patterns of conduct.[137] Lacey and Pickard adopt this clinical-diagnostic model of analysis for the justification of official responses to crime more generally. Their theory is initially founded on the fact that, although 64 per cent of male and 50 per cent of female offenders have a personality disorder,[138] traditional retributive theories of punishment overlook this, choosing to focus solely

132 See, e.g., P Spivack and S Raman (2008), 150: '[T]he effect of DPAs has created the "New Regulators" as the Department of Justice has fashioned for itself a new role of "focusing more on prospective questions of corporate governance and compliance, and less on the retrospective question of the entity's criminal liability".'

133 See, e.g., Nicola Lacey and Hanna Pickard (2013).

134 Ibid., 3.

135 Ibid.

136 Ibid., 12.

137 Ibid., 13: 'Most forms of effective therapy thus involve not only responsibility but accountability: a demand that patients must answer and explain themselves to clinician or group, together with the imposition of negative consequences, if they fail to change problematic behaviour.'

138 Ibid., 11.

and exclusively on the fact that such offenders are—in spite of their disorder—still (to an extent) capable of manifesting responsible agency. What if one were to bring offenders' mental disorders back into the justificatory picture, in terms of what a theory of punishment must account for? Then, for Lacey and Pickard, 'reform, rehabilitation, reduction of crime, and, correspondingly, public protection . . . may all be furthered by sentencing practices that follow the clinical model in holding offenders responsible and accountable without the stigmatizing and exclusionary effects of affective blame'.[139]

The focus of this original but controversial theory might seem far removed from our present concerns, but in fact it is highly relevant. It bolsters the claim made in Section 6.2 above that achieving 'just deserts' should not generally feature as a goal in the soundest theory of a penitential response to corporate wrongdoing. Perhaps, as its primary goal, the state should be asking not what kind of punishment of a company would meet the demands of just deserts, slaking a thirst for revenge: the goal of classical liberals and dirigiste social-democratic thinkers. Instead, the state should be considering what punitive measures would—to recall Lacey and Pickard's words, echoing the approach of Baldwin[140]—incentivize 'choosing to alter entrenched maladaptive patterns, and effecting this choice even in the face of inclinations to revert to old habits'.[141] The theory is a powerful one, in relation to individual offenders—perhaps the majority—suffering with some kind of mental disorder or disability, and it has considerable appeal where one is concerned with corporate offenders who are (in the language of Chapter 4) 'positive responders' or 'proactive learners'. Even so, a question arises over its adequacy in dealing in a morally appropriate way with the full range of (corporate) offenders, in a context in which offending constitutes a breach of membership rules, as explained in Section 6.4 above.

So far as individual companies are concerned, as Ian Vickers et al put it, in their study of small-firm responses to health and safety regulation:

> [Firms'] attitudes and behaviour need to be seen as the outcome of the interactions between a complex set of internal and external factors that lead them to differ widely in the priority they accord to health and safety and their responsiveness to statutory legal requirements.[142]

As we saw in Chapter 4, the corporate compliance landscape is not only populated by proactive learners and positive responders, whose law-abiding disposition is part of the ideal-type of a company on which rests the liberal-welfarist model of corporate criminal liability defended in this book. For firms in these categories, a

[139] Ibid., 21.
[140] See also the approach of Julia Black, described in Section 6.3 above.
[141] Nicola Lacey and Hanna Pickard (2013), 12. For a further critique of retributive theories in the corporate crime context, see Sam Buell (2020).
[142] Ian Vickers et al (2005), 160.

purely forward-looking, broadly educational, and restorative regulatory approach, tailored to their individual circumstances, might be the right approach. However, the compliance landscape also contains 'avoider-outsiders' and 'minimalist reactors'.[143] Even if a purely forward-looking, individualized, rehabilitative, and reparative approach to the latter types of firms is also to some extent appropriate, is it also sufficient? In answering that question, we need to bear in mind that, unlike an individual offender who cannot withdraw from society itself to avoid obligations breach of which may lead to sanctions, an avoider-outsider firm can simply choose to disengage from a market if the barriers to dishonest quick profit-making are too high, with a view to re-entering it if the barriers are subsequently lowered.

Related to this point is the deontological aspect of the membership rules institutional context of corporate offending, discussed in Section 6.4 above. As indicated earlier, lawful participation in the market by companies is achieved through voluntarily becoming part of the Companies Act 2006–governed corporate 'membership' scheme, and thereby impliedly agreeing to abide by membership rules. As argued earlier, such rules include wrongdoing-focused rules, such as those forbidding certain kinds of harmful or risky conduct engaged in by someone on company business. Purely forward-looking, individualized theories of punishment are rich in detail about how to deal on a case-by-case basis with offending and offenders after an offence, and that is of great importance. However, the voluntary, membership rule–governed nature of corporate participation in the marketplace provides sufficient (deontological) reasons for companies to commit to safeguarding steps and programmes, intrinsic to fair market participation, *in advance of* being caught in acts of wrongdoing that involve disregarding such steps and programmes.

In that respect, the nature of the state's response to corporate wrongdoing must account for two things in the membership rules context of securing corporate commitment to fair competition. First there is the fact that, for 'avoider-outsiders' or 'minimalist reactors', it may be only the threat of adverse consequences or hard treatment (as some element of a punitive response) when caught in wrongdoing that may tip the balance in favour of more or less reluctant law-abidingness. Secondly, as discussed earlier, there is the distinct possibility that 'proactive learners' or 'positive responders', who value law-abidingness in the membership rules context, may have their commitment to it undermined or seriously diminished if they believe would-be lawbreakers are inadequately incentivized to conform to the law.[144] As

[143] See ibid., and the discussion in ch 4.

[144] See John Finnis (1980), 262: 'There is the need of the actually or potentially recalcitrant (which includes most members of society, in relation to at least some activity or other) to be given palpable incentive to abide by the law when appeals to the reasonableness of sustaining the common good fail to move. And there is the need to give the law-abiding the encouragement of knowing that they are not being abandoned to the mercies of criminals . . . and that to comply with the law is not be a mere sucker: for without this support and assurance, the indispensable co-operation of the law-abiding is not likely to be continued.' Finnis goes on to justify the infliction of punishment by appeal to a theory of just deserts, which is not a theory endorsed or adopted here.

I have already said, a morally rich justification for a punishment system cannot be entirely limited by the normative framework within which 'punishment' is subjectively understood by law-abiding (corporate) citizens. Nonetheless, individualized, purely forward-looking approaches to the state's response to corporate wrongdoing simply do not do enough to explain how such a response can function as an ex ante incentive for non-offenders to conform to membership rules, alongside legitimating ex post efforts to help offenders change their behaviour and attitudes for the better.

6.7 Corporate Moral Impact: Contextualizing Penitential Activity

Let it be granted that the marketplace participation membership rules are more likely to be respected and obeyed, if members accept that the state is committed to ensuring that corporate persons are deterred ex ante from engaging in certain kinds of rule-breaking conduct by the threat of adverse consequences visited on them if they do engage in such conduct. It does not follow that the deterrent quality of the adverse consequences plays a pivotal role in giving value to threatening or implementing those adverse consequences. When someone is caught engaging in membership rule-breaking criminal conduct, we might consider that subsequently being compelled, by way of adverse consequence, to engage in certain kinds of victim- or community-focused activity is not simply a means of securing a deterrent effect on others: the 'penance of (moral) diminishment'.[145] Still less is it about what that person 'justly deserved': a moral irrelevance.[146] Instead, the requirement to engage in such activity is what subsequently legitimates the state's investment in the wrongdoer ex post to seek change in their future behaviour and attitudes. What is it that gives the imposition of adverse consequences (in the form of intrinsic value–generating activity) that legitimating quality? It is the redemptive potential of the offender's activity as—in the eyes of the state—an adequate form of atonement: the 'penance of (moral) growth'.[147]

Seen in isolation, 'atonement' may be thought of as what I myself decide to do, to make up for some wrong done, whether or not my efforts to atone are acknowledged or requested by anyone else. However, this solipsistic conception of atonement is unstable and contentious. That is because what I decide is enough by way of atonement may, quite simply, be so wholly inadequate as not to amount to atonement in any meaningful sense at all (or, contrariwise, perhaps I am being too hard on myself, in the circumstances). The solipsistic conception is at odds with the idea

[145] On the distinction between the penance of (moral or spiritual) diminishment and the penance of (moral o spiritual) growth, see Bede Benjamin Bidlack (2021).

[146] See the discussion in Victor Tadros (2017), 230–31, and the discussion of the work of Nicola Lacey and Hanna Pickard (2013) in Section 6.6 above.

[147] Bede Benjamin Bidlack (2021).

that atonement gains authenticity through its endorsement as such by the person or authority in ultimate control of the (broken) membership rules, where that person or authority has a moral stake in the offender's redemption.[148] To achieve redemption is to do what the (membership rules) authority accepts is sufficient to make up for the wrong done and to wipe the slate clean, putting things right between the parties. Atonement and redemption are closely connected, because the latter may not authentically be achieved in the absence of the former.[149] Nonetheless, there is more to redemption than the acknowledgement that, by undergoing some process or engaging in some form of conduct, an offender will atone for their wrong.[150] Unless, as a wrongdoer, I also accept that I did something wrong, show remorse, and form a determination not to reoffend, no amount of atonement is likely to gain me redemption.[151] That explains my insistence at the beginning of Section 6.1 above that a penitential theory of appropriate state response to corporate wrongdoing is an integrated theory, one that includes attitude impact, and not a theory focused exclusively on securing penitential activity impact—however wholeheartedly engaged in—for a wrong done in the past.

Most importantly, thus, when the state insists that the offender atone through enduring penitential commitment, as part of the journey towards redemption, it does not treat the offender merely as a means to a deterrent end. Rather, the state uses the requirement of atonement to justify morally its wholehearted investment in the part of that journey that involves working with the offender as an end in themselves: to change their attitudes, and hence their behaviour, for the future.[152] It is only against that background that the possibility of having to undertake such an atoning journey towards redemption can be understood as something that tips

[148] https://www.ewtn.com/catholicism/library/appropriate-penances-4438 (last accessed 22/06/2023). See, further, in relation to the idea of punishment as 'penance', RA Duff (2003).

[149] In an article refining his duty-based justification for punishment, Tadros appeals to the idea that if an offender cannot serve to protect their victim from harm (e.g. because the victim was killed in D's attack), D should nonetheless seek to 'redeem' themselves by (say) protecting others from similar harms. Victor Tadros (2017), 247. However, it is unclear to what extent Tadros means to put stress on the idea that it is redemption, as opposed to atonement, that D must seek, as Tadros neither defines redemption nor mentions atonement.

[150] For example, in the Catholic Church, the sacrament of reconciliation—what I am calling redemption—involves three things: contrition, confession, and accepting the penance (the act of atonement): see https://www.ewtn.com/catholicism/library/appropriate-penances-4438 (last accessed 22/06/2023). So, society's relationship will always in some sense remain broken with an unrepentant offender who refuses to regard their punishment as a form of atonement for wrong, and does not seek to redeem themselves.

[151] This point is revealed by prosecutorial practices of offering what might be called 'atonement discounts' for companies that self-report in relation to wrongdoing, take pre-emptive steps to reform company practices, and cooperate with the authorities in any investigation: see the discussion of the issue in House of Lords (2019), ch 7.

[152] Of course, in relation to individual offending discussed by Lacey and Pickard, when offending is wholly explained by mental disorder, then atonement is inappropriate: one should proceed straight to the question of what can help to cure the disorder whilst protecting the offender and the public. To the extent that an act is only in part explained by mental disorder (Lacey and Pickard's starting point), a state might simply set a lower bar for atonement and redemption or, in trivial cases, simply waive the requirement.

the balance in favour of law-abidingness, for those not otherwise inclined to obey, and hence to reassure the law-abiding of the value of their law-abidingness. There is, though, another moral dimension to atonement (requested by the state), conceived of as a legitimation of the state's investment in changing offenders' attitudes and behaviour as part of the redemption journey. This concerns the value of the penitential activity in which the offender is actually required to engage.

Just now I spoke about the redemptive potential of the offender's penitential activity as—in the eyes of the state—an adequate form of atonement: the 'penance of (moral) growth'. How is this potential to be realized, in such a way that punishment does not treat offenders merely as means to a punitive end? Answering that question requires us to reflect on the relationship between victim-focused and community-focused common good creation, as forms of punishment. The US sentencing guidelines for the so-called community service provide a useful focus in this respect. Part 8B1.3 of the 2023 version says:

> An organization can perform community service only by employing its resources or paying its employees or others to do so. Consequently, an order that an organization perform community service is essentially an indirect monetary sanction, and therefore generally less desirable than a direct monetary sanction. However, where the convicted organization possesses knowledge, facilities, or skills that uniquely qualify it to repair damage caused by the offence, community service directed at repairing damage may provide an efficient means of remedying harm caused. In the past, some forms of community service imposed on organizations have not been related to the purposes of sentencing. Requiring a defendant to endow a chair at a university or to contribute to a local charity would not be consistent with this section unless such community service provided a means for preventive or corrective action directly related to the offense.

Two points should be made about this provision. The first is that it is wrong to suggest that community service is nothing more than an 'indirect' monetary sanction. To describe it in such a way is to focus purely on its extrinsic value (the expenditure of money), and to ignore its intrinsic value (the penitential activity for which the money pays). Secondly, the provision appears to define community service narrowly, in terms of purely victim-focused reparation of damage (*restitution in integrum*), in order to exclude from its scope seemingly unconnected charitable activity (such as endowing a chair); but that contrast risks being too sharp.

To focus on the examples given in the guidelines, there may be in principle a difference between requiring a corporate wrongdoer to endow a chair and requiring it to become involved in the activities of a local charity. In a case where a company has polluted a river, as well as involving victim-focused environmental restoration of the immediately affected environment, appropriate reparation should be seen as extending to such community-focused activity as, for example, boosting the activities and facilities for (say) the regional Royal Society for the Protection of Birds or local groups involved in river conservation, even though the latter are not 'victims' of the pollution in the ordinary sense.[153] Such community-focused penitential activity has important morally symbolic value. However, it is also a way of expressing acceptance of and atoning for wrongdoing by engaging in valuable activity that derives part of its value from being a 'materially' contextual—and not merely an 'abstractly' contextual—counterpart to the wrongdoing.

To some extent, penal systems may try morally to contextualize standard just deserts-based punishments, to provide a humanitarian dimension to the process. So, the amount that someone is fined can be linked to an assessment of their means, or electronic tagging designed to enforce restrictions on movement can be devised such that someone can continue to care for a relative living some distance away. In relation to penitential activity, the law may adopt one of three positions. First, penitential activity may be required that lacks *any* appropriate moral context. It will lack such a context when it is completely unrelated to offending. An extreme example would be requiring a firm guilty of bribery to become involved in funding a project to land astronauts on Mars. By contrast, secondly, penitential activity may be 'abstractly' contextual. It takes this form when it does no more than reflect or relate to the legal character of the offence committed. An example would be where an offender guilty of fraud is required to endow a chair in fraud studies, or to provide advice to a government anti-fraud agency. Depending on the nature and circumstances of an offence, it may be appropriate to require an offender to atone by engaging in abstractly contextual penitential activity. Thirdly, there is 'materially' contextual penitential activity.

Materially contextual penitential activity is the ideal-typical response to criminal wrongdoing of the liberal-welfarist state. Penitential activity is materially contextual when it comes in one of two forms. First, it may directly reflect or be related to harm done or risk posed to a victim by the offence: as where an offender restores damage done to the place in which the victim lives. For obvious reasons, victim-focused penitential activity may in many instances be a highly appropriate form of materially contextual penitential activity. Secondly, though, penitential activity is also materially contextual when it coerces the offender into engaging in activities that would be the hallmark of the good corporate citizen in the liberal-welfarist state, in relation to their workplace or trading environment. For example, a good corporate citizen operating in an area with a fragile natural environment will not

[153] See, e.g., Peter Kellett (2020). In that regard, it should be noted that, when deciding on what is in effect a requirement for community-focused penitential activity, the US Department of Justice has approved the undertaking by the wrongdoer of 'supplemental environmental projects', which involve some kind of nexus, between the violation and the proposed project. The Department of Justice provided that such a nexus could be established when the proposed project had been designed to reduce the likelihood of similar violations, the proposed project reduced the adverse impacts to which the violation contributed, and finally, the proposed project reduced the overall risk potentially affected by the violation at issue. See the discussion in Sam Hickey (2021), 410–12.

only take care not to damage that environment, but will also do something—however small—to sustain its viability. Similarly, a good corporate citizen operating in a jurisdiction that struggles to control business corruption will not only avoid engaging in corruption, but will also do something—however small—to contribute to the fight against such corruption. Penitential activity can be materially contextual when it involves requiring the offender to commit themselves to copying the actions of the good corporate citizen of the liberal-welfarist state.

Suppose that a wealthy UK corporate wrongdoer is found guilty of bribery overseas in Redland. As part of a DPA agreed with the prosecution authorities, the company might seek to atone by endowing a chair in anti-corruption studies at a university close to its UK headquarters, and then perhaps following that up (a more 'active' part of its atonement) by itself promoting the study of anti-corruption measures in the United Kingdom nationwide. However, valuable though such atonement is, it is morally thin or unsophisticated because it is only an abstractly contextual counterpart to the company's wrongdoing. As a counterpart to the wrongdoing, the atonement lacks a materially contextual dimension capable of realizing its full moral significance. This could only come through penitential activity that is connected to Redland itself, whether or not we can say that (e.g. for compensation purposes) Redland was a 'victim' of the company's offending. An example of penitential activity that was meant to (but did not) embody a materially contextual element was the £30 million settlement reached between the SFO and defence contractor BAE Systems, in relation to illicit payments regarding the supply in 1999 of an air-traffic radar control system in Tanzania. BAE agreed that most of the settlement would be used to fund educational projects in Tanzania, including the purchase of desks, textbooks, and teacher instruction manuals for elementary schools.[154] Such a settlement is not morally inappropriate or irrational. However, whilst the settlement had the virtue of benefitting the affected jurisdiction, it does not meet the criteria just set out for being materially contextual penitential activity. That is because what the company was required to do is unrelated to its offending. An abstractly contextual form of penitential activity in this case would have involved BAE in becoming actively involved in strengthening international bodies involved in anti-corruption. A materially contextual form of penitential activity in the case would have involved BAE becoming involved in strengthening integrity safeguards in procurement and contracting within Tanzania itself.

Other settlements have seen the Department of Justice require a corporate wrongdoer to support public infrastructure in an affected jurisdiction, to donate money to charities, or to create a foundation.[155] Such settlements have the potential to meet the criteria for materially contextual penitential activity. By contrast, in the *Siemens AG* case in 2009, it was found sufficient that the company paid

[154] See the discussion in Andrew B Spalding (2014), 1410–11.
[155] See the discussion in Sam Hickey (2021), 411.

$100 million over fifteen years to support anti-corruption work in general, even though the wrongdoing had concerned corruption in relation to a World Bank project in Russia.[156] Such a settlement is controversial because the community-focused penitential activity demanded is only an abstractly contextual counterpart to the wrongdoing. So, it lacks the materially contextual moral significance that anti-corruption work in (or relating to) Russia itself would have had, even if it would not be right to describe Russia as in any sense having been a victim of the offending.[157] Even so, in one respect, the Siemens AG settlement lived up to the ideal of penitential activity, in that Siemens AG *itself* become involved in delivering on the anti-corruption work. The company launched the 'Siemens Integrity Initiative', which involved inviting international and non-governmental organizations, along with universities, to apply to Siemens for funding for projects that would 'promote business integrity and fight corruption'.[158] In that sense, at least, the settlement did exemplify some of the ideals of community-focused penitential activity for which I have been arguing: the active, creative engagement of the offender in the penitential activity.

6.8 Morally Active Penitential Activity and Punishment Over Time

Whilst it is possible that an individual may 'feel' the negative financial impact of paying a substantial fine, fines are not commonly aimed at producing such a (hard to measure) feeling. The punitive intent of a fine is financial and 'momentary', in that what matters is that at T2, the wrongdoer is £X poorer as a result of making payment to the state, than they were at T1 when the £X fine became due. By contrast, in the case of imprisonment,[159] part of the intended punishment is the non-momentary element of what might be called 'endurance'. For the length of their sentence, the offender must undergo or suffer the inevitable deprivations and pains of imprisonment (inevitable, to some extent, even in the most enlightened and humane of regimes).[160] An intrinsic value–generating account of penitential

[156] See the discussion in ibid., 412.

[157] In that respect, I agree with Sam Hickey (2021), 413, who rightly cautions that 'enforcement agencies [should] first determine whether a nexus exists and only then consider whether reparations can be provided to some other area of public outlay if either no nexus can be identified or there is some other compelling reason to not provide reparations to whichever segment of society was harmed'.

[158] Ibid., 412.

[159] Regrettably, this will also be true of many forms of community penalty imposed on individuals.

[160] So, for example, if someone sentenced to two years' imprisonment immediately fell into a coma, from which they did not awake until the date for their release, it could not be said that they had 'endured' or 'suffered' imprisonment even if they had spent the period of the coma in (say) a prison hospital. That is to not say, necessarily, that it would then be right for them to be forced to start the period of imprisonment afresh (stigma attaches to anyone who has spent time as a prisoner). The point is simply that a key element of the punishment constituted by imprisonment would have been missed out, during the coma period.

activity involves turning on its head the element of 'endurance' in non-momentary punishment that is associated with negativity and moral passivity. It seeks to make the wrongdoer use their own human and organizational resources to engage in an active, creative, value-generating course of conduct: a course of conduct that involves moral imagination and dedicated effort or persistence over time (perhaps, in some cases, over the entire course of the corporate wrongdoer's life).

The existing regime of DPAs reflects the need to have non-momentary forms of penalty: kinds of penalty that have traditionally been unavailable as punishments of the court. Currently, it is possible for the SFO to require a company, as a part of its DPA, to agree to the appointment of an external monitor for up to three years, to 'assess and monitor [the corporate's] internal controls, advise of necessary compliance improvements that will reduce the risk of future recurrence of the conduct subject to the DPA and report specified misconduct to the [relevant] prosecutor'.[161] However, it is clear that, useful though such a measure may be in some cases,[162] it is narrowly focused on crime prevention. So, it is not directed at involving the company in intrinsically valuable penitential activity. After all, one gets no moral credit—even if one avoids blame—simply for ensuing that one complies with laws prohibiting engagement in *mala in se*. Even so, it is possible to imagine the remit of such a monitor being extended to include the supervision of intrinsically valuable projects engaged in by the corporate wrongdoer.[163] For example, under the broad supervision of the Environment Agency, offenders causing pollution damage in England and Wales, who accepted an Enforcement Undertaking, made amends locally for the harm they caused through some £11,500,000 contributed towards specific environmental projects between 2011 and 2018.[164] In the United States, corporate probation has sometimes been imposed explicitly as a form of (morally active) 'corporate penance'.[165] As mentioned at the beginning of the chapter, a bakery company involved in price fixing has been ordered to bake for charitable organizations,[166] and an electricity company convicted of price fixing was required to employ several former felons.[167]

These sentences can be considered largely symbolic, in moral as well as financial terms; but as we have seen, in the modern era, fines and penalties currently run

[161] DPA Code, https://www.cps.gov.uk/sites/default/files/documents/publications/DPA-COP.pdf, para 7.12.

[162] https://globalinvestigationsreview.com/guide/the-guide-monitorships/fourth-edition/article/monitorships-in-the-united-kingdom#footnote-023 (last accessed 17/07/2024).

[163] In relation to corporate fraud and corruption, over time, funds could be built up to finance an independent 'corporate outreach' office, which would have the task of devising and overseeing the delivery of such projects, once they had been agreed between the prosecutor and the wrongdoer.

[164] Peter Kellett (2020), 192. This example obviously involves victim-focused as much as community-focused penitential activity, but these tend to blend into one another in the case of environmental damage.

[165] *US v Wright Contracting Co*, 563 F Supp 213, 214 (1983), discussed in Richard Gruner (1988).

[166] *US v Danilow Pastry Co Inc*, 563 F Supp 1159 (SDNY 1983).

[167] *US v Richards Elec Supply Co*, 604 F Supp 126 (SD Ohio 1984).

into the tens or hundreds of millions of pounds. A genuinely transformative difference could be made to so many lives and communities, if such fines were turned into intrinsically value-generating forms of penitential activity involving victim or community benefit, and engaging the offender's wholehearted commitment to making that difference. As the problematic example at the outset of the chapter is meant to indicate, the era of the 'mega fine' needs to be radically reconceived, as one in which the state ceases to pursue the morally passive and ultimately self-serving goals of extracting supposedly justly deserved penalties, and instead requires offenders to engage creatively in the 'penance of moral growth'.

BIBLIOGRAPHY

Akerlof, George A, '"The Market for Lemons": Quality Uncertainty and the Market Mechanism' (1970) 84(3) Quarterly Journal of Economics 488–500.

Amodu, Tola, *The Determinants of Compliance with Laws and Regulations with Special Reference to Health and Safety: A Literature Review* (London: Health and Safety Executive, 2008).

Arena, Marika, Arnaboldi, Michela, and Azzone, Giovanni, 'The Organizational Dynamics of Enterprise Risk Management' (2010) 35(7) Accounting, Organizations and Society 659–75.

Arlen, Jennifer, 'The Potentially Perverse Effects of Corporate Criminal Liability' (1994) 23(2) Journal of Legal Studies 833–67.

Ashworth, Andrew, 'The Scope of Criminal Liability for Omissions' (1989) 105 Law Quarterly Review 424–59.

Ashworth, Andrew, *Sentencing and Criminal Justice*, 4th edition (Cambridge: Cambridge University Press, 2005).

Ashworth, Andrew, *Positive Obligations in Criminal Law* (Oxford: Hart Publishing, 2013).

Ashworth, William, 'The Late Victorian Economy' (1966) 33(129) Economica 17–33.

Association of Certified Fraud Examiners, *Occupational Fraud: A Report to the Nations* (2022), https://acfepublic.s3.us-west-2.amazonaws.com/2022+Report+to+the+Nations.pdf (last accessed 20/08/2025).

Atiyah, PS, *Vicarious Liability in the Law of Torts* (London: Butterworths, 1967).

Ayers, Ian, and Braithwaite, John, *Responsive Regulation: Transcending the Deregulation Debate* (Oxford: Oxford University Press, 1992).

Baker, Dennis, ed, *Glanville Williams & Dennis Baker Treatise of Criminal Law*, 5th edition (London: LexisNexis, 2021).

Baldwin, Robert, 'The New Punitive Regulation' (2004) 67(3) Modern Law Review 351–83.

Bant, Elise, 'Systems Intentionality: Theory and Practice', in Elise Bant (ed), *The Culpable Corporate Mind* (Oxford: Hart Publishing, 2023), 183–207.

Bant, Elise, and Faugno, Rebecca, 'Corporate Culture and Systems Intentionality: Part of the Regulator's Essential Toolkit' (2024) 23(2) Journal of Corporate Law Studies 345–74.

Basu, Anuradha, 'Entrepreneurial Aspirations among Family Business Owners: An Analysis of Ethnic Business Owners in the UK' (2004) 10(1) International Journal of Entrepreneurial Behaviour & Research 12–33.

Basu, Anuradha, and Altinay, Eser, 'The Interaction between Culture and Entrepreneurship in London's Immigrant Businesses' (2002) 20(4) International Small Business Journal 371–93.

Bean, Bruce W, and MacGuidwin, Emma H, 'Expansive Reach—Useless Guidance: An Introduction to the U.K. Bribery Act 2010' (2012) 18 ILSA Journal of International and Comparative Law 323–46.

Bechhofer, F, et al, 'Small Shopkeepers: Matters of Money and Meaning' (1974) 22 Sociological Review 465–82.

Bello Y Villarino, José-Miguel, and Bronitt, Simon, 'AI-Driven Corporate Governance: A Regulatory Perspective' (2024) 33(4) Griffith Law Review 355–74, https://doi.org/10.1080/10383441.2024.2405752.

Bennett, GCJ, 'Institutional Abuse of Older People: The Regularity of Institutional Scandal and Calls for the Government to Appoint a Health Service Commissioner Specifically for Institutional Care' (1999) 6(9) British Journal of Therapy and Rehabilitation 420–23.

Bennett, Robert J, Smith, Harry, Montebruno, Piero, and Van Lieshout, Carry, 'Changes in Victorian Entrepreneurship in England and Wales 1851–1911: Methodology and Business Population Estimates' (2021) 64(7) Business History 1211–43.

Berman, Mitchell N, 'Blameworthiness, Desert and Luck' (2021) *Noûs* 1.

Better Regulation Executive, *Lightening the Load: The Regulatory Impact on UK's Smallest Businesses* (London: BRE, 2010).

Bidlack, Bede Benjamin, 'Not for Myself Alone: Atonement and Penance After Daoism', in Catherine Cornille (ed), *Atonement and Comparative Theology* (Oxford: Oxford University Press, 2021), 78–102.

Bird, Robert C, and Park, Stephen Kim, 'Turning Corporate Compliance into Competitive Advantage' (2017) 19(2) University of Pennsylvania Journal of Business Law 285–339.

Bisschop, Lieselot, et al, 'Examining the Multifaceted Harms of Corporate and White-Collar Crime' (2025) 83(16) Crime, Law and Social Change 15–23.

Black, Julia, 'Critical Reflections on Regulation' (2002) 27 Australian Journal of Legal Philosophy 1–35.

Blackburn, Robert, 'Small Businesses in the UK: From Hard Times the Great Expectations' (2002), https://core.ac.uk/download/pdf/13789.pdf (last accessed 08/09/2025).

Blackstone, Sir William, *Commentaries on the Laws of England*, 4 vols (Oxford: Clarendon Press, 1765–69).

Blair, Margaret M, and Stout, Lynn A, 'A Team Production Theory of Corporate Law' (1999) 85(2) Virginia Law Review 247–328.

Bonnifassi, Stéphane, et al, *The Role of Victims in Negotiated Settlements: Working Paper 2* (Paris: International Academy of Financial Crime Litigators, 2024).

Bradgate, J Robert, and Howells, Geraint G, 'Food Law in the United Kingdom' (1991) 46 Food, Drug, Cosmetic Law Journal 447–66.

Braithwaite, John, 'Reintegrative Shaming' (2016), http://johnbraithwaite.com/wp-content/uploads/2016/05/2000_Reintegrative-Shaming.pdf (last accessed 20/08/2025).

Braithwaite, John, 'Restorative Justice and Reintegrative Shaming' in Cecilia Chouhy, Joshua C Cochran, and Cheryl Leo Jonson (eds), *Criminal Justice Theory: Explanation and Effects*, Vol 26 (London: Routledge, 2020), 281–305.

Brett, David, 'How the FTSE 100 Has Changed Over 33 Years' (30 June 2017), https://www.schroders.com/en/uk/private-investor/insights/markets/how-the-ftse-100-has-changed-over-33-years/ (last accessed 08/08/2019).

Brettschneider, Corey, 'Rights within the Social Contract: Rousseau on Punishment', in Austin Sarat, et al (eds), *Law as Punishment, Law as Regulation* (Oxford: Oxford University Press, 2011), 50–76.

Brickey, Kathleen F, 'Corporate Criminal Accountability: A Brief History and an Observation' (1982) 60(2) Washington University Law Review 393–423.

British Institute of International and Comparative Law, *A UK Failure to Prevent Mechanism for Corporate Human Rights Harms* (London: BIICL, 2020).

Brudner, Alan, 'Agency and Welfare in the Penal Law', in Stephen Shute, John Gardner, and Jeremy Horder, *Action and Value in the Criminal Law* (Oxford: Clarendon Press, 1993), 21–54.

Buchanan, James M, 'An Economic Theory of Clubs' (1965) 32(125) Economica 1–14.

Buell, Samuel W, 'The Responsibility Gap in Corporate Crime' (2017) 12 Criminal Law and Philosophy 471–91.

Buell, Samuel W, 'Criminally Bad Management', in Jennifer Arlen (ed), *Research Handbook on Corporate Crime and Financial Misdealing* (London: Edward Elgar, 2018), 59–86.

Buell, Samuel W, 'Retiring Corporate Retribution' (2020) 83(4) Law and Contemporary Problems 25–46.

Carpenter, Alfred, 'Presidential Address: Sanitary Inspectors' Conference', (1890–91) 111 Public Health 141–45.

Carrol, Archie B, 'The Pyramid of Corporate Social Responsibility: Toward the Moral Management of Organizational Stakeholders' (1991) 34(4) Business Horizons 39–48.

Carroll, Archie B, 'Corporate Social Responsibility: The Centerpiece of Competing and Complementary Frameworks' (2015) 44 Organisational Dynamics 87–96.

Carter, Sara, et al, 'Women's Business Ownership: A Review of the Academic, Popular and Internet Literature with a UK Policy Focus' (2000–01) 1 Annual Review of Progress in Entrepreneurship 66–157.

Census 2001, 'UK Business: /Activity, Size and Location' (2019), https://www.ons.gov.uk/businessindustryandtrade/business/activitysizeandlocation/bulletins/ukbusinessactivitysizeandlocation/2019 (last accessed 08/01/2025).
Chalmers, James, and Leverick, Fiona, 'Fair Labelling in Criminal Law' (2008) 71(2) Modern Law Review 217–46.
Chalmers, James, and Leverick, Fiona, 'Tracking the Creation of Criminal Offences' [2013] Criminal Law Review 543–60.
Chaplin, Julia Elizabeth, 'The Origins of the 1855–6 Introduction of General Limited Liability in England' (PhD thesis, University of Easy Anglia, 2016), https://ueaeprints.uea.ac.uk/id/eprint/64258/1/ThesisRevisions2.pdf (last accessed 20/01/2025).
Chen, James, 'Subsidiary Company: Definition, Example, and How it Works' (2023), https://www.investopedia.com/terms/s/subsidiary.asp (last accessed 14/07/2023).
Chourou, Lamia, Himick, Darlene, and Saadi, Samir, 'Regulatory Uncertainty and Corporate Social Responsibility' (2023) 55(B) Finance Research Letters 104020.
Clarkson, CMV, 'Kicking Corporate Bodies and Damning Their Souls' (1996) 59(4) Modern Law Review 557–72.
Coase, Ronald, 'The Nature of the Firm' (1937) 4(16) Economica 386–405.
Coffee, John C Jr, ' "No Soul to Damn: No Body to Kick": An Unscandalized Inquiry into the Problem of Corporate Punishment' (1981) 79(3) Michigan Law Review 386–459.
Coffee, John C Jr, 'Crime and the Corporation: Making the Punishment Fit the Corporation' (2022) 47(4) Journal of Corporate Law 963–89.
Collins, Hugh, *Marxism and Law* (Oxford: Oxford University Press, 1982).
Collins, Hugh, 'Employment as a Relational Contract' (2021) 137 Law Quarterly Review 426–50.
Cooley, Dennis R, 'Understanding Social Welfare Capitalism, Private Property, and the Government's Duty to Create a Sustainable Environment' (2009) 89 Journal of Business Ethics 351–69.
Conti, Sergio, and Giaccaria, Paolo, 'Enterprise Organisation, Hierarchies, Networks and Competitive Environments', in Sergio Conti and Paolo Giaccaria (eds), *Local Development and Competitiveness*, Vol 59 (Berlin: Springer, 2001), 35–64.
Cope, J, 'Entrepreneurial Learning from Failure: An Interpretative Phenomenological Analysis' (2011) 26(6) Journal of Business Venturing 604–23.
Copp, Stephen, and Cronin, Alison, 'The Failure of Criminal Law to Control the Use of Off Balance Sheet Finance During the Banking Crisis' (2015) 36(4) The Company Lawyer 99–123.
Corruption Watch, *Compensating Victims for the Harm of Overseas Corruption: Discussion Paper* (London: Corruption Watch, 2019).
Costley, Tom, and Gorasia, Monika, *Public Attitudes to Roads in England: Wave*, Vol 3 (London: Department of Transport, 2014).
Council of the European Union, *Proposal for a Directive of the European Parliament and of the Council on Corporate Sustainability Due Diligence and Amending Directive (EU) 2019/1937* (Brussels: Council of the European Union, 2024).
Croall, Hazel, 'Who Is the White-Collar Criminal?' (1989) 29(2) British Journal of Criminology 157–74.
Cronin, Alison, 'The Important Role of Civil Class Actions in the Enforcement of Corporate Criminal Law' (2024) 6 Journal of Economic Criminology 100106.
Crook, Tom, 'Sanitary Inspection and the Public Sphere in Late Victorian and Edwardian Britain: A Case Study in Liberal Governance' (2007) 32(4) Social History 369–93.
Cunningham, Sally, 'Punishing Drivers Who Kill: Putting Road Safety First?' (2007) 27(2) Legal Studies 288–311.
Dagger, Richard, 'Social Contracts, Fair Play, and the Justification of Punishment' (2011) 8(2) Ohio State Journal of Criminal Law 341–68.
Dan-Schmidt, Kenneth G, 'An Economic Analysis of the Criminal Law as a Preference-Shaping Policy' [1990] Duke Law Journal 1–38.
Davies, Kevin E, *Between Impunity and Imperialism: The Regulation of Transnational Bribery* (Oxford: Oxford University Press, 2019).

Department for Business, Energy and Industrial Strategy, *Challenges Businesses Face When Complying with Regulation*, BEIS Research Paper No 2020/043 (London: DBEIS, 2020).

Department for Business, Innovation and Skills, *A Guide to Legal Forms for Business* (London: DBIS, 2011a), https://assets.publishing.service.gov.uk/government/uploads/system/uploads/attachment_data/file/31676/11-1399-guide-legal-forms-for-business.pdf (last accessed 20/03/2025).

Department for Business, Innovation and Skills, *Sources of Economic Growth* (London: DBIS, 2011b).

Department for Business and Trade, 'Estimating Numbers of Unregistered "Active" Companies Not Included in the Business Population: Research and Analysis' (2023), https://assets.publishing.service.gov.uk/media/65169ee56dfda6000d8e3881/estimating_numbers_of_unregistered_active_companies_not_included_in_the_business_population_estimates.pdf (last accessed 03/05/2025).

Department of Trade and Industry, *Reform of the Ultra Vires Rule: A Consultative Document* (London: HMSO, 1986).

Department of Transport, *Public Opinion Survey on Traffic and Road Use* (London: Department of Transport, 2020).

Diamantis, Mihailis E, 'The Extended Corporate Mind: When Corporations Use AI to Break the Law' (2020) 98(2) North Carolina Law Review 893–932.

Diamantis, Mihailis E, 'The Corporate Insanity Defence' (2021) 111 Criminal Law and Criminology 1–30.

Diamantis, Michailis E, 'How to Read a Corporations; Mind', in Elise Bant (ed), *The Culpable Corporate Mind* (Oxford: Hart Publishing, 2023), 209–28.

Diamantis, Mihailis E, and Thomas, Robert, 'But We Haven't Got Corporate Criminal Law!' (2022) 47(4) Journal of Corporate Law 991–1008.

Dorling, Danny, et al, *Criminal Obsessions: Why Harm Matters More Than Crime*, 2nd edition (London: Centre for Crime and Justice Studies, 2005).

De Sousa, Susana Aires, and Laufer, William S, 'The State's Responsibility for Criminal Justice' (2022) 47(4) Journal of Corporate Law 1109–25.

D'Souza, Mark, 'The Corporate Agent in Criminal Law–An Argument for Comprehensive Identification' (2020) 79(1) Cambridge Law Journal 91–119.

Duff, RA, 'Penance, Punishment and the Limits of Community' (2003) 5(3) Punishment and Society 295–312.

Duff, RA, 'Towards a Theory of Criminal Law?' (2010) 84 Proceedings of the Aristotelian Society 1–28.

Duff, RA, 'Relational Reasons and the Criminal Law' (2012) 2 Oxford Studies in Philosophy of Law 175–208.

Duff, RA, 'Punishment as Communication', in Jesper Ryberg (ed), *Oxford Handbook of Punishment Theory and Philosophy* (Oxford: Oxford University Press, 2024), 90–112.

Easterbrook, FH, and Fischel, DR, *The Economic Structure of Corporate Law* (Cambridge, MA: Harvard University Press, 1991).

Environment Agency, *Dealing with Contaminated Land* (2016), https://assets.publishing.service.gov.uk/media/5a80ab47ed915d74e622fc4a/State_of_contaminated_land_report.pdf (last accessed 13/08/2025).

Esping-Andersen, Gøsta, *The Three Worlds of Welfare Capitalism* (Princeton, NJ: Princeton University Press, 1990).

European Union, *Food Safety in the EU* (2018), https://european-union.europa.eu/priorities-and-actions/actions-topic/food-safety_en (last accessed 07/08/2025).

Evans, DM, *The Commercial Crisis 1847–1848* (London: Letts, Son and Steer, 1848).

Feargrieve, Duncan, and Squires QC, Dan, *The Negligence Liability of Public Authorities* (Oxford: Oxford University Press, 2019).

Feinberg, Joel, *Harm to Others* (Oxford: Oxford University Press, 1987).

Financial Conduct Authority, *FCA Practitioner Panel Survey: 2022–2023 Report* (July 2023), https://www.fca.org.uk/publication/research/fca-practitioner-panel-joint-survey-2023.pdf (last accessed 14/09/2025).

Financial Conduct Authority, *Final Notice to Starling Bank* (2024), https://www.fca.org.uk/publication/final-notices/starling-bank-limited-2024.pdf (last accessed 20/09/2025).

Financial Reporting Council, *Corporate Governance Code* (2024), https://media.frc.org.uk/documents/UK_Corporate_Governance_Code_2024_kRCm5ss.pdf (last accessed 20/08/2025).

Finkelstein, Clare, 'Punishment as Contract' (2011) 8 Ohio State Journal of Criminal Law 319–40.

Finnis, John, *Natural Law and Natural Rights* (Oxford: Clarendon Press, 1980).

Fisher, Talia, 'Economic Analysis of Criminal Law', in Markus Dubber and Tatjana Hörnle (eds), *The Oxford Handbook of Criminal Law* (Oxford: Oxford University Press, 2014), 38–58.

Fisse, Brent, 'Complicity in Regulatory Offences' (1968) 6 Melbourne University Law Review 278–307.

Fisse, Brent, 'Reconstructing Corporate Criminal Fault: Deterrence, Retribution, Fault and Sanctions' (1983) 56(6) Southern California Law Review 1141–246.

Fisse, Brent, 'Sentencing Options Against Corporations' (1990) 1(2) Criminal Law Forum 211–58.

Francis, Ronald, and Armstrong, Anona, 'Ethics as a Risk Management Strategy: The Australian Experience' (2003) 45 Journal of Business Ethics 375–85.

Friedman, Milton, 'The Social Responsibility of Business is to Increase Its Profits', *The New York Times* (1970), 17.

Friedman, Nick, 'Corporate Liability Design for Human Rights Abuses: Individual and Entity Liability for Due Diligence' (2021) 41(2) Oxford Journal of Legal Studies 289–320.

Fries, Alexander, Kammerlander, Nadine, and Leitterstorf, Max, 'Leadership Styles and Leadership Behaviours in Family Firms: A Systematic Literature Review' (2021) 12(1) Journal of Family Business Strategy 100374.

FTSE, *Women Leaders Review* (2024), https://ftsewomenleaders.com/wp-content/uploads/2024/04/ftse-women-leaders-report-final-april-2024.pdf (last accessed 12/09/2025).

Fuller, Lon, *The Morality of Law*, revised edition (New Haven, CT: Yale University Press, 1969).

Gardner, John, 'On the General Part of the Criminal Law', in RA Duff (ed), *Philosophy and the Criminal Law: Principle and Critique* (Cambridge: Cambridge University Press, 1998), 205–56.

Gardner, John, 'Wrongs and Faults', in AP Simester (ed), *Appraising Strict Liability* (Oxford: Oxford University Press, 2005), 51–80.

Gardner, John, *Offences and Defences: Selected Essays in the Philosophy of Criminal Law* (Oxford: Oxford University Press, 2007).

Gardner, Simon, 'Rethinking Family Property' (1993) 109 Law Quarterly Review 263–300.

Getzler, Joshua, 'Use of Force in Protecting Property' (2005) 7(1) Theoretical Enquiries in Law 131–66.

Gilchrist, Gregory, 'Individual Accountability for Corporate Crime' (2018) 34(2) Georgia State University Law Review 335–55.

Glazebrook, Peter, 'A Better Way of Convicting Businesses of Avoidable Deaths and Injuries' (2002) 61(2) Cambridge Law Journal 405–22.

Gleason, Kimberly, Kannan, Yezen H, and Rauch, Christian, 'Fraud in Startups: What Stakeholders Need to Know' (2022) 29(4) Journal of Financial Crime 1191–221.

Glowka, Gundula, Kallmünzer, Andreas, and Zehrer, Anita, 'Enterprise Risk Management in Small and Medium Family Enterprises: The Role of Family Involvement and CEO Tenure' (2021) 17(2) International Entrepreneurship and Management Journal 1213–31.

Gobert, James, 'Corporate Criminality: Four Models of Fault' (1994) 14(3) Legal Studies 393–410.

Gobert, James, and Punch, Maurice, *Rethinking Corporate Crime* (London: Butterworths, 2003).

Godfrey, Brian, Killeen, Neil, and Moloney, Kitty, 'Data Gaps and Shadow Banking: Profiling Special Purpose Vehicles' Activities' (2015) 3 Central Bank Quarterly Bulletin 48–60.

Goss, David, *Small Business and Society* (London: Routledge, 1991).

Government Finance Function, *Risk Appetite Guidance Note* (London: Crown Copyright, 2021).

Grady, Mark F, 'A New Positive Economic Theory of Negligence' (1983) 92(5) Yale Law Journal 799–830.

Gross, Charles, 'The Court of Pie Powder' (1906) 20(2) The Quarterly Journal of Economics 231–49.

Gruner, Richard, 'To Let the Punishment Fit the Organization: Sanctioning Corporate Offenders through Corporate Probation' (1988) 16(2) American Journal of Criminal Law 1–106.

Haldane, Richard Burdon, *Reign of Relativity* (London: John Murray 1921).

Harris, Ron, *Industrialising English Law: Entrepreneurship and Business Organisation 1720–1844* (Cambridge: Cambridge University Press, 2000).

Hart, HLA, *The Concept of Law* (Oxford: Clarendon Press, 1961).

Hart, HLA, *Punishment and Responsibility: Essays in the Philosophy of Law*, 2nd edition (Oxford: Oxford University Press, 2008).

Hasnas, John, 'The Centenary of a Mistake: One Hundred Years of Corporate Criminal Liability' (2009) 46(4) American Criminal Law Review 1329–58.

Hayek, FE, *The Constitution of Liberty* (Chicago, IL: Chicago University Press, 1960).

Hayek, FE, *The Road to Serfdom*, Bruce Caldwell (ed) (Chicago, IL: University of Chicago Press, 2007).

Hawkins, Keith, *Law as a Last Resort: Prosecution Decision-Making in a Regulatory Agency* (Oxford: Oxford University Press, 2003).

Health and Safety Executive, *Annual Report and Accounts 2022/23*, HC 1599 (London, 2022–23).

Hedrick, Todd, *Reconciliation and Reification: Freedom's Semblance and Actuality from Hegel to Contemporary Critical Theory* (Oxford: Oxford University Press, 2018).

Hertstein, Bastian, Berry, Matthew, and Brown, Sam C, 'Deferred Prosecution Agreements in Jersey: Ways to Buttress the Castle: A Comparative Analysis of Regimes for Deferred Prosecution Agreements in Jersey and England and Wales' (2024) 3(3) Journal of Economic Criminology 100046.

Heyd, David, 'Supererogation', in Edward N. Zalta (ed), *The Stanford Encyclopedia of Philosophy* (Winter 2019 Edition), https://plato.stanford.edu/archives/win2019/entries/supererogation/ (last accessed 06/08/2025).

Hickey, Samuel J, 'Remediation in Foreign Bribery Settlements: The Foundation of a New Approach' (2021) 21(2) Chicago Journal of International Law 367–416.

HM Government, *Insight into Awareness and Impact of the Bribery Act 2010 among Small and Medium Sized Enterprises* (2015), https://assets.publishing.service.gov.uk/media/5a809f87e5274a2e8ab5134c/insight-into-awareness-and-impact-of-the-bribery-act-2010.pdf (last accessed 10/10/2025).

HMRC, *Understanding Evasion by Small and Medium-Sized Businesses*, HM Revenue and Customs Research Report 433 (London, 2017).

Hohfeld, Wesley Newcomb, 'Fundamental Legal Conceptions as Applied in Judicial Reasoning' (1917) 26(8) Yale Law Journal 710–70.

Hollingsworth, Kathryn, 'Responsibility and Rights: Children and Their Parents in the Youth Justice System' (2007) 21(2) International Journal of Law, Policy and the Family 190–219.

Holmes Jr, Oliver Wendell, 'The Path of the Law' (1897) 10 Harvard Law Review 457–78.

Holmstrom, Bengt, and Milgrom, Paul, 'Multitask Principal-Agent Analysis: Incentive Contracts, Asset Ownership and Job Design' (1991) 7(1) Journal of Law, Economics and Organisation 24–52.

Home Office, *Economic Crime and Corporate Transparency Act 2023: Guidance to Organisations on the Offence of Failure to Prevent Fraud* (2024), https://assets.publishing.service.gov.uk/media/67f8ef1845705eb1a1513f35/Failure+to+Prevent+Fraud+Guidance+-+English+Language+v1.6.pdf (last accessed 20/07/2025).

Honoré, AM, *Responsibility and Fault* (Oxford: Hart Publishing, 1999).

Horder, Jeremy, 'Gross Negligence and Criminal Culpability' (1997) 47(4) University of Toronto Law Journal 495–532.

Horder, Jeremy, *Excusing Crime* (Oxford: Oxford University Press, 2004).

Horder, Jeremy, 'Bribery as a Form of Criminal Wrongdoing' (2011) 127(1) Law Quarterly Review 37–66.

Horder, Jeremy, *Homicide and the Politics of Law Reform* (Oxford: Oxford University Press, 2012).

Horder, Jeremy (ed), *Ashworth's Principles of Criminal Law*, 10th edition (Oxford: Oxford University Press, 2022).
Horder, Jeremy, 'Control Over Land and Criminal Pollution: Empress Car Reconsidered' [2024] Criminal Law Review 230–46.
Horder, Jeremy, 'Corporate Criminal liability under the Economic Crime and Corporate Transparency Act 2023' [2025a] Legal Studies 1–16.
Horder, Jeremy, 'Corporate Criminal Liability under the Crime and Policing Bill 2025: A Critique of the "Senior Manager" Regime' [2025b] Criminal Law Review 449–68.
Horder, Jeremy, and Watts, Gabriele, 'The Scope of Liability for Failure to Prevent Economic Crime' [2021] Criminal Law Review 851–65.
Horder, Jeremy, and Watts, Gabriele, 'Senior Corporate Managers' Criminal Liability for the Crimes Committed by Their Employees or Agents', in Melissa Bone, JJ Child, and Jonathan Rogers (eds), *Criminal Law Reform Now: Proposals and Critique*, Vol 2 (Oxford: Hart Publishing, 2024), 87–107.
House of Lords, *The Bribery Act: Post-legislative Scrutiny* (London, 2019).
Howorth, Carole, and Kemp, Martin, *Governance in Family Business: Evidence and Implications* (York: University of York, 2019).
Humber Authorities Food Liaison Group, *Food Safety Act 1990: Guidelines on the Defence of Due Diligence* (1991), https://www.reading.ac.uk/foodlaw/pdf/due_diligence_guidelines.pdf (last accessed 04/09/2025).
Ibbotson, David, *A Historical Introduction to the Law of Obligations* (Oxford: Oxford University Press, 2001).
INSEAD, *The Institutionalisation of Family Firms: Europe* (New York: Clayton Dubilier & Rice, 2020).
International Labour Organisation, *Profits and Poverty: The Economics of Forced Labour* (Geneva: ILO, 2024).
Ireland, Peter W, 'The Rise of the Limited Liability Company' (1984) 12(3) International Journal of the Sociology of Law 239–60.
Jardon, Carlos M, 'Satisfaction Level and Competitiveness in Subsistence Small Businesses' (2018) 56(5) Management Decision 25–35.
Jefferys, JB, 'Trends in Business Organization in Great Britain since 1856, with Special Reference to the Financial Structure of Companies, the Mechanism of Investment and the Relations between Shareholder and Company' (Unpublished PhD thesis, University of London, 1938).
Jenkins, TA, *Parliament, Party and Politics in Victorian Britain* (Manchester: Manchester University Press, 1996).
Johnson, Paul, *Making the Market: Victorian Origins of Corporate Capitalism* (Cambridge: Cambridge University Press, 2010).
Kahan, Dan M, 'Social Meaning and the Economic Analysis of Crime' (1998) 27(2) The Journal of Legal Studies 609–54.
Kalmenovitz, J, 'Regulatory Intensity and Firm-specific Exposure' (2023) 36(6) Review of Financial Studies 3311–47.
Kamenka, E, and Erh-Soon Tay, A, 'Beyond Bourgeois Individualism; the Contemporary Crisis in Law and Legal Ideology', in E Kamenka and RS Neale (eds), *Feudalism, Capitalism and Beyond* (London: Edward Arnold, 1975), 15–30.
Kelemen, R Daniel, and Menon, Anand, 'The Politics of EC Regulation', in Stephen Weatherill (ed), *Better Regulation* (Oxford: Hart Publishing, 2007), 175–189.
Kellett, Peter, 'Securing High Levels of Business Compliance with Environmental Laws: What Works and What to Avoid' (2020) 32(1) Journal of Environmental Law 179–94.
Kennedy, JP, 'Sharing the Keys to the Kingdom: Responding to Employee Theft by Empowering Employees to be Guardians, Place Managers, and Handlers' (2016) 39(4) Journal of Crime and Justice 512–27.
Khanna, VS, 'Corporate Criminal Liability: What Purpose Does It Serve?' (1996) 109(8) Harvard Law Review 1477–1534.
Kitching, John, 'Better Regulation and the Small Enterprise', in Stephen Weatherill (ed), *Better Regulation* (Oxford: Hart Publishing, 2007), 155–74.

Korkka-Knuts, Heli, 'Evaluating Corporate Accountability for Human Rights Violations: The (Uncertain) Efficacy of Administrative Sanctions under the EU Sustainability Due Diligence Directive' (2024) 35 European Business Law Review 481–502.
Kostal, RW, *Law and English Railway Capitalism 1825–1875* (Oxford: Clarendon Press, 1994).
KPMG, *Supply Chain Fraud* (2017), https://assets.kpmg.com/content/dam/kpmg/bm/pdf/2017/04/supply-chain-fraud.pdf (last accessed 04/08/2025).
Lacey, Nicola, *State Punishment* (London: Routledge, 1988).
Lacey, Nicola, and Pickard, Hannah, 'From the Consulting Room to the Court Room? Taking the Clinical Model of Responsibility without Blame into the Legal Realm' (2013) 33(1) Oxford Journal of Legal Studies 1–29.
Laird, Karl, 'The Criminal Finances Act 2017: An Introduction' [2017] Criminal Law Review 915–39.
Laufer, William S, 'Corporate Liability, Risk Shifting, and the Paradox of Compliance' (1999) 52(5) Vanderbilt Law Review 1341–95.
Law Commission, *Reforming Bribery*, Report No 313 (London, 2008).
Law Commission, *Criminal Liability in Regulatory Contexts*, CP No 195 (London, 2010).
Law Commission, *Corporate Criminal Liability: A Discussion Paper* (London, 2021).
Law Commission, *Corporate Criminal Liability: An Options Paper* (London, 2022).
Law Commission, *Aviation Autonomy: Consultation Paper* (London, 2024).
Local Better Regulation Office (2012), https://assets.publishing.service.gov.uk/media/5a7ca35ae5274a38e5755d0a/0353.pdf (last accessed 06/11/2025).
Local Better Regulation Office, *Regulation and Growth* (2016), https://assets.publishing.service.gov.uk/media/5a758828ed915d731495ab1e/12-688-regulation-and-growth.pdf (last accessed 12/09/2025).
Löfstedt, Ragnar E, *Reclaiming Health and Safety for All: An Independent Review of Health and Safety legislation* (London: Department of Work and Pensions, 2011).
Lund, Dorothy S, and Sarin, Natasha, 'Corporate Crime and Punishment: An Empirical Study' (2021) 100(2) Texas Law Review 285–320.
Luskin, Robert, 'Caring About Corporate "Due Care": Why Criminal *Respondeat Superior* Liability Outreaches Its Justification' (2020) 57(2) American Criminal Law Review 303–30.
Marcketti, Sara B, Niehm, Linda S, and Fuloria, Ruchita, 'An Exploratory Study of Lifestyle Entrepreneurship and Its Relationship to Life Quality' (2006) 34(3) Family and Consumer Sciences Research Journal 241–59.
Marshall, TH, *Citizenship and Social Class* (London: Pluto Press, 1992 [first published 1949]).
Martinez, Christian R, 'The Curious Case of Lawrence Hoskins: Evaluating the Scope of Agency under the Anti-Bribery Provisions of the FCPA' (2020) 53(2) Columba Journal of Law and Social Problems 211–45.
Marx, Karl, Capital Punishment', *New York Daily Tribune* (18 February 1853), reprinted in Marx, Karl, and Engels, Friedrich, *Gesamtausgabe (MEGA)*, Vol 12 (Berlin: Dietz, 1984), 15–17.
Mazzacuva, Federico, 'Justifications and Purposes of Negotiated Justice for Corporate Offenders: Deferred and Non-prosecution Agreements in the UK and US Systems of Criminal Justice' (2014) 78(3) Journal of Criminal Law 249–62.
McNaughton, David, and Rawling, Piers, 'Honouring and Promoting Values' (1992) 102(4) Ethics 835–43.
Micheler, Eva, *Company Law: A Real Entity Theory* (Oxford: Oxford University Press, 2021).
Mill, JS, *Principles of Political Economy*, Vol 1 (London: John W Parker, 1848).
Miller, CJ, Harvey, Brian W, and Parry, Deborah L, *Consumer and Trading Law: Text, Cases and Materials*, 2nd edition (Oxford: Oxford University Press, 1998).
Ministry of Justice, *The Bribery Act 2010: Guidance* (London, 2010).
Moore, Michael S, *Placing Blame* (Oxford: Oxford University Press, 1997).
Morabito, Vince, 'Tax or Penalty: The Latest Sequel' (1999) 2(6) Journal of Australian Taxation 391–407.
Morgan, Phillip, 'Vicarious Liability for Group Companies: The Final Frontier of Vicarious Liability?' (2015) 31(4) Professional Negligence 276–99.

Murdoch, Iris, *The Sovereignty of Good* (London: Ark Publishing, 1970).
National Audit Office, *A Short Guide to Regulation* (2017), https://www.nao.org.uk/wp-content/uploads/2017/09/A-Short-Guide-to-Regulation.pdf (last accessed 11/07/2025).
Neyers, JW, 'A Theory of Vicarious Liability' (2005) 43(2) Alberta Law Review 287–322.
Nicholson, Catherine, and Young, Bob, 'The Relationship between Supermarkets and Suppliers: What are the Implications for Consumers?' (2012), https://www.law.ox.ac.uk/sites/default/files/migrated/the_relationship_between_supermarkets_and_suppliers.pdf (last accessed 06/11/2025).
Niggol Seo, S, *The Economics of Globally Shared and Public Goods* (London: Elsevier, 2020).
Norrie, Alan, 'Legal and Social Murder: What's the Difference?' [2018] Criminal Law Review 531–42.
Note, 'Developments in the Law—Corporate Crime: Regulating Corporate Behaviour Through Criminal Sanctions' (1979) 92 Harvard Law Review 1227–75.
Nurse, Angus, 'Contemporary Perspectives on Environmental Enforcement' (2022) 66(4) International Journal of Offender Therapy and Comparative Criminology 327–44.
Ó Floinn, Micheál, Farmer, Lindsay, Hörnle, Julia, and Ormerod, David, *Transformations in Criminal Jurisdiction* (London: Bloomsbury, 2023).
Oberdiek, John, 'The Wrong in Negligence' (2021) 41(4) Oxford Journal of Legal Studies 1174–96.
Office for National Statistics, *Long-term Trends in UK Employment: 1861 to 2018* (2019), https://www.ons.gov.uk/economy/nationalaccounts/uksectoraccounts/compendium/economicreview/april2019/longtermtrendsinukemployment1861to2018/pdf (last accessed 13/10/2025).
Office of Communication (OFCOM), *Regulatory Enforcement Guidelines for Investigations* (London, 2022).
Office of the UN High Commissioner for Human Rights, *The Corporate Responsibility to Respect Human Rights: An Interpretive Guide* (Geneva, 2012).
Organisation for Economic Co-operation and Development (OECD), *Implementing the OECD Anti-Bribery Convention in Canada: Phase 4 Report (2023)*, https://www.oecd.org/corruption/anti-bribery/canada-phase-4-report.pdf (last accessed 08/08/2025).
Oxford Economics, *The True Cost of Compliance* (London: LexisNexis, 2024).
Pan, Eric J, 'A Board's Duty to Monitor' (2010) 54(3) New York Law School Law Review 717–40.
Parker, Christine, *The Open Corporation: Effective Self-Regulation and Democracy* (Cambridge: Cambridge University Press, 2014).
Parker, D, et al, 'Driving Errors, Driving Violations and Accident Involvement' (1995) 38(11) Ergonomics 1036–48.
Parker, Jeffrey S, 'Criminal Sentencing Policy for Organizations: the Unifying Approach of Optimal Penalties' (1989) 26(3) American Criminal Law Review 513–62.
Parry, Deborah L, 'Judicial Approaches to Due Diligence' [1995] Criminal Law Review 695–710.
Paternoster, Raymond, and Sipson, Sally S, 'Sanction Threats and Appeals to Morality: Testing a Rational Choice Model of Corporate Crime' (1996) 30(3) Law and Society Review 550–72.
Peck, Frank, et al, *Business Perceptions of Regulatory Burden* (2012), https://assets.publishing.service.gov.uk/media/5a79c32340f0b670a80253f3/12-913-business-perceptions-of-regulatory-burden.pdf (last accessed 22/09/2025).
Pettit, Philip, *Republicanism: A Theory of Freedom and Government* (Oxford: Clarendon Press, 1997).
Pinto QC, Amanda, and Evans, Martin, *Corporate Criminal Liability*, 2nd edition (London: Sweet & Maxwell, 2008).
Pound, Roscoe, *The Spirit of the Common Law* (Boston, MA: Marshall Jones, 1921).
Poynder, John, *Literary Extracts*, Vol 1 (London: J Hatchard & Son, 1844).
Pratt, John, and Miao, Michelle, 'Risk, Populism, and Criminal Law' (2019) 22(4) New Criminal Law Review 391–433.
Qureshi, Fiza, et al, 'Revisiting the Nexus among Foreign Direct Investment, Corruption and Growth in Developing and Developed Markets' (2021) 21(1) Borsa Istanbul Review 80–91.
Ramsay, Peter, 'The Responsible Subject as Citizen: Criminal Law, Democracy and the Welfare State' (2006) 69(1) Modern Law Review 29–58.

Rasmusen, Eric, 'Stigma and Self-Fulfilling Expectations of Criminality' (1996) 39(3) Journal of Law and Economics 519–43.

Raz, Joseph, *The Authority of Law* (Oxford: Clarendon Press, 1979)

Raz, Joseph, *The Morality of Freedom* (Oxford: Clarendon Press, 1986).

Raz, Joseph, *Practical Reason and Norms* (Oxford: Oxford University Press, 1999).

Reed, M, 'Railways and the Growth of the Capital Market', in M Reed (ed), *Railways in the Victorian Economy: Studies in Financial and Economic Growth* (Newton Abbot: David and Charles, 1969), 231–63.

Reiman, J, *The Rich Get Richer and the Poor Get Prison: Ideology, Class and Criminal Justice*, 5th edition (Boston, MA: Allyn and Bacon, 1998).

Report from the Select Committee on Laws Respecting Joint Stock Companies (Parliamentary Paper, 1844, 354, VIII).

Rich, Sylvia, 'Can Corporations Experience Duress? An Examination of Emotion-Based Excuses and Group Agents' (2019) 13(1) Criminal Law and Philosophy 149–63.

Rich, Sylvia, 'Moral Entanglement in Group Decision-Making: Explaining an Odd Rule in Corporate Criminal Liability' (2024) 18(1) Criminal Law and Philosophy 1–17.

Rix, MS, 'Company Law: 1844 and Today' (1945) 55(218) Economic Journal 242–60.

Roberts, John, McNulty, Terry, and Stiles, Philip, 'Beyond Agency Conceptions of the Work of the Non-Executive Director: Creating Accountability in the Boardroom' (2005) 16(1) British Journal of Management 5–26.

Robson, JM (ed), *The Collected Works of John Stuart Mill*, Vol 3 (Toronto: University of Toronto Press, 1965).

Salach, Ali, *Corporate Criminal Liability in England and Wales* (London: House of Commons Research Briefing, 2022), https://researchbriefings.files.parliament.uk/documents/CBP-9027/CBP-9027.pdf (last accessed 04/08/2025).

Salguero-Caparrós, F, et al, 'Management of Legal Compliance in Occupational Health and Safety. A Literature Review' (2020) 121(1) Safety Science 111–18.

Sarpong, David, and Adams, Kweku, 'The Mabey and Johnson Bribery Scandal: A Case of Executive Hubris' (2019), https://ray.yorksj.ac.uk/id/eprint/3060/1/The%20Mabey%20and%20Johnson%20bribery%20Scandal%20A%20Case%20of%20Executive%20Hubris.pdf (last accessed 14/06/2025).

Sayre, FB, 'Criminal Responsibility for the Acts of Another' (1930) 43(5) Harvard LR 689–723.

Scanlon, TM, *What We Owe to Each Other* (Harvard, MA: Harvard University Press, 1999).

Schaefer, Marcela E, 'Should a Parent Company be Liable for the Misdeeds of Its Subsidiary? Agency Theories under the Foreign Corrupt Practices Act' (2019) 94(6) New York University Law Review 1654–87.

Schwartz, Jennifer, et al, 'Financial Prominence and Financial Conditions: Risk Factors for 21st Century Corporate Financial Securities Fraud in the United States' (2021) 39(3) Justice Quarterly 612–41.

Sealy, L, 'The Director as Trustee' (1967) 83(1) Cambridge Law Journal 83–103.

Searle, John R, 'The Problem of Consciousness', in Antti Revonsuo and Matti Kamppinen (eds), *Consciousness in Philosophy and Cognitive Neuroscience* (London: Routledge, 1994), 93–104.

Searle, John R, 'Animal Minds' (1995) XIX(1) Midwest Studies in Philosophy 206–19.

Sepinwall, Amy J, 'Faultless Guilt: Toward a Relationship-based Account of Criminal Liability' (2017) 54(2) American Criminal Law Review 521–78.

Sheppard, Dean A, 'Learning from Business Failure: Propositions of Grief Recovery for the Self-employed' (2003) 28(2) Academy of Management Review 318–28.

Shute, Stephen, Gardner, John, and Horder, Jeremy (eds), *Action and Value in Criminal Law* (Oxford: Clarendon Press, 1993).

Simester, AP, 'Is Strict Liability Always Wrong?', in AP Simester (ed), *Appraising Strict Liability* (Oxford: Oxford University Press, 2005), 21–50.

Simester, AP, *Fundamentals of Criminal Law: Responsibility, Culpability and Wrongdoing* (Oxford: Oxford University Press, 2021).

Simon, Herbert A, 'Rational Choice and the Structure of the Environment' (1956) 63(2) Psychological Review 129–38.

Singla, Shikhar, 'Regulatory Costs and Market Power' (2023), https://shikharsingla.com/files/reg.pdf (last accessed 09/09/2025).

Smallbone, David, et al, 'Small Business Responses to a Major Economic Downturn: Empirical Perspectives from New Zealand and the United Kingdom' (2012) 30(7) International Small Business Journal 754–77.

Smith, KJM, Lawyers, *Legislators and Theorists: Developments in English Criminal Jurisprudence 1800–1957* (Oxford: Clarendon Press, 1998).

Soltwisch, Brandon William, 'Comparing Maximizing and Satisficing Decision-Making Styles: The Impact on Managerial Performance' (2017), https://www.hippocampus.si/ISBN/978-961-7023-12-1/82.pdf (last accessed 12/02/2025).

Spalding, Andrew B, 'Corruption, Corporations, and the New Human Right' (2014) 91(6) Washington University Law Review 1365–428.

Spencer, Herbert, *Railway Morals and Railway Policy* (London: Longman, Brown, Green, & Longmans, 1855).

Spivack, P, and Raman, S, 'Regulating the 'New Regulators': Current Trends in Deferred Prosecution Agreements' (2008) 45(6) American Criminal Law Review 150–93.

Spotlight on Corruption, 'Regulators failing to hold senior executives to account for economic crime, new analysis reveals' (7 February 2024), https://www.spotlightcorruption.org/hold-senior-executives-to-account/ (last accessed 03/01/2026).

Stark, Findlay, *Culpable Carelessness* (Cambridge: Cambridge University Press, 2016).

Storey, David J, *Entrepreneurship and the New Firm* (London: Routledge, 1982).

Strickland, Pat, and Beard, Jacqueline, 'The Duty of the Police to Enforce the Law' (2013), https://researchbriefings.files.parliament.uk/documents/SN04230/SN04230.pdf (last accessed 07/11/2025).

Sullivan, GR, 'The Attribution of Liability to Limited Companies' (1996) 55(3) Cambridge Law Journal 515–46.

Sullivan, GR, 'Doing without Complicity' (2012) 2(2) Journal of Commonwealth Criminal Law 199–231.

Sutton A, and Wild, R, 'Small Business: White Collar Villains or Victims?' (1985) 13(3) International Journal of the Sociology of Law 247–59.

Tadros, Victor, *Criminal Law Theory* (Oxford: Oxford University Press, 2002).

Tadros, Victor, *The Ends of Harm: The Moral Foundations of Criminal Law* (Oxford: Oxford University Press, 2011).

Tadros, Victor, 'Punishment and the Appropriate Response to Wrongdoing' (2017) 11(2) Criminal Law and Philosophy 229–48.

Taylor, Russell, *Economic Crime and Corporate Transparency Bill HL Bill 96 of 2022–23* (House of Lords Research Briefing, 2 February 2023), https://lordslibrary.parliament.uk/research-briefings/lln-2023-0008/, 2 (last accessed 23/09/2025).

Thomas, W Robert, 'The Conventional Problem with Corporate Sentencing (and One Unconventional Solution)' (2021) 24(3) New Criminal Law Review 397–432.

Thompson, Grahame, 'The Enterprise as a Dispersed Agency' (1982) 11(2) Economy and Society 233–56.

Thomson, J Jarvis, 'Causation: Omissions' (2003) LXVI(1) Philosophy and Phenomenological Research 81–98.

Tombs, Steven, '@workplace Harms and the Illusions of Law', in Paddy Hillyard et al (eds), *Criminal Obsessions: What Harm Matters More than Crime* (London: Crime and Society Foundation, 1995), 41–61.

Tombs, Steve, 'Review: *Law as Last Resort: Prosecution Decision Making in a Regulatory Agency* by Keith Hawkins' (2004) 31(2) Journal of Law and Society 276–79.

Tombs, Steve, 'Workplace Harm and the Illusions of Law', in Danny Dorling et al (eds), *Criminal Obsessions: Why Harm Matters More Than Crime*, 2nd edition (London: Centre for Crime and Justice Studies, 2005), 41–61.

Tombs, Steve, and Whyte, David, *The Corporate Criminal* (London: Routledge, 2015).

Transparency International, *How to Bribe: A Typology of Bribe-Paying and How to Stop It* (London, 2014).

Turner, John D, *The Development of English Company Law before 1900*, QUCEH Working Paper Series No 2017–01 (Belfast: Queen's University Centre for Economic History, 2017).

Tuttle, Evan, 'Re-examining the Vicarious Criminal Liability of Corporations for the Wilful Crimes of their Employees' (2021) 70(1) Cleveland State Law Review 121–58.

Ucbasaran, Deniz, Shepherd, Dean A, Lockett, Andy, and Lyon, John, *Life after Business Failure: The Process and Consequences of Business Failure for Entrepreneurs*, Warwick Business School Working Paper No 117 (Warwick: Warwick Business School 2012).

UK Finance, *2021 Half-Year Fraud Update* (London, 2021).

UK Joint Committee on Human Rights, *Human Rights and Business 2017: Promoting Responsibility and Ensuring Accountability*, Sixth Report of Session 2016–17 (5 April 2017), https://publications.parliament.uk/pa/jt201617/jtselect/jtrights/443/443.pdf (last accessed 05/05/2025).

United Nations, 'Corporate Human Rights due Diligence: Emerging Practices, Challenges and Ways Forward' (2018), https://www.ohchr.org/sites/default/files/Documents/Issues/Business/ExecutiveSummaryA73163.pdf (last accessed 09/06/2025).

US Department of Justice, *A Resource Guide to the US Foreign Corrupt Practices Act*, 2nd edition (New York, 2020).

US Environmental Protection Agency, 'Consideration of Cumulative Impacts in EPA Review of NEPA Documents' (1999), https://www.epa.gov/sites/default/files/2014–08/documents/cumulative.pdf (last accessed 15/09/2025).

Velasquez, Manuel, 'Debunking Corporate Moral Responsibility' (2003) 13(4) Business Ethics Quarterly 531–62.

Vickers, Ian, et al, 'Understanding Small Firm Responses to Regulation: the Case of Workplace Health and Safety' (2005) 26(2) Policy Studies 149–66.

Voyiakis, Emmanuel, *Private Law and the Value of Choice* (Oxford: Oxford University Press, 2017).

Waldron, Jeremy, 'Moments of Carelessness and Massive Loss', in David G Owen (ed), *The Philosophical Foundations of Tort Law* (Oxford: Oxford University Press, 1997), 387–408.

Wasserstrom, Richard A, 'Strict Liability in Criminal Law' (1959–60) 12(5) Stanford Law Review 731–55.

Weber, Max, *Economy and Society: An Outline of Interpretive Sociology*, G Roth and C Wittich (eds) (Berkeley, CA: University of California Press, 1978 [first published in 1921]).

Weisman, Dov, 'Reasonable Precaution for the Individual' (2014) 88(3) St John's Law Review 653–720.

Weissmann, Andrew, and Newman, David, 'RE-thinking corporate Criminal Liability' (2007) 82(2) Indiana Law Journal 411–45.

Wells, Celia, *Corporations and Criminal Responsibility*, 2nd edition (Oxford: Oxford University Press, 2001).

Wells, Celia, 'Corporate Crime: Opening the Eyes of the Sentry' (2010) 30(3) Legal Studies 370–90.

Wells, Celia, 'Corporate Failure to Prevent Economic Crime: a Proposal' [2017] Criminal Law Review 426–38.

Welsh, John A, and White, Jerry F, 'A Small Business Is Not a Little Big Business' (July 1981), https://hbr.org/1981/07/a-small-business-is-not-a-little-big-business (last accessed 09/05/2024).

Welsh, RS, 'The Criminal Liability of Corporations' (1946) 62(4) Law Quarterly Review 345–65.

Wetzel, Linda, 'Types and Tokens' (Stanford Encyclopedia of Philosophy, first published 28 April 2006), https://plato.stanford.edu/entries/types-tokens/ (last accessed 21/01/2026).

Wetzel, Linda, 'Types and Tokens', in Edward N Zalta (ed), *The Stanford Encyclopedia of Philosophy* (Fall 2018 Edition), https://plato.stanford.edu/archives/fall2018/entries/types-tokens/ (last accessed 22/08/2025).

White, Robin, ' "Civil Penalties": Oxymoron, Chimera and Stealth Sanction' (2010) 126(4) Law Quarterly Review 593–616.

Williams, Bernard, *Ethics and the Limits of Philosophy* (London: Fontana, 1985).

Williams, Glanville, 'Criminal Omissions: The Conventional View' (1991) 107(1) Law Quarterly Review 86–112.
Wilson, Charles, 'Economy and Society in late-Victorian Britain' (1965) 18(1) The Economic History Review 183–202.
Wilson, Sarah, 'Law, Morality and Regulation: Victorian Experiences of Financial Crime' (2006) 46(6) British Journal of Criminology 1073–90.
Winn CRN, 'The Criminal Liability of Corporations' (1929) 3(4) Cambridge Law Journal 398–414.
Wolf, Susan, 'The Legal and Moral Responsibility of Organisations', in J Roland Pennock and John William Chapman (eds), *Criminal Justice* (New York: New York University Press, 1985), 267–86.
Woody, Karen, 'No Smoke and No Fire: The Rise of Internal Controls Absent Anti-Bribery Violations in FCPA Enforcement' (2017) 38(5) Cardozo Law Review 1727–68.
Wray, Christopher A, 'Corporate Probation under the New Organizational Sentencing Guidelines' (1992) 101(8) Yale Law Journal 2017–42.
Wray, Christopher A, 'Corporate Probation under the New Organizational Sentencing Guidelines' (2017) 101 Yale Law Journal 2017–42.
Xie, Jianhua, 'An Explanation of the Relationship between Artificial Intelligence and Human Beings from the Perspective of Consciousness' (2021) 4(3) Cultures of Science 124–34.
Yaeger, Peter Cleary, 'Management, Morality, and Law: Organizational Forms and Ethical Deliberations', in Frank Pearce and Laureen Snider (eds), *Corporate Crime: Contemporary Debates* (Toronto: University of Toronto Press, 1995), 147–64.
Zedner, Lucia, 'Reparation and Retribution: Are They Reconcilable?' (1994) 57(2) Modern Law Review 228–48.

INDEX

For the benefit of digital users, indexed terms that span two pages (e.g., 52–53) may, on occasion, appear on only one of those pages.